THE SPANISH STAGE

IN THE TIME OF

LOPE DE VEGA

BY

HUGO ALBERT RENNERT, Ph.D. (Freiburg i. B.)

DOVER PUBLICATIONS, INC.
NEW YORK

This Dover edition, first published in 1963, is
an unabridged and unaltered republication of the
text of the work first published by the Hispanic
Society of America in 1909. The "List of Spanish
Actors and Actresses, 1560-1680" appended to the
first edition has been omitted in this new edition.

Library of Congress Catalog Card Number: 63-19513

Manufactured in the United States of America

Dover Publications, Inc.
180 Varick Street
New York 14, N.Y.

PREFACE

LITTLE more than a decade has elapsed since the attention of scholars has again been directed to the history of the Spanish stage, and their labors have been rewarded with most unexpected success. While these results have been due to the work of a number of investigators—Sanchez-Arjona, Cotarelo, Restori, and others—it is to the late Dr. Cristóbal Pérez Pastor's patient and unwearying researches that we are especially indebted. The mass of material which he has brought to light will always form the foundation upon which others must build. For nearly a century, or since the appearance of Pellicer's work upon the Spanish stage in 1804 (excepting the very important matter contributed by Schack in the *Nachträge* to his *Geschichte der dramatischen Literatur und Kunst in Spanien*, 1854), little of importance had been done by scholars in this field until very recent times. About ten years ago Pérez Pastor began investigations in the Archives of Madrid and other Spanish cities that have yielded the richest results, and to these the present volume is greatly indebted. The labors of this distinguished investigator have, moreover, shown that the first volume of Pellicer's *Tratado Historico sobre el Origen y Progresos de la Comedia y del Histrionismo en España*, Madrid, 1804, is, upon the whole, trustworthy as far as

it goes, and, since a number of documents to which Pellicer had access seem to have disappeared, his work is still
valuable.

It was with the purpose of utilizing the latest researches
of the scholars above mentioned, and such other information as has come to my knowledge, that the present account of the Spanish stage was undertaken.

The amount of material for such a work is now large.
I have not attempted to chronicle every known fact, and
whether I have always chosen what is most important,
must be left for others to judge. Frequent references will
be found in the course of the succeeding pages to the stage
history of other countries, especially of England and
France, with the view of throwing some light upon the
points under discussion. They may, it is hoped, be not
unwelcome to the reader.

CONTENTS

vii

TO THE MEMORY OF

MY MOTHER

MAY 19, 1835—JUNE 5, 1899

Death is the end of life; ah, why
Should life all labour be?
Let us alone.   Time driveth onward fast,
And in a little while our lips are dumb.
Let us alone.   What is it that will last?
All things are taken from us, and become
Portions and parcels of the dreadful Past.

Tennyson.

INTRODUCTION

It has been said that the dramatic literature of Spain in the sixteenth and seventeenth centuries exceeded that of all other European nations combined, and this is, perhaps, no exaggeration. Lope de Vega, the great founder of the national drama, who heads the list with about fifteen hundred plays, would alone suffice for an entire nation. He is followed by Tirso de Molina and Luis Velez de Guevara, with about four hundred plays each, and by other playwrights whose productivity is almost as remarkable. Of the vast dramatic output of this period it has been estimated that fully one half is lost beyond recovery. Of Lope de Vega's repertory about two thirds has perished; of Tirso de Molina's and Velez de Guevara's about four fifths has disappeared, and of all the great dramatists of the Golden Age perhaps Calderon is the only one whose literary baggage has descended to us almost in its entirety.[1]

Theatrical representations became exceedingly popular in Spain in the last decades of the sixteenth century, and with the establishment of the first permanent theaters in Madrid—the *Corral de la Cruz* in 1579 and the *Corral del Príncipe* in 1582—the passion for the theater increased, and it was not long before all the larger cities possessed fixed *corrales* or theaters, and few towns were so small that they were not occasionally visited by strolling players. In all matters pertaining to the stage, however,

---

[1] Concerning the drama in England, W. W. Greg (*Henslowe's Diary*, Vol. II, London, 1908, p. 146) says: "We may, I think, conclude with some confidence that the total output of the Elizabethan Age was between 2000 and 3000 [plays] and probably not very far removed from the mean. This is, of course, exclusive of masques." He gives about 650 as the total number of plays extant from Elizabeth's accession to the outbreak of the civil war (1558–1642).

Madrid was always paramount. Upon this point the evidence is overwhelming. The importance of Valencia as a theatrical center has been much exaggerated, and while a *corral* may have existed in that city as early as 1566, there is no positive record of one till 1582 or 1583. As the dramatists of the so-called Valencian school were all followers of Lope de Vega (its activity can be dated back no farther than Lope's residence in that city in 1588), so, too, the Valencian stage was at all times ruled by that of Madrid. In the capital all the large companies of players were organized; here all the celebrated managers (*autores de comedias*) and actors lived, and from this source all the cities of Spain, as well as the capital of Portugal, drew for their theatrical representations.

After Madrid, the most flourishing theatrical center, on account of its wealth and commercial importance, was undoubtedly Seville, and hence, in the following account of the Spanish stage, I have confined myself almost exclusively to these two cities, not only because of their prime importance, but also for the no less potent reason that here the sources flow much more freely than elsewhere.

As regards the city of Valencia it may not be out of place to give here such information as is furnished by the rare little book *El Teatro de Valencia desde su Origen hasta nuestros Dias,* por D. Luis Lamarca, Valencia, 1840. Concerning theatrical representations in that city Sr. Lamarca says that "to Valencia belongs the indisputable glory of having been the first city in Spain in which dramas were represented in the vulgar tongue," and mentions that in April, 1394, there was performed in the Palacio del Real a tragedy entitled *L'hom enamorat y la fembra satisfeta,* written by Mosen Domingo Mascó, counselor of the King, Don Juan I.[1]

A few years afterward, in 1412, on the occasion of the

[1] See also Wolf, *Studien zur Geschichte der spanischen und portugiesischen Nationalliteratur,* Berlin, 1859, p. 584.

festivities celebrated by the city in honor of the visit of the King, Don Fernando, among other things four *entramesos nuevos* were enacted. Lamarca says that these were probably *carros triunfales,* which are now known by the name of *rocas;* and upon these *carros* were represented *pasos* or mysteries, for in the *deliberacion* of March 7, 1415, it was decreed to pay to "Mosen Juan Sist, presbitero, *per trobar é ordenar les cobles é cantilenes ques cantaren en los entramesos de la festividad de la entrada del Sor. Rey, Reyna é Primogenit,*" thirty florins, "*é igual suma á Juan Perez de Pastrana, per haber de arreglar é donar el só á les dites cantilenes é haber fadrins que les cantasen é ferlos ornar*" (p. 10). This, the author says, is proof of the Valencian origin of the term *entremes.* As early as the middle of the fifteenth century the city had paid *juglares* (*juglares asalariados*) to represent the public festivals, as is shown by a *deliberacion* of August 28, 1487, when the city appointed "Juan Alfonso para una plaza de juglar de la ciudad, que se hallaba vacante por muerte de Martin Alfonso; expresando, que se le concedia con los emolumentos y trajes pertenecientes á dicho oficio" (*ibid.*), and he continues: "Los misterios en lengua lemosina que se representan todavia por las calles en la vispera y dia del Corpus y en especial el de *Adam y Eva,* que ántes de salir de la procession se ejecuta sobre el carro ó *roca* de la Santisima Trinidad, bajo los balcones de la casa de ayuntamiento, son una memoria de aquellas primitivas representaciones."

As to the playhouses of Valencia, Sr. Lamarca calls attention to the fact that Jovellanos was in error in stating that in 1526 the Hospital of Valencia possessed a theater in that city, and states that many years passed before the Hospital had any interest in the *casa de Comedias.* The evidence for an early theater in Valencia he finds in the circumstance that in 1566 the street now called *calle de la Tertulia* was called the *carrer de les Comedies.* The fact is, however, that the Hospital, in 1582, finding itself in straits for funds, the Marquis of Aytona, then Viceroy of the kingdom of Valencia, decreed on September 15 of that year that the companies of players which came from various parts to Valencia could only represent in the place appointed by the Hospital. This concession was confirmed by the Cortes of Monzon in 1585.

From a *deliberacion* of November 6, 1584, it appears that, for a short time prior to this date, a theater had been established in a house of Ana Campo, "situada cerca dels *Santets*," in which Alonso de Cisneros had represented for three months (p. 18).

These, however, were only provisional theaters, and on May 4, 1584, the permanent theater in the *Vall-cubert* was finished. This, Sr. Lamarca declares, was in the Plaza de la Olivera, now called the Plaza de las Comedias, for a *deliberacion* of November 6, 1584, shows that N. Velazquez represented "*farsas* en la casa *que te lo dit spital pera dit efecte á la Olivera.*" At this time the entrance fee was 4 *dineros*, and a *silla* cost seven. This famous *Casa de la Olivera* existed for thirty-four years, until 1618, when it was torn down and rebuilt. While rebuilding comedias were again represented in the house called *dels Santets*, over against what is to-day the church of St. Thomas, where performances had formerly taken place. The *Teatro de la Olivera* was opened on November 3, 1619, when the first representation took place in the new structure, and here they were continued until 1715, when it was rebuilt anew.

In 1622 the dramatist Jacinto Maluenda was *alcaide* of this *casa de comedias*, and moved to the house in the theater called *del Autor*, "which he was to occupy and to exercise the duties of his office, receiving all the returns and profits from the sale of waters, sweets, fruits," etc., "*del modo y manera que fins huy ho han tengut tots sos antepasats.*" (*Ibid.*, p. 63.) In 1650 representations were forbidden by royal decree. In June, 1662, we find José Carrillo and his company representing forty comedias in Valencia. Performances continued to take place in the *Teatro de la Olivera* until it was demolished in 1750, at the instance of the archbishop, D. Andrés Mayoral.

With this brief notice of the theater at Valencia we now turn our attention to the stage of Madrid, first casting a retrospective glance over the early religious representations in the peninsula.

THE SPANISH STAGE

CHAPTER I

Early religious representations. The festival of Corpus Christi. The secular drama. Lope de Rueda. Torres Naharro. Early secular representations.

So far as the representation of secular dramas in Spain is concerned, we need go back no further than Lope de Rueda, who is, in fact, the first professional actor-manager whose name has been preserved in the theatrical annals of Spain. To him and to Torres Naharro, Lope de Vega, the great creator of the Spanish national drama, has ascribed the beginnings of the comedia.[1] On the other hand, any discussion of the representations of the religious drama in the peninsula must necessarily revert to a much more remote period.

The earliest definite notices of popular representations in Spain, it may be observed here, all concern the celebra-

[1] In his *Loa de la Comedia,* Agustin de Rojas tells us that the comedia had its beginning in the city of Granada, at the time when the Catholic kings expelled the Moriscos from Spain (1492), and says that the comedia was begun by Juan de la Enzina, "who was the first and of whom we have three eclogues" (p. 120). And, again, he says that "the use of the comedia began to be discovered" when Columbus discovered the New World (p. 121). He states that Enzina himself represented them to "the Almirante y Duquessa de Castilla y de Infantado." But as Cañete remarks: "Encina estuvo muy lejos de ser representante, y mucho menos *autor de Compañías cómicas* en el sentido que posteriormente ha dado á este frase el tecnicismo teatral. Poetas coetáneos de nuestro salmantino [Encina] como Pedro de Vega, vendían ya sus *coloquios pastoriles,* que entonces *se practicaban mucho,* á los representantes *que andaban por el reino, que fueron los pri-*

3

tion of the festival of Corpus Christi, which was first instituted by Urban IV. in 1264.[1] Most of our information
concerning these festivals has been obtained from the
Archives of the larger Spanish cities, and that these
notices have been recorded is due to the fact that such
festal representations were given at the command and expense of the corporations of the various municipalities.
In this respect the Spanish Archives seem to be unusually
rich, and they throw much light on the character of these
early representations and on the manner in which they
were produced. It may not be without interest, therefore,
to cast a glance, though it be a very hasty one, at these
early religious representations, i.e., before the middle of
the sixteenth century.[2]

According to Sanchez-Arjona the Archives of Barcelona
contain accounts of the celebrations of the festival of
Corpus Christi covering the first two thirds of the fifteenth
century, i.e., down to 1462. This festival was first introduced into Spain at Gerona by Berenger de Palaciolo, who
died in 1314. It was celebrated with great solemnity in
Seville during the fifteenth century, the cathedral chapter

meros que salieron á recitar públicamente. Asi lo expresa Juan López
Osorio, en una obra historica muy anterior á las de Rojas y Méndez, y su
dictámen es más digno de crédito en este punto." (*Teatro completo de
Juan del Encina,* Edicion de la Real Academia Española, ed. by Manuel
Cañete, Madrid, 1893, p. xxxviii.) Of these actors, however, we have no
knowledge.

[1] That representations—secular as well as religious—must have taken
place in Spain at a period considerably antedating those mentioned in the
text, is evinced by the *Siete Partidas* of Alfonso X., which were probably
written between 1252 and 1257. Partida I, Tit. VI, Ley 34, is a very important document for the history of the early Spanish drama, to which
attention has frequently been called. From it Schack has drawn the
following conclusions: (1) That in the middle of the thirteenth century
religious as well as secular representations were well known in
Spain; (2) that they took place as well within as without the church;
(3) that they were represented not only by clerics, but also by laymen;
(4) that acting was followed as a profession (*Erwerbszweig*); (5) that
the plays were represented not only in pantomime, but were also spoken.
(*Geschichte der dramatischen Literatur und Kunst in Spanien,* Frankfurt
am Main, 1854, Vol. I, p. 114.)

[2] For an account of the origin of the religious drama and of the *autos*

defraying the expenses of the representations, which took place on what was called *la roca*, which the cathedral books (*libros de fabrica*) describe as a kind of platform (*andas*) carried by twelve men and on which were those persons who represented Maria, Jesus, Saints Dominick and Francis, and the four evangelists. "There were, besides, six angels and eight prophets, who were playing (*tañendo*); we do not know whether they were upon the *roca*, but rather presume that they went on foot like the devils and the angels who came forth and performed a sort of dance." As early as 1454, or a hundred years before Lope de Rueda, Sanchez-Arjona gives the names of two of these performers, Beatriz and Diego Garcia, who were paid twenty-five maravedís for dancing (*que iban rillendo*). It is very likely that the persons engaged for these early representations were merely mountebanks and strolling players; in fact, in the same year forty maravedís were paid by the corporation to "Juan Canario, a *juglar*, and his companion, who appeared on the *roca*, besides ten maravedís for coming to this city."

In Zaragoza, in 1414, on the car or float for the representation which Don Enrique de Aragon (generally, but wrongly, called the Marquis of Villena) had arranged to celebrate the nuptials of the King, Don Fernando *el Honesto*, there was represented "a great castle with four towers at the sides, and in the middle a higher one, with a wheel in its center which gave motion to the whole device (*armazon*), and showed successively the various allegorical personages who graced it."[1]   These castles seemed

sacramentales, see, in addition to the first volume of Schack, *Geschichte der dramatischen Literatur und Kunst in Spanien,* the introduction by Eduardo Gonzalez Pedroso to Vol. 58 of the *Biblioteca de Autores Españoles,* and Sanchez-Arjona, *Anales del Teatro en Sevilla,* Seville, 1898. See also Wolf, *Studien zur Geschichte der spanischen und portugiesischen Nationalliteratur,* Berlin, 1859, pp. 556 ff.

[1] For an account of this piece (written in Limousin, not in Castilian), which is ascribed to the Marquis of Villena, see Schack, *Nachträge,* p. 2, and Wolf, *Studien,* p. 583 and note.

to have figured largely in these representations, for in 1454 "one Pedro Gonzalez, the friend who makes castles," was paid for erecting one on the *roca,* which must have been a similar device to the one used by the Marquis of Villena. Despite the exalted purpose with which these festivals were celebrated, the earthly needs of the performers were not overlooked, as is evinced by an entry in the books of the cathedral of Seville, in which the expenses of the festival were kept. Here we find, among other items, one "for wine for the angels and prophets." (Sanchez-Arjona, p. 4.) Again, in 1462, in addition to the item "gloves for Mary," nine maravedís were paid "for another pair of gloves, together with a wound for St. Francis." In 1497, besides an increased number of personages on the *roca,* other innovations were made. Two reals were paid to each of six trumpeters and to a drummer and a tambourine-player. "A gilded sun was provided at a cost of ten reals, besides twelve diadems for the apostles; keys for St. Peter, which cost two reals; eighteen little gilded lamps and two hundred and thirty roses gilded and plated with leaves of tin (*lata*) to adorn the sky in which is God the Father, the gilding at two maravedís and for the plating one maravedí." In that year "Mary wore a gilded star, God the Father a tiara, Jesus Christ a diadem, and St. Dominick a lily." It is very likely, as Sanchez-Arjona remarks, that during the fifteenth century these festivals were chiefly in charge of the various guilds, and he adds that, to judge by the titles of these *autos* and the notices of them which have been preserved, these representations with which the festival of Corpus Christi was then celebrated "had no direct relation to the sublime mystery which is commemorated on that solemn day, and down to the middle of the sixteenth century we find no *auto* which unites all the distinctive characteristics of the *autos sacramentales.*" He refers here to the *Farsa llamada Danza de la Muerte,* written by Pedraza, a native of Segovia, and cloth-shearer (*tundidor*) by trade, and first printed in 1551.[1] It was doubtless represented in that city by the guild of *tundidores*, since at that time the cars for representation were in charge of the guilds and officers of the city, who took part in the processions, preceded by a standard, bearing the ensigns of the respective guilds. This was also the case in Seville, where, besides the care of the cars, the well-cleaners had charge of the decoration of the "*tarasca*," the *ganapanes* looked after the "giants," and an enormous St. Christopher was furnished by the glovers. (*Ibid.*, p. 8.) In Seville these *autos* were represented at Corpus by the various guilds and at their expense until 1554, when they were undertaken by the city, which also assumed all the charges of the representations.[2] At this time, says

[1] The earliest *auto* bearing a definite date, that has survived, is Gil Vicente's *Auto de San Martinho*, written and represented in 1504; "la mas antigua, entre quantas poseen fecha auténtica, de dramas castellanos, hechos para solemnizar la fiesta del Sanct. Sacramento." (Gonzalez Pedroso, in *Bibl. de Autores Españoles*, Vol. 58, p. xvii.) That there is, however, much uncertainty concerning the chronology of Vicente's works, has been shown by Stiefel, who makes it apparent that the *Auto da Fama*, for instance, was written after 1519 and perhaps not before 1525, though the date 1510 is assigned to it. (*Archiv für das Studium der neueren Sprachen* (1907), p. 192.) It should be added that, while the *Auto de San Martinho* was represented at Corpus Christi, it had nothing to do with the glorification of the doctrine of transubstantiation; and is not, therefore, an *auto sacramental*. Fitzmaurice-Kelly says: "Hernán López de Yanguas est peut-être le premier qui ait écrit un véritable *auto* dans sa *Farsa sacramental en coplas* (1520)." (*Littérature espagnole*, Paris, 1904, p. 174.) The *Farsa* of Pedraza is republished by Pedroso, *loc. cit.*, p. 41. On López de Yanguas, see Cañete, *Teatro español del Siglo XVI*, Madrid, 1885, pp. 61 ff.

[2] The manuscript collection of *Autos, Farsas*, etc., of the Biblioteca Nacional, to which reference is made by writers upon this subject, has been published by Rouanet, under the title *Coleccion de Autos, Farsas y Colloquios del Siglo XVI*, Madrid, 1901, in four volumes. It consists of ninety-six pieces. The editor says: "Les diverses compositions du recueil pourraient se diviser en trois classes: 1° sujets empruntés à la Bible (Ancien et Nouveau Testament); 2° sujets pris dans la légende ou la vie des saints. Les uns et les autres portent le nom d'*autos*. 3° Sujets allégoriques, désignés sous le nom de *farsas*. Il est à noter ici que, vers la fin du XVIe ou le commencement du XVIIe siècle, le mot *auto* n'était l'équivalent ni d'*auto sacramental*, ni d'*auto al nacimiento*, et ne s'appliquait pas exclusivement aux représentations en l'honneur de l'Eucharistie ou de la Nativité, mais à toute œuvre dramatique *en un act*. Si on voulait chercher dans le *Codice* de Madrid le

Sanchez-Arjona, it was the custom to place the Holy Sacrament in the middle of the principal chapel in the church, and the town council and cathedral chapter having occupied the stage or platform (*tablado*), placed between the two choirs, the representation of the *auto* took place, after which divine service was held. The mass and sermon being concluded, the dances were presented in the same place in which the *auto* had been given, and there they remained dancing before the Holy Sacrament until evening, when the procession, of which they formed a part, emerged from the church. (*Ibid.*, p. 9.) Meanwhile the deputies appointed by the city to take charge of the festival assigned the places where the representations were to take place, and once designated, fixed the arms of the city over them, so that, the representations within the cathedral and before the chapters being concluded, the players might go in their "cars" to perform the *autos* in all the places indi-

prototype des *autos sacramentales* tels qu'on les conçut plus tard, c'est parmi les *farsas* qu'on le trouverait. Les *autos*, au contraire, y apparaissent comme une forme encore rudimentaire des *comedias divinas*." (*Ibid.*, p. x.) Forty years before, Wolf, in speaking of this same collection, had said that from their nature these pieces must have been represented outside the church, and that in the *farsas sacramentales* the special, allegorical form of the *auto sacramental* is already found developed, while the pieces which in this collection are called *autos* mostly treat of the lives of heroes of the Old and New Testaments, of saints, etc., and may be considered the forerunners of the so-called *comedias divinas*. "Moreover," he says, "it may be confidently asserted that the ancient religious drama in Spain was divided, as in France and England, into two principal classes: historical representations of sacred history (Mysteries or Miracle-plays) and moral-allegorical pieces (Moralities). From the former the *comedias divinas* were afterward developed, and from the latter the *autos* (in the signification which was afterward exclusively confined to this name)." (*Studien zur Geschichte der spanischen und portugiesischen Nationalliteratur*, Berlin, 1859, p. 602, quoting Schack, Vol. I, p. 243.) A piece similar to those contained in the collection edited by Rouanet, and which, moreover, bears a definite date, was written by Sebastian de Horozco of Toledo, and is printed in his *Cancionero*, Seville, 1874, p. 148. It is entitled "Representacion de la Parabola de Sant Mateo á los veinte Capítulos de su sagrado Evangelio; la qual se hizo y represento en Toledo en la Fiesta del Sanctíssimo Sacramento por la Santa Iglesia. Año de 1548 años." It also begins with an "Argumento" or *prefacio*, as the author calls it.

cated by the arms of the city. (*Ibid.*) So the procession moved from street to street and received the name, in popular phrase, of the "Festival of the Cars"—*La Fiesta de los Carros*.[1] Toward the close of the sixteenth century the *auto* received a new and powerful impulse through Lope de Vega, seconded by other writers; an impulse that was epoch-making in the annals of this species of composition, which developed in regularity and brilliancy, at the cost, perhaps, as Sr. Sanchez-Arjona says, of its former tenderness and simplicity, and putting an end to the *autos viejos,* works of transition between the farces of the fifteenth and early sixteenth centuries and the eucharistic representations of the seventeenth century, in which they constituted one of the richest and most varied manifestations of the dramatic muse.[2]

Throughout the seventeenth century the *autos sacramentales* were represented publicly in the streets of Spain,[3] the performances moving from place to place, as directed by the authorities of the cities, under whose auspices and at whose expense they were given. And it is in Benavente, in 1554, that we first hear of Lope de Rueda, when he represented an *auto* in that city. Lope de Rueda is the earliest *autor de comedias* (head of a company of players) in Spain of whom we have any knowledge. His is a famous name in the annals of the Spanish theater, of which he was one of the founders. Indeed, his great successor, Lope de Vega, frequently alludes to his illustrious namesake as the first to bring the *comedia,* as it was afterward known, upon the public stage. To Lope de Rueda the name *autor* was rightly applied; he was an author as well as actor and wrote the farces and comedies which he and his little company performed in the public squares.

[1] Ticknor, *History of Spanish Literature,* Boston, 1888, Vol. II, pp. 291 ff.
[2] Sanchez-Arjona, *Anales,* p. 8.
[3] For the representation of *autos* in the theaters, see below, Chapter XIV.

Born in Seville, probably in the second decade of the sixteenth century, he at first followed the trade of a gold-beater. The earliest documentary notice concerning him is of the year 1554, when, as just stated, he represented an *auto* at Benevente in honor of Philip the Second, on his passage through that town on his way to England.[1] On August 15, 1558, we find him in Segovia performing *una gustosa comedia* at the dedication of the new cathedral of that city.[2] In 1559 his company represented two *autos* at Seville, *El Hijo pródigo* and *Navalcarmelo*,[3] and the instrument dated April 29, 1559, is still preserved in the Archives of Seville, in which Juan de Coronado, the *mayordomo* of the rents and properties of the city, is commanded to pay to Lope de Rueda, "residing in this city, forty ducats, on account of seventy ducats,[4] which he is to receive for two representations, to be given on two cars (*carros*), with certain figures, on Corpus Christi; the one *Navalcarmelo*, the other *El Hijo pródigo*, with all the costumes of silk and other things that may be necessary," etc. Attached is the receipt of Lope de Rueda,

[1] The best account of Lope de Rueda and his works is to be found in Cotarelo y Mori, *Lope de Rueda y el Teatro Español de su Tiempo,* Madrid, 1901, and in the same writer's introduction to the *Obras de Lope de Rueda,* published by the Spanish Academy, Madrid, 1908, 2 vols. See also Cortés, *Un Pleito de Lope de Rueda,* Madrid, 1903, and on the sources of Rueda's plays, the excellent article of Professor Arthur L. Stiefel, *Lope de Rueda und das Italienische Lustspiel,* in the *Zeitschrift für Romanische Philologie,* Vol. XV.

[2] "A la tarde, celebradas solenes visperas en un teatro que estava entre los coros. . . . Luego la compañia de Lope de Rueda, famoso comediante de aquella edad, representó una gustosa comedia." (Diego de Colmenares, *Historia de Segovia,* Madrid, 1640, Cap. XLI, p. 516.)

[3] This *auto* is still extant and has been published by Rouanet in the *Coleccion de Autos, Farsas y Coloquios del Siglo XVI,* Vol. II, Madrid-Barcelona, 1901. In the introduction to Vol. I (p. xii), M. Rouanet says: "No. LIX, l'*Auto de Naval y Abigail* est précisément celui que Lope de Rueda composa en 1559 pour la Fête-Dieu de Seville."

[4] For some years after this seventy ducats seems to have been the usual price for an *auto*. In May, 1580, seventy ducats each were paid for the *autos* of that year by the chapter of Toledo, Alonso Rodriguez receiving 210 ducats for three *autos* and Melchor de Herrera 140 ducats for two *autos*. (Pérez Pastor, *Bulletin Hispanique* (1906), p. 78.)

dated May 9, 1559, acknowledging the payment of forty
ducats, and signed by his own hand.[1]

The court having moved from Valladolid to Madrid,
we find Lope de Rueda in the latter city on September 24,
1561, married to a Valencian woman. After a short stay
in Madrid, in which his company seems to have been very
unfortunate—for he was obliged to leave part of his theatrical wardrobe in pawn for a debt—he left for Valencia,
whence he returned to Seville, where, on July 18, 1564,
Juana Luisa, "daughter of Lope de Rueda and his wife
Rafaela Anxela," was baptized.[2]

A very curious document,[3] which throws an interesting
light upon the early theatrical career of Lope de Rueda, is
a lawsuit brought by "Lope de Rueda and Mariana de
Rueda, his wife," on July 6, 1554, in Valladolid, against
Juan de la Cerda, the heir and successor of Don Gaston de
la Cerda, Duke of Medinaceli, for services rendered by
the wife to the latter. It appears that about the year
1546, two women, who earned their living by singing and
dancing, arrived from Aragon in the town of Cogolludo,
where Don Gaston was residing. The Duke was so pleased
with one of these singers that he admitted her to his service. She was called Mariana, and we are told that she
fulfilled with extreme solicitude her duty of amusing the
Duke. She remained in his service six years, "dedicating
herself exclusively to furnishing him with recreation, singing and dancing in his presence whenever it suited his
caprice, and giving him always *grande placer e contenta-
miento.*" Mariana seems to have been an excellent singer
and dancer, and, according to the testimony of one of the
witnesses, "*es en extremo unica e sola en lo que hace.*" At
all events, she greatly pleased the old Duke, "who admitted her to his chamber, *le daba de comer en su propio*

[1] Sanchez-Arjona, *Anales,* p. 11.
[2] Cotarelo, *Lope de Rueda,* p. 38, note.
[3] See Cortés, *Un Pleito de Lope de Rueda,* Madrid, 1903.

plato, and lavished gold and silver upon her, and in his solicitude not to be separated from her, he used to take her with him on his hunting parties." In order the better to accompany the Duke, "now on foot and now on horse," Mariana had her locks shorn and dressed in male attire. While her position, in the circumstances, might be regarded as rather equivocal, it should be added that one of the witnesses "affirmed under oath, and insisted upon it, that Mariana tried to please the Duke and to serve him in all that she could *como muger honrada.*" It appears that the old Duke died owing Mariana considerable money, and sometime after her marriage to Lope de Rueda she determined to sue for the amount due her. The testimony at the trial shows that when suit was brought (1554) she had been married to Lope de Rueda for about two years. As Mariana entered the Duke's service in 1546 and remained six years, she must have married Lope de Rueda directly after she left the Duke. This lawsuit lasted from July, 1554, until March, 1557, during which time Lope de Rueda was living with his wife, Mariana, in Valladolid.

.The testimony of some of the witnesses in this case affords a glimpse of Lope de Rueda's company at this time. The first witness was Pedro de Montiel, "a silk-spinner (*hilador de sieda*), being in this court [Valladolid] and a member of the company of Lope de Rueda." Another witness was Gaspar Diez, *musico,* who testified that "whenever the said Lope de Rueda represents a comedy, he calls him and pays him [the witness] well for playing the *biguela* in the said comedy," etc. Francisco de la Vega, *musico e tañedor* of Valladolid, and Alonso Centino, *danzante,* also testified, the latter saying that he was not in Rueda's company because he [the witness] was married.

It appears, therefore, that Lope de Rueda was twice married, first in 1552 to Mariana, a strolling singer and dancer, and sometime in 1563 or earlier to Rafaela Anxela. Two years before this, in 1561, he is said to have repre-

sented the *autos* at Corpus in Toledo, and on October 4
and November 28, 1561, he received one hundred reals
each for two comedias acted at the instance of the Queen,
Doña Isabel de la Paz.[1] He died at Cordoba shortly
after March 21, 1565, the date of his testament.[2]

To Bartolemé de Torres Naharro and Lope de Rueda
belongs the singular honor of having been the "first inventors" of the comedia in Spain; Torres Naharro was the
first Spaniard to write comedias in the manner in which
they were afterward taken up and brought to the highest
development of artistic form by Lope de Vega.[3] His
comedias are in verse, while Rueda's are in prose. Naharro has been strangely overlooked by those early Spanish
writers who touch upon the drama. Juan de la Cueva
does not mention him, nor does Agustin de Rojas. Cervantes notes him briefly in the "Canto de Caliope" in his
Galatea, as does Lope de Vega in the dedication of his
comedia *Virtud, Pobreza y Muger,* in 1624, where he
says: "In Spain the rules of art are disregarded; not
through ignorance—for the first inventors [of the comedia
in Spain], Rueda and Naharro, who have scarcely been
dead eighty years, observed them—but through following

---

[1] Cotarelo, *Lope de Rueda,* p. 37, note.

[2] *Ibid.,* p. 39.

[3] The most distinguished of living critics of the Spanish drama, Sr.
Menéndez y Pelayo, says this of our author: "Bartolomé de Torres Naharro, inferior á otros contemporáneos suyos en dotes poéticas, habia nacido
hombre de teatro, y en esta parte les aventaja á todos. Compárense sus
obras con cuanto inmediatamente las precedió en nuestra escena: con las
églogas, farsas y representaciones de Juan del Enzina (sin excluir las últi-
mas y mas complicadas); con las de Lucas Fernández, Francisco de Madrid, Diego de Avila y Martin de Herrera; y aun con todo lo que Gil
Vicente compuso antes de la Comedia del Viudo, que es de 1514, açaso
influida ya por los ensayos de nuestro autor; y nos parecerá que entramos
en un mundo nuevo, y que fué un paso de gigante el que Torres Naharro
dió en el camino de la buena comedia" (p. lxxxviii). Again: "Complicó
ingeniosamente la trama, en tres por lo menos de sus piezas; atendió por
primera vez al estudio de las costumbres, y si no llegó á la comedia de
carácter, fué por lo menos el fundador de la comedia de intriga"
(p. xciii). (Introduction to the *Propaladia* of Torres Naharro, Vol. II,
Madrid, 1900.)

the bad style introduced by those who succeeded them."
Juan de Timoneda, as Schack has observed, is the earliest
Spanish writer to couple the names of Torres Naharro and
Lope de Rueda as the founders of the Spanish drama, calling attention to the fact that the works of Torres Naharro
are in verse, while the comedies of Lope de Rueda are in
prose.[1]

Lope de Rueda's historic importance lies in his invention of the *paso*—a dramatic interlude turning on
some simple episode: a quarrel between Torubio and
his wife Águeda concerning the price of olives not yet
planted, an invitation to dinner from the penniless licentiate Xaquima, etc.　Mr. Fitzmaurice-Kelly, in his brief but
admirable summary of Rueda's achievement, says: "Rueda
had clearly read the *Celestina* to his profit; and his prose,
with its archaic savor, is of great purity and power. . . .
Considerable as were Rueda's positive qualities of gay
wit and inventive resource, his highest merit lies in this,
that he laid the foundation stone of the actual Spanish
theater, and that his dramatic system became a capital
factor in his people's intellectual history."[2]　And Sr.
Menéndez y Pelayo says: "The positive and eminent merit
of Lope de Rueda is not in his dramatic conception, nearly
always foreign, but in the art of the dialogue, which is a
treasure of popular diction, picturesque and seasoned as
well in his *pasos* and *coloquios sueltos* as in those which can
be culled from his comedias.　This episodical part is really
the very essence of them.　This is what Cervantes admired

---

[1] The works of Lope de Rueda, which Timoneda began to publish at
Valencia in 1567, are now accessible in the two volumes edited by the
Marqués de la Fuensanta del Valle in the *Coleccion de Libros Españoles
raros ó curiosos,* Madrid, 1895–96, and in the new edition of the Spanish
Academy, just issued in two volumes (Madrid, 1908), edited by Emilio
Cotarelo.　For the above allusion, see the edition of 1895, Vol. I, p.
153. The *Propaladia* of Torres Naharro has also been reprinted, with an
excellent introductory essay by Menéndez y Pelayo, in two volumes, in the
Libros de Antaño, Madrid, 1880 and 1900; the second volume containing
the introductory essay.

[2] *History of Spanish Literature,* New York, 1898, p. 169.

and in part imitated not only in his *entremeses* but also in the picturesque portion of his novels."[1]

Of Lope de Rueda, Rojas says:

> "Digo que Lope de Rueda,
> Gracioso representante,
> Y en su tiempo gran poeta,
> Empeçó á poner la farsa
> En buen uso y orden buena,
> Porque la repartió en actos,
> Haziendo *introito* en ella
> Que agora llamamos *loa*," etc.
>
> (*Viage entretenido* (ed. 1603), p. 123.)

As Pellicer had already observed,[2] Rojas does not seem to have been acquainted with the *Propaladia* of Torres Naharro, first published at Naples in 1517, since he ascribes the introduction of the *introito* or *argumento* to Rueda, though it had been used by Naharro nearly half a century before. Nor is Rojas correct in saying that Rueda divided his *farsas* into acts. The only division of his plays is into scenes. Cañete calls Naharro "padre y fundador de la comedia española."[3]

Of the plays of Naharro numerous editions appeared after the first one at Naples: at Seville in 1520, 1526, 1533, and 1545; one at Toledo in 1535, and one at Antwerp without date, but probably about 1550. According to Menéndez y Pelayo,[4] the *Propaladia* was first placed upon the *Index Expurgatorius* in 1559, and an *edicion castigada* was issued at Madrid in 1573, one at Antwerp

---

[1] Introduction to his edition of the *Comedias de Alonso de la Vega*, Dresden, 1905, p. xiv. He says further: "Lope de Rueda, con verdadero instinto de hombre de teatro y de observador realista transportó á las tablas el tipo de la prosa de la *Celestina*, pero aligerándole mucho de su opulenta frondosidad, haciendole mas rápido é incisivo, con toda la diferencia que va del libro á la escena."

[2] *Tratado historico sobre el Origen y Progresos de la Comedia y del Histrionismo en España*, Madrid, 1804, Vol. I, p. 22.

[3] *El Teatro español del Siglo XVI*, p. 112.

[4] *Propaladia*, Madrid, 1900, Vol. II, p. lxxv.

in the same year, and again at Madrid in 1590, though, according to the same distinguished critic, other editions, unexpurgated, were published between 1559 and 1573. This list of editions evinces considerable vogue for the *Propaladia,* though its influence on the Spanish drama at this period does not seem to have been proportionate. Still, those who are most competent to give an opinion in the matter declare that Naharro's influence was wide and immediate.[1]

However this may be, it was in the plays of Naharro and Rueda that Lope de Vega, with the eye of genius, saw the coming comedia, and in them it had its beginnings, as he himself tells us. Hence the career of Lope de Rueda, who was both actor and playwright, is of especial interest to us. Cervantes, born in 1547, is the most important witness we have among Spanish poets concerning Lope de Rueda. He saw him in the flesh. We can imagine Cervantes as a boy of ten or twelve standing in the square of Valladolid gazing with unfeigned delight at the somewhat crude and boisterous farces enacted, with due accompaniment of horse-play, doubtless, by Lope de Rueda and his little company of strolling players.[2] They made an endur-

---

[1] *Propaladia,* Vol. II, pp. cxlv *et seq.;* Schack, *Geschichte der dramatischen Literatur und Kunst in Spanien,* Frankfurt am Main, 1854, Vol. I, pp. 194 ff.; Cañete, *El Teatro español del Siglo XVI,* Madrid, 1885, p. 206; Ticknor, *History of Spanish Literature,* Boston, 1888, Vol. I, p. 209; Vol. II, p. 54. As long ago as 1749 Blas Nasarre said of our author: "Pero Bartolomé de Torres Naharro, que floreció por el mismo tiempo debaxo del Pontificado de Leon X, debe ser tenido por el primero que dió forma á las Comedias vulgares; las suyas se representaron en Roma," etc. (*Comedias y Entremeses de Miguel de Cervantes,* Madrid, 1749.) A list of pieces which were printed in the first half of the sixteenth century, containing several not mentioned by any writer on the Spanish drama, has been published by Emilio Cotarelo y Mori, *Catálogo de Obras dramaticas impresas pero no conocidas hasta el presente,* Madrid, 1902. See also *Anales de la Literatura española,* ed. Bonilla y San Martin, Madrid, 1904, p. 236. A long list of sixteenth-century pieces had been given many years ago by Gayangos in his Spanish translation of Ticknor, Vol. II, pp. 523–550. See also Cañete, *El Teatro español del Siglo XVI,* pp. 55 ff.

[2] Lope de Rueda evidently gave a performance whenever an audience could be collected, both in the morning and afternoon, for at the close of

ing impression on his boyish mind. From that time forth he was in the thrall of the stage, and never afterward, through all his long and checkered career, even when in his generous, valiant optimism he must have acknowledged that his plays were failures, was he able to shake off entirely the spell of the theater. After the lapse of more than half a century, in the prologue to the volume of his *Comedias* (1615), the old hero of Lepanto, whose name was now the greatest in all the literature of Spain, falls into one of his delightfully reminiscent moods and gives us an animated description of the primitive performances of Lope de Rueda's little band of strollers. The account is now much worn by constant usage, but Cervantes is the only eye-witness who has left anything on paper, and his narrative must serve once more here.

In the time of this celebrated Spaniard [Lope de Rueda] all the properties of a theatrical manager were contained in a sack (*costal*), and consisted of four white pelices trimmed with gilded leather, and four beards and wigs, with four staffs, more or less. The plays were colloquies or eclogues between two or three shepherds and a shepherdess. They were set off by two or three *entremeses,* either that of the "Negress," the "Ruffian," the "Fool," or the "Biscayan," for these four characters and many others the said Lope acted with the greatest skill and propriety that one can imagine. At that time there were no *tramoyas* (theatrical machinery) nor challenges of Moors or Christians either afoot or on horse. There were no figures which arose or seemed to arise from the center of the earth through the hollow of the stage, which at that time consisted of four benches arranged in a square, with four or five boards upon them, raised about four spans from the ground, nor did clouds with angels or souls descend from the skies. The furnishings (*adorno*) of the stage were an old woolen blanket drawn by two cords from one side to the other, which formed what is called a dressing-room (*vestuario*), behind which were the musicians, sing-

his *Eufemia* he invites his audience "only to go and eat their dinners and to return to the square, if they wish to see a traitor beheaded, a loyal man freed," etc. (*Obras de Lope de Rueda*, Madrid, 1896, Vol. I, p. 88.)

ing some old ballad without the accompaniment of a guitar. . . .
Lope de Rueda was succeeded by Nabarro, a native of Toledo,[1]
famous as an impersonator of the cowardly ruffian; he improved
somewhat the setting of the comedia (*levantó algun tanto mas el
adorno de las Comedias*), and instead of a bag for the costumes
used chests and trunks. He brought the musicians from behind the
curtain, where they formerly sang, out upon the stage, removed
the beards of the players, for up to that time no actor appeared upon
the stage without a false beard, . . . except those who represented
old men or other characters which required a facial disguise. He
invented stage machinery (*tramoyas*), thunder and lightning, challenges and battles, but these never reached the excellence which we
see now, etc.

Continuing, Cervantes mentions his own plays, *Los
Tratos de Argel, La Destruycion de Numancia,* and *La
Batalla Naual,* which were then seen in the theaters of
Madrid, and speaks of the innovations introduced by him,
such as reducing the comedias from five acts to three;
representing for the first time upon the boards the "imag-
inations and hidden thoughts of the soul and moral abstrac-
tions," etc.

All this is very interesting, but the accuracy of Cervantes's statements has been questioned because they
apparently do not agree with facts that are known from
other sources.[2] There can be no doubt that Cervantes is
mistaken when he says that he first reduced the comedia
from five acts to three. This had been done by Francisco

---

[1] Of this *autor,* Pedro Nabarro, one play survives, *La Marquesa Saluzia,
llamada Griselda,* a drama in four acts in verse. From a unique copy,
dated 1603, Dr. C. B. Bourland has reprinted it in the *Revue Hispanique*
(1905).

[2] Juan Rufo, another eye-witness of the performances of Rueda, cor-
roborates the testimony of Cervantes as regards the rudeness of the stage at
that time. In his *Seiscientas Apotegmas, y otras obras en verso* (Toledo,
1596), fol. 266, v., he says:

> "Quien vió, apenas ha treinta años,
> de las farsas la pobreza,
> de su estilo la rudeza,
> y sus mas que humildes paños."

de Avendaño as early as 1553. Besides, Schack cites a rescript promulgated by Charles V. in 1534 against extravagance in dress, "which is to extend likewise to players —men and women—musicians and other persons who take part in comedias by singing and playing."[1] Schack observes that this decree not only shows that the representation of comedias in Spain had reached a high degree of refinement at that early date, but that women also appeared upon the stage at that time, while later, under Philip the Second, women's rôles were played by boys.[2]

Another curious notice referring to the same period is found in the *Ingeniosa Comparación entre lo antiguo y lo presente,* by the Bachiller Villalón, which first appeared in 1539. The author says that never since the creation of the world had "the comedias which we call *farsas* been represented with such subtlety and ingenuity as nowadays." He speaks of six men who are regularly in the pay (*asalariados*) of the church of Toledo, of whom the two principal ones, named Correa, are such remarkable actors that he says he would spend a large sum of money or go begging in order to see them, "though they should be many miles from here."[3]

It cost but a copper to see the show:

"Una ó dos comedias solas,
como camisas de pobre,
la entrada á tarja de cobre,
y el teatro casi á solas."
                    (Quoted by Wolf, *Studien,* p. 606.)

[1] Pragmatica de Carlos V. y Doña Juana, su madre, hecha en Toledo en el año de 1534 (Lib. VII, Ley 1, Tit. 12 de la Nueva Recopilacion): "Item mandamos que lo que cerca de los trages está prohibido y mandado por las leyes de este titulo, se entienda asi mismo con los comediantes, hombres y mugeres, musicos y las demas personas que assisten en las comedias para cantar y tañer, las quales incurren en las mismas penas que cerca desto estan impuestas.'' (*Geschichte der dramatischen Lit. u. Kunst in Spanien*, Vol. I, p. 198, note.)

[2] See below, Chapter VI.

[3] "Pues en las representaciones de comedias que llamamos farsas, nunca desde la creación del mundo se representaron con tanta agudeza é industria como agora, porque viven seys hombres asalariados por la Iglesia de

However, neither the rescript of Charles V. in 1534, nor the account given by Villalón in 1539, seem to me to invalidate in the slightest degree the narrative of Cervantes. The decree of 1534 relates, almost certainly, to the elaborate representations that were given at public and church festivals, indeed Villalón states explicitly that the players whom he had seen were regularly in the pay of the church of Toledo. So far as we know there were no fixed *corrales* or theaters in Spain at this early period nor for many years thereafter. We may be quite sure that the little company of Lope de Rueda (he died in 1565) never acted upon a permanent stage. Juan Rufo, quoted above, alludes to the "cruel inn-yard" and its furnace-heat in summer, while the memory of the icy winter blasts still makes him shiver.[1] Surely strolling players, acting even a quarter of a century before this, were not at all likely to be attired in such magnificent costumes as to bring them under the ban of the "Pragmatica" of Charles V. Hence the representations against which the rescript of 1534 was directed were undoubtedly the religious dramas that were acted in the public squares or within the churches, or perhaps in the open space without the church. Moreover, all the evidence furnished by the comedia itself tends to corroborate and validate the account given by Cervantes. It may be said with a great degree of probability that the stage accessories in the public theaters of

Toledo, de los quales son capitanes dos que se llaman los *Correas,* que en la representación contrahazen todos los descuydos y avisos de los hombres, como si Naturaleza, nuestra universal madre, los representasse alli. Estoy tan admirado de los ver, que si alguno me pudiera pintar con palabras lo mucho que ellos en este caso son, gastara yo grandes summas de dineros ó mendicando fuera por los ver, aunque estuvieran mil leguas de aqui." (Page 180 of the reprint by the Sociedad de Bibliófilos Españoles, 1898, and quoted by Menéndez y Pelayo in his introduction to the *Propaladia* of Torres Naharro, Vol. II, p. cl, Madrid, 1900.) See also Cañete, *Teatro español,* p. 95, note.

[1] "Porque era el patio cruel,
fragua ardiente en el estio,
de invierno un elado rio,
que aun agora tiemblan dél."

Spain down to almost the beginning of the seventeenth century were of a very simple and elementary kind. Two or three musicians had been substituted for the ballad singers, some simple devices to indicate locality and the introduction of crude stage machinery. Indeed, in spite of the improvements introduced upon the stage by Cervantes himself and to which he alludes with evident pride in the *Prologue* above quoted, we need go no further than his own plays to show the primitive character of the stage machinery of his day. To represent thunder and lightning, we read the following stage direction in his *Numancia:* "Under the stage they make a noise with a barrel full of stones and discharge a rocket."[1]

That representations were given in Spain, at this early period, in which there was, in all probability, much display of costume, there is other evidence to prove. The comedias of Torres Naharro, as we have seen, were published as early as 1517, and Italian comedies were not impossibly known in Spain at this time or not long thereafter. As we shall see (below, p. 29), one Muzio, with his company of Italian players, had taken part in the Corpus festival at Seville in 1538. The earliest known account of the performance of an Italian comedy in Spain is dated 1548, when one of Ariosto's comedies was represented at Valladolid on the occasion of the marriage of the Infanta Doña Maria, daughter of Charles V., to Maximilian, Prince of Hungary. It was performed "with such apparatus and scenery as are used at Rome in the representation of comedies," and was "a royal and sumptuous affair."[2] Creizenach, commenting on this, says: "This is also the first known instance in Spain of the use of the scenic arrange-

---

[1] "Hagase ruido debaxo del tablado con un barril lleno de piedras, y disparese un cohete volador." (*Numancia,* Act II, Scene II, p. 195, ed. of 1784.)

[2] Pellicer, Vol. I, p. 31. The latter's authority, as Stiefel (*Zeitschrift für Roman. Phil.,* XV, p. 319) remarks, is Caluete de Estrella, *Felicissimo Viaje del Principe Phelippe . . . ,* Anvers, 1552, fol. 2b.

ments of the Renaissance, the sight of which was evidently a matter of the first importance to the narrator, for he does not even mention the title of Ariosto's comedy. Towards the close of the same year, Philip II., the successor of Charles, saw a comedy performed at Milan, with the greatest refinement and luxury of scenic decoration, and after he had ascended the throne (1556), according to a later account, Antonio Vignali of Siena, a member of the *Academia degli Intronati,* is said to have produced Italian comedies at his court. Still, after this time we hear of no great lords or rich corporations in Spain instituting such elaborate productions. These were naturally beyond the reach of the professional actor, but the latter had found, even as Torres Naharro before him, many a useful hint in the Italian comedy." [1] Furthermore, we read that in 1561, on the occasion of the marriage of Guglielmo, Duke of Mantua, to Eleonora of Austria, the celebrated "scultore del re di Spagna," Leon Leoni of Arezzo, was sent to Mantua "a inventare e porre in ordine qualche bellissimo apparato ed invenzione." [2]

These representations, with their wealth of costume and decorations, were Italian comedies, and were performed privately by Italian players, before the King or his great nobles. They had nothing to do with plays in the market-places, for theaters, so far as we have any information, were then unknown in Spain. But during the great church festivals or on other solemn occasions, here,

---

[1] *Geschichte des neueren Dramas,* Vol. III, p. 167. See also *ibid.,* Vol. II, p. 297. Stiefel (*l. c.*), and after him Creizenach, quotes Scipio Bargagli, *Commedie degli Accademici Intronati,* Vol. II, p. 494, as follows: " 'Arsiccio intronato (i.e. Vignali), con onore stato conosciuto infino dalla remotissima Spagna, mentre in buonissimo grado vi servì Filippo il Secondo là regnante, a diletto di cui fece alla guisa Italiana, ivi non prima conosciuta, rappresentare, dal regal tesoro illustrate, più e chiarissime commedie, dalla ricca e piacevolissima vena del suo felice e tanto universale ingenio scaturite.' " According to this, as Creizenach observes, these representations must have taken place between 1556 and the time of Vignali's death (1559), while "regnante" Philip might be taken as early as 1543.

[2] D'Ancona, *Origini del Teatro Italiano,* Vol. II, p. 416, note.

doubtless, as in religious or festal representations in other countries, the costumes were often very elaborate and costly. Schack mentions such a representation at Valladolid, on June 5, 1527, at the christening of the Infanta Philip. On this occasion the *auto* of the "Baptism of St. John" was performed.[1] The same author, quoting Ortiz de Zuñiga, *Anales de Sevilla,* ed. of 1796, Vol. III, pp. 339 ff., mentions a magnificent representation given in Seville in the previous year (1526) in honor of the marriage of Charles V with the Princess Isabel of Portugal, and also the *autos* represented at Corpus in 1532, likewise at Seville. Schack remarks that it is very probable that allegorical figures appeared in these *autos,* though this fact is not expressly stated.[2]

In 1563 there was represented at Plasencia, at the festival of Corpus Christi, the tragedy of *Nabuco Donosor,* with elaborate scenic display (*con gran aparato*), "and when the children were thrown into the furnace, it seemed so real that some persons believed that they were actually thrown in."[3]   Seven years after this, in 1570, we find the

---

[1] See the passage from Sandoval, *Historia de Carlos V.,* Valladolid, 1604, Bk. XVI, quoted by Schack, *Geschichte,* Vol. I, p. 200. On page 403, indeed, he mentions some elaborate religious representations which were given a quarter of a century earlier, in 1501, in honor of the Palsgrave, afterward Kurfürst Friedrich II. He quotes from Hubertus Thomas of Lüttich, *Annales de vita et rebus gestis Friderici II.,* Francof., 1624 (German: *Spiegel des Humors groszer Potentaten,* Schlensingen, 1628). Speaking of the "pomphaften dramatischen Spielen" given in Barcelona, he says: "Da war angestellt ein gemachter Himmel, dabei man auch die Hölle sah, sehr schrecklich und grausam.   Dabei wurden viele Historien gespielt, welche fast an die vier Stunden währten."   "In Perpignan sahen wir Stücke aus dem alten und neuen Testament, Paradies und Hölle waren da gleich prächtig zu schauen, und vier Stunden lang gab man da ein schauerliches Stück zu sehen.   Die Engel in weiszen Kleidern, die Teufel in Gold und Silber stattlich angethan stritten mit einander; unter gewaltigem Krachen und Platzen sprangen die Raketen und es gab einen Höllenlärm, als bewegten sich Himmel und Erde.   Zuletzt kam Judas und erhing sich an einem Fenster, ward auch sobald mit einem Feuerstrahl getroffen und verschwand, dasz ihn Niemand mehr sahe."

[2] *Ibid.,* pp. 202, 203, and p. 205 for a list of early *autos.*

[3] Sanchez-Arjona, *Anales,* p. 16.   See also the account of the elaborate representation in 1578, in the public square of Plasencia, of *El Naufragio*

students of the college of San Hermenegildo representing a tragedy entitled *San Hermenegildo,* in which there were thirty-four characters, besides soldiers, pages, etc. While this was a festival performance given under the direction of the Fathers of the Company of Jesus, and not a representation in a public theater, we have here one of the earliest descriptions of stage scenery, and hence it is of interest.

The stage was about five feet (*un estado*) in height and thirty-nine feet square. On the front was a large door of fine architecture, representing the city of Seville, on the frieze of which was a shield with the letters S. P. Q. H. At the two sides of this door ran a handsome canvas of a wall with its battlements, forth from which, projecting a distance of three feet, arose towers somewhat higher, of which the tower on the left served as the prison of San Hermenegildo, while the one on the right was the castle for the entertainments. On the sides of these two towers sufficient room remained for the exit of those personages who were represented as belonging outside of Seville, such as the King Leovigildo and others, for through the middle gate only those entered and departed who were supposed to be from Seville, like San Hermenegildo,[1] etc.

Juan de Malara, the reputed author of this tragedy, was, as is well known, an imitator of the ancient comic poets, as opposed to the popular style of Lope de Rueda. But it were useless to cite other religious or festal representations. We have already passed beyond the period of Lope de Rueda, and our chief reason for citing such spectacles is (as this is not a history of the drama) to show that, while they were not uncommon during the

de Jonas profeta, in Cañete, *El Teatro Español del Siglo XVI,* p. 139, and of the *Representacion* of Francisco de las Cuebas in Alcalá in 1568. (*Ibid.,* p. 323.) This shows, as Sr. Cañete says, that "'el aparato escénico de los dramas religiosos era en toda España lujosísimo durante el siglo XVI." A copy of this *Representacion* of Cuebas is before me, made by my colleague, Dr. Crawford, who purposes publishing it shortly.

[1] Sanchez-Arjona, *Anales,* p. 41.

time of Lope de Rueda and even long before, they cannot serve in support of the statements of some writers that during this period the costumes and accessories of the popular theater in Spain were of an elaborate and sumptuous character. For such spectacles as we have mentioned had nothing to do with the performances of strolling players in the market-places, and hence a "pragmatica" of 1534 could not have had them in view. We are therefore safe in accepting the account of Cervantes in regard to Lope de Rueda's performances as essentially true.

CHAPTER II

The *corrales* of Madrid. The *Corral de la Pacheca.* The *Corral de Burguillos.* The *Corral de Puente.* The foundation of the two famous theaters: The *Corral de la Cruz* and the *Corral del Príncipe.*

MADRID became the capital of Spain in 1560. Strolling players had certainly appeared there long before this date, but with the rapid growth of the city in wealth and population, which naturally ensued when it became the official center of the kingdom, it was necessary to find some fixed place where these companies of players could perform. The establishment of permanent theaters in Madrid was, at the outset, connected with an event that seemed to have but a remote relation to public amusements.[1] In 1565 a number of charitable citizens of Madrid founded a fraternity called the *Cofradia de la Sagrada Pasión,* the primary object of which was merely to feed and clothe the poor; but, under the auspices of the King and the Council of Castile, their field was soon widened, and a hospital for poor women suffering from fever, "because there was no other hospital for this purpose in the capital," was founded in the calle de Toledo. In order to increase the funds of the hospital the President of Castile, Cardinal Espinosa, and the Councilors granted to the *Cofradia* the privilege

---

[1] Schack, *Geschichte der dramatischen Literatur und Kunst in Spanien,* Vol. I, p. 264, remarks that such a connection between public amusements and religious or charitable foundations seemed natural enough to the Spanish mind; that it seemed equally natural to the English mind, we shall see further on. The theater being supported by the public, it does not appear so very strange, after all, that it should contribute to the public charities.

of providing a place for the representation of all comedias given in Madrid, and of appropriating to their pious purposes the funds thus obtained.[1] Two years after this, in 1567, another fraternity was founded called the *Cofradia de Nuestra Señora de la Soledad,* with charitable aims of greater scope than those of the older fraternity. The *Cofradia de la Soledad* bought a house near the Puerta del Sol and fitted it up as a hospital. The places designated for theatrical representations by the *Cofradia de la Pasion* were three: a square or *corral* in the Calle del Sol; another belonging to Isabel Pacheco, in the Calle del Príncipe,[2] and a third in the same street—a *corral* leased from one Burguillos—which afterward passed into the control of the *Cofradia de la Soledad.* For in 1574 the latter brotherhood also petitioned for the right to furnish a place for the representation of comedias in order to maintain its hospital,[3] and the matter ended in a compromise with the

[1] If now we cast a glance at theatrical affairs in London, we find that in March, 1573-4, the Lord Chamberlain (Earl of Essex) requested that one Mr. Holmes might appoint places for plays and interludes within the city. "The Mayor and aldermen replied that it would hurt their liberties so to do, and that it was unfitting for any private person to hold such an office. They had had preferable offers of a similar nature, *for the relief of the poor in the hospitals;* they would accept these, if any." (Fleay, *Chronicle History of the London Stage,* 1559-1642, London, 1890, p. 45.) And an Act of the Common Council of London provided that all plays performed in the city should first be licensed . . . and that of the money taken there should be applied to the relief of the sick poor such sums as shall be agreed on. (*Ibid.,* p. 46.) Again, on October 8, 1594, Lord Hunsdon wrote to the Lord Mayor asking permission for his players to play at the Cross-Keys, "as they have been accustomed [i.e., before 1592]. They will play from 2 P. M. to 4, instead of beginning at 4 or 5, . . . and be contributory to the parish poor." (Halliwell-Phillipps, *Illustrations,* p. 31. See also Collier, *Annals of the Stage,* Vol. I, p. 216, and *Henslowe's Diary,* ed. W. W. Greg, Vol. II, p. 77.)

[2] There is a notice of a performance here in 1568: "En miercoles á 5 de Mayo de 1568 años entró a representar Velazquez en el Corral desta casa: ha de dar seis reales cada dia de los que representare." (Pellicer, *Tratado historico,* Vol. I, p. 48. *El Corral de la Pacheca,* by Ricardo Sepúlveda, Madrid, 1888.)

[3] Among the reasons on which they based their petition were that "comedians were people coming and going to the court [Madrid], and as they were not to remain therein longer than eight or ten days, they performed freely wherever they listed, and making use of this and wishing to do a

older fraternity, the *Cofradia de la Soledad* acquiring the *corral* of Burguillos. Both brotherhoods finally decided to join forces and petitioned Dr. Antonio de Aguilera, Councilor of Castile and deputy for the administration of the said hospitals, that two thirds of the profits accruing from these *corrales* should go to the *Cofradia de la Pasion,* and the remaining third to the *Cofradia de la Soledad;* the expenses to be shared in the same proportion. This agreement of the two brotherhoods was approved by Dr. Aguilera on June 7, 1574.

These *corrales*—a name that down to our own day has remained synonymous with playhouse—were originally, before they were transformed into theaters, the yards of houses.[1] In the rear was the stage; the larger part of the audience viewed the performance standing in the courtyard, while the windows of the principal building and of the surrounding houses served as boxes for the more distinguished spectators. Arrangements for the comfort of actors and audience were at first, naturally, very crude. The stage, as well as the whole court-yard, had no roof nor any kind of protection against sunshine or rain. If the weather was unfavorable the representation was either suspended or brought suddenly to a close.[2]

As early as 1574 a company of Italian players under

good work and a charity to the brotherhood of *La Soledad,* Alonso Rodriguez and other comedians were representing comedias to aid in the bringing up of foundlings, in the *Corral de Burguillos,* which the brotherhood had provided, and for which it had paid." (Pellicer, *Tratado,* Vol. I, p. 50.)

[1] So in England the immediate predecessor of the playhouse was the inn-yard. Until 1576, Fleay says, public performances in London were given in inn-yards, of which there were five. (See also Collier, *Annals,* Vol. I, p. 36.)

[2] Schack, Vol. I, p. 266. Under date of December 10, 1579, we read: "No hubo representacion en ningun corral por haber llovido mucho." (Pérez Pastor, in *Bull. Hispanique* (1906), p. 76.) Moreover, when there were but few people in the *corral* the managers refused to give a performance. "27 de Agosto de 1579.—No hubo representacion en la calle del Lobo (*Corral de Puente*) porque Cisneros estaba ausente, ni en la *Pacheca* porque Ganasa no quiso representar al ver que habia poca gente en el corral, y se devolvió el dinero á las personas que habian entrado." (*Ibid.,* p. 74.)

Alberto Nazeri de Ganassa[1] presented plays at Madrid
(mostly in pantomime, as it appears), and in the same year
Ganassa succeeded in having a theater erected in the *Corral
de la Pacheca*. "For while comedias had already been
represented in the said *corral,* it was wholly open, and the
stage, raised seats, and *patio* were exposed to the inclem-
ency of the weather, so that when it rained no performance could be given." And in 1574 the theater was built
by two carpenters, using the "tablados, lienzos y otros
pertrechos del Corral de la Pacheca," and also the awn-
ings which had been made to shade the stage of this *corral*
from the sun.[2]

The agreement was that a theater and stage should be
built, wholly covered by a roof, and that this theater
should be leased for a period of nine or ten years, etc., the

---

[1] Concerning Ganassa, who had a company of players in France in September, 1571, see Baschet, *Les Comédiens Italiens,* Paris, 1882, pp. 18–25,
and Sanchez-Arjona, *Anales del Teatro en Sevilla,* Sevilla, 1898, p. 47. As
Ganassa appeared in Seville in 1575 in the *Corral de Don Juan,* the
corrales of the latter city were probably established as early as those of
Madrid. (Sanchez-Arjona, *Anales,* p. 53, and see below.) Ganassa seems
to have been at the head of the company called the *Gelosi* as early as 1572,
and to him is probably due the invention of the second *Zanni* or Arlecchino.
Scherillo says: "La compagnia, che sembra avesse già allora (1572) il titolo
dei *Gelosi,* era condotta da un bergamasco Alberto, noto pel suo nome o
soprannome di Ganassa; al quale, oltre tutto il resto, si deve fors' anche
l'invenzione della parte e del nome del secondo Zanni, cioè dell' Arlecchino."
(*La Commedia dell' Arte,* in *La Vita Italiana del Seicento,* Milano, 1895,
p. 451.) It appears that a company of Italian players had visited Spain as
early as 1538, when one Muzio, "Italiano de la Comedia," was in Seville,
taking part in the festival of Corpus Christi. (Sanchez-Arjona, *Anales,*
p. 47, note.) The petition of Muzio, which is found in Vol. VI of the
Escribania de Cabildo of the municipal Archives of Seville, is as follows:
"Los Italianos que sacaron los carros en la fiesta del Corpus Cristi suplican a V. S. que, pues es costumbre de repartir joyas a quien mas buena
voluntad y obras mostrare en tal dia, que habiendo ellos hecho todo lo que
pudieron, sean V. S. tan benignas que, aunque en ellos haya poca parte de
merecimientos, puedan gozar della, y en todo sea, como suplican, con
aquella brevedad que el favor de V. S. y sus necesidades requieren, a fin
que se puedan ir a su viaje, e quitarse de los gastos, que son muchos, que
hasta agora han tenido para aguardar tan señalada merced."—Muzio,
Italiano de la Comedia. (*Ibid.,* p. 47, note.) Stiefel (*Zeitschrift für
Roman. Phil.,* Vol. XV, p. 320) conjectures that Lope de Rueda may have
joined this company of Muzio's, and it is not improbable.

[2] Pellicer, *Tratado historico,* Vol. I, p. 54.

rent being fixed at ten reals per day. But, in fact, the roof
covered only the stage and the sides of the *patio;* the sole
covering of the latter was an awning to shade the spectator from the sun. From this *patio* the rank and file—the
vulgo or *gente del bronce*—viewed the play, standing. On
account of the clamor and uproar they made, they were
called *mosqueteros.* So in France "the boisterous and
vulgar" stood, as did the "groundlings" in the pit of the
inn-yards of London.

Ganassa further agreed to perform two comedias for
the benefit of the theater, to advance 600 reals toward the
erection of it—to be returned to him at the rate of ten reals
per day (the rental of the playhouse)—and agreed besides
to give sixty performances.

Of the plays performed by Ganassa and his Italian company, Pellicer says: "Representaban comedias italianas,
mimicas por la mayor parte, y bufonescas, de asuntos
triviales y populares. Introducian en ellas las personas
del Arlequino, del Pantalone, y del Dotore."[1] This was
the Italian *commedia dell' arte.* Ganassa seems to have
made several journeys to Spain with his company, for
after this first visit in 1574, he appeared again in June and
July, 1579 (see below, p. 31), at the *Corral de Puente,*
and also in the beginning of the following year in the
Pacheca and again during the years 1581 and 1582,[2] and
in the *Corral del Príncipe* in 1584.[3] He seems to have
visited Spain again in 1603, according to Pellicer,[4] though
his statements are not clear on this point. We may be
quite sure that the financial success reaped by Ganassa
and his players, to which Ricardo de Turia (Don Pedro

---

[1] *Tratado historico,* Vol. I, p. 53.
[2] Under date of December 31, 1581, we find the curious notice that
"Saldaña did not perform on this day, because he and his company were at
the *Teatro de la Cruz* to see the Italians." (See Pérez Pastor, in *Bull.
Hispanique,* April–June, 1906, p. 149, and Appendix A.)
[3] See below, p. 43.
[4] Vol. I, pp. 57 and 72.

Juan de Rejaule y Toledo)[1] alludes many years afterward, induced other Italian actors to try their fortunes
upon Spanish soil. To these we shall recur further on.
The *Corral de la Pacheca*, as stated above, was in the
Calle del Príncipe.. The increased demand for theatrical
representations, however, now induced the same *Cofradias*
to rent another *corral*, belonging to Cristóbal de la Puente,
in the Calle del Lobo, which they furnished with benches
and *gradas* or raised seats, and fitted it up for the performance of comedias. Besides, another *corral* was provided by the fraternities for Francisco Osorio, a theatrical
manager, who came to Madrid with his company in June,
1579. To Osorio was assigned the *Corral de Valdivieso*
by the then *comisario de comedias*, Francisco de Prado,
"and the said Osorio has bound himself to build a stage
and two platforms (*tablados*) at the sides, at his own cost,
and the profits arising therefrom shall be for the hospitals,
without any deductions being made, and besides the said
Osorio is to give ten reals for every day that he performs,
and to-day [June 7, 1579] is the first day that the said
Osorio represents, while also on this day Salcedo represents in the *Corral de la Pacheca* and Ganassa in the
Puente."[2] We learn, moreover, that Osorio only gave performances on June 7, 8, and 9, when, on account of the
small number of spectators, he abandoned the *corral*. On
Sunday, June 7, 1579, the Hospital de la Pasion received,
as its two-thirds share from the performances of Ganassa,
who was representing in the *Corral de Puente*, and from
Salcedo, in the *Corral de la Pacheca*, two hundred and
twenty-one reals and ten maravedís, and on June 8 and 9
these receipts were one hundred and fifty-six reals twelve

---

[1] In his *Apologetico de las Comedias españolas*, prefixed to the second part
of *Norte de la Poesia Española*, etc., Valencia, 1616, he speaks of "el famoso
comico Ganaça, que en la primera entrada que hizo en ella [España] robo
igualmente el aplauso y dinero de todos." I possess an excellent copy of
this very rare book.

[2] Pérez Pastor, in *Bull. Hispanique*, 1906, p. 72, and see also Appendix A.

maravedís, and one hundred and ninety-five reals ten maravedís respectively. Ganassa and Salcedo also represented on Trinity Sunday, and on June 18 we learn that Ganassa had gone to Toledo for the festival, while Salcedo was engaged in the festival at Madrid, so that there were no representations in the *Corral de Puente,* where Ganassa had performed, nor in the *Pacheca,* which Saldaña had occupied. On June 24 Ganassa returned from Toledo and again performed in the *Puente,* and on June 28 and 29 in the *Pacheca.* On July 2 Ganassa appeared in the *Pacheca* "and declared that he had been given a license by the Council of Madrid to perform two days in each week."[1] In these *corrales* various *autores* or theatrical managers gave performances, among them Ganassa, Cisneros, Alonso Rodriguez "el Toledano," Jerónimo Velazquez, Francisco Salcedo, Rivas, Juan Granado, Alonso Rodriguez of Seville, Saldaña, and others.[2]

Of these directors of companies many wrote farces or comedias,[3] and the term *autor* was therefore strictly appropriate to them at this time. It was not till some years afterward that the title *autor de comedias* came to mean

[1] The representations during the three next succeeding years will be found in Appendix A. The list is copied from the very important article by Dr. Pérez Pastor, in the *Bull. Hispanique,* 1906.

[2] Pellicer mentions Alonso Velazquez among these early *autores,* but according to Sanchez-Arjona, *Anales,* p. 98, this *autor de comedias* was not born till 1572.

[3] Of these *autores* Antonio de Villegas is said to have written fifty-four comedias and forty *entremeses,* according to Pellicer, Vol. I, p. 116. The latter quotes Rojas, *Viage entretenido,* p. 54, as his authority, but Pellicer's mistake was pointed out by Barrera (*Catálogo,* p. 493) nearly fifty years ago. Rojas evidently meant that these comedias and *entremeses* formed the repertory of Villegas, not that he wrote them. None of the comedias attributed by Pellicer to Antonio de Villegas was written by him. *Callar hasta la Ocasion,* which Pellicer ascribes to Alonso de Cisneros, was, according to Barrera, written by Don Juan Hurtado y Cisneros. Pellicer also mentions Gaspar Vazquez, an actor (perhaps the lessee of the *Corral del Príncipe* in 1583, mentioned below, p. 41), who, in the opinion of Tamayo de Vargas, in his *Biblioteca manuscrita,* is the author of a comedia entitled *La Costanza* (Alcalá de Henares, por Sebastian Martinez, 1570).

merely a theatrical director, an *impresario*.[1] We have seen that, after paying the *autor* and his company, the average net proceeds of a single representation varied, at this early period, from 140 to 200 reals, which went to the hospitals of the city. It may be mentioned here that in 1583 Philip II. granted to the "Royal House of Incurables" at Naples half the proceeds derived from the public performances of comedias in that city.[2]

Performances in these *corrales* always took place in the afternoon. At first they were limited to Sundays and feast-days, but with the growing demand for such spectacles, two representations were authorized during the week, on Tuesdays and Thursdays, and sometimes they continued for fifteen or twenty days before Shrovetide. On Ash Wednesday the theaters were closed till Easter, and in 1580 plays were not resumed until September 11, when Rivas began in the *Pacheca*.[3]

All representations took place in these *corrales* until the *Cofradías* erected their own permanent theaters, the first one in the Calle de la Cruz in 1579, the other in the Calle del Príncipe in 1582.[4]

Let us turn now to these permanent theaters. A site having been purchased in the Calle de la Cruz on October 12, 1579, for 550 ducats, the wood, benches, and other properties were moved from the *corral* of Cristóbal de la Puente, and a new theater was fitted up.[5] It is interesting

[1] Caramuel, writing in the latter half of the seventeenth century, says: "*Autor de Comedias* apud Hispanos non est qui illas scribit aut recitat, sed qui Comicos alit et singulis solvit convenientia stipendia." (*Rhythmica* (second ed. Campaniæ, 1668), quoted by Schack, *Nachträge*, p. 25.)

[2] Croce, *I Teatri di Napoli*, p. 56.

[3] For details see Appendix A.

[4] Performances continued to take place in the old *corrales*, however, for some time after the establishment of the two permanent theaters. There is record of a representation in the *Pacheca* in January, 1583, and in the *Corral de Puente* on February 18, 1584. See Appendix A.

[5] "Martes 8 de Diciembre [1579]:—En este dia se notificó á Cristóbal de la Puente, dueño del corral de la Calle del Lobo, que tienen alquilado las cofradias, que cesaba este arrendamiento y que los asientos, tablados y

to note that the building and the expenditures of this new theater, or *Corral de la Cruz*, as it was called, were in charge of Getino de Guzman, who had been the surety for Cervantes's mother, Doña Leonor de Cortinas, for his redemption from Algerine captivity.[1]

The *Corral de la Cruz* had not yet been completed when the first comedia was represented therein on Sunday, November 29, 1579, by the companies of Juan Granado and Jerónimo de Galvez.[2]

Though on December 8, 1579, as we have just seen, the *Corral de Puente* had been stripped of its benches, etc., Cisneros again began to represent in it on January 28, 1580; and we find him there again on February 11 and 18,[3] and according to Pellicer[4] on February 1, 1584. It is clear, however, that the new *Corral de la Cruz*[5]

pertrechos que a costa de las cofradias se habian hecho en dicho corral se trasladarian al nuevo teatro de la calle de la Cruz ya por evitar gastos ya tambien porque Francisco Salcedo, que representaba en la calle del Lobo, se ha ausentado." (Pérez Pastor, *Bull. Hispanique,* Jan., 1906, p. 75.)

[1] *Bull. Hispanique* (1906), p. 76. Cervantes alludes to the relation existing between the theaters and the "Brotherhoods of the Hospitals" in his *Entremes del Retablo de las Maravillas,* where Chanfalla says: "Yo señores mios soy Montiel, el que trae el retablo de las marauillas; hanme embiado a llamar de la Corte los señores cofrades de los hospitales, porque no ay autor de comedias en ella, y perecen los hospitales, y con mi yda se remediara todo." (*Ocho Comedias,* etc., Madrid, 1615, fol. 244.)

[2] "Yo Francisco de Olea doy fee . . . en como hoy domingo 29 dias del mes de Noviembre de 1579 años fue el primero dia que se representó en el corral que las cofradias de la Sagrada Pasion y Nuestra Señora de la Soledad tienen en esta dicha villa en la calle de la Cruz, en el qual asi mismo representó la primera vez Juan Granado y Galvez, autores de comedias, esta ultima vez que vinieron a esta corte sin que hubiesen representado en el ni en otro corral donde se acostumbra hacer las dichas comedias otra vez desta postrera venida . . . Francisco de Olea." (Pérez Pastor, *Bull. Hispanique,* Jan., 1906, p. 75.)

[3] *Ibid.,* pp. 77, 150. See Appendix A.

[4] Vol. I, p. 80.

[5] In 1576, three years before the building of the *Corral de la Cruz,* "the first London theater properly so called, the *Theatre,* was built by James Burbadge, one of Leicester's players. It was situate in Halliwell or Holy Well, in the parish of St. Leonard's, close to Finsbury fields. In 1577 we find another theater called the *Curtain* erected close to the *Theatre,* both being in the same fields." (Fleay, *Chronicle History of the London Stage,* p. 37.) "When Shakespeare came to London (1586?) there were two

and the *Corral de la Pacheca* now became the favorite playhouses, and were leased by the most famous *autores:* Ganassa, Galvez, Granado, Saldaña, Jerónimo Velazquez, Cisneros, Alonso Rodriguez, Salcedo, and others. On October 29, 1580, all representations in Madrid were suspended on account of the death of the Queen, Doña Ana, and the theaters were closed until November 30, 1581, when Ganassa and his Italian players again appeared at the *Corral de la Cruz.*[1]

The success of the *Corral de la Cruz* and the desire to be relieved of the rent which they were paying for the *Corral de la Pacheca* induced the *Cofradia de la Soledad y Niños expositos,* in 1582 (February 19), to buy a number

theaters in London and its suburbs: the *Theatre* and the *Curtain,* both in Shoreditch. In February, 1592, a third playhouse, the *Rose,* was opened by the manager Philip Henslowe. It was situated on the Bankside in Southwark and was doubtless the scene of Shakespeare's pronounced success alike as an actor and dramatist. In 1594 he [Shakespeare] was connected with another theater at Newington Butts [see now Greg, in *Henslowe's Diary,* II, pp. 72 and 85]; and later (1595–1599) he returned to the *Theatre* and *Curtain.* The latter playhouse was kept up till after his death, but the *Theatre* was torn down in 1599, and most of the materials were used by the Burbadges in the erection of the *Globe* on the Bankside. From the opening of this theater until Shakespeare gave up acting, it appears to have been the only one [with the *Blackfriars*] with which he was regularly connected. The *Blackfriars* theater, originally a dwelling-house converted into a theater by James Burbadge in 1596, was in the City, not far from the northern end of Blackfriars bridge. The *Times* building is now on this site." (Collier, *Works of Shakespeare,* Vol. I, p. 80.) Between July 22, 1596, and April 17, 1597, *Romeo and Juliet* was acted at the *Curtain* by the company known as Lord Hunsdon's servants. (See Ordish, *The London Theatres,* p. 100.) According to the same writer Shakespeare's *Henry V.* was first performed at the *Curtain* in 1599, "presumably by the Burbadge-Shakespeare company." (*Ibid.,* p. 84.) Ordish says that after the accession of James I., in 1603, the Chamberlain's company—which Shakespeare had joined before Christmas, 1594 (*ibid.,* p. 169)—acted only at the *Globe* and at the *Blackfriars.* (*Ibid.,* p. 103.) Greg suggests that Shakespeare may have been a member of Lord Strange's company (which became the servants of Baron Hunsdon, Lord Chamberlain, after the death of Lord Strange, then Earl of Derby, in 1594) as early as April, 1593, though Shakespeare's name does not occur in the list of the company, as he was not a shareholder. (*Henslowe's Diary,* Vol. II, p. 74.)

[1] "30 Noviembre 1581.—Ganasa representó en la Cruz y fue el primer dia que hubo comedia despues de la muerte de la reina Ana. 'Y de todo el aprovechamiento de la comedia, sin la representacion [i.e., the rental paid by

of houses near the latter *corral,* in the Calle del Príncipe, for which they paid the owner, Dr. Alaba de Ibarra, physician to Philip II., the sum of 800 ducats.[1] Here they built a theater after the pattern of the *Corral de la Cruz:* this was the *Corral del Príncipe,* which, with the *Corral de la Cruz,* were, after 1584, the only public theaters of Madrid.[2] Their glory, in the annals of the modern drama, is surpassed only by the *Globe* and *Blackfriars* in London. And it is a curious coincidence that the dramatic careers of the great creators of the English and Spanish dramas began at about the same time. Lope de Vega, born in 1562, began to write for the public stage about 1585. Shakespeare, born in 1564, came to London in 1586(?), and became attached to one of the theaters. Each rose to the topmost height in the dramatic art of his country, and while the wide gulf that separates Shakespeare from his contemporaries does not exist in the case of Lope de Vega, the superiority of the latter among the dramatists of his own country is now undisputed. Lope de Vega had his Sessa, and Shakespeare his Southampton, yet neither ever received aid or encouragement from his

the players], se allegaron doscientos y sesenta reales y medio de que cupo a la cofradia de la Soledad de la tercia parte que lleva noventa reales y cinco maravedis, y a la Pasion le cupo de sus dos tercias partes ciento y ochenta reales y doce maravedis.' " (Pérez Pastor, *Bull. Hispanique* (1906), p. 148.)

[1] "Escritura de venta de dos pares de casas y corrales otorgada por el Dr Alava de Ibarra, médico de S. M., por sí y como legítimo administrador de su hijo D. Juan, en favor de los diputados de la cofradía de Na Sa de la Soledad y Niños expósitos, en la calle del Príncipe, por precio de 800 ducados. Madrid, 19 Febrero 1582.—Ventà de las dos tercias partes de las casas de la calle del Príncipe que fueron del Dr Alava de Ibarra otorgada en favor de los diputados de la cofradía de la Pasión por los de la cofradía de la Soledad y Niños expósitos en precio de 200,000 maravedises. Madrid, 10 Marzo 1582." (*Ibid.,* p. 152.)

[2] I prefer to use the term *Corral del Príncipe* and not *Teatro,* because *Corral* was the only term applied to these theaters for many years after their foundation. Antonio Armona, in his *Memorias cronologicas,* a manuscript in the Biblioteca Nacional at Madrid, says that these buildings began to be called *teatros* in 1608. They were still called *corrales* in 1611 (*Bull. Hisp.* (1907), p. 376) and certainly as late as the middle of the seventeenth century. (Pellicer, Vol. I, p. 108.)

sovereign. There is no proof at hand of personal patronage extended to Shakespeare by either Elizabeth or James,[1] nor did Philip the Third or Philip the Fourth bestow any favor upon Lope.[2] Neither poet seems to have been mindful of the glory he had reaped in the field of the drama, while each took a peculiar pride in his other poetical compositions. Shakespeare polished the verse of his *Venus and Adonis* and his *Rape of Lucrece,* and Lope laid the last file on his epics and sonnets, while both strangely neglected those works which have since been the delight of mankind. Lope's achievement in the drama was too stupendously vast to receive much pruning or revision at his hands, while Shakespeare never troubled himself about the fate of his plays after they were once in print. I cannot forbear quoting the words of Collier in this regard: "Shakespeare probably superintended the passage through the press of his two poems, *Venus and Adonis* and *Lucrece,* but it is our conviction that, as far as regards any of his plays, he never corrected a line of them after they were in type. Even with respect to the two dramas that with most show of probability may be said to have been published entire, in order to check the sale of imperfect, mutilated, and surreptitious copies— *Romeo and Juliet* and *Hamlet*—we feel persuaded that their author was in no way instrumental in the issue of the more authentic copies. . . . After his plays had answered their purpose on the stage, he seems to have been utterly reckless of their fate."[3]

[1] Ward, *History of English Dramatic Literature,* London, 1899, Vol. I, p. 501.

[2] This statement must be mildly qualified in view of a document recently published by Dr. Cristóbal Pérez Pastor, *Bulletin Hispanique* (1908), p. 253: "Ordenareis que se paguen a Lope de Vega Carpio ciento y cincuenta ducados de que la Reyna Nuestra Señora le hizo merced por el servicio que le hizo de la comedia de *El Vellocino dorado,* y esto se pagará por donde se acostumbran pagar cosas deste genero. Dios guarde al Sr. Contralor. Madrid, 3 de Noviembre 1626.—El duque y conde de Benavente. (Arch. de Palacio.—Espectaculos públicos y privados.)" But even here it will be seen that the sum was granted by Philip the Fourth's young queen.

[3] *Memoirs of Actors,* pp. 66, 67.

"If any one should cavil about my comedias and think that I wrote them for fame, undeceive him and tell him that I wrote them for money."[1] So wrote Lope in the autumn of 1604. From all that we know of Shakespeare, it is clear that his plays also were written merely for money, and that for him they had no further interest save the profit to be derived from them. Lope de Vega, indeed, in his later years, when he realized that his chief claim to be remembered by posterity lay in his comedias, did make an attempt to correct his plays for the press, and beginning with Part IX (1617), they were printed under his supervision.[2]

On the other hand, Shakespeare's indifference to the fate of his plays continued till the end of his life. *The Tempest* was probably the latest drama that he completed, and it was written, as it appears, early in 1611—at all events, it was well known in the autumn of that year. Moreover, Lee says: "While there is every indication that in 1611 Shakespeare abandoned dramatic composition, there seems little doubt that he left with the manager of his company unfinished drafts of more than one play which others were summoned at a later date to complete. His place at the head of the active dramatists was at once filled by John Fletcher, and Fletcher, with some aid possibly from his friend Philip Massinger, undertook the working up of Shakespeare's unfinished sketches."[3]

Shakespeare lived five years after this date, in retirement at Stratford. We are told that until 1614 he made frequent visits to London, but he does not seem to have had sufficient regard for his plays to revise and correct them. He continued to draw his income from them, and in his quiet days at "New Place" his thoughts must often

---

[1] See my *Life of Lope de Vega*, Glasgow, 1904, p. 154, note.
[2] In the following year, in Part XI of his *Comedias*, Lope gives the number of plays he had then written as eight hundred.
[3] Sidney Lee, *Shakespeare's Life and Work*, p. 135.

have reverted to the scenes of his great dramatic triumphs, yet he allowed the plays on which his great fame rests to go through the world, not in the perfection in which they issued from his pen, but lame and halt and disfigured, as chance might change and shape them, regardless of their fate.[1] So there is some justification, it would seem, for Pope's couplet on Shakespeare:

> For gain, not glory, wing'd his roving flight,
> And grew immortal in his own despite.

While it has not been without interest, perhaps, to thus point out coincidences and parallels in the careers of the two greatest dramatic geniuses of the modern stage, the comparison closes with a contrast. Lope de Vega was a priest, Shakespeare an actor,—almost the two extremes of the social scale in their day. Lope was the lion of Madrid, the "Phenix of Spain," whose fame had spread far and wide, and whom men came from distant lands to see. Shakespeare enjoyed no such renown among his fellow-countrymen. In the fullness of his powers, at the age of forty-seven, he withdrew from the theater, well provided with the goods of this world, to lead a life of ease and retirement in the quiet of his birthplace. Lope remained in harness, a veteran of seventy-three, battling till the end, on the scene of his early triumphs. His generous hospitality, his unstinted charity, kept his purse-strings ever open, and the last years of his life found him often dependent upon his patron for the necessities of his humble household.

IN 1582, as we have seen, the second of the famous theaters of Madrid—the *Corral del Príncipe*—was erected in

---

[1] "He allowed most mangled and deformed copies of several of his greatest works to be circulated for many years, and did not think it worth while to expose the fraud, which remained in several cases undetected, as far as the great body of the public was concerned, until the appearance of the folio of 1623." (Collier, *Shakespeare's Works*, Vol. I, p. 142.)

the Calle del Príncipe. The deputies of the brotherhoods seem to have proceeded with great circumspection in the building of this new theater. An expense-book was kept, and the work was begun on Monday, May 7, 1582. Of these building expenses the *Cofradia de la Pasion* paid two thirds and the *Soledad* one third, just as they shared the profits, the former contributing 200 ducats and the latter 100 ducats toward the expense. Pellicer gives the following description of the theater: "A platform or stage was built, a green-room, raised seats (*gradas*) for the men, portable benches to the number of ninety-five, a gallery for the women, stalls and windows with iron gratings, passageways, and a roof to cover the *gradas*. Finally the *patio* was paved and an awning was stretched over it which protected against the sun, but not against the rain." Four stairways were also erected, "one to ascend to the women's gallery, with its balustrade of brick and plaster, its wooden steps and its partitions of plaster around the lower part, and the same above, so that the women who went up the said stairway and were in the balcony could not communicate with the men," etc.[1] In addition three other stairways were built, "ascending to the seats of the men [in the galleries?] and to the green-room (*vestuario*),[2] and also a stall or box in the *corral*, whereby women entered to a window which looked upon the stage."

[1] Andres Aguado [the builder of the theater] "se obligó á hacer quatro escaleras, una para subir al corredor de las mugeres, con sus pasamanos de ladrillo y yeso, y sus peldaños de madera labrados, y sus cerramientos al rededor de yeso por la parte de abaxo, y por la de arriba ni mas ni menos, de manera que las mugeres que subiesen por la dicha escalera y estuviesen en el dicho corredor, no se puedan comunicar con los hombres: y de la mesma manera otras tres por donde se sube á los asientos de los hombres y al vestuario: y asimesmo un aposento en el Corral por donde entran las mugeres para una ventana que cae al dicho Teatro . . . y un tejado á dos aguas encima de la dicha ventana hasta el caballete del tejado del aposento de la calle." (*Tratado Historico*, Vol. I, p. 68.)

[2] From this it appears that the green-room was on the floor above the stage. If this were so, a change must have been made later, for an examination of the comedias of Lope de Vega shows that the *vestuario* must have been at the back of the stage and on both sides of it, i.e., on the same

So impatient was the public for these spectacles that the theater was opened before its completion, on September 21, 1583, when [Antonio?] Vazquez and Juan de Ávila represented therein.[1] The proceeds of this performance, including the ten reals paid by the players for the rent of the theater for that day, amounted to seventy reals, "for neither the *gradas,* nor the *ventanas,* nor the *corredor* were yet finished." (*Ibid.,* p. 69.) Adjoining the *Corral del Príncipe* on one side was the house of Doña Juana Gonzalez Carpio, afterward the wife of Francisco Alegria, one of the lessees of the theaters of the city. To Doña Juana the brotherhoods paid one hundred ducats annually for allowing a passage to be made through her house for a women's entrance to the theater. Payment was made by giving her two *aposentos,* one in the *Cruz* and one in the *Príncipe.*[2]

The proceeds of a single representation at this time generally amounted to about three hundred reals, after deducting expenses. Seeing the large pecuniary gains derived by the two fraternities from the theaters, the Council of Castile in December, 1583, decreed that the General Hospital of Madrid should henceforth have a share in the proceeds. Besides the charge for admission to the theater or *corrales,* the privileges for the sale of water, fruit, *aloja,* and confections were an additional source of income to the fraternities.[3]

Schack[4] gives the following description of the *corrales* or theaters of that time:

floor. See my article "On the Staging of Lope de Vega's Comedias," in the *Revue Hispanique,* 1907. Concerning the *Coliseo* of Seville, Sr. Sanchez-Arjona (p. 152) says: "En su origen el *vestuario* del *Coliseo* estaba lindando con la casa de D. Diego Dávalos, y las puertas que daban paso á los espectadores muy próximas al tablado y *vestuario.*"

[1] Pellicer, Vol. I, p. 69.

[2] *Ibid.,* p. 70.

[3] The privilege of selling water, fruit, etc., in the two theaters of *La Cruz* and *El Príncipe* was granted to Francisco Briceño on March 23, 1587; he paying on each day that a comedia was acted five reals for each theater, until St. Michael's day of the said year. (Pellicer, Vol. I, p. 82.)

[4] *Geschichte,* etc., Vol. I, p. 369.

The *corrales* were, as we have said, court-yards where the backs of several houses came together. The windows (*ventanas*) of the surrounding houses—provided, as is the Spanish custom, with iron railings or latticework, and then called *rejas* or *celosias*—served as boxes or stalls; a much larger number of these windows than originally existed in the buildings were especially constructed for this purpose. If these boxes were situated in the upper stories, they were called *desvanes* (attics) ; the lowest row of windows above the ground, however, were called *aposentos,* a name that, in a wider sense, seems also to have been applied to the *desvanes.* These *aposentos* (apartments or rooms) were really spacious rooms, as the name implies. The windows were, like the houses to which they belonged, sometimes the property of others, and if not rented by the fraternities, were entirely at the disposition of their owners, who, however, had to pay annually a specified sum for the privilege of seeing the plays from them.[1] Beneath the *aposentos* was a row of seats, raised like an amphitheater, and called *gradas;* in front of these was the *patio,* a larger open space whence the *vulgo* saw the play standing. In front of the *patio,* and nearest the stage, stood rows of benches called *bancos,* presumably also under the open sky, like

---

[1] In 1635 permission was given to Don Rodrigo de Herrera to open a window looking into the *Corral del Príncipe,* he paying to the lessees of the theater the sum of thirty ducats (330 reales vellon) annually. (Pellicer, Vol. I, p. 70; Sepulveda, *El Corral de la Pacheca,* p. 89.) This privilege was also granted in the same year to Don Pedro de Aragon, who, having purchased in the Calle del Príncipe a house which already had two *aposentos* looking upon the *Corral de las Comedias,* wished to open another window between the two. (Sepulveda, p. 90.) This notice is interesting in view of a picture published by Sepulveda (p. 18), representing the *Teatro del Príncipe* in 1660. I do not know the provenance of this picture, but it corresponds in every detail to the description in the text as given by Schack. It represents a rectangular space inclosed on the two longer sides by houses with grated windows, and with a raised stage occupying the further end. The whole space is open to the sky, except the portion over the stage and extending some distance beyond it, which is covered by a canvas awning. In the middle space or pit are a number of benches, which cover about half the ground immediately in front of the stage. The rest of the open space or *patio* is free, and is the place from which the groundlings or *mosqueteros* saw the play, while standing. On the left, beginning level with the ground, are rows of terraced seats—the *gradas* mentioned above. These are protected by a small roof supported by pillars. These seats were partitioned off from the pit. The stage seems to have had a slightly projecting roof. Of course the women's gallery (*cazuela*) does not appear in the picture.

the *patio,* or protected only by a canvas covering. The *gradas* were under a projecting roof at the sides. In the rear of the *corrales,* i.e., in the part furthest from the stage, was the gallery set apart for women, especially of the lower classes, and called the *cazuela* or stewpan, also called *corredores de las mugeres* or gallery for women. The more refined women patronized the *aposentos* or *desvanes.*[1]

Women were, apparently, no less eager to see a comedia than men, and when Jerónimo Velazquez, in February, 1586, determined to give a morning performance for women only, no less than seven hundred and sixty flocked to the theater, but on hearing of this the Council of Castile stopped the performance and confiscated the proceeds for the benefit of the hospitals.

We have seen above (p. 33, n. 4) that representations continued in the older *corrales* even after the new theaters —the *Cruz* in 1579, and the *Príncipe* in 1583—had been opened. On February 1, 1584, according to Pellicer,[2] Saldaña performed in the *Corral de Puente,* Cisneros in the *Cruz,* and Ganassa in the *Corral del Príncipe,* and on Sunday, February 5, Ganassa appeared in the *Príncipe,* Velazquez in the *Cruz,* and Cisneros in the *Corral de Puente.* It seems to result from a document published by Pellicer[3] that before 1587 all the other *corrales* had passed out of existence, except the *Corral de la Cruz* and the *Corral del Príncipe.* The success of Ganassa and his Italian company, to which we have already alluded, doubtless induced other Italian players to visit Spain. Ganassa had appeared in the *Corral de la Cruz* on February 23,

---

[1] Malone, speaking of the London theaters, says: "What was called the *pit* in the private theaters, like the one in Blackfriars, was called the *yard* in the public ones, as the Globe. The former theaters were inclosed by a roof, and the latter were open, except the stage, which was covered by a thatched roof. In the *pit* were benches for the spectators, while in the *yards* the groundlings stood." (*Historical Account of the English Stage.* See also Collier, *Annals of the Stage,* Vol. III, p. 335.)

[2] Vol. I, p. 80.

[3] *Ibid.,* p. 81.

1582. Four days afterward, on February 27, we find a
notice that Ganassa did not represent because he had been
put in prison.[1] On June 29, 1582, we find that "an Italian
performed acrobatic feats in the *Pacheca* and continued
performing with his tumblers until St. James' day," and on
August 24, 1582, *los Italianos nuevos* represented a
comedia at the *Pacheca*.[2] They again appeared on September 29 and 30, on October 17 and 18, and on November 1. From the fact that they are called "the new Italians," it is very probable that this company was not
Ganassa's. In 1587 and 1588 we find another company
of Italian actors in Madrid (or was it the company of
1582?) under the management of the brothers Tristano
and Drusiano Martinelli.[3] This is undoubtedly the Italian
company that was performing at the *Corral del Príncipe*
in November and December, 1587, and for some time
thereafter. Lope de Vega was a frequent visitor at this
time to these plays by the "Italians," or the "Comedia of
the Harlequin."[4]

It is, moreover, very probable that in his early career as
a dramatist Lope was much influenced by the *commedie
dell' arte* which he saw represented by these Italian
companies. The name of the male lover in these *commedie,* Fulvio, Valerio, Ottavio, Leandro, Fabricio, Cin-
thio, etc., and of the female lover, *la comica accesa,*

[1] See Appendix A.
[2] It is not likely that two companies of Italians were acting in Madrid at
the same time, and I presume that these *Italianos nuevos* were the same
as the company called *Los Corteses* (*I Cortesi*), who represented in the
Pacheca on August 26, 1582, and again on September 2, 8, 9, 16, 21, 23, 29,
and 30, and at various times down to November 15 of the same year.
(*Bulletin Hispanique* (1906), p. 152. See Appendix A, under year 1582.)
[3] D'Ancona, *Origini del Teatro Italiano,* Vol. II, p. 479. Drusiano Martinelli was in England with a company of players in 1577. Collier says:
"There was an Italian *commediante* named Drousiano, and his company,
in London, in January, 1577-78. The nature of their performances is not
anywhere stated, but it is possible that they might represent some extem-
pore comedies." (*Annals of the Stage,* Vol. III, p. 398, note.)
[4] Rennert, *Life of Lope de Vega,* pp. 27 ff. Drusiano Martinelli was a
famous *Arlecchino*. (See D'Ancona, *Origini del Teatro Italiano,* Vol. II,

Isabella, Lucinda, Leonora, etc., we find very frequently in the comedias of Lope. Besides, there is much similarity in the situations in many of Lope's *comedias de capa y espada,* or comedies of intrigue, and the ordinary *commedia dell' arte.* In the latter they recur from piece to piece with inconsiderable changes, each with the same mistakes, the same quarrels, the same night scenes, where one person is taken for another in the darkness; the same misunderstandings—*scene equivoche,*[1] etc.

Lope de Vega, seeing these plays almost daily, at the very beginning of his dramatic career, could hardly have failed to be influenced by them. Indeed, Clemencin remarks that the comic figure, *Trastulo,* in these farces of the Italians may have suggested to Lope the character of the *gracioso.*[2]

One of the members of Martinelli's company whom Lope saw in 1587 was undoubtedly the "Madama Angelica," wife of Drusiano, a celebrated actress and at that time a member of the company called *I Confidenti.*[3] In a letter of Drusiano Martinelli, published by D'Ancona,[4] he

p. 497, and Scherillo, *La Commedia dell' Arte,* in *La Vita Italiana nel Seicento.* Milano, 1895, p. 475.)

[1] See Mantzius, *History of Theatrical Art,* Vol. II, p. 228.

[2] Cervantes, *Don Quixote,* ed. Clemencin, Madrid, 1833, Vol. IV, p. 126, note. See also his very interesting note on the *bobo* of the comedia, *ibid.,* p. 64. That Lope de Vega was an assiduous visitor of the theater, carefully observing the striking situations, is also asserted by Ricardo de Turia in his *Apologetico de las Comedias Españolas,* prefixed to the *Norte de la Poesia española,* Valencia, 1616. He says: "El Principe de los Poetas Comicos de nuestros tiempos, y aun de los pasados, el famoso y nunca bien celebrado Lope de Vega, suele oyendo asi Comedias suyas como agenas, aduertir los pasos que hazen marauilla y grangean aplauso; y aquellos aunque sean impropios imita en todo, buscandose ocasiones en nueuas Comedias, que como de fuente perenne nacen incesablemente de su fertilissimo ingenio," etc.

[3] See below, p. 143. That both Drusiano and Tristano Martinelli were in Spain in this and the following year is shown by a letter which the former wrote to his mother, dated August 18, 1588, in which he says: "Staremo tutto quest' anno qui in Spagna." (Rasi, *I Comici Italiani,* Firenze, 1897, Vol. II, p. 104.) For his wife Angela or Angelica, see also *ibid.,* p. 16.

[4] *Origini del Teatro Italiano,* Vol. II, p. 479.

signs himself "husband of Mª Angelica," and from another letter [1] it appears that Mª Angelica was quite as frail as most of her sister-actresses. In a document of 1587 [2] her name is given as Angela Martineli; she, Angela Salomona, and *La Francesquina* (Silvia Roncagli) seem to have been the only women then in the company of the *Confidenti*. [3]

[1] *Origini del Teatro Italiano,* Vol. II, p. 523.
[2] See below, p. 143.
[3] Pérez Pastor, *Nuevos Datos,* p. 21. This company had been in Paris in 1584–85. (Moland, *Molière et la Comédie Italienne,* p. 41.)

CHAPTER III

The *corrales* of Seville. *Las Atarazanas. La Alcoba. San Pedro.*
The *Huerta de Doña Elvira.* The *Coliseo. La Monteria.*

TURNING now to another city, to Seville, we find more
detailed information concerning the public theaters or
corrales than was available in the case of Madrid. In
Seville, as already noted, *corrales* seem to have been established at about the same time that we first find them in
Madrid. The *Corral de Don Juan* was in existence as
early as 1575; here the Italian Ganassa performed in that
year, "and those who went to see the comedias of Ganassa
in the *Corral de Don Juan* paid an entrance fee of half a
real; a real for each chair (*silla*) and a cuartillo (=¼
real) for each seat on the *bancos.*"[1] In 1578 the *Corral
de las Atarazanas* was built, followed by that of the *Huerta
de la Alcoba* and the *San Pedro* (the latter apparently
ceased to exist after 1610), besides one mentioned by
Rodrigo Caro, which was in the Collacion de San Vicente,
and lastly, and perhaps the most famous of all, that of
Doña Elvira.[2] During the seventeenth century two others

[1] Sanchez-Arjona, *Anales del Teatro en Sevilla,* 1898, p. 51. From this
work the account in this chapter is taken.
[2] There were other *corrales* in Seville besides those here mentioned, according to Sanchez-Arjona. "Mateo de Salcedo y Juan Cano arrendaron
en 1600 unas casas que hubieron de servir de posada para los comediantes,
y en cuyo patio hicieron un teatro con algunos aposentos de tablas, 'sin
otra mezcla que la trabazon,' y los autores que venian á Sevilla 'negociaban
representar sus comedias en el dicho teatro y casa de Salcedo, sin haber
habido otra licencia de la Ciudad.'" Besides this *corral* there were "las
casas del coliseo del *Duque de Medina Sidonia* (situadas en la plaza del
Duque)" and "el corral de *San Pablo,* próximo sin duda al convento de
este nombre, de cuyos corrales no tenemos más noticias que esta ligera refe-
rencia." (*Ibid.,* pp. 502, 503.)

47

were built: the *Coliseo* and *La Monteria,* "notable for their construction and famous in the annals of the theater."

"With the establishment of fixed *corrales de comedias,*" says Sanchez-Arjona, "as well in the capital as in Seville and other cities of importance, and with the increased fondness of the people for theatrical representations, the number of professional actors also continued increasing, and as, down to this time, those who furnished the text for the *autos*[1] also represented them, or, at all events, intrusted their representation to persons who were not professional players, from this time there began to take charge of these representations *autores de comedias,* as the chiefs or directors of the companies were called, and a distinction was established between the writer and the player."[2]

Of the *Corral de Don Juan* nothing seems to be known beyond the fact just stated, that Ganassa acted therein with his company of Italians in 1575.[3] The *Corral de las Atarazanas,* which was built in 1578, was of wood and was constructed by Diego de Vera, lessee of the *huerta de las Atarazanas,* at a cost of two thousand ducats, upon a spot once occupied by a rubbish-heap in the *huerta.* It passed out of existence in 1585, when a mint was built on its site. On petition to the city, the builder and lessee, Diego de Vera, who had had a lease for eighteen years, at an annual rental of 150 ducats, was permitted to erect a new *corral* with the wood and materials of the old one, in the *huerta de*

---

[1] The word *auto* was first applied to any and every play; then, the meaning becoming narrower, an *auto* was a religious play, resembling the medieval Mysteries (Gil Vicente's *Auto de San Martinho* is probably the earliest piece of this type). Finally, a far more special sense was developed, and an *auto sacramental* came to mean a dramatized exposition of the Mystery of the Blessed Eucharist, to be played in the open on Corpus Christi day. (Fitzmaurice-Kelly, *History of Spanish Literature,* p. 327.)

[2] *Anales del Teatro en Sevilla,* p. 54, *sub anno* 1575. See above, p. 32.

[3] It stood upon the site of what is to-day the Iglesia de los Menores, and derived its name from its owner, Don Juan Ortiz de Guzman. (*Ibid.,* p. 51.)

la Alcoba, likewise upon a spot that had once been a dung-heap. It was in the *Corral de las Atarazanas* that two comedias by Juan de la Cueva, *La Libertad de España por Bernardo del Carpio* and *La Libertad de Roma por Mucio Scévola,* were first performed, the former by Pedro de Saldaña, the latter by Alonso de Capilla.[1]

The *Corral de Doña Elvira* was in existence as early as 1579, for in that year, according to the same writer, three plays by Juan de la Cueva were first represented therein by the company of Alonso Rodriguez. Their titles are: *La Muerte del Rey Don Sancho y Reto de Zamora por D. Diego Ordoñez; El Saco de Roma y Muerte de Borbon y Coronacion de nuestro invicto Emperador Carlos V.,* and the tragedy *Los siete Infantes de Lara.* Besides, the following four plays, also by Juan de la Cueva, were represented this year in the same *corral* by the company of Pedro de Saldaña: *El Degollado, El Tutor, La Constancia de Arcelina,* and the tragedy *La Muerte de Ayax Telamon sobre las armas de Aquiles,* in which, Cueva says, Saldaña played the part of Ajax admirably.[2]

The *Corral de Doña Elvira* was situated in the parish of the *Sagrario,* near the residence of the Count of Gelves, at the mouth of the *Borceguineria,* with an entrance through two small streets (*callejas*) near the *Plazuela del Pozo Seco.*[3] The *corral* was so called because it was built on the property of Doña Elvira de Ayala, wife of the admiral

[1] Sanchez-Arjona, p. 60.

[2] *Ibid.,* p. 64. This *corral* was originally called *La Huerta de Doña Elvira.*

[3] It may not be without interest to note that in 1619 (and doubtless before this) the *Corral de Doña Elvira* belonged to the Counts of Gelves. In that year there was some litigation concerning this *corral,* and the Count of Lemos is mentioned as administrator (*curador*) of "la condesa de gelbes doña Catalina de Portugal." (*Ibid.,* p. 196.) Doña Leonor de Milan, wife of D. Alvaro de Portugal, second Count of Gelves, was the divinity of Fernando de Herrera's verses, whom he celebrates under the name "*Luz.*" She died either shortly before or after September 29, 1581, the date of her husband's death. Their eldest son, D. Jorge Alberto de Portugal, born in 1566, died in 1589, "sans laisser de posterité." The Doña Catalina mentioned above was probably his widow. See Coster, *Fernando de Herrera (El Divino),* pp. 112 ff.

D. Alvar Perez de Guzman, and daughter of the great Chancellor of Castile, Pero Lopez de Ayala.[1] It consisted of a spacious *patio* surrounded by numerous *aposentos* (rooms or boxes) and a *cazuela,* having its entrance through the Calle del Agua, opposite the Calle del Chorro. Perhaps originally the *patio* was open to the sky, and only the *aposentos* and the *cazuela* were covered, as in other *corrales* of the time. But, if this was the original arrangement, the *corral* was probably completely covered afterward, for in 1617 it was directed that "toda la armadura [framework, truss] que *cubre* el dicho *coral de Doña Elvira,* juntamente con los colgadizos [shed, shed-roof] de los lados," should be torn down.[2] Still, it is probable that the *armadura* may have merely protected the stage.

In a document existing in the Archivo del Alcázar of Seville, dated October 10, 1585, Diego de Vera, lessee of the *Corral de las Atarazanas,* is described as the gardener of the *huerta de la Alcoba,* for which he paid a yearly rental of 450 ducats, and in consideration of the permission to build a theater on the grounds he agrees to pay an additional 150 ducats, or 600 ducats annually.[3] The theater, called *El Coliseo* (the street in which it stood still bears the name), was finished in 1607, and was leased at the beginning of the following year for the term of six years to Diego de Almonací, at a yearly rental of 3250 ducats, the city reserving fourteen *aposentos,* which were leased to Luis de Aguilar, for the same term, at 800 ducats annually. The price of the *aposentos* was fixed at six reals each for every representation. At this time, it seems, there were only two other *corrales* in Seville, besides

[1] Sanchez-Arjona, p. 65. The *corral* must have been built on property belonging to the descendants of Doña Elvira de Ayala, for if she was the daughter of Pedro Lopez de Ayala she must have been dead about two hundred years at this time, as her father, the great Chancellor, died in 1407. See Salazar de Mendoza, *Origen de las Dignidades seglares de Castilla y Leon,* Madrid, 1794, p. 278.

[2] *Ibid.,* p. 65.

[3] See above, p. 48.

the *Coliseo,* namely, the *Doña Elvira* and the *San Pedro.* We learn, moreover, that in 1608 less than one hundred and fifty comedias were represented in the city, "on account of the rains, the dog-days, Lent, and for lack of theatrical companies."[1] Indeed, it is said that, on an average, the period during which performances were given in a *corral* did not exceed four months in the year, after deducting Sundays, Lent, the summer months (in which no plays were given), the rainy days, and other occasions. The price of the *sillas* in the theaters at this time was half a real; a seat on the *bancos* one real, and the *aposentos* six reals each.

The *Coliseo,* though the latest and largest of the *corrales* in Seville, was originally without a roof, as we learn from the fact that those living in the immediate neighborhood used to gather on the tops of their houses to view the performance, "thus occasioning considerable loss and much noise."[2] It was a wooden structure, which must have been very poorly built, for portions of it had to be repaired and rebuilt in 1614. It was, on its reconstruction, provided with 250 seats with backs (*sillas de respaldo*) and 50 benches covered with leather and having stuffed backs (*taburetes con asientos de vaca y los espaldares aforrados de baldana con sus clavos de hierro negros*). The interior was supported by twenty Doric columns, with bases and capitals of white marble; these were ten feet high, the first gallery having twenty columns, likewise of marble, seven feet high. In this gallery were the twenty-nine *aposentos,* the guard-rails of which were of iron, and above this another gallery or *corredor.* Here the *ventanas* were situated, each more than two and a half yards high and one and a half yards wide, in the wall in the side of the house of the Marquis of Ayamonte. The object of these *ventanas* was to give light to the *corral,* which, unlike other theaters of the

[1] Sanchez-Arjona, p. 133. [2] *Ibid.,* p. 152.

time, was covered by a roof and painted ceiling. Besides
the *patio*, in which the representations took place, there
was another space, forming an entrance, the floor of which
was paved with stone and likewise decorated in marble.
The principal entrance was also of marble, surmounted by
the arms of the city. In the body of the house (*patio de
las representaciones*) were placed fixed benches (*bancos*)
and the *sillas de respaldo* and *taburetes* above mentioned.
The work of rebuilding, though begun in 1614, progressed
slowly, and the theater was finally leased for 6500 ducats
annually, on condition that the lessee should finish it by
Easter of 1616.[1] It appears that, in spite of the large
amount of money expended in the construction of the
Coliseo, its acoustic properties were defective, and the
autores coming to Seville preferred the *Corral de Doña
Elvira*, although the latter was now in poor condition and
in need of repairs.

These two *corrales* were the only ones in Seville in which
performances were now given, and so great was the pref-
erence for the older of them (*Doña Elvira*) that in 1617
Juan Acacio, after representing for some time in the
Coliseo, petitioned that his company might now pass to
the *Doña Elvira* (in which Pedro Llorente's company was
then performing), on account of the few people who visited
the *Coliseo*, and that representations be given alternately
by the two *autores* for fixed periods in the two *corrales*.[2]
Such, however, was the unsafe condition of the *Doña
Elvira* (the roof and other portions of which were in
imminent danger of falling, according to an examination
made by a commission) that it was resolved to tear down
this *corral* in part and rebuild it. Accordingly, Pedro de
Valdes, who was then (February, 1617) representing with
his company in the *Doña Elvira*, was notified to cease,
under a penalty of 200 ducats. Valdes objected on account of the large amount that he had expended for
apariencias especially made for a comedia already an-

[1] Sanchez-Arjona, p. 174.   [2] *Ibid.*, p. 183.

nounced, and the threat to close the theater was not carried into effect, though it is to be presumed that some repairs were made in the building, for in the following May, Pedro Llorente was still performing therein.

At this time the yearly rental of the *Corral de Doña Elvira* was 3700 reals, plus one half the profits, the other half going to the lessee.[1]

As the residence of the Marquis of Ayamonte, in the Plaza de la Regina, adjoined the *Coliseo,* the city granted him the privilege of making a private entrance to one of the *aposentos,* "in view of the fact that his party-wall had been used without expense to the theater; that he had furnished water from one of his private fountains, and had otherwise aided in the construction of the said *corral.*" This *aposento* was to be enjoyed by him and his successors without cost.

Lope de Vega's *Obras son Amores,* an *auto* written in 1615, but not yet performed, was represented in Seville in this year (1618), he receiving 600 reals for it.

The number of persons frequenting the theater having greatly diminished, to the serious loss of all concerned, and especially of the city and of the dependent charities, it was resolved to close the *Corral de Doña Elvira* and to restrict all performances to the *Coliseo.* No representations were to be given in the *Doña Elvira* after January 1, 1620, and the rental of the *Coliseo* was increased 400 ducats annually, to counterbalance the loss occasioned by the closure of the *Doña Elvira.*

It was customary, says Sanchez-Arjona, to represent the *autos* of the festival of Corpus Christi in the *corrales,* which was an additional source of profit to the theatrical managers. This year (1619) they were represented in the *Doña Elvira* by the companies of Juan Acacio and Diego Vallejo, and a poster announcing a performance on June 5, 1619, is still preserved in the Archivo del Ayuntamiento of Seville.[2]

[1] Sanchez-Arjona, p. 185. [2] See below, p. 133.

On the afternoon of July 25, 1620, the *Coliseo* was completely destroyed by fire during the performance of Claramonte's comedia *San Onofre ó el Rey de los Desiertos,* by the company of Juan Bautista and Juan Jerónimo Valenciano. Fifteen or sixteen persons, mostly women and children, lost their lives. The actors all escaped, the one who played the part of San Onofre running into the street almost nude, "with a bunch of ivy (*mata de yedra*) for small-clothes (*por paños menores*). On seeing him in this strange guise, he was pursued by a shouting crowd of little boys until he reached his house, which, unfortunately, was some distance off." [1]

While some of the good citizens of Seville looked upon the burning of the *Coliseo* as a visitation of the wrath of the Almighty, the municipal authorities, considering the loss which the city had sustained in its revenues, viewed it in a different light and resolved to rebuild the theater. Meanwhile all theatrical performances were confined to the *Doña Elvira,* which had been condemned and ordered to be torn down after January 1, 1620, as we have seen. As a matter of fact, representations did not cease in the *Doña Elvira* on January 1, and the lessee at the time, Luis de Leon,[2] continued to give performances in it.

On March 31, 1621, Philip the Third died, the theaters were closed, and all representations were suspended until July 28, not a castanet being heard at the performance of the *autos* of that year.[3]

The city, having resolved, in 1622, to rebuild the *Coliseo,* which had been destroyed by fire in 1620, hit upon a rather novel expedient. The new theater was to be leased for a period of nine years, the lessee to pay 2000 ducats annually, to build the theater at his own expense, and to be recouped from the receipts. The lease was adjudged to Juan Bautista de Villalobos, apparently a man

---

[1] Sanchez-Arjona, p. 212.
[2] *Ibid.* In *Nuevos Datos,* p. 174, this name is given as Luis de Lesa.
[3] Pellicer, Vol. I, p. 161.

of straw, put up by Diego de Almonacid. The rent was to begin on January 1, 1623; the theater to be finished, according to plans furnished by the city, on the first day of Pascua Florida of 1624. The prices for admission to the various localities in the theater were fixed as follows: one real for each *banco* (which was to hold at least three persons), 24 maravedís for a *silla*, 18 maravedís for a *taburete*, 6 reals each for the *aposentos* which were entered through the *corral*, and 12 reals for each *aposento* entered from the outside of the *corral*, because persons using the latter were to pay nothing at the entrance. Out of these 12 reals, however, the lessee was obliged to pay the theater's share in the maintenance of the public prison and such other imposts as were payable out of the entrance money. In addition, the lessee was entitled to his share of the takings at the second door. In the *patio* eight or nine fixed benches were to be placed for those who only paid the entrance fee.[1]

In order to determine the rental to be paid, the following curious statistics were drawn up, showing the amounts produced and the expenses incurred. It is one of the most important documents concerning the early Spanish theater which we possess, and is as follows: Representations can only be given on 198 days out of the 365 in a year, since none can be given on the remaining 167 days, for the following reasons:

46 days during Lent.

77 days for the months of July, August, and half of September, when no *autores* come to Seville.

34 for the Saturdays, on which days no performance can be given.

10 days to be allowed for the making of *apariencias* (stage machinery); for St. Sebastian's and St. James's day; because of few spectators and on account of rain.

167 days.

[1] Sanchez-Arjona, *Anales*, p. 218.

There remain 198 days for representations, "rather less than more, for none have been deducted for the time that elapses between the coming and going of the various *autores*."

The lessee's share for these 198 days is: From the entrance fee of each person he receives 5 maravedís, "and as it is notorious that many persons enter who do not pay, it is calculated that, taking one day with another, about 350 persons will pay each day, which, at 5 maravedís, amounts to 51½ reals."

From each *silla* he receives 6 cuartos (=24 maravedís) and from each *taburete* 4½ cuartos (=18 maravedís), and taking into account those for which nothing is received, it is estimated that 40 *sillas* and 20 *taburetes* will be paid for daily, which amounts to 39 reals.

From each *banco* the lessee receives one real, and counting that on an average thirty-two are rented daily, this amounts to 32 reals.

Of the twenty-eight *aposentos,* supposing that on an average twelve are rented, and taking these at an average rate of 9 reals each, produces 108 reals daily.

Estimating the rental of the right to sell water, sweets, fruit, *aloja* (a kind of mead), etc., at 8 reals per day, it gives a total of 238½ reals daily, which, for 198 days, amounts to 47,223 reals. Besides, during Lent and at other times it is customary to have in the *Coliseo* puppet-shows or pantomimes (*títeres*) and other games, and these produce about 1000 reals yearly. The living-rooms in the residence portion of the *Coliseo* (which are also one of the benefits accruing to the lessee) are worth 600 reals each year. This makes the total annual receipts of the lessee 48,823 reals.

Payments and expenditures: The amount expended in sending for the various *autores,* for sums advanced to them, and for cost of *apariencias* and other expenses, 5 reals for each day of representation. To the person who takes the money at the first entrance, 8 reals daily; to the person in charge of the *sillas* and *bancos*, 6 reals daily; to the person who hires the *aposentos* on the right-hand side, 6 reals; to the one who hires the *aposentos* on the left, 6 reals daily. To the *autor* representing, an average of 64½ reals daily as an *ayuda de costas*.[1] To the poor of the prison, one sixth of the proceeds of the *aposentos, sillas,* and *bancos* (together 179 reals), that is, 29½ reals. This makes a total daily expenditure of 125 reals, or in 198 days 24,750 reals. Adding to this the interest on the sum expended in the erection of the *Coliseo,* about 10,000 ducats, which amounts to about 10 reals per day, or 3650 reals for the year, the total amount of expenditures is about 28,400 reals. Deducting this from the receipts, 48,823 reals, leaves a profit of about 20,423 reals annually. If, therefore, the *corral* were rented for 1600 ducats (17,600 reals), it would leave a sufficient profit to the lessee. We have seen that it had been rented to Juan Bautista de Villalobos for 2000 ducats annually.

In 1626, in the former Alcázar of Seville, in the spacious "patio de la Monteria" a new theater was built called *La Monteria*. The *corral* was leased to Diego de Almonací, the younger (*el mozo*), "who shall cause to be constructed on his own account, and according to the plans made by Bermudo Resta, a *corral* for the representation of comedias, he to enjoy the profits for the space of ten years, to begin with the day of Pascua de la Resurreccion." The condition of the agreement was that the amount ex-

---

[1] Besides this amount the *autor* received his share of the money taken at the door. This, however, does not seem to have been the usual practice. It was customary for the lessee of the theater to give a fixed sum to the *autor* of the company for each performance. As an instance we may mention that Diego de Almonacid, lessee of the *corrales* of Seville in 1619, had signed an agreement in that year, whereby Hernan Sanchez de Vargas and his company were to give sixty representations in the *Coliseo*, the said Sanchez to receive 1000 reals for each performance. These representations were actually given by the company of Cristóbal Ortiz de Villazan. (*Nuevos Datos,* p. 177.)

pended by the lessee, under the supervision of the *oficiales* of the Alcázar, was to be deducted from the rent, which was fixed at 850 ducats annually, Almonací agreeing to finish the *corral* by the next ensuing Pascua Florida, the contract being dated December 6, 1625.

As already stated, the theater was to be built at the sole expense of the lessee, "who was to enjoy all the profits there might be from the street entrance to the second door of *La Monteria,* as well as what might be taken from the admissions, *bancos, sillas, aposentos,* or any other thing which might or ought to be profitable." [1] Only one real was to be charged for each *silla* as well as for each *banco* (perhaps this means for each seat on a *banco,* as they held three persons); six reals for the *aposentos* (boxes or stalls) entered from within, and twelve reals for those entered directly from the street, because persons using the former also had to pay an entrance fee. It was stipulated that there should be two *alguaciles,* each to be paid ten reals daily, at the joint expense of the lessee and the *autor;* one of these officers to be stationed at the first entrance, the other at the entrance for women. The building was to be of wood and all the *aposentos* and passages to be paved with brick; the *aposentos* to be furnished with partitions and iron railings and lattices or blinds. The whole to be whitewashed and the *aposentos* to be provided with doors, locks, and keys. The structure was oval,[2] with two rows or series of *aposentos,* situated on the right and left of the principal entrance. There were thirty-four *aposentos,* sixteen above and eighteen below, of which four were reserved for the Alcázar. Above the *aposentos* was the *cazuela* (stewpan), or place set apart

---

[1] "Que acabado el corral el arrendador habia de gozar de todos los aprovechamientos que hubiere ó pudiese haber desde la puerta de la calle hasta la segunda puerta de la Monteria, asi lo que se cobrase de entradas, bancos, sillas," etc. (Sanchez-Arjona, p. 250.)

[2] This was the first oval theater, to my knowledge. All others had been rectangular in shape.

for women. The *patio,* in which the *sillas* and *bancos* were placed, was of earth firmly rammed, and the whole *corral* was covered by a wooden roof. The building also contained living-rooms for the *autor* or for the players. Its total cost was over 183,000 reals.[1] This sum, which represents a purchasing power to-day of about $45,000, will give some idea of the character of the new theater, *La Monteria.* The first representation in it took place on May 25, 1626.

The *Corral de Doña Elvira,* which had its entrance in the Calle del Agua, opposite the Calle del Chorro, had long been in need of repairs. Like the rest of the older theaters of the time, it consisted of a spacious *patio* open to the sky, surrounded by covered *aposentos* and a covered *cazuela.* The more convenient situation of *La Monteria* (though it was not very far from the *Doña Elvira*), and the fact that the former was a new and much handsomer structure, gradually caused the public to neglect more and more the *Doña Elvira,* which was finally closed and torn down. A part of it was converted into a tavern, the remaining ground being used for games. Later, cards and dice were played here, and the place became the haunt of ruffians and vagabonds. Finally, in 1679, an asylum for poor priests was built on its site.

In 1629 *La Monteria* was leased to Domingo de Roças for six years at 1450 ducats annually. While the *Coliseo* was to have been finished by Easter, 1624, as we have

---

[1] The very interesting memorandum, preserved in the Archivo del Alcazar, is as follows: "Importe de la madera 63,730 reales. Materiales 35,587. La clavazon 18,091. Raspadores, aserradores, traida de maderas y materiales, jornales al carpintero Felipe Nieto y sus oficiales y al albañil Gabriel Marin y sus oficiales y peones 50,985. En lucir el frente del teatro y otras paredes, solar los dos aposentos del vestuario de ladrillo, igualar á pisón el suelo del patio, hacer unas gradas, tarimas y otras obras de arbañileria y carpinteria, y por último el escudo, columnas y la *Fama* que se pintó encima del teatro, por cuya pintura sòlo se abonaron mil reales—4000. Planchas de hierro y abrazaderas para la seguridad y firmeza de la obra y hierramientas, etc., 11,000 reales," making a total of 183,393 reals. (Sanchez-Arjona, *Anales,* p. 252.)

seen, the building was not actually completed until 1631. Much of what had been built in this long interval by the lessees was so badly done that the city determined to tear it down and build it anew. An agreement was made with Alonso de Vergara to construct a new theater. He was to pay 1400 ducats yearly for ten years, the cost of the new building to be deducted from the rent. A further condition was that the structure must be finished by Easter, 1632. Rodrigo Caro describes this magnificent and costly building, "worthy of all esteem and praise," as "the finest of its kind in Spain, and capable of holding between four and five thousand spectators, all of whom were equally able to see and hear."[1]

In 1636 *La Monteria* was leased to Miguel de Molina for six years at an annual rental of 1450 ducats (15,950 reals), to be paid in three payments.[2] In the following year Antonio de Prado, *autor de comedias,* agreed with the lessee of the *Coliseo* to give sixty performances, from the second day of Easter till Corpus, receiving 200 reals for each performance as an *ayuda de costas;* of these 12,000 reals 4000 were to be paid on signing the contract, and the balance on Palm Sunday.

On October 4, 1659, the *Coliseo* was again destroyed by fire, only the front wall and a few rooms (in which actors lived) remaining of the famous edifice. It may be noted that the two companies of players in Seville in the following year (1660) were managed by women. These *autoras* were Francisca Lopez and Juana de Cisneros.

[1] *"El Coliseo* tenia tres órdenes de aposentos, de balconería de hierro, unos sobre otros, trabados en estribos de magnífica y costosa sillería, cubierto el alto de un artesón igual por techo, con rica pintura, para las representaciones que se hacen al pueblo, con tanta distinción para diferentes personas de hombres y mujeres, que no pueden embarazarse unos á otros, y tan capaz su disposición que caben cuatro á cinco mil personas, pudiendo gozar todas igualmente de la vista y oído de su teatro; obra digna de toda estimación y alabanza por la mejor de España de las de su genero," etc. (*Antigüedades de Sevilla,* fol. 25 v, quoted by Sanchez-Arjona, p. 270.)

[2] In 1642 *La Monteria* was leased to Antonio Correa at a yearly rental of 13,000 reals *vellon.*

The *Coliseo* was rebuilt in 1676. Three years later both theaters were closed on account of the plague. A portion of *La Monteria* was then used as a stable, in which, on May 3, 1691, a fire broke out, and the whole *corral* was reduced to ashes, "causing it to disappear forever."[1]

How soon after 1679 representations were resumed in the *Coliseo* is uncertain. It is not likely, however, that any performances were given in it until 1692, when permission was granted to a company of acrobats and sleight-of-hand performers to represent therein. These performances found such favor that women used to go to the theater early in the morning to secure a seat. On November 12, 1698, during the performance of Mescua's comedia *El Esclavo del Demonio,* a woman in the *cazuela* raised a cry of fire. In the attempt to escape from the building a number of women were killed, and thereafter all theatrical representations in the *Coliseo* were forbidden, which interdict lasted till after the middle of the eighteenth century.[2]

---

[1] Sanchez-Arjona, p. 495.

[2] Concerning the theater in Valladolid, Sr. Cortés says: "El patio de comedias se hallaba situado en el mismo sitio donde aún existe el teatro antiguo (plaza de las Comedias). Su administracion correspondia á la cofradía de S. José, con el directo apoyo del Ayuntamiento, que tenia su *aposento* propio para presenciar las representaciones." (*Noticias de una Corte literaria,* Valladolid, 1906, p. 30.)

CHAPTER IV

Music in the *corrales*. Dancing. Spectators on the stage. Various dances and *bayles* at Corpus Christi. The *Zarabanda, Chacona, Escarraman*, etc.

ABOUT the middle of the sixteenth century, in the time of Lope de Rueda, as we have seen, the music accompanying the plays acted in the public squares was provided by one or two persons "who sang an old ballad without the accompaniment of a guitar," behind a woolen blanket, which served as a curtain, and which separated the dressing-room (*vestuario*) from the stage.[1] It was Pedro Navarro of Toledo, Cervantes tells us, "who brought the musicians, who formerly sang behind the curtain, upon the public stage."[2] Here they played before and after the performance of the farce or between the acts of a

---

[1] See above, p. 17. Rojas, speaking of the time of Lope de Rueda, says that a guitar was played behind the curtain:

> "Tañian una guitarra
> Y esta nunca salia fuera
> Sino a dentro."
> (*Viage entretenido*, ed. 1603, p. 124.)

[2] "Sucedio a Lope de Rueda Nabarro, natural de Toledo, el qual . . . sacò la musica que antes cātaua detras de la manta al teatro publico." (*Ocho Comedias*, etc., Madrid, 1615, "Prologo al Lector.") "El teatro publico" evidently means the stage. As late as 1671 the musicians of Molière's troupe were concealed from the spectator: "Jusques icy [15 Auril, 1671] les musiciens et musiciennes n'auoient point voulu parroistre en public; ils chantoient à la Comedie dans des loges grillées et treillissées, mais on surmonta cet obstacle, et auec quelque legere despance on trouua des personnes qui chanterent sur le Theatre à visage descouuert, habillez comme les Comediens, scauoir . . ." etc., and he gives the names of eight musicians. (*Registre de La Grange*, Paris, 1876, p. 124.) In the London theaters, the "band," as Malone calls it, "sat in an upper balcony, over

comedia. As I have nowhere found any special place designated for the musicians, it is probable that they occupied the stage during the whole of the best period of the comedia. Indeed, as the principal part of their entertainment consisted of singing, they could not have been stationed elsewhere.

In 1593 we find that a comedia was performed "with its *entremeses* and with its music of a *viola* and guitars,"[1] and we are told that later the music consisted of "two or three violins and an oboe." Even in the middle of the seventeenth century theatrical companies in Spain rarely contained more than four or five musicians. Most of the actresses were also dancers (*bailarines*), and every company contained persons who were designated especially as dancers, while most players were hired both to act and dance.

In the company of the famous Alonso Riquelme, a favorite *autor* of Lope de Vega, we find the following musicians in 1607: Luis de Quiñones, *musico y representante;* Vega; Francisco Martinez; Leon, *musico y bailarin;* Marigraviela, *musica y representanta;* Maria de los Angeles, *musica y representanta,* and Juan Catalan, *musico y representante.*[2] Here the term *musica,* in the case of the actresses, probably meant merely *singer.* In 1619, when the comedia was almost at its apogee, the company of Diego Vallejo contained but two musicians, and the same number were in the companies of Juan Acacio and Cristóbal Ortiz.[3] By 1640 the number of musicians in a company seems to have been greatly increased. In

what is now called the stage-box," and was not placed "between the pit and the stage," until 1667. (*Historical Account of the English Stage,* Basil, 1800, pp. 120, 123.)

[1] Pérez Pastor, *Nuevos Datos,* p. 37. Minsheu says *viola* is the same as *vihuéla,* "an instrument called a viall, sometimes a bandore," and defines *Vihuéla de árco* as "a viall de Gamba, or a great viall that men set between their legs to play on." (*Spanish Dictionary,* London, 1599.) Clemencin says: "*Vihuela* en lo antiguo era distinto de *guitarra,* y habia vihuela de mano y de arco." (*Don Quixote,* ed. 1833, Vol. V, p. 423.)

[2] Sanchez-Arjona, *Anales,* p. 126.

[3] *Ibid.,* pp. 203, 204.

that year the first five actresses in the company of Antonio de Rueda have added to their names the word *musica,* and in two of these cases the word *arpa* is also used; four men musicians are also in the company, one of them being *maestro de la musica* and two being harpists. As this company represented the *autos* in Seville in that year, the large number of musicians may be due to that fact.[1]

Upon the English stage more attention seems to have been paid to instrumental music, where it was likewise played between the acts; the instruments chiefly used were trumpets, cornets, hautboys, lutes, recorders, viols, and organs. Malone[2] cites the following stage directions from Marston's *Sophonisba,* acted at the Blackfriars theater in 1606: "The ladies draw the curtains about Sophonisba;—the *cornets* and *organs* playing loud full musicke for the act. . . . *Organ* mixt with *recorders,* for this act. . . . *Organs, viols,* and voices play for this act. . . . A *base lute* and *treble viol* play for this act." And in *Henslowe's Diary*[3] we read: "Lent unto Richard Jonnes the 22 of desember 1598 to bye a basse viall & other enstrementes for the companey, x x x x s."

It is well known that in the Elizabethan theater the gallants frequently took seats upon the stage;[4] whether this

---

[1] In 1631 Luisa de Guevara agreed to play third parts in the company of Juan Martinez and also first musical parts (*primera parte de musica*) (Pérez Pastor, *Nuevos Datos,* p. 220) ; and in 1633 Alonso Gonzalez Camacho agreed to play the violin, dance, and *poner los tonos* in the company of Fernan Sanchez de Vargas during the octave of Corpus for 500 reals, a very considerable amount. (*Ibid.,* p. 233; see also *ibid.,* p. 246.) Every company also contained a prompter (*apuntador*).

[2] *Historical Account of the English Stage,* Basil, 1800, p. 120, note.

[3] Edited by W. W. Greg, London, 1904, Vol. I, p. 100.

[4] "Whether therefore the gatherers [Spanish = *cobradores*] of the public or private playhouse stand to receive the afternoones rent, let our Gallant (hauing paid it) presently aduance himself up to the throne of the Stage. I mean not into the Lords roome . . . but on the very Rushes where the Comedy is to daunce. . . . By sitting on the Stage, you haue a signed patent to engrosse the whole commodity of Censure; may lawfully presume to be a Girder; and stand at the helme to steere the passage of *scænes,* etc. . . . By sitting on the stage, you may (with small cost) purchase the deere acquaintance of the boyes; haue a good stiole for six pence," etc. (Dekker,

custom prevailed in Spain in the early period we are unable to determine.[1] I find no evidence of spectators being admitted to the Madrid stage at any time. That they occupied seats on the stage in Seville is shown by an incident recorded by Sanchez-Arjona. On May 31, 1635, in the theater *La Monteria,* the company of Salvador Lara and Maria Candau, his wife, was representing the burlesque comedia *Casarse por defender.* In the second act there is a passage which necessitates the drawing of swords, and one of the actors, Antonio de Rueda, accidentally wounded in the face a boy who was sitting on the stage viewing the performance, and who promptly ran out of the theater shouting, "Confession, confession, they have

The Gul's Horne-Booke, London, 1609, chap. vi.) From the three legs of the stools here mentioned, they were called *tripos.* Wallace says that "the fad of sitting on the stage came into vogue with the Blackfriars in 1597. . . . It was a custom in no other theater in Elizabeth's reign." He adds that it was imitated afterward by two other private theaters, the Cockpit (1617) and Salisbury Court (1629), but that it was never tolerated at the Globe or at any public playhouse, and was abolished sometime prior to September 14, 1639. (*The Children of the Chapel at Blackfriars 1597-1603,* Lincoln, Nebraska, 1908, pp. 130 ff.) According to this writer the custom spread from England to France.

[1] From the *Argumento* which precedes the *Auto de la Ungion de David* (second half of the sixteenth century), one might infer that at the representations of the short *autos* or farces of that time the spectators were in the habit of gathering upon the platform or stage. This *Argumento* is as follows: " . . . El acostunbrada atençion que en semejantes casos se rrequiere pide el autor, para que con ella entiendan claramente la obra; y porque siento qu'el profeta [one of the characters] sale, le quiero desocupar el sitio, suplicando a vs. mds. suplan nuestras faltas." (*Coleccion de Autos, Farsas,* etc., ed. Rouanet, Vol. I, p. 315.) Bapst says that the custom of the *élégants* sitting upon the stage was unknown in France in the middle of the sixteenth century. (*Essai sur l'histoire du Théâtre,* Paris, 1893, p. 146.) But it was evidently in vogue in 1661, for in that year Molière, in the opening lines of *Les Fâcheux,* denounces this reprehensible practice, and four years later he again complains of it at the performance of the tragi-comedy *La Coquette ou le Favori* at Versailles: "Le Vendredy 12 Juin, [1665] la Troupe est allée à Versailles par ordre du Roy, où on a joué le Fauory dans le jardin, sur un theastre tout garny d'orangers, Mr de Moliere fist vn prologue en marquis ridicule qui uouloit estre sur le theastre malgré les gardes, et eust une conuersation risible auec vne actrice qui fist la marquise ridiculle, placée au milieu de l'assemblée." (*Registre de La Grange,* Paris, 1876, p. 74.) Voltaire also alludes to "la foule des spectateurs confondues sur la scène avec les acteurs" on the

killed me." The wound was a slight one, and the barber, we are told, made "la primera cura."[1]

As early as the beginning of the Christian era Spanish women were celebrated as dancers,[2] and as far as modern times are concerned, Ticknor truly observes that "dancing has been to Spain what music has been to Italy, a passion with the whole population." As Cervantes says:

> There never yet has been a Spanish woman
> Who was not born into this world a dancer.[3]

From the King down, everybody danced, and it was said of the grave and somber Philip the Third that "he dances very well and it is the thing that he does best and enjoys most."[4]

occasion of the first performance of his *Sémiramis*. (*Dissertation sur la Tragédie Ancienne et Moderne* (seconde partie), in *Oeuvres Complètes*, Paris, 1823, Vol. III, p. 111.) According to Despois this practice did not cease in France till 1759. See his interesting note in *Oeuvres de Molière* (ed. des Grands Écrivains de la France), Paris, 1876, Vol. III, p. 36, and Fischmann, *Molière als Schauspieldirektor*, in *Ztft. für Franz. Sprache und Lit.* (1905), p. 30.

[1] Sanchez-Arjona, *Anales*, p. 296.

[2] Spanish dancers were famous among the Romans, the lascivious dances of the women of Cadiz being especially mentioned by Juvenal and Martial. Mariana, in his chapter on the *Zarabanda,* says: "las mugeres que hacian este baile de deshonestidad las llamaban en Roma gaditanas, de Cádiz, ciudad de España, donde se debió de inventar en aquel tiempo." (*Contra los Juegos publicos,* cap. xii.) Martial's words are:

> *"Nec de Gadibus improbis puellae*
> *Vibrabunt sine fine prurientes*
> *Lascivos docili tremore lumbos."*

See also the eleventh Satire of Juvenal, the passage beginning: *Forsitan expectes ut gaditana canoro,* etc.

[3] "No ay muger Española que no salga
del vientre de su madre bayladora."
La gran Sultana, Act III. (*Ocho Comedias,* Madrid, 1615, fol. 130, v.)

[4] See the very interesting *Cuadros viejos* of Julio Monreal, Madrid, 1878, the chapter entitled "Los Bailes de antaño." In Lope's *El Maestro de Danzar* (written in 1594), Tebano says:

> "Verdad es que es el danzar
> El alma de la hermosura,
> Que mas que el rostro procura
> Persuadir y enamorar.

Music and dancing seem to have been indispensable accompaniments of the comedia from the earliest times. They were also a necessary part of all religious festivals and representations, and we may be sure that no *auto* was performed without music and dancing for the delectation of the spectators. One of the earliest documents preserved in the Archives of Madrid concerning these dances is dated May 17, 1574, when Alfonso de Silva, dancing-master, agreed to present four dances at the festival of the Holy Sacrament;[1] and in 1579 Jusepe de las Cuevas produced a dance "representing the battle of Rodrigo de Narvaez with the Moor Abindarraez" at the festival of Corpus Christi, and also a dance of the "Seven Virtues and Seven Sins."[2] These dancers were frequently Portuguese, and in 1587 one Hurtado, at the Corpus festival in Seville, exhibited a car "with five Portuguese women, with their *tamboriles and sonajas*[3] and instruments, who are to dance, play, and sing along the streets through which the procession is to pass";[4] and in 1590 eight ducats were paid to Leonor Rija, a mulatto, to appear upon a car at Corpus in Seville, and dance, sing, and play the guitar, *sonajas* and *tamboril,* together with four other mulatto women and two men.[5] In the same city at the Corpus festival of 1591, two sleight-of-hand perform-

> Que aquel ágil movimiento
> Muestra con mayor afeto
> Un sentimiento secreto
> Que nos muestra sentimiento."
> (Act I, Scene IV, ed. Hartzenbusch, II, p. 73.)

[1] Pérez Pastor, *Nuevos Datos,* p. 9.

[2] *Ibid.,* p. 12.

[3] *Tamboril* = timbrel or tabor; *sonajas* = "a kind of instrument the country people dance to, being a round, flat frame of wood, with both sides covered with parchment like a drum, not above six inches diameter, and not above two inches between the parchments, and round the frame horse-bells or loose brass plates are set; this they shake with the one hand and strike it with the other to make a rustical musick." (Delpino's *Spanish Dictionary,* London, 1758.)

[4] Sanchez-Arjona, *Anales,* p. 77.

[5] *Ibid.,* p. 81.

ers, with living birds, "according to the custom of the Italians," with music and ballads "in the sacred style," took part.[1] For a dance at the Corpus festival of 1609 the Villa de Madrid paid 1550 reals to Andres de Nájera. This was a *danza de cascabel,* entitled "The dance of Gayferos and rescue of Melisendra," to consist of nine personages: "four Frenchmen, four Moors, and the infanta Melisendra; also an enchanted castle, a horse of painted pasteboard (*papelon*), and Don Gayferos." A description of the rich costumes of the dancers follows, and we are told that the castle is to be provided with hinges, so that it may be opened where desired.[2] In 1611 there is mentioned a "Dance of King Alonso,"[3] and in 1623 a dance called "The History of the Marquis of Cañete."

[1] Sanchez-Arjona, p. 82. For other dances at the Corpus festival at Madrid in the closing years of the sixteenth century, see below, pp. 74, 75.

[2] Pérez Pastor, *Nuevos Datos,* p. 113. "Las *danzas de cascabel* eran para gente que puede salir á danzar por las calles. Y hubiera sido indecente que asistiesen á ellas los maestros. Era danza muy diversa de la *de cuenta* que era para Príncipes y gente de reputacion." (*Don Quixote,* ed. Clemencin, Vol. VI, p. 273.) Clemencin's source for this statement was probably Juan de Esquivel, *Discursos sobre el Arte del danzado,* Sevilla, 1642, who tells us that Philip IV. was extremely fond of dancing: "El Rey nuestro Señor, á cuya obediencia se postran los dilatados términos del mundo, aprendió este arte, y quando le obra, es con la mayor eminencia, gala y sazon que puede percibir la imaginacion mas atenta." He mentions the most famous dancing-masters of the time, among them Antonio de Almenda, of Madrid, Philip's teacher, José Rodriguez Tirado of Seville, Antonio de Burgos, Juan de Pastrana, and others. On fol. 30, v., he says that "*jácara, rastro, zarabanda y tarraga* son una misma cosa." He always speaks with contempt of the "bailes populares, á los que llaman danzas," as unworthy of gentlemen. On fol. 44, v., he says: "Todos los maestros aborrecen á los de las danzas *de cascabel,* y con mucha razon porque es muy distinta á la *de quenta* y de muy inferior lugar, y ansi ningun maestro de reputacion y con escuela abierta, se ha hallado jamas en semejantes chapandacas y si alguno lo ha hecho, no habrá sido teniendo escuela, ni llegado á noticia de sus discípulos, porque el que lo supiese rehusará serlo de allí adelante, porque la danza *de cascabel* es para gente que puede salir á dançar por las calles, y á estas danças llama por gracejo Francisco Ramos, la tarasca del dia de Dios," etc. (Gayangos, in the Spanish translation of Ticknor's *History,* Tomo III, p. 458.)

[3] This seems to have been a very ancient dance. Cervantes alludes to it at the close of his entremes *El Rufian viudo* as:

"El Rey don Alonso el Bueno,
Gloria de la antiguedad."

In 1634 costumes were hired from Alonso de la Vega, *autor de comedias,* for a dance in the town of Mejorada, the sum paid being 150 reals, besides a skin (*bota*) of wine of half a gallon, and a hen, "which are to be presented to the said *autor* by the *mayordomos* of the Lady of the Rosary of the said town";[1] and in 1637 we read of a sword dance (*danza de espadas*) to be performed in the town of Valdemoro.[2]

Dances or *bayles,* and short interludes, called *entremeses,* were inseparable from the comedia. Most of the players in a theatrical company, as already observed, also sang and danced, besides acting in the comedia, and many of the contracts between manager and player stipulate that the player is to act, sing, and dance (*para representar, cantar y bailar*). Of the nature of these *bayles* we know very little, except that many of them were *deshonestos.*[3] They were always accompanied by words or by singing;[4] the three or four most celebrated *bayles,* at least, having each its particular air, to which the later ones were often sung. They were frequently of such a loose and licentious nature that they caused great scandal and obliged the

---

It is mentioned in the *Tragicomedia de Lysandro y Roselia* (Salamanca(?), 1542). See *Coleccion de Libros españoles raros ó curiosos,* Vol. III, Madrid, 1872, p. 225, and Pellicer's note to his edition of *Don Quixote,* Madrid, 1797, Vol. IV, p. 102.

[1] Pérez Pastor, *Nuevos Datos,* p. 238.

[2] On the *danza de espadas,* see Leon-Pinelo, *Velos antiguos y modernos,* Madrid, 1641, fol. 112, v.

[3] Gonzales de Salas makes the following distinction between *danzas* and *bailes:* "Dances are measured and grave movements in which the arms are not used, but the feet only. *Bailes* admit of freer gestures of the arms and feet at the same time." (*Nueva Idea de la Tragedia antigua,* Madrid, 1778, p. 171.) See, however, Pellicer's note to *Don Quixote,* Pt. II, chap. xlviii, on the distinction between *bailar* and *danzar.*

[4] "Assi tambien lo vemos en nuestros Theatros, pues unas veces Danzan i Bailan solo al son de los instrumentos, i otras veces al son de lo que con los instrumentos cantan las voces. I lo que mas es, los mismos que danzan i bailan, cantan juntamente, primor i elegancia en estos ultimos años [before 1633] introducida, i sumamente dificultosa, siendo fuerza que estorbe, para la concentuosa harmonia de la voz, el espiritu alterado i defectuoso con los ajitados movimientos." (Gonzales de Salas, *ibid.,* p. 173.)

brated were the *Chacona* and the *Escarraman*. Cervantes and Lope de Vega were both great admirers of the popular dances, and the former has introduced a *chacona* in his novel *The Illustrious Kitchen-maid,* which is danced by muleteers and Galician girls, the refrain of which is:

> The *Chacona* is a treasure:
> Makes of life a real pleasure.

The third stanza is as follows:[1]

> Oft that noble dame *Chacona,*
> With the Saraband allied,
> Has put our carking cares to rout
> And the black bitch has defied.
> Oft *Chacona* makes its entry
> Through the chinks of convent cell,
> And that tranquil virtue flutters
> Which in sacred haunt should dwell.
> Often those who most admire it
> Rail against *Chacona's* charm,
> For the fool is ever eager,
> And the loose imagine harm, etc.[2]

But the *Chacona* and the *Escarraman* were no less vigorously opposed by the clergy than the *Zarabanda* had been.

Lerma, before Philip III. and his court in 1618, ending with "the scandalous and voluptuous dance of the *Zarabanda.*" (*History of Spanish Literature,* Vol. II, p. 519, note.) This also shows that the dance continued in vogue despite all opposition. In fact, as Pellicer (Vol. I, p. 138) says: "la Zarabanda quedó tan mal muerta que aun vivia y pirueteaba en los Corrales de Madrid el año de 1640."

[1] Cervantes, *The Exemplary Novels,* translated by N. Maccoll, Glasgow, Gowans & Gray, 1902, Vol. I, p. 55.

[2] "Qué de veces ha intentado
    Aquesta noble señora
    Con la alegre Zarabanda,
    El pésame, y perra mora
    Entrarse por los resquicios
    De las casas religiosas," etc.

It should be observed here that the *pésame* and the *perra mora* were also *bayles.* The *Escarraman* is danced in Cervantes's *entremes* entitled *El Rufian biudo.*

In 1613 we find the Catalan Jesuit, P. Juan Ferrer, speaking of them in these terms: "In a certain city in Spain there was current at one time one of those songs which they call the *chacona,* of such licentiousness that it created the greatest scandal, and now there are songs which they call *escarraman,* sung in this city [Barcelona], that have been produced in the theaters with such lewdness that even the admirers of the comedia were scandalized thereby, and many left the theater to avoid hearing them."[1]

Besides the three *bayles* or dances just mentioned, which

---

[1] Cotarelo y Mori, *Controversias,* p. 253. The *Chacona* is defined as a "Son ó tañido que se toca en varios instrumentos, al cual se baila una danza de cuenta con las castañetas, muy airosa y vistosa, que no sólo se baila en España en los festines, sino que de ella la han tomado otras naciones, y le dan este mismo nombre." (*Dic. de Aut.*) In the very rare volume, "*Norte de la Poesia Española ilustrado del Sol de doze Comedias (que forman Segunda Parte) de laureados Poetas Valencianos,* etc. Año 1616. Impreso en Valencia: En la Impresion de Felipe Mey," there are found, at the end of Ricardo de Turia's comedia *La Fé pagada,* "tres famosas Chaconas para cantar," of which the first is as follows:

"Assi vida, vida bona,
vida vamonos a Chacona.
Acuerdome un tiempo quando
dulce, y amada Señora,
la noche me halló en tus braços,
y en ellos el Alba hermosa.
Y en medio destos contentos,
aunque mejor diria glorias,
con la grana de tus labios
mescle mis dos amapolas.
Y aunque acertaron a hallarse
dos lenguas en cada boca,
en un profundo silencio
pasamos la noche toda.
Ay quanto un amor se aumenta,
y una aficion se acrisola
entre sauanas suaues,
y entre las obscuras sombras.
Alli en bonança tranquila
olas de estorbos se cortan,
los uracanes de celos
su fuerça, y poder aflojan.
Los escollos de desdenes
en dulce puerto se tornan,
y los baxios de ausencia
del gran Neptuno en la concha.

Y con tener sesgo el mar,
y tener el viento en popa,
no nauega mal quien puede
nauegar legua por hora.
Que del trabajo del vaso
por ser materia porosa,
sudan mastiles y jarcias,
y los velames se mojan.
Que en semejante ocasion
sudaran hasta las rocas;
tal es el dulce trabajo,
y la apacible congoja.
Los prosperos vientos cesan,
y asesan con vozes roncas
los pechos que el pecho dieron
al agua del amor sabrosa.
Falta el viento, y el aliento
antes de salir se ahoga,
quedando el Vagel rendido
en una calma amorosa,
hasta que refresca el viento,
y la gente se alboroça,
continuando el viage
hasta arribar a las costas.
Asi vida, vida bona," etc.

were the most popular, Pellicer mentions a number of other "bayles antiguos": the *Turdion, Pavana, Madama Orliens, Pie de gibao, Rey Don Alonso el Bueno,* etc., and of what he calls the "populares y truanescos," he gives a long list, including the *Carreteria, Hermano Bartolo, Pollo, Perra Mora, Canario,*[1] etc. That these dances were in vogue at about the same time is shown by the fact that the *Canario, Rey Don Alonso el Bueno, Coscolina, Repulida, Pizpita, Chiquinaque, Mostrenca, Juan Claros el galan, Zambapalo, Pésame dello, Gallarda, Villano,* and others are mentioned by Cervantes in the *Escarraman* which he has introduced into his interlude *El Rufian biudo.*[2]

Many other curious dances are mentioned by Pérez Pastor, which were performed at the Corpus Christi festival in Madrid: in 1584 the *Danza de Radamante, Reinaldos, Roldan, Oliveros* and *Montesinos,* and the *Llegada de Eneas á Cartago;*[3] in 1592 the *Danza de seis Abestruces y seis Muchachos zapateadores* and the *Danza de la Recuperacion de España;*[4] in 1596 the *Danza del Robo de Elena* and *Danza de Villanos y Villanas;*[5] in

[1] *Tratado historico,* Vol. I, p. 126, and p. 137 for a long list of *bayles* that were danced to the air of the *Zarabanda.*

[2] Lope de Vega laments the disappearance of these old dances, and mentions another, *La Alemana:* "se van oluidandose . . . las danças antiguas, con estas acciones gesticulares, y mouimientos lasciuos de las Chaconas, en tanta ofensa de la virtud de la castidad, y el decoroso silencio de las damas. Ay de ti Alemana, y Pie de Gibao, que tantos años estuuistes honrando los saraos!" (*La Dorotea,* Madrid, 1632, Act I, Scene VII, fol. 40.) Góngora, in one of his ballads, says there is no dance like the *Gallarda:*

> "Que quiere doña Maria
> Ver bailar á doña Juana
> Una *Gallarda* española,
> Que no hay danza mas gallarda."

The stately gravity with which the *Gallarda* was danced is described at some length by Calderon in his *El Maestro de Danzar,* Jornada II, Scene XXV. See Monreal, *Cuadros viejos,* Madrid, 1878, p. 85. In a French work on dancing, Arbeau's *Orchésographie,* published at Maçon in 1588, the *Tordion* and *Gaillard* are described as being danced exactly alike. See Shakespeare's *Much Ado about Nothing,* ed. by Dr. Horace Howard Furness, Philadelphia, p. 65, note 69.

[3] *Nuevos Datos,* p. 15.   [4] *Ibid.,* p. 33.   [5] *Ibid.,* p. 43.

1598 a *Danza de Portugueses;*[1] in 1599 a *Danza de veintequatro Sátiros y Fábulas y un Sileno,* danced on the occasion of the entrance of the Queen into Madrid.[2] I presume that these were all what were called "Danzas habladas."[3]

It appears that down to the close of the sixteenth century and perhaps even later, these dances at the Corpus festivals were performed and the expenses were borne by the various guilds. In March, 1599, there was an agreement between the company of tavern-keepers (gremio de taberneros) and Jusepe de las Cuevas to represent the "danza de los caballeros para la entrada de la Reina";[4] and in April of the same year Juan Granado is to give the dance *La Boda á lo sayagües* by order of the blacksmiths, and the *Danza de los Dioses,* to be paid for by the shoemakers, and the *Danza de la Pandorga,* performed by the joiners and inn-keepers (cajoneros y mesoneros).[5] Besides, the "gremios" or guilds of "cabestreros, esparteros, zurradores," and "curtidores" represented dances at Corpus in Madrid in 1599.[6]

---

[1] *Nuevos Datos,* p. 48.

[2] *Ibid.,* p. 349.

[3] See *Don Quixote,* Part II, chap. xx, and Clemencin's note. Delpino defines a *Danza hablada* as "a dance composed of many persons, with dresses suitable to represent any passage in history." (*Spanish Dictionary,* London, 1758.)

[4] *Nuevos Datos,* p. 49.   [5] *Ibid.,* p. 50.   [6] *Ibid.*

CHAPTER V

The staging of the comedia. English court plays. The *Entertaining Journey* of Rojas. Alonso Lopez Pinciano on staging. The stage. The curtain. Scenery. Stage machinery. *Apariencias.* *Tramoyas.* The French stage. Private representations.

IN any discussion of the stage or scenic arrangements of the early Spanish theater the distinction between *autos* and other festival or court performances, on the one hand, and those which took place in the public *corrales,* on the other, must always be borne in mind. In the former, as already observed, there was often an elaborate display of scenery and ornamentation even before the middle of the sixteenth century, while the public theaters or *corrales* were almost destitute of scenery, in our acceptation of the word. And this, we know, was also the case in England in Shakespeare's time.[1] Cunningham[2] gives some curious information concerning the private representations at the English court. As early as 1571, after mentioning several plays, the last of which is *Paris and Vienna,* "shewen on Shrovetewsdaie at night by the children of Westminster," we read: "All whiche vi playes being chosen owte of many and ffownde to be the best that then were to be had; the same also being often perused and necessarely corrected & amended by all thafforseide officers. Then they being so orderly addressed, were likewise throwghly apparelled & furnished with sun-

---

[1] See the interesting articles by G. F. Reynolds in *Modern Philology,* Vols. II and III (1904–5).

[2] *Extracts from the Accounts of the Revels at Court,* London (Shakespeare Society), 1842.

dry kindes and sutes of Apparell & furniture, ffitted and garnished necessarely & answerable to the matter, person & parte to be played. Having also apt howses, made of canvasse, fframed, ffashioned & paynted accordingly as might best serve theier severall purposes" (p. 13).

1573 (it may be noted that in this year Italian players are mentioned at Windsor, *ibid.*, p. 79) : "Mrs. Dane for Canvas to paynte for howses for the players & for other properties as Monsters, great hollow trees & suche other," etc. (p. 54).

1574: There is frequent mention of frames and canvas as early as this year, and also the following entry: "Pulleys for the Clowdes and curteynes . . . Dubble gyrte to hange the soon in the clowde," etc. (p. 90).

1578: "For a hoope and blewe Lynnen cloth to mend the clowde that was borrowed and cut to serve the rock in the play of *The burnyng Knight,*" etc. (p. 147).

1579: *"The History of Serpedon* shewen at Whitehall on Shrovetewesdaye at night enacted by the Lord Chamberleyns servants wholly furnyshed in this office whereon was ymployed for head attyres for women and Scarfes xi ells of Sarcenett, a greate Cittie, a wood, a castell and vi payre of gloves" (p. 156). Colors for painting scenery are mentioned in this year: "William Lyzarde for sondry things by him browght into the office. Syse, cullers, pottes, nayles and pensills used and occupyed upon the payntinge of vii Cities, one villadge, one Country howse, one battlement, iiii axes, a Braunche, lillyes, and a mount for Christmas iii Holidaies" (p. 162).

1580: "A *Storie of Pompey,* enacted in the hall [Whitehall], on twelfnighte whereon was ymployed newe, one great citty, a senate howse, and eight ells of double sarcenet for curtens and xviii paire of gloves" (p. 167).

1584: " *The History of Felix & Philomena* shewed and enacted before her highnes by her Ma^tes servauntes on the sondaie next after neweyeares daie, at night at Grenewiche, whereon was ymploied one battlement & a house of canvas." Lastly, in the same year we read: "A pastorall of *Phillyda & Choryn* . . . whereon was ymployed . . . one greate curteyne and scarfs for the nymphes, one mountayne and one greate cloth of Canvas" (p. 188).

All these were court performances and had nothing to do with the public theaters in England, which at this time had probably advanced no further than those of Spain. To these we now return.

There can scarcely be a doubt that down to about the last decade of the sixteenth century (i.e., even a few years after Lope de Vega had begun to write for the stage) the public theaters of Madrid possessed only the most primitive stage machinery and appliances, and no scenery in our sense of the word. This view, however, is not in accord with an opinion expressed by Schack, though this distinguished writer's other statements upon the subject can hardly be reconciled with the assertion to which we refer, which is as follows: "According to Rojas, therefore, the improvements in scenic arrangements had progressed to such an extent by about 1580 that comedias were performed in which were represented miraculous visions, artistically contrived scenes, and alarms of war, and even horses were brought upon the stage." [1] Schack bases this statement upon the following lines of the "Loa de la Comedia" contained in the *Viage entretenido* of Rojas: "Now they made inflated verses, wore costumes of cloth, satin, and velvet, and silken stockings. They wrote [comedias] in three acts and introduced challenges; they sang by two and threes, and women acted. The time arrived when *comedias de apariencias* (i.e., with scenic effects) and lives of saints and plays with

[1] "So war, nach Rojas, die Vervollkommnung der scenischen Vorrichtungen um 1580 schon so weit gediehen dasz man Comödien mit Wundererscheinungen, Coulissenkünsten und Kriegslärm aufführte und sogar Pferde auf die Bühne brachte." (*Geschichte der dramatischen Literatur u. Kunst in Spanien*, Vol. I, p. 308.)

stage machinery came into vogue, and among these, farces in which battles were represented. Pedro Diaz then wrote his comedia *El Rosario*, which was good, and Alonso Diaz his *San Antonio*, and finally there was not a poet in Seville who did not write a comedia about some saint. Then they sang by threes and fours; the women were beautiful and dressed in male attire, and gallantly and well made up they stepped upon the stage, adorned with pearls and chains of gold. Now horses were brought upon the stage, a feat never seen until this time, nor was this the least of them. All these things passed away, and then came our day, which may be called the Golden Age, to judge by the point reached by comedias, actors, plots, conceits, epigrams, inventions, novelties. . . . What, that has not already been done, can they do who come after us? What can they invent that is not already invented?" etc.[1]

Important as the *Viage entretenido* is in many respects,

---

[1] After mentioning Artieda's *Los Encantos de Merlin* (now lost), Lupercio's tragedies, the *Semiramis* of Virués, and the *Conde Loco* of Morales (v. Barrera, *Catálogo*, pp. 517, col. 1, and 527), Rojas continues:

"Hacian versos hinchados,
    Ya usaban sayos de telas
    De raso, de terciopelo,
    Y algunas medias de seda.
Ya se hacian tres jornadas,
    Y echaban retos en ellas,
    Cantaban á dos y á tres,
    Y representaban hembras.
Llegó el tiempo que se usaron
    Las comedias de apariencias,
    De santos y de tramoyas,
    Y entre estas farsas de guerras,
Hizo Pedro Diaz entonces
    La del *Rosario*, y fué buena,
    San Antonio Alonso Diaz,
    Y al fin no quedó poeta
En Sevilla que no hiciese
    De algun santo su comedia:
    Cantabanse á tres y á quatro,
    Eran las mugeres bellas,

Vestianse en habito de hombre,
    Y bizarras y compuestas,
    A representar salian
    Con cadenas de oro y perlas.
Sacábanse ya caballos
    A los teatros, grandeza
    Nunca vista hasta este tiempo,
    Que no fué la menor de ellas.
En efecto este pasó,
    Llegó el nuestro, que pudiera
    Llamarse el tiempo dorado,
    Segun al punto en que llegan
Comedias, representantes,
    Trazas, conceptos, sentencias,
    Inventivas, novedades, . . .
    . . . .
¿ Qué harán los que vinieron
    Que no sea cosa hecha?
¿ Qué inventarán, que no esté
    Ya inventado? cosa es cierta," etc.

(*El Viage entretenido*, Madrid, 1603, pp. 127, 128.)

Rojas then mentions the appearance of Lope de Vega, *La fenix de nuestros tiempos*, and after him *El Divino* Miguel Sanchez.

it was not the purpose of its author to write a history of the Spanish stage. It was composed, as the title indicates, for the mere entertainment and pastime of the reader. Rojas, in all probability, took no great pains to be precise and accurate in his statements. What he wrote slipped from his pen without much thought of chronology. His statements should not be taken *al pie de la letra*. Moreover, his experience on the stage was limited, according to his own statement, to about three years. Of Pedro Diaz and his comedia *El Rosario*, mentioned by Rojas, we know nothing, but Alonso Diaz is said by Sanchez-Arjona (*Anales*, p. 86) to be the author of an *auto* entitled *Santa Maria Egipciaca*, for which he received thirty ducats when it was represented by the company of Gaspar de Porres at Seville in 1594. Alonso Diaz was, therefore, a contemporary of Lope de Vega. His *San Antonio* was doubtless one of that large class of *comedias de santos* which greatly depend for their effect on the use of *apariencias* and *tramoyas*, quite primitive stage machinery at that time, we may be sure. As Morel-Fatio says: "Les pièces, en effet, où était représentée la vie d'un saint se prêtaient particulièrement au jeu de cette machinerie primitive qui enchantait le peuple." The same writer quotes Cristobal Suarez de Figueroa (*El Passagero*, Alivio iii), who says: "En las comedias de cuerpo (pièces à grand effet par opposition à celles dites *de ingenio* ou *de capa y espada*) que, sin las de reyes de Hungria o principes de Transilvania, suelen ser de vidas de santos, intervienen varias *tramoyas* o *apariencias*, singular añagaza para que reincida el poblacho tres o quatro vezes con crecido provecho del autor."[1] That skilful engineers or machinists were employed by the public theaters in staging such plays at the time alluded to by Rojas, is not at all probable.

---

[1] *Bulletin Hispanique*, October–December, 1901, p. 481. See also Clemencin's note to his edition of *Don Quixote*, Madrid, 1833, Vol. III, p. 407, and Suarez de Figueroa, *Passagero*, ed. 1617, ff. 104–106.

Concerning the assertion of Rojas, "Sacabanse ya caballos" (horses were now brought out upon the stage), there is no dramatist prior to 1602 to whom this could particularly refer, so far as I know, except Lope de Vega.[1] In the latter's *La Serrana de la Vera*, *El Sol parado*, and *La Varona Castellana*, all written before 1603, and in *El primer Faxardo*, perhaps also before that date, a horse appears on the stage. According to Luis Fernández Guerra,[2] it was Andres de Claramonte particularly who was fond of bringing horses upon the stage in his plays. He says: "Gozabase en aderezar muchas de sus comedias con desafios á caballo y en pasear sobre hipógrifos de carne y hueso á las hermosuras dc bastidores por en medio de lo más turbulento y alegre de la concurrencia. . . . Esto dió lugar á que Ana Muñoz, obligada en uno de sus dramas á salir á caballo por el patio, alborotado el corcel con la algaraza de los mosqueteros, malparió un varon." As Claramonte is mentioned by Rojas[3] among those actors who had (at least as early as 1602) written *farsas, loas, bayles*, etc., it is not improbable that the allusion may be to him. In any event, it carries us no further back than the time of Lope de Vega, who was a contemporary of Claramonte's. Moreover, Miguel Sanchez, *el Divino*, who is mentioned after Lope de Vega, was undoubtedly one of Lope's predecessors. Hence the period to which Rojas refers cannot be "about 1580," as Schack had supposed, but was, in all probability, more than a decade later.[4]

[1] In *El gallardo Español* by Cervantes, Act I, is the stage direction: *Entra Alimuzel a cauallo, con lanza y adarga*. And in *La Casa de los Zelos*, Act I: *ha de entrar por el patio Angelica la bella sobre un palafren*. These plays may date before 1592. Tirso de Molina also not infrequently introduced horses upon the stage, though at a much later date.

[2] *Don Juan Ruiz de Alarcon*, p. 186.

[3] *Viage entretenido*, p. 131.

[4] It is interesting here to note the observations of a very acute and learned writer, Alonso Lopez Pinciano, concerning the decorations of the stage, the costumes, etc., written about 1595 or perhaps a little before. From a reference to two of the older Spanish *autores de comedias*, it has been considered that, though published in 1596, the work alluded to was written at least

We may readily believe that with the appearance of a genius like Lope (who wrote plays at twelve, but perhaps did not begin to write for the public stage until about 1585) the progress in the comedia was accompanied by a corresponding advance in staging. Yet it seems reasonably safe to say that, even for some years after Lope began his career as a playwright, the decorations and scenic effects in the public theaters of Spain were very primitive. As Schack observes, any attempt at optical illusion was wholly out of the question. "Nor was there a curtain in front of the stage, from which it follows that, at the beginning of a piece, the stage could not be occupied by groups [of players], but the actors had to enter before the eyes of the spectators." An examination of the comedias

ten years earlier. (Schack, Vol. I, p. 299, says that it was written shortly after 1580.) The passage is: "When I see the placards of Cisneros or Galvez, I cannot help going to see them, and while I am in the theater I neither feel the cold in winter nor the heat in summer." But we know now that Jerónimo Galvez was acting at least as late as 1590 and probably later, while Alonso de Cisneros did not die till September 10, 1597. It is probable, therefore, that our author's remarks refer to about the time that his work was published. This work is in the form of a conversation between the author and his friends Ugo and Fadrique, and consists of a number of letters written by the author to one Don Gabriel and the replies of the latter thereto. In the thirteenth and last letter *de los actores y representantes,* Don Ugo remarks: "So far as the action is concerned, the person, the time, and the place ought to be considered, for it is clear that a different decoration and dress or costume is required for a prince than for a servant, and different ones for youths and old men. Wherefore the second consideration, that of time, is very important, for the Spain of to-day demands a different decoration and dress from the Spain of a thousand years ago, and hence it behooves to examine carefully histories which throw light upon the costumes of the times, and we should likewise take note of the various countries, for in each they have different kinds of dress. The actor should observe these matters carefully, for the poet rarely pays any attention to them, generally writing the poem to be read rather than to be represented, leaving those matters that refer to the action to the actor, whose business it is to represent. Whence it is to be inferred that the good actor (especially the chief of a company) ought to know much of fiction (*fabula*) and of history, so that, in accordance with the difference in time, besides the costumes of the persons in the action, there is required a corresponding decoration for the theater itself, besides the necessary machinery, which ought to be in conformity with the poem: if it be pastoral, there should be woods; if the action take place in a city, there should be houses; and so in accordance with the other differences, the theater should have its various decora-

of Lope de Vega proves the truth of this assertion, as regards the theaters of Madrid, and that there was no outer curtain in the theater at Valencia is shown by a number of plays by Valencian dramatists which appeared in a volume entitled *Norte de la Poesia española*, Valencia, 1616.[1] This statement seems to be contradicted by a passage at the close of Lope de Vega's *La inocente Sangre*, published in Part XIX of his *Comedias*, the *Aprovacion* of which is dated 1622. Here one of the characters, Mendo, says:

> "Corre essa cortina, y desse
> fin a los Carauajales," etc.

Five players are on the stage, and the curtain is drawn to conceal them from the audience. It is possible, however, that this, too, was a curtain farther back on the stage. Unfortunately, we do not know the date of this

tions (*ornato*). And in the machinery there should be much excellence (*primor*), for there are some machines which are fitting for a miracle and others for different purposes, and they have their differences according to the persons, for an angel must appear to be flying and a saint going through the air with joined feet, and both must descend from on high, while the demon ascends from below. . . . In a word, the actor should observe and study the various machinery and artifices, so that suddenly, as if by a miracle, a person be made to appear: by magic art, if terrestrial; without it, if the person be divine." (*Philosophia Antigua*, ed. 1596, pp. 522, 523.)

[1] Lope's *El Rey Bamba* (written before 1603) shows clearly that there was no outer curtain. At the close of the play the King is lying dead upon the stage, when Atanarico says:

> "Cojamos el cuerpo en ombros
> y luego el entierro se haga,
> dando fin a la comedia
> y vida y muerte de Bamba."
> (*Comedias*, Part I, Valladolid, 1604, fol. 116, v.)

And in his *La Quinta de Florencia*, Part II, 1609, we read at the end: "*Vanse todos por su orden, con que se da fin a la Comedia.*" At the close of Aguilar's play, published in the *Norte de la Poesia española*, entitled *El Mercader Amante*, is the stage direction: *Entranse todos, y se da fin a la Comedia del Mercader Amante*. Ricardo de Turia's *Burladora burlada* concludes with the stage direction: *Entranse todos cada uno por su puerta, dandose con esto fin a la famosa Comedia*, etc. The same author's *La belligera Española* and Aguilar's *La Fuerça del Interes* close with similar stage directions. These would, of course, have been unnecessary had there been an outer curtain.

play. Though not printed till 1622, Lope says in his
dedication that he had written it years ago: "Años ha que
escriui este suceso."

There was a curtain at the back of the stage, like the
traverses of the Elizabethan theater, which could be drawn
aside to represent a tent, bedchamber, chapel, etc.[1] The
sides of the stage were also hung with curtains, as the
stage directions abundantly show.[2]

Cervantes even tells us that the curtains were of green
baize, and they must have been arranged, upon occasions,
in such a manner that the spectator could see behind
them.[3]

In the background, raised some distance from the
stage, was a gallery (*lo alto del teatro*), which served for

---

[1] In the first act of Lope de Vega's *El Asalto de Mastrique* (*Comedias,*
Part IV, 1614), we read the stage direction: *Corrase una tienda, o cortina,
y veanse sentados el Duque de Parma, etc. . . . los soldados se arrimen al
Teatro.* Afterward: *Cierrese la tienda, y los soldados digan:*

> "*Soldado:* Parece que ya se van
> de la tienda."

In *El Marmol de Felisardo,* Act III (written before 1604), occurs the stage
direction: *Corre Tristan la cortina, detras de la qual está Elisa,* etc., and in
Las Pobrezas de Reynaldos (also before 1604), Act II: *Corren una cortina,
y descubrese una Capilla con un altar,* etc. So near the close of Act III of
Guillen de Castro's *La Tragedia por los Celos* (1622) the curtain that was
drawn to show the dead body of Margarita de Hijar was doubtless at the
rear of the stage. And in Ricardo de Turia's *La Burladora burlada*
(printed in 1616), Act III, Laura says:

> "Detras deste tapiz rico
> pienso escuchallas."

This is followed by the stage direction: *quedase detras de la cortina.*

[2] See *La Burladora burlada,* cited in the previous note. Also in Alarcon's
El Desdichado en fingir (one of his earliest plays, written probably before
1600), at the close of a scene in Act II, is the direction: *Vanse, y escondense
detras de una cortina.* In Act III of Tirso de Molina's *La fingida Arcadia,*
a stage direction seems to show that a curtain sometimes covered the whole
rear of the stage. The direction is: *Tocan trompetas,* etc. *Cáese abajo todo
el lienzo del teatro y quede un jardin lleno de flores y yedra.* This is a late
play, however, certainly after 1621, for in it Tirso mentions Lope de Vega's
La Filomena, which appeared in that year. For further examples see my
article "The Staging of Lope de Vega's Comedias," in the *Revue Hispanique,* Vol. XV, 1907.

[3] In *La Gran Sultana* we find the stage direction: *Parece el Gran Turco*

various purposes; for example, to represent the walls of a city, the balcony of a house, a tower, a mountain, etc. In the above article I have collected many examples under the various headings: "A wall or tower at the back of the stage," "A window," "A balcony," etc., which show that the "balcony" was merely a gallery at the upper part of the back of the stage, which was covered by a hanging curtain, so that there was no essential difference in the representation of a wall, a tower, a window, or a balcony. That a gallery ran along the back of the stage, perhaps a continuation of the gallery occupied by the spectators, appears from stage directions in a number of plays.[1]

The stage, Schack observes, was not nearly so deep as that of the modern theater, but was rather wide. "Its decorations consisted of curtains of a single color, hung at the sides and in the background, leaving the various entrances free. These represented now a room, now a hall or a street, now a garden or a forest, without any visible change."[2] Continuing, the same writer observes: "With this simple arrangement those pieces were played the action of which was supposed to take place in ordinary domestic and civil life, chiefly therefore the *comedias de capa y espada,* but especially those in which the stage did not essentially enter into the action of the play and where the imagination of the spectator could be relied upon. Whether more machinery was to be used or not

detras de unas cortinas de tafetan verde . . . descubrese la cortina: parece el Gran Turco. (*Comedias,* etc., Madrid, 1615, fol. 121.)

[1] In Tirso de Molina's *Doña Beatriz de Silva,* Act I: *Tiros de Artilleria; musica de todo genero; fiestas de dentro, y saca Silveria sobre los corredores de arriba, a un lado una bandera con las armas de Portugal y Castilla.* Afterward we read: *Al otro lado saca arriba Olivenza otra bandera,* etc. Finally: *Entranse los de arriba.* This comedia was written about 1618, according to Cotarelo. See additional cases cited below, p. 94, note 1.

[2] These statements require some modification. That there were at least two doors at the back of the stage, always called *puertas,* is shown by every comedia. In the above article on the staging of Lope's plays, numerous instances are given to show that trees were represented on the stage either painted on canvas hanging at the sides, or single trees or groups of trees on frames standing on the stage. Some examples are cited below.

was left to the discretion of the theatrical manager. This depended especially upon whether the play in question, from its subject-matter, necessitated scenery and was such that all could not be left to the imagination. In such cases the objects which would otherwise have to be imagined were actually brought before the eye, and the plays in which such apparatus had to be employed, beyond the simple curtains, and in which the costumes were richer and costlier, were called *comedias de teatro*. Decorations, however, in the modern sense of the word, or a regular change of scene, were wholly unknown."[1]

For most scenes, as just remarked, a simple curtain sufficed, and this was used to represent the most diverse localities. "If the stage was unoccupied for a moment and persons came upon it through another entrance, a change of scene had to be imagined by the spectator, though none was visible on the stage, and this was irrespective of the entrances or exits of the characters." Schack cites several instances of this: Act II of Calderon's *El Alcayde de si*

[1] Schack, *Geschichte der dram. Lit. u. Kunst in Spanien*, Vol. II, p. 120. Spaniards, according to Caramuel, considered changes of scene superfluous, as neither the exactness of the thought, nor the elegance of the diction, nor the splendor of the production, depended upon them. He says: "Scenarum mutationes Hispani superfluas judicant: quas tamen Itali esse necessarias supponentes in theatri fabricâ pro unicâ interdum Comoedia magnam summam ducatorum impendunt. Et hic, si loquamur sincere, inconsequenter Hispani laborare videmur: quoniam hinc leges scribendi Comoedias ab Antiquis latas fastidimus, inde scenarum mutationes quasi superfluas judicamus, cum tamen haec duo non subsistant. Cur non volumus ut nostrae Comoediae subsint Veterum legibus? Quia falsae hypothesi leges a Veteribus prolatae insistunt. Putabant ipsi Comoedias Viris tantum doctis scribi, et coram doctis tantum agi, cum tamen certum sit et nos supponimus, illas scribi vulgo et coram numeroso vulgo repraesentari. Et cur non volumus mutare Scaenas? Quia ab earum mutatione conceptuum subtilitas, verborum elegantia et nitor prolationis non dependent. Ecce severas scribendi Comoedias leges negligimus, nam illae representantur propter vulgus, qui illas leges non capit: et ecce Scenarum mutationes negligimus, nam docti, quorum est, de conceptuum et versuum nitore judicare, ut bona laudent carmina, hoc impendio non indigent. Ego hoc auderem discurrere. Seu doctis seu indoctis scribantur Comoediae, debent Scenae mutari et apparentiae quas vocant admitti: illarum enim varietate doctorum et indoctorum oculi dilectantur." (J. Caramuelis, *Primus Calamus,* Tom. II, quoted by Schack, *Nachträge,* p. 28.)

mismo opens in a park; the second scene is a forest; enter three peasants and Antona, who says that Benito has assured her that on her return to the forest she will find his love "more firm than this oak." Nothing has been said to intimate a change of scene when Federico enters, and in a dialogue with Roberto says: "Is not some one knocking? *Roberto:* Yes. *Federico:* Then go and open the door," and the stage direction follows: "Federico sits down in a chair; enter Marguerite," whereby a change to the interior of the castle is to be supposed by the spectator.[1]

In Lope de Vega's *Los Embustes de Fabia*, Aurelio has been in the chamber of his mistress and has not left the stage, when he says: "Here is the palace and there Nero, our Emperor, appears, for the poet has permitted this expedient to be employed, since, if the Emperor should not enter now, the narrative would be so vague that nobody would understand it."[2] A better example to illustrate the point under discussion could hardly be found. We do not know when *Los Embustes de Fabia* was written, but it was one of Lope's early plays, for it is mentioned in the list in the first edition of his *Peregrino en su Patria,* and hence must be earlier than 1604. A notable instance of where a change of scene is indicated merely by the actor's going

---

[1] Schack, *Geschichte,* etc., Vol. II, p. 121. It should be noted that this incident was first referred to by Damas Hinard, that excellent scholar to whom Spanish literature owes so much. In his *Chefs-d'œuvre du Théâtre Espagnol, Calderon,* 2e Série, Paris, 1841, note to p. 316, he says: "Nous étions tout-à-l'heure dans le parc, et tout-à-coup nous voilà transportés dans l'interieur du château. Comme Frédéric et Roberto n'ont pas quitté le théâtre, il nous est impossible d'indiquer un changement de scène. Mais enfin le lecteur est averti, nous sommes maintenant dans le château de Belflor, ou de Miraflor."

[2] "Este es el palacio, acá sale
Neron, nuestro Emperador,
Que lo permite el Autor
Que desta industria se vale;
Porque si acá no saliera
Fuera aqui la relacion
Tan mala y tan sin razon
Que ninguno lo entendiera."
(*Comedias,* Part XXV, Zaragoza, 1647, fol. 537.)

in one door and coming out of another is furnished by *La Española de Florencia,* a comedia wrongly ascribed to Calderon. The example is of especial interest because of the comparatively late date of the play, which was probably written between 1630 and 1635.[1] Schack further remarks: "That the stage did not always realize what one should suppose, even in the so-called *comedias de teatro,* results from the speeches of the characters, who frequently indicate the locality, which would have been unnecessary if it had been actually brought before the eyes of the spectator. Only when the progress of the action could not well be otherwise indicated was recourse had to such expedients of the scenic art as were available. Such cases were mostly left to the judgment of the theatrical manager, inasmuch as the poets only gave directions in the most necessary cases. The

[1] "*Salen Carlos y Gerardo.*

Gerardo: Ya hemos llegado á casa.
Carlos: ¡ Ay, Gerardo, qué el pecho se me abrasa!
Lucrecia: Cavalleros, si el cielo
á piedad os inclina, tened duelo
de una muger, si noble, desdichada,
que llega de su suerte atropellada
á pedir vuestro amparo.
Valgame vuestra casa de reparo,
que en tanta desventura
mi honor vuestra nobleza me assegura.
Entranse Carlos y Lucrecia.
Carlos: Entrad, Señora en ella.
Gerardo: ¡ Por Dios, qué la muger parece bella !
No seria en mi amo dicha poca,
si por ésta oluidasse [á] la otra loca.
Entranse, y salen por la otra puerta todos tres.
Carlos: Ya estamos en la posada."
(*Comedias Escogidas,* Vol. XII, Madrid, 1658, Jornada II, fol. 105.)

Jornada III furnishes a similar instance:
"*Salen Cesar y Valerio.*
Cesar: Ya á casa á buscaros me boluia,
Carlos; yo os hallo, ¡qué gran dicha es mia!
Lleguemos á la entrada.
Lucrecia: Lida, aquesta ocasion es apretada.
Carlos: Ya en vuestra casa estamos."

I quote these passages at length on account of the scarcity of this comedia. Dr. M. Rosenberg purposes publishing a critical edition of it shortly.

staging of plays was therefore very arbitrary."[1] A decoration which happened to be at hand was sometimes used in cases where it was not necessary, while in other instances, where the required apparatus was lacking, an appeal was unreasonably made to the imagination of the spectator.

Moreover, the freedom exercised in the matter of scenery can hardly be exaggerated. "There was no thought of any actual illusion—of any deception of the senses. The painting of scenery according to the rules of perspective, so that the stage should have some appearance of reality, was wholly unknown. A few houses or trees painted on pasteboard or linen did duty for a street or a forest, while the simple curtain in the background or the sides remained unchanged. After such a decoration had been set upon the stage, no particular care was taken to remove it at the end of the scene, and frequently it had to suffice to indicate another similar place."

There can scarcely be a doubt that simultaneous scenery was used upon the Spanish stage, as it was used at the same period in the Elizabethan theater. In the representation of Calderon's *El Alcayde de si mismo* it is very probable that a tree was represented upon the stage at the opening of the second act and was not removed until its close.

In Alarcon's *El Dueño de las Estrellas* (1618?), toward the close of Act III, the scene is supposed to represent a street at night. The King and Palante appear before the house of Marcela. Palante gives a sign, and we have the stage direction: *Asomase Marcela a una ventana.*

"*Marcela:* ¿Es Palante? *Palante:* Si. *Marcela:* Ya voy.
(*Vase a abrir la puerta.*)"

Presently Palante says: "Ya está á la puerta Marcela.

(*Aparece Marcela en la calle.*)
Marcela: Entrad. *Rey:* Marcela querida, etc.
Marcela: Seguidme. (*Vanse de la calle, y dando la vuelta por detras del teatro, entranse despues en la sala* [*de Marcela*].)"

That is, the actors merely pass out on one side of the stage and enter on the other, and the scene is supposed to change from a street to a room in Marcela's house.

[1] For a detailed account see my article already referred to, in the *Revue Hispanique* for 1907.

"Sometimes a change of scene was indicated by simply drawing a curtain aside, whereby the essential object became visible, the rest of the stage remaining unchanged, only a small scene, as it were, stepping out of the larger one. In this way it is frequently supposed that from the foreground, which represents a street or a room, one can look into the interior of a house or into another apartment. How little attention was given to the probability of a scene may be observed from the fact that not seldom the stage represented a field of great dimensions, in which the personages traverse long distances, so that the scene was actually to be considered movable. Thus, in the first act of Calderon's *Dos Amantes del Cielo*,[1] one of the characters, Chrysanthus, is represented as being in the grove of Diana; then it is supposed that he goes thence deeper into the mountains; he describes the wild, mountainous country which he is now approaching, without leaving the stage for a moment. A change of scene could not have taken place here; the same trees and perhaps hills which had at first served for a grove were afterward taken to represent the wilder mountain region."

Another and similar case is the following: "when the personages upon the stage are supposed to be moving forward and have reached an object which attracts their attention and which enters into the action of the play, a back or side curtain is drawn in order to permit this to appear. Examples are frequent. At the beginning of Lope's *Arauco domado* a number of soldiers are wandering in the neighborhood of a South American seaport. They are on their way to the public square, where a Corpus Christi procession is to pass under a triumphal arch; when they arrive at the spot, the scene is opened by withdrawing a curtain, and a glimpse is afforded of the arch and the holiday crowd."[2] So in Tirso de Molina's *El Burlador de Sevilla*

---

[1] The date of this play is unknown: it was written before 1651.
[2] Schack, *ibid.*, p. 123. For a similar scene, see Lope's *La Prueba de los*

(written before 1630), Don Juan and his servant are roaming the streets of Seville, and after they have been upon the stage a considerable time, the statue of the Comendador, Don Gonzalo de Ulloa, is suddenly disclosed.

Sometimes the place of action is mentioned in the dialogue at the beginning of a scene; more rarely by a stage direction.[1] But the stage remained the same, there was no visible change, whether the action was transported to Florence, Rome, or Hungary. Indeed, there is often great difficulty in distinguishing interior from exterior scenes. Many scenes, in fact, are entirely unlocalized, and here, as in the Elizabethan drama, "vagueness of localization" is a fundamental fact.[2]

Besides, it must be borne in mind that costume was a

Amigos (1604), Act III, in the article above mentioned on *The Staging of Lope de Vega's Comedias*, p. 7, and *La Fé rompida* (before 1604), Act I, *ibid.*, p. 9.

[1] In Lope de Vega's *Rey Bamba* (Part I, 1604), Act II:

> "*Rodrigo:* Esta es la Vega famosa,
> del Tajo la plaça llana
> y aquesta de Galiana
> la morada deleytosa."

In Lope's *Comedia del Molino* (Part I, 1604), Act III:

> "*Rey:* Que gente es esta que camina al bosque,"

showing that a grove is intended.

Lope's *La Quinta de Florencia* (Part II, 1609), Act I:

> "*Alexandro:* Hermosa ciudad Florencia."

Coello's *El Conde de Sex* (a late play, probably about 1635), Act II, at the beginning:

> "*Cosme:* Aora, á Londres llegamos,
> y ya a palacio venimos?"

Place indicated in stage direction: Lope de Vega, *La Escolastica zelosa* (Part I, 1604), Act III: "Sale Marico solo de camino en Alcala." Lope, *La Burgalesa de Lerma* (1613), Act I: "Salgan en Madrid Clauela y Lucia." Lope, *De Cosario a Cosario* (Part XIX, 1623), Act I: "Salen en la calle Mayor Celia, dama," etc. Lope, *Peribañez y el Comendador de Ocaña* (Part IV), Act I: "El Comendador en casa con ropa, y Luxan lacayo." Numerous cases could be cited; see the above-mentioned article in the *Revue Hispanique* for 1907.

[2] See an excellent article by William Archer in the *Quarterly Review*

very important means, and frequently the only one, of indicating a change of scene. Many examples could be quoted. In Lope de Vega's *La Fé rompida*,[1] at the opening of Act I we find the stage direction: "[Enter] Luzinda as a huntress with a javelin and Alberto, peasant," showing that a wood is to be imagined by the spectator. In *Los Comendadores de Cordoba*,[2] Act I, near end: "Enter D. Fernando with cloak and buckler, as if at night."

In the rear of the stage were two doors. It is quite probable, indeed, that there were three, the middle door being in a recess (*nicho*) in front of which a curtain could be drawn. This was certainly the case later, as Calderon's *El Encanto sin Encanto*[3] shows. While the exact date of this play is unknown, it was performed, in all probability, before 1635.

The dressing room, or *vestuario,* occupied the two sides and the back of the stage. It is evident from a number of stage directions that an actor could enter upon the stage directly from the *vestuario.* In fact, when a man was killed upon the stage he generally managed to fall into the dressing-room. In Cervantes's *El gallardo Español,* Act III, we read the stage direction, "They fall

for April, 1908, p. 447, who very pertinently says: "The category of place imposed itself but faintly and intermittently on the mind of the Elizabethan play-goer: a fact which the believers in the habitual indication of scenes by placards, and even by painted cloths, would do well to note. . . . We believe that *vagueness of localization* of the Elizabethan drama to be a fundamental fact which cannot be fully realized until the student has dismissed modern editions from his mind, and gone back to the original texts."

[1] *Comedias,* Part IV, Madrid, 1614.

[2] *Comedias,* Part II, Madrid, 1609.

[3] Jornada I, stage direction: *Escondense los dos en la puerta de en medio, y sale el Gobernador,* etc. Jornada II, *Los dos se pasen, y sale al paño Serafina, Libia,* etc. Jornada III, *Arrimanse al nicho, suena ruido en la otra puerta,* etc. That painted canvas was then used, is evinced by the following direction: Jornada II: *Vanse las dos, y abriendose una puerta, que estará pintada de muralla, y que convenga con lo demas.* The term *bastidores* also occurs in this piece. While I have seen no edition of this play earlier than 1760, the stage directions are probably unchanged, as this edition is not divided into scenes. For the date of this play, see Schmidt, *Die Schauspiele Calderon's,* Eberfeld, 1857, p. 59.

within the dressing-room"; [1] in Lope de Vega's *La Ocasion perdida* (written before 1604): "Enter Leoncio . . . then the Princess . . . all come close to the canvas (*lienço*) of the *vestuario*." [2]

That the *vestuario* was separated from the stage by a canvas (*lienço*) results from a number of stage directions, and also that it contained doors, for it is very probable that the doors mentioned in these stage directions sometimes referred, not to the two doors at the back of the stage, but rather to doors at the sides, for it is clear that the stage could be entered from the two sides, which were provided with hangings at first and afterward were evidently of canvas. [3]

Many of Lope de Vega's earliest comedias, being comedies of intrigue, required no theatrical accessories of any kind except a balcony or window. These balconies, which served also for windows or towers, seem to have been, as already stated, a continuation of the gallery or *corredor* of the theater, and extended behind the hangings or parti-

[1] *Comedias*, Madrid, 1615, fol. 26. In Lope's *El Capellan de la Virgen* (printed in Part XVIII, 1623), Act II, is the stage direction: *Vase desatinado a caer en el vestuario.*

[2] *Entra Leoncio, Pinabelo, . . . y la Princessa detras, llega Doriclea a besarle las manos, y arrimanse todos al lienço del vestuario, descubiertos.* (*Comedias*, Part II, Madrid, 1609, fol. 37, v.)

[3] In Lope de Vega's *La Obediencia laureada* (Part VI, 1615), Act I, stage direction: *Mira hacia el vestuario.*

> "*Carlos:* A cielos, dos bultos veo,
> mas parece, yo lo creo,
> lienço de Ninfas pintadas" (fol. 11).

Lope de Vega, *La Imperial de Oton* (Part VIII, 1617), Act III, stage direction: *Entrense, y con musica descubran el lienço del vestuario . . . y Margarita en lo alto.* Lope, *El Amante agradecido* (Part X, 1618): *Veanse dos medias barcas con sus ramos a la puerta del vestuario*, etc. *La bella Aurora* (printed in Part XXI, 1635), Act II: *Las dos huyendo se pongan en dos tramoyas, que estaran en dos partes del lienço del vestuario*, etc. In Alarcon's *La Cueva de Salamanca* (perhaps the first of his works, and written about 1599, according to Hartzenbusch), Act I, a cord is stretched across the stage to trip an alguacil, and the stage direction reads: *Atan el cordel atravesando el vestuario*, where evidently the back of the stage only is meant. But near the close of Act II is the stage direction: *Sale Lucía y un Ganapan, con un cajon de la estatura de un hombre; ponelo en pie a raiz del*

tion which separated the sides of the stage from the auditorium.[1]

It is, perhaps, needless to remark that Lope de Vega did not divide his comedias into scenes, nor did any of the older dramatists. The only division that they made was into three acts. These scenes are the work of later editors. It is equally superfluous to add that, for the purposes of an examination like this, the editions of these later editors are absolutely useless. Recourse should be had only to the original editions, and these only have been consulted in the present examination.[2]

The appeal to the imagination of the spectator for a change of scene is sometimes made in words, by the poet. Cervantes, in his *Rufian dichoso*, Act II, says:

> To the auditor it matters
> Little that I in a moment

vestuario. Afterward we read: *Abre el cajon, y sale del Don Diego; que el cajon ha de tener la espalda tambien hecha puerta, que se abre hacia el vestuario, de suerte que la gente no lo eche de ver; y asi, cuando doña Clara cierra el cajon, abren la puerta trasera, y quitan la estatua y entra don Diego.* In the same author's *La Manganilla de Melilla* (written in 1616–17), Act III, is the stage direction: *Coge Acen del vestuario un hombre vestido como Pimienta* [one of the characters of the play], *y echalo por un escotillon, y Pimienta aparece luego en lo alto del vestuario.* These stage directions, it should be added, however, are taken from the edition of Hartzenbusch in the *Bibl. de Autores Españoles.* The existence of a side curtain is shown very clearly in Lope's *La Reina Doña Juana de Napoles* (Part VI, 1615), Act I. The Queen, Ludovico, and Tancredo are in a garden; as Isabela enters, the stage direction reads: *Escondese la Reyna detras del paño y sale Isabela,* a strange confusion. For other examples, see above, p. 84, note, Ricardo de Turia's *La Burladora burlada,* and the article mentioned above.

[1] See the previous note. But other cases may be cited: In Lope de Vega's *Los Torneos de Aragon* (Part IV, 1614), Act III, is the following stage direction: *Chirimias y sientanse en un corredor, que tome todo lo alto del Teatro, el Rey de Aragon,* etc. In Alarcon's *El Examen de Maridos,* written at the beginning of 1625 or earlier, Act III, is the direction: *Sale Ochauo en el corredor mas baxo, y salta al teatro.* So it reads in Lope's *Comedias,* Part XXIII, Çaragoça, 1633, fol. 59. In the *Comedias de Alarcon,* ed. Hartzenbusch, we find: *Desde un tejado muy bajo salta al suelo y caese.* See also Lope's *El Amor Vandolero,* Act II, and *El Favor agradecido,* Act II.

[2] The one exception is especially noted above.

Pass from Germany to Guinea,
Though from off this stage I move not.
Human thought, indeed, is nimble;
Well may they accompany
Me with it, where'er it may be,
Without losing me or tiring.[1]

Yet it must not be inferred from what has just been said that no attempt at verisimilitude was made—that nothing was done to aid the imagination of the spectator. There is abundant and indisputable evidence to the contrary. A garden was represented on the stage; of this there are numerous instances;[2] or a fountain,[3] or rocks and mountains.[4] Trees were represented on the stage, either painted on canvas or by set pieces. Many examples might be cited.[5]

[1] "Muy poco importa al oyente
Que yo en un punto me passe
Desde Alemania a Guinea
Sin del teatro mudarme.
El pensamiento es ligero;
Bien pueden acompanarme
Con él, do quiera que fuere,
Sin perderme ni cansarse."

Comedias, Madrid, 1615, fol. 97. See also the closing lines of his comedia *Pedro de Urdemalas, ibid.*, fol. 220.

[2] In Lope de Vega's *La Ocasion perdida* (before 1604), Act II, stage direction: *La Princesa detras de un muro baxo, y dentro se vea como jardin.* Act III: *Assomase la Infanta en lo alto del jardin.* So in *La octava Maravilla* (Part X, 1618), Act II: *Esté un jardinillo en el teatro, y salga el Rey con un escardillo.* For further examples, see the article above mentioned.

[3] Lope de Vega's *La Quinta de Florencia* (Part II, 1609), Act II, stage direction: *Ha de estar en el tablado una fuente, donde ha de auer estado todo este tiempo Laura, junto a ella hinchando el cantarrillo.*

"*Laura:* Por estas ramas me voy.
Sale Belardo.
Belardo: Estos los marmoles son
de aquellas fuentes hermosas."

[4] Lope de Vega's *El Animal de Ungria* (Part IX, 1617), Act I: *Subese el Niño en una peña.* *El Principe despeñado* (1602), Act II: *Va baxando por la sierra la Reyna doña Eluira en habito de Saluage con una piel, y parece en medio de la sierra, y prosigue.*

[5] Lope de Vega's *San Isidro labrador de Madrid* (Part VII, 1617), Act II: *Vease un arbol con algun algodon encima, que parezca neuado, y unas palomas en el.*

In one instance a fort[1] was represented by a painted canvas, and again a castle.

From the examples just cited it may be inferred that painted scenery, at all events in Lope de Vega's later years, was not unknown to the public stage, but that it was not movable on rollers or slides, we may be reasonably sure.

A most important matter, to be borne constantly in mind when treating of the staging of plays, is that of chronology. Only where we know the exact date of a play or a reasonably approximate date can it furnish us with helpful and reliable evidence. For here a matter of a very few years may make a vast difference in scenic appliances.

Lope de Vega wrote for the public theater for half a century, and naturally there were many innovations upon the stage in the course of his long career. In the *Prologo del Teatro a los Letores*, prefixed to Part XI (1618) of his *Comedias*, the Theater (i.e., the stage), speaking, says: "Despues que a viua fuerça de tantas, y tan diferentes comedias de varios Poetas, como en mi se han representado (Letor amigo, o enemigo, como tu quisieres) he aprendido a hablar, aunque compuesto de tablas, y lienços, con mas trampas que un hombre que no tiene de que pagar, ni verguença de deuer, descanso con quexarme de los muchos sinrazones que mis dueños padecen, y a mi me hazen." From this we see that *lienços*, or canvases for scenery, were getting to be of frequent use.

Again, in the *Prologo Dialogistico*, prefixed to Part XVI (1623), the Theater says: "I have come to great misfortune, and I presume that it is due to one of three reasons: either because there are no good actors, or because the poets are bad, or because the auditors lack understanding; for the managers avail themselves of machinery, the poets

---

[1] Lope de Vega's *Pobreza no es Vileza* (written in 1624 or earlier), Act II: *Salen despues de auer tocado caxas soldados, y el Conde de Fuentes, aura en el teatro un fuerte pintado de canteria.* See also *El Casamiento en la Muerte* (Part I, 1604), Act III, and *La Vitoria del Marques de Santa Cruz* (before 1618), Act II.

of the carpenters, and the auditors of their eyes." Further: "But to return to the common people, I say that they are justly moved by this machinery to delight the eyes, but not by that of the Spanish comedia, where the figures rise and descend so clumsily, and animals and birds appear in like manner, which the ignorance of the women and the rude mechanics among men come to see."[1]

Lope's complaint is significant, moreover, inasmuch as it shows that a great change had come over his audiences early in the third decade of the seventeenth century. The *vulgo* now went to see the play, not to hear it; the comedia had become a spectacle for the eyes. And so the play degenerated and the splendor of scenery and stage setting increased, until in the eighteenth century we come to a playwright like Comella, in whose comedia *Cristóval Colon,* Act I, we find the following stage direction: "Jardin magnifico, adornado de macetas cenadores, y fuente grande en el medio, con asientos al rededor, el foro representa el Palacio con su galeria y escaleras, para baxar; la galeria estará adornada de macetas de flores. Aparece la Reyna sentada, y las Damas repartidas, cogiendo flores," etc. Here we find the term *bastidor* (wing of stage scenery),[2] and at the end of the act, the direction: *Cae el telon,* the drop-curtain falls.

The help of stage machinery of various kinds, under the name of *artificios, invenciones, apariencias,* and *tramoyas,* had been invoked in the religious representations of Spain since very early times. One of the primary requisites was a trap-door, and with these the public stages were early provided. In the performance of the *autos* of Corpus Christi the *apariencias* formed a very important feature of the festival and were frequently of the most elaborate character, the municipalities expending large sums of

[1] *Life of Lope de Vega,* Glasgow, 1904, p. 289.
[2] *Bastidores* or wings were in use long before this, and we find them mentioned at the beginning of 1643 among the stage appliances at *La Monteria,* Seville. (Sanchez-Arjona, p. 364, and see above, p. 92, note 3.)

money in their preparation. Upon the stage of the public theaters, on the other hand, we may well imagine that the *apariencias* or *tramoyas* were of a more crude and inexpensive kind. Still, Lope de Vega, as we have seen, early complained of the great importance attached to stage machinery, and he again refers to the work of the stage carpenter in the Prologue to Part XIX of his *Comedias* (Madrid, 1623). Here, too, in a dialogue between the Poet and the Theater, the former says: "Since they use *apariencias,* which they call *tramoyas,* I do not care to publish my comedias." He never concealed his contempt for the arts of the scene-painter and the machinist. As Mr. Fitzmaurice-Kelly says: "Lope needed no scene-painters to make good his deficiencies. In *¡Ay Verdades! que en Amor* (1625), he laughs at the pieces

> en que la carpintería
> suple concetos y trazas." [1]

Likewise in *Don Quixote* (Part I, chap. xlviii), the Canon, in the course of his remarks on the drama of the day, says: "Y aun en las [comedias] humanas se atreven á hacer milagros, sin mas respecto ni consideracion que parecerles que allí estará bien el tal milagro y *apariencia* como ellos llaman, para que gente ignorante se admire y venga á la comedia." *Apariencia* or *tramoya* was, therefore, the technical term for stage machinery, and commenting on this passage, Clemencin says: "*Apariencia* es tramoya ó máquina teatral para representar trasformaciones ó acontecimientos prodigiosos." [2]

The term *appearances* was also used on the English

---

[1] *Chapters on Spanish Literature,* London, 1908, p. 182. See also the close of Lope's *Epistola á Pablo Bonnet,* the verses beginning:

> "El Teatro de España se ha resuelto
> En aros de cedazos y clauos."

[2] Edition of Madrid, 1833, Vol. III, p. 409. In 1633, when Gonzalez de Salas published his *Nueva Idea de la Tragedia antigua,* he spoke of the

stage. When Cartwright's *Royal Slave* was presented before the King and Queen at Oxford, in August, 1636, the changes of scene then produced by Inigo Jones were called "appearances." They were eight in number, but whether they were effected by sliding frames covered with canvas, or by falling curtains now technically called "drops," is not stated.[1]

We may be quite sure that theatrical machinery had made no greater advances in the public theaters than the stage decoration. That this machinery was still very rudimental and imperfect, even after the middle of the seventeenth century, is evinced by the accounts published by Francis van Aerssen, Madame d'Aulnoy, and other travelers in Spain.

From the above instances we are enabled to form a fairly clear conception of the resources (or perhaps it were better to say the limitations) of the Spanish stage in the time of the great creator of the Spanish drama. They also furnish information that is not without importance as to the arrangement of the Spanish stage. It did not project into the theater, as did the Elizabethan stage, and its two sides were provided with hangings (*paños*), behind which the actors could retire, and from which they could make their entrances.

The stage setting of the French theater at this time was quite different from that in use in Spain and England, and in the time of the playwright Hardy it was that of the Mysteries of the Middle Ages. With slight modifications this system reigned for nearly a hundred years at the Hôtel de Bourgogne, the only public theater in Paris during the second half of the sixteenth and the first thirty

word *tramoya* as if it had been but lately introduced: "las *Machinas* de la Scena, las appariencias quiero decir, i ingeniosos artificios, a quien vulgarmente los Nuestros llaman con un vocablo nuevo *Tramoias.*" (Edition of Madrid, 1778, Vol. I, p. 248.) This seems to show that the work was written some years before the date of its publication.

[1] Collier, *Annals of the Stage*, London, 1831, Vol. III, p. 372.

years of the seventeenth century.[1] This stage of the Mysteries consisted of two parts: the *mansions* and the stage proper, or the free space between and in front of the *mansions*. These *mansions* were simply houses or buildings to which the action was transported during the play. Thus one might represent the house of the Virgin at Nazareth, another the temple at Jerusalem, another the palace of Pilate, which formed so many *mansions* in the Mystery of the Passion. In other words, the simultaneous scenery of these religious plays of the Middle Ages was transferred to the public stage, which was divided into several regions, and France might be represented by one corner of the theater, Turkey by the other, and Spain in the middle of the stage. Indeed, the author of the *Traité de la disposition du poème dramatique* (1637), quoted by Rigal,[2] says: "Il ne faut pas introduire ni approuver la règle qui ne represente qu'un lieu dans la scène." It is this system to which Corneille objected in his *Examen de Mélite* (1629), when he says: "Common sense, which has been my sole guide, gave me sufficient aversion to this horrible confusion, which placed Paris, Rome, and Constantinople on the same stage, to reduce mine to a single city."[3] Here, too, we are told that a wood was represented merely by a little foliage, an encampment by half a tent, and that the sea and the mountains "were absolutely lacking in majesty."[4] "Besides the permanent decorations and those which appeared only at certain times in the performance, the players used also more or less ingenious machinery, but whether these *trucs* were always successful, is more than we care to affirm."[5] That this stage setting as late as 1642 was very crude and far from satisfactory is shown by the complaints made by d'Aubignac concerning the manner in which his tragedy

---

[1] Rigal, *Le Théâtre français avant la période classique*, Paris, 1901, pp. 238 ff.

[2] *Ibid.*, p. 246.   [3] *Ibid.*, p. 247.   [4] *Ibid.*, p. 252.   [5] *Ibid.*, p. 255.

La Pucelle d'Orléans was staged. Bapst says that in 1634 the stage at the Hôtel de Bourgogne was ornamented with pilasters, cornices, moldings, arabesques, etc. "It was the Italian stage setting on a small scale . . . there were three doors, one at the back and one on each side, without counting the *lucarnes.*" The canvases were painted in perspective. In 1635 representations took place by daylight, without lamps. At the beginning of the seventeenth century a police ordinance fixed half-past four o'clock in the afternoon as the closing hour of the spectacles in winter. In the middle of the seventeenth century the Opera, Molière, and the Comédie Française had no place for their performances except the tennis courts, which must have been most unsatisfactory, both optically as well as acoustically, to both auditors and actors.[1] In these tennis courts, transformed into theaters, the rich and the nobility occupied boxes or stalls, while "the less fortunate public stood in the part of the building that was not occupied by the stage."[2]

The poverty of scenic effects upon the Spanish stage applies, as already stated, only to the public theaters, like the *Cruz* and the *Príncipe* in Madrid, where an entrance fee was paid. The representations which took place in the palaces of great nobles (these representations were called *particulares*),[3] and those given before the King in his private theaters (see below, Chapter X), were generally accompanied, as we may readily imagine, by ingenious and costly scenic effects and stage machinery.

[1] Bapst, *Essai sur l'histoire du Théâtre,* Paris, 1893, p. 167.
[2] *Ibid.,* p. 171.
[3] In October, 1602, Antonio Granados represented a comedia before D. Diego Gomez, "who was sick with quartan fever," receiving 200 reals (Pérez Pastor, *Nuevos Datos,* p. 353); in February, 1603, Nicolas de los Rios received 300 reals for a comedia which he represented before the Duke of Lerma, "en la Huerta de la Ribera del Pisuerga" (*ibid.,* p. 353); and in November, 1603, the same *autor de comedias* received, for going from Valladolid to Tordesillas, and representing four comedias before the King, 1200 reals, besides 371 reals for expenses. This was, apparently, also a festival given by the Duke of Lerma. (*Ibid.,* p. 354.)

We read, for instance, that in 1618 Luis Velez de Guevara's comedia *El Caballero del Sol* was performed by the company of Baltasar Pinedo in the house of D. Juan Gaytan de Ayala, in the Calle de Atocha, "with the same *invenciones* and stage arrangement with which this comedia was represented in the garden of his Excellency the Duke of Lerma." This latter representation was, doubtless, intended solely for the delectation of the Duke's friends. The performance in the house of D. Gaytan de Ayala, however, is the only one that I have found recorded, in which an admission fee was charged, and from which other profits accrued to the person giving the comedia. The details are so curious that I transcribe them. The document is in the form of an agreement between D. Juan de Vidaurre, Captain in Ordinary to his Majesty in Madrid and his *entretenido* in that city, and the lessees of the profits which result to the hospitals from the performance of comedias, reciting that the said comedia is to be given by the company of Pinedo in Ayala's house. "That the said D. Juan de Vidaurre is to provide the said *invenciones* and to erect, at his own cost, in the said house and yard, the theater and boxes (*aposentos*) and seats (*gradas*) necessary for the men as well as the women to hear the said comedia. Likewise that the said lessees are to give to the said D. Juan forty ducats, in part payment of the expenses. Likewise that all that may result by way of profit during the whole time the said comedia is to be given in the said *corral*—deducting the share of the said Baltasar de Pinedo, *autor*—as well from the entrance fees as from the *aposentos,* and all other profits, are to be divided equally between the said lessees and the said D. Juan, but the forty ducats which the said Baltasar de Pinedo is to give to the said D. Juan are to belong solely to the latter. All the fruits and confections while the festival lasts are to be sold by Roque Hernandez, who is also to receive eight reals, one half to be paid by the said lessees and one half by the said D. Juan. Likewise the said forty ducats are to be returned by the said D. Juan, unless he erect the said theater and gradas in eight days."[1]

[1] Pérez Pastor, *Nuevos Datos,* pp. 164, 165.

CHAPTER VI

Costumes. Their impropriety. Their magnificence. Costumes in the *autos sacramentales*. Performances in the public theaters. Prices of admission. The audiences. The *mosqueteros*. Women in the *cazuela*. Ruffianism in the theaters. Seats in the *corrales*.

As there was little thought of verisimilitude in the stage setting, so, as regards the costumes worn by the players, there was no pretense to historical accuracy. All characters appeared in the Spanish costume of the time. This is due to a peculiarity—shared in a measure by the drama of other nations at the time (particularly the English), but eminently characteristic of the Spanish drama— that is, the tendency to translate everything which it represents into the present and actual in which it moves: that the remotest past and the strangest occurrences are transformed into the national usages and customs, and that what is most foreign is changed, as it were, to something essentially Spanish. The single exception was in the case of plays founded upon Spanish history or legend, —here only an attempt was made to reproduce the spirit of a bygone age.[1]

[1] "Ein ganz eigenthümlicher, nirgends in gleicher Stärke hervortretender Zug der spanischen Comödie nun besteht darin, dasz sie in Allem, was sie vorführt, sich die nächste Gegenwart und Umgebung, in der sie selbst lebt, abspiegeln läszt: dasz sie die fernste Vorzeit, die fremdeste Begebenheit in die heimische Sitte und Gewohnheit hinüberzieht und selbst das Entlegenste durch Umwandlung gleichsam zum spanischen Nationalgut macht. Gewisz ist diese Art, die Gegenwart zur Grundlage der Darstellung zu machen, die einzige, wie ein wahres Nationalschauspiel entstehen kann. Denn das Drama, das vor allem auf lebhafte Anregung seiner Zuhörerschaft bedacht sein musz, wird durch alles Entlegene, nicht unmittelbar Verständliche in seiner lebendigen Wirkung beeinträchtigt, und vermag die Begebenheiten

As Ticknor says, "Coriolanus was dressed like Don John of Austria, and Aristotle came on the stage with a curled periwig and buckles on his shoes, like a Spanish Abbé."[1] Only the most obvious distinctions were made: a Moor, naturally, would appear in the traditional costume, or, at all events, in a turban and long mantle, for these were known to the audience, but the Roman wore a short cloak and sword. Lope de Vega, in his *Arte nuevo de hacer Comedias* (1609), complains of the impropriety of Romans wearing breeches upon the Spanish stage, for Greeks and Romans, as he says, appeared with cloak and sword, in the national costume.[2] But this reproach applies not only to the Spanish drama, but to all others of the time as well. Concerning the French theater we are told: "Le même costume, cheveux tombants, cuirasse collant au corps, avec tonnelets, brodequins et casque à panache, sert à tous les rôles historiques, depuis David et Salomon

---

und Verhältnisse früherer Zeiten oder ferner Länder nur insofern zu gebrauchen, als es sie mit der Gegenwart verknüpfen und seinen Zuschauern in nächste Nähe rücken kann. Nur die Stoffen aus der nationalen Geschichte oder Sage hat sich daher die spanische Comödie bemüht, sich genau in den Geist und Ton vergangener Zeiten zu versetzen, weil diese der lebenden Generation noch mannigfach vertraut und gegenwärtig waren; die Geschichten des classischen Alterthums und des Auslandes dagegen finden wir durchaus phantastisch und in der Art behandelt, dasz die spanische Nationalität, die Sitte und Sinnesart der Gegenwart überall durchklingt." (*Geschichte der dramatischen Literatur und Kunst in Spanien*, Vol. II, pp. 79, 80; cf. also *ibid.*, pp. 29, 30.) These remarks, it seems to me, apply with almost equal force to the Elizabethan drama. An audience totally ignorant of the facts of history was responsible for such a condition and requisite for its maintenance. Hence the glaring anachronisms that occur in the plays of Lope, Shakespeare, and other dramatists of the period passed unnoticed. There was, for instance, no hesitancy in introducing firearms upon the stage in a play, the action of which took place long before gunpowder was invented, if the effect of the action were heightened thereby.

[1] *History of Spanish Literature*, Vol. II, p. 539.

[2] The stage directions, however, abundantly show that some regard was had, here also, for the fitness of things. The costume, being an indication of rank, helped to tell the story. Apart from the very obvious fact that the peasant always appeared in a costume suited to his station (examples: Lope de Vega, *Llegar en Ocasion* (Part VI), fol. 12, v.: *Salen Fenisa, y Otauio con gauan de labrador. El mejor Maestro el Tiempo* (Part VI), Act III: *Sale Oton de villano con un azadon*, etc., etc.), we find such stage

jusqu'à Charles V."[1] Of course the Roman citizens of
Shakespeare's time wore the English costume then in
vogue, and we know that, in the middle of the eighteenth
century, Garrick appeared as Macbeth in a powdered wig
and knee-breeches. In Spain, too, this carelessness as to
costume was maintained until far into the eighteenth century. D. José Clavijo y Fajardo, speaking of the *autos* in
1762, says: "Who could help laughing aloud on seeing a
Levite appear, in the first age of man (*en la primera edad
del hombre*), dressed like a priest and wearing a miter?
It would be hard to say which were the greater nonsense,
to introduce a Levite at that period or to clothe him in
this manner."[2]

When it is said, however, that the costumes had little
or no regard for historical accuracy, it by no means implies
that they were not magnificent and costly.[3] On the contrary, there is ample evidence to prove that Spanish actors
and actresses were exceedingly extravagant in the matter
of costumes, and the amount of money expended upon
them often shows an improvidence which has been a characteristic of the theatrical profession in all times. In 1589
Sebastian de Montemayor, an *autor de comedias* or theatrical director, and Ana de Velasco, his wife, paid 100
ducats (= 1100 reals) for a rich skirt and jacket ("precio

directions as: *Salen dos alabarderos, vestidos como Tudescos, con su bota
de Vino.* (Lope de Vega, *Urson y Valentin,* Part I, 1604, fol. 171.) In *El
Hijo de Reduan* (Part I), Act I: *Entra Gomel con un alquizel* [Moorish
cloak] *de alarde, y un bonete colorado, y unas abarcas de pellejos* (fol. 143).
Servir con mala Estrella (Part VI, 1616), Act I: *Salen Rugero de Valoes y
Turin su criado de camino a lo Frances.* Cervantes, *La Gran Sultana,* Act
I, opening: *Sale Doña Catalina de Oviedo Gran Sultana vestida a la Tur-
quesca,* and a little later: *Salen Madrigal de cautiuo, y Andres en abito de
Griego.*

[1] Bapst, *Essai sur l'histoire du Théâtre,* p. 176.

[2] Cotarelo y Mori, *Controversias,* p. 159. The same writer says: "Un
Elias vestido muy pobremente, con mucha barba y zapatos encarnados con
galón de oro ya lo habíamos visto en los *Tres Prodigios del Mundo,* pero
Cristo peinado de *ala de pichón,* con polvos y corbatin, esto estaba reservado
para aumentar las deformidades de los autos."

[3] The theatrical wardrobe was, perhaps, the manager's heaviest item of

de una basquiña y un manteo ricos, para representar").[1]
In 1602 Melchor de Leon paid 330 reals for a skirt of
straw-colored satin ("basquiña de razo pajizo").[2]   In
1607 Baltasar Pinedo paid 550 reals for hats, feathers,
and silks.[3] In 1610 Diego Lopez de Alcaraz paid 240
reals for a costume "de paño de mezcla aceitunada," or
mixed cloth of an olive color.[4] In 1617 Jusepe Jiménez
and his wife Vicenta de Borja, players in the company
of Baltasar Pinedo, paid 440 reals for a skirt and
waist of grosgrain with silk lace ("basquiña y
jubon de gorgoran con pasamanos de seda").[5] In
1619 Juan Bautista Muñiz and his wife Eugenia Osorio
paid 2400 reals for a costume of greenish-gold sateen with
gold lace and edging of red sateen with trimmings of gold
fringe, lined with red taffeta silk ("vestido de raso de oro
verde con pasamanos de oro y pestañas de raso encarnado
y alamares de peinecillo de oro forrado en tafetán encarnado").[6] In 1636 Pedro de la Rosa, theatrical director,
bought from Bartolomé Romero and his wife Antonia
Manuela, both players, "un calzon de ropilla y ferreruelo
[short cloak, without cape] de lana parda, bordado de
coronas y palmas de oro y plata, y las mangas del jubon
de canutillo [embroidery] de plata," for 3600 reals.[7]
One may form some conception of this extravagance,
bearing in mind that the average price received by Lope
de Vega for a comedia, at the height of his popularity,
was 500 reals.

Sometimes, indeed, the costumes used in the representation of the *autos sacramentales*—which were given at
the expense of the municipality—were so costly that

expense. A conception of the splendor of the costumes in Spain at the
beginning of the seventeenth century may be formed from the "Memoria
del hato para representar" sold by Baltasar Pinedo to Juan Granados, on
April 25, 1605, printed in the *Bull. Hispanique*, 1907, pp. 369–371.
[1] Pérez Pastor, *Nuevos Datos*, p. 337.
[2] *Ibid.*, p. 78.   [3] *Ibid.*, p. 101.   [4] *Ibid.*, p. 119.
[5] *Ibid.*, p. 163.   [6] *Ibid.*, p. 181.   [7] *Ibid.*, p. 251.

the actors petitioned the city for an extra sum to defray this expense, alleging that the costumes were useless for any other purpose. This the town council frequently did, in one case paying 200 reals.[1] Many instances are recorded where actors and actresses were granted a special sum by the town council, as a prize for having particularly distinguished themselves in the performance of an *auto* either by their acting or costume.

While the principal players possessed their own costumes, the *autores de comedias* provided them for the lesser members of their companies. Frequently, also, a town, in order to give a dance or comedia for some festival, hired the costumes from some *autor*. So in 1597 the clothes and costumes ("ato y vestidos de farsa") of Gaspar de Porres were hired; in 1634 Sanchez de Vargas hired out his costumes for a dance in the town of Mejo-

---

[1] Sanchez-Arjona, *Anales*, pp. 307 and 322. The value of Spanish money in the sixteenth and seventeenth centuries is a very difficult matter to ascertain even approximately, as it varied so much from time to time. The only Spanish coins with which we have to deal are the ducado, the real, and the maravedí. There is an excellent article on the maravedí in the *Revista de Archivos* for March–April, 1905. The ducado = 11 reals, and the real plate = 34 maravedís. Minsheu's *Spanish Dictionary*, London, 1599, tells us that a *ryall plate* = sixe pence = 34 maravedís. The maravedí, which was at first a gold coin, became in the time of Philip III (1598–1621) a copper coin of very small value. And just here occurs the difficulty. Seldom is it stated whether the *real vellon* (copper) or the *real de plata* (silver) is meant, the real plate being equal to two reals copper. It would seem, however, that at one time there was little difference between the *real de plata* and the *real vellon*. As an example: under date of Valladolid, September 1, 1604, Gaspar de Porres, *autor de comedias*, bound himself to pay to the Brotherhood of the *Niños Expositos* of that city 2000 reals silver, which he had received in *vellon* from the treasurer of the Brotherhood (*Nuevos Datos*, p. 88). This may be explained by a note which I find in Gallardo, *Ensayo*, Vol. III, p. 1150: "Al principio deste año (1604) se quilataron las monedas de vellon en todos los reinos de Castilla, doblandose el valor para socorro de S. M. y se pregonó con graves penas en esta cibdad (Cordoba) a 29 de Marzo que no corriese la moneda sino quilatada." Again, in 1612, Juan de Morales Medrano, *autor de comedias*, promises to repay 1000 reals, which he had borrowed, "in silver and not in *vellon*." (*Nuevos Datos*, p. 129.) I believe that the silver real of the double value of the *real vellon* is called the *real de plata doble*. (See *Nuevos Datos*, p. 160.) An account of the value of money at a later period (1667) is furnished by a work entitled *Hispania Illustrata, or the Maxims*

rada.[1] In 1636 Andres de la Vega hired out to Pedro de la Rosa, to be returned after the festival of Corpus, a costume of Moses, a *ropon* for Aaron, a *capuz* for a Jew, and a *ropon* for a Moor, together with eight cloaks of taffeta, for 2500 reals.[2] In 1636 Mariana de Aparicio agreed with Andres de la Vega to play second parts in his company, he to furnish the costumes.[3] Andres de la Vega seems to have been possessed of a rich and extensive theatrical wardrobe, which he frequently hired out.[4] Some idea of the extent and quality of the wardrobe of a prominent theatrical manager in the middle of the seventeenth century is furnished by the list of the effects of Jacinto Riquelme, which were attached in 1652 to compel the performance of a contract to act in the *Corral de La Monteria* in Seville.[5] In this list are included all the properties, scenery, and machinery necessary to represent what were called *comedias de apariencias*, "besides the costumes for the fools and peasants."[6]

It may not be without interest to note here that in 1608

---

of the Spanish Court, etc., London, 1703. On p. 53 we find: "In 1667, 500 *doblones* = £450 sterling. A *doblon* = 4 pieces of 8 = 74 *reales vellon*, and that a real plate = 6d. and a *real vellon* = 2½d." From such data as I have been able to gather, I infer that the purchasing power of a real in the early seventeenth century was about five times its value in present money, i.e., that a real plate = about 25 cents. So we are told that in Molière's time, which was nearly half a century later, money was worth five times as much as at present, i.e., in 1654 *six cents livres = trois mille francs*. (Soulié, *Recherches sur Molière*, p. 68.) A convenient norm for the value of money in Spain at the close of the sixteenth century is furnished by an instrument dated March 26, 1596, by which Baltasar Pinedo, *autor de comedias*, agrees to pay to Gabriel Rubio, tailor, of Madrid, 24 ducats = 264 reals, for board and lodging for six months for himself and servant, at the rate of 4 ducats per month, i.e., 11 reals per week, for two persons. (*Nuevos Datos*, p. 43.) The great depreciation of money during the reign of Philip IV., and the many attempts to regulate its value, render any definite general statement impossible.

[1] *Nuevos Datos*, p. 238.   [2] *Ibid.*, p. 252.   [3] *Ibid.*, p. 258.

[4] See *ibid.*, pp. 269, 271.

[5] Sanchez-Arjona, *Anales*, pp. 398 ff. For a list of the properties and costumes of Diego Lopez de Alcaraz in 1602, see *Nuevos Datos*, p. 63.

[6] "Todo el jato que llaman ornato del vestuario, paños y maromas, y vestidos de villanos y bobos, y garruchos y hierros y tramoyas."

Shakespeare was proprietor of the wardrobe and properties of the Blackfriars theater, besides owning four shares, which brought him in £133 6s. 8d. "These properties, we may conclude, he lent to the company for a certain consideration."[1]

When in financial straits, a condition that has ever been familiar to the followers of Thespis, the mainstay of the player or manager was the wardrobe, which he could always pawn with some money-lender.[2]   A curious case is that of Lorenzo Hurtado de la Camara, who in 1639 paid 1000 reals to redeem a costume which he had pawned to the convent of S. Juan de Dios in Ocaña.[3]   Indeed, with very few exceptions, both *autores de comedias* and actors seem to have been almost constantly in debt, as the many obligations and agreements collected by Pérez Pastor amply show. To compel the payment of a debt, recourse was had to the very efficacious remedy of clapping the debtor into prison. Not infrequently, as the records prove, did this misfortune befall the theatrical manager and actor of those days. In 1601 Rodrigo Osorio, *autor de comedias,* was imprisoned at Madrid for a debt of 700 reals, being released on the guaranty of his son-in-law Diego Lopez de Alcaraz and his daughter Magdalena Osorio to pay the debt;[4] and in 1605 Alonso de Riquelme, a famous *autor,* was imprisoned in Valladolid for a debt of 900 reals.[5]

[1] *Shakespeare's Works,* ed. Collier, Vol. I, p. 191. Greg (*Henslowe's Diary,* II, p. 130) says: "The wardrobe of a company appears to have been a complicated affair; part, like the stage properties, belonged to the company in general, that is to say, was the common property of the sharers, while part belonged to individual actors. Thus, we find Pembroke's men pawning their 'parel in 1593, and Edward Alleyn buying Jones's share in the common stock of playing-apparel, etc., belonging to Worcester's men in 1589," etc.

[2] A list of the theatrical wardrobe of the stranded company of Jerónimo de Amella, seized for debt in Valencia in 1628, is given in the *Bull. Hispanique,* 1906, p. 377.

[3] *Nuevos Datos,* p. 315.

[4] *Ibid.,* p. 54.

[5] *Ibid.,* p. 91. (See also *Bull. Hisp.* (1907), p. 374.)

With the passing of the *Corral de Puente*, about 1584, the theaters of Madrid were reduced to two, the *Corral de la Cruz* and the *Corral del Príncipe*. These continued to be the only public theaters in Madrid till the close of the seventeenth century. The King had his own private theaters, and from an account of the events which happened at court between 1599 and 1614, written by the historian Luis Cabrera de Córdoba, it follows that private performances of comedias must have taken place in the King's palace, the Alcázar, as early as the beginning of the seventeenth century. Besides this stage, which was erected in one of the rooms of the palace, Philip the Third, in 1607, caused a theater to be built in the *Casas del Tesoro*, near the palace.[1]

Dramatic performances in the public theaters always took place in the afternoon, at three o'clock in summer and at two in winter.[2] By an ordinance of 1608 it was provided that the doors of the theaters[3] should not be opened

---

[1] Cabrera says under the date, Madrid, January 20, 1607: "Háse hecho en el segundo patio de las casas del Tesoro un teatro donde vean sus Magestades las comedias, como se representan al pueblo en los corrales que estan deputados para ello, porque puedan gozar mejor de ellas que quando se les representa en su sala, y asi han hecho alrededor galerias y ventanas donde esté la gente de Palacio, y sus Magestades irán allí de su Cámara por el pasadizo que está hecho, y las verán por unas celosías." (*Relaciones de las Cosas sucedidas en la Corte de España desde el Año 1599 hasta 1614*, edited by D. Pascual de Gayangos, Madrid, 1857, p. 298.) It appears that Philip IV., in 1622, the year after his accession to the throne, entertained the project of building another theater in Madrid. (Pérez Pastor, *Nuevos Datos*, p. 191. See below, p. 237.)

[2] Court performances, on the other hand, were generally given at night; this was also the rule in England. (Malone, *Historical Account of the English Stage*, p. 185.)

[3] Don Luis Fernandez-Guerra, in his excellent biography of Alarcon, p. 181, says that the *Corral de la Cruz* had seven doors and the *Príncipe* eight, "cada cual para su objeto, ya de subir á los aposentos, ya para el escenario y su servicio, ahora para entrada de hombres, ahora para las mugeres; cuál, la de la alojeria; una, la del cocheron; y la última, la de la taberna." His authority for this statement is Armona, *Memorias cronológicas*. The latter work, because of the recent publications of Pérez Pastor and Cotarelo, is now of little importance. I have a copy of portions of it, and under the caption "Visita que en el año de 1606 se hizo por el visitador del Real Hospedaje, etc. Año de 1606," it is stated that the *Corral del Príncipe* has

until noon, and that representations should begin, during the six months beginning October 1, at two o'clock, and during the remaining six months at four in the afternoon, "in such a manner that the performance may be concluded an hour before nightfall," and the *comisarios* and bailiffs were to take particular care that this proviso be fulfilled. The same ordinance likewise provided that posters should be put up to indicate clearly the comedias which were to be represented each day.[1] The same provisions are again found in the "Regulations for the Theaters," issued in 1641, to which we shall recur in a succeeding chapter. A performance generally lasted from two to three hours.[2]

The price of admission to the *corrales* varied at different

eight doors, the first to ascend to the *aposentos* and the other five (*sic*) for entrance, but there is besides "a casa con dos puertas en que hay una tienda y taberna." These two doors evidently did not give access to the theater. Likewise in 1638 there were only six entrances. In the "Visita general que se hizo el año de 1606," to the Calle de la Cruz, we find: "*Corral de la Cruz*. Por no estar labrado no se taso," which I do not understand. In 1638 there were seven(?) doors: one to the *Alogeria*, two to the *aposentos*, one for women, and another entrance is described as a coach-house (*cochera*). The latter is probably accounted for as follows: in 1631 the King commanded that his entrance to the *Corral de la Cruz*, which was the property of the Duke of Medina de las Torres, should be changed to a more retired and more decent place. In April, 1631, a *corral* was taken which belonged to D. Fernando Segura in the Plazuela del Angel, and an entrance made, so that the coach of the King could be driven to the stairway, a rent of 2000 reals yearly to be paid. Since, in doing this, a part of the property of Doña Potencia de Quesada would have to be occupied, it was necessary to rent this also for 75 ducats yearly. (*Averiguador*, Vol. I, p. 171.) This entrance was still in existence in 1653.

[1] Cotarelo y Mori, *Controversias*, p. 623.

[2] "La comedia aora empeçamos,
De aqui á dos horas saldremos,
Quando ya estará acabada,
Que todo lo acaba el tiempo."
(*Loas* to *Comedias* of Lope de Vega, Part I, Valladolid, 1604, p. 3.)

And again:

"Boluamos á lo importante,
Que es el silencio pedido,
Por tres horas no cabales."
(*Ibid.*, p. 7.)

times. What it was in Madrid in the latter part of the sixteenth century, we learn from a document dated March 6, 1589, published by Pellicer.[1] According to this, "every person who entered to see the said comedias paid for his seat 4 quartos (= 16 maravedís), and at the entrance, besides what he gives to the players, he pays another quarto, in such manner that each person who enters the comedia pays 5 quartos, besides what he gives to the players."[2] In Seville, "those who went to see the comedias of Ganassa in 1575 at the *Corral de Don Juan* paid half a real entrance, one real for each *silla*, and a cuartillo (= one fourth of a real) for each seat on a *banco*."[3] About 1585 the price of a seat on the *bancos* in the *Corral del Príncipe* was a half-real.[4] This price was afterward increased, but in April, 1602, the court being no longer in Madrid (it was removed to Valladolid in January, 1601, and did not return to Madrid till the end of January, 1606), the town council of Madrid again lowered the prices and declared: "that the *autor* (manager) receive from each man and woman, at the entrance, 12 maravedís; and that the General Hospital receive, as it had received, two maravedís from each person at the entrance."[5] Thus the entrance fee for the *mosqueteros* (who stood in the *patio*), and for the women, was 14 maravedís, or a little less than half a

---

[1] *Tratado historico,* Vol. II, p. 191.

[2] "El Hospital General de Madrid tiene dos Corrales, donde se representan Comedias, y cada una de las personas que entran á ver las dichas Comedias, dan por el asiento en que se asientan quatro quartos, y á la entrada, ademas de lo que se da á los Comediantes, se da otro quarto: por manera que son cinco quartos los que cada uno de los que entran en la Comedia paga, demas de lo que dan á los Comediantes," etc. These 5 quartos (= 20 maravedís) were therefore the *limosnas,* or alms, which was the share of the hospitals from each one who entered the *corrales;* and in addition to this the spectator had to pay a sum to the manager of the players. This charge the theologians, to whom it was referred, did not consider excessive in view of the fact that four and even six reals were at that time paid in Madrid for a seat to see a bull-fight. (*Ibid.,* p. 195.)

[3] Sanchez-Arjona, *Anales,* p. 51.

[4] *Life of Lope de Vega,* p. 28.

[5] Pérez Pastor, *Nuevos Datos,* p. 73.

real. The price of the *sillas* and seats on the *bancos* (which held three persons) was probably the same as before, or one real. The court having returned to Madrid in January, 1606, another decree was issued, dated March 21, 1606, in which the deputies of the Brotherhoods were called upon to fix the price of admission to the *corrales,* restoring the prices in vogue when the court left Madrid. They agreed that from the first day of *Pascua de Resurreccion* every man admitted to the *gradas* was to pay 16 maravedís, and every woman who entered the large compartment for women (*cazuela*), 20 maravedís, which included the quarto (=4 maravedís) for the General Hospital; each *aposento* was 12 reals and each *banco* [seat on a *banco?*] one real; each of the *celosias* which has its entrance through the house of the Condesa de Lemos, 12 reals, and that likewise the General Hospital should receive at the entrance doors of the *corrales* a quarto from each person, and the same from the persons who occupy the *aposentos,* "which are the prices which are ordinarily paid when the court is in Madrid."[1]

[1] Pellicer, *Tratado Historico,* etc., Vol. I, p. 88. Information concerning the price of admission to the English theaters of the period is not very definite. Malone says: "The galleries or *scaffolds* and that part of the house which in private theaters was named the pit, seem to have been at the same price, and probably in houses of reputation, such as the *Globe* and that in *Blackfriars,* the price of admission into those parts of the theater was *six pence,* while in some meaner playhouses it was only a penny, in others two pence. The price of admission into the best *rooms* or boxes was, I believe, in Shakespeare's time a shilling; though afterward [about 1640] it appears to have risen to two shillings, and half a crown. At the *Blackfriars* theater the price of the boxes was, I imagine, higher than at the *Globe.*" (*Historical Account of the English Stage,* pp. 77–79.) As regards the English actors in Germany, Creizenach gives the following prices of admission to their performances: "In Ulm and Frankfort the ordinary price was 2 Kreuzer; in the former city at first 1 Kreuzer; in Strassburg 3 Kr., though the players would have preferred a Batzen (=4 Kr.); later, in 1618, it was 1 Batzen. In Cologne 2–4 Albus (Albus=2 Kr.). In Memmingen in 1600 it was 4 Kr. In Nürnberg at first ½ Batzen, afterward as high as 6 Kr. In Münster in 1599, one *Schilling.* The difference in price is probably due to the fact that in some instances the cost of the seat is included. Where this is not the case, the price given is for entrance only, an additional sum being required for a seat. In Frank-

In the ordinance of 1608 we find that every person who entered the theater paid 5 quartos ($=$ 20 maravedís) at the door, men as well as women, of which 5 quartos the *autor* received 3, and the hospitals of Madrid 2 quartos.[1]

In the *Corral de Doña Elvira* at Seville, in 1610, the price of a *silla* was half a real and the *banco* one real, and each *aposento* 6 reals.[2] Here 8 maravedís was the amount exacted from each entrance fee for the benefit of the city hospital.[3] This seems to have been in addition to the regular charge for entrance. This admission fee I infer to have been 16 maravedís ($=$ 4 quartos), from the petition of Juan Jerónimo Valenciano, an *autor de comedias,* who, in 1625, sets forth that the lessees of the *Coliseo* had refused to advance him and his company the customary sum as an *ayuda de costa,* and he therefore begs that he be given a license to perform in Triana, within the walls, in such place as he may find, receiving 4 quartos from each person.[4]

In 1617 the price of a *silla* in the *Coliseo* or the *Doña Elvira* was 4 quartos, while the *banco* remained at one real. It was particularly specified in the leases of these theaters

fort in 1601 the entrance was 8 Pfennig, and 4 Pfennig additional for a seat in the gallery, which is designated as a preferred place in 1610. In 1613 the Council of Nürnberg fixed the entrance fee at 3 Kr., besides 3 Kr. for a seat in the gallery. In 1611 at Ulm only 2 Kr. could be charged, and in 1611 the Council of Frankfort declared that a scale of prices must be hung outside the theater door. Here, too, overcharges were frequent, and in 1599 Sackville had to pay a fine of 20 Florins for overcharging. At Leyden in 1608 the players were obliged to give half their receipts for the support of poor orphans, the guardians of the orphans furnishing a person at the outer door to collect this amount." (*Die Schauspieler der Englischen Comedianten,* pp. xvii–xix.) Concerning the theaters in France, a police ordinance of 1609 forbade actors charging more than five *sous* to the pit and ten to the boxes and galleries. These prices were still in vogue about 1620, but in 1634 they seem to have been about nine or ten *sous* for the pit and nineteen or twenty for the boxes, while in 1652 it was fifteen *sous* for the pit. (Rigal, *Le Théâtre français avant la Période classique,* pp. 156, 157.)

[1] Cotarelo y Mori, *Controversias,* p. 624.

[2] Sanchez-Arjona, *Anales,* p. 144.

[3] *Ibid.,* p. 147.   [4] *Ibid.,* p. 241.

that no spectator be allowed to bring into the theater any seat or chair; the entrance fee entitled to standing room only. Admission to the *aposentos,* which were numbered, was by a numbered ticket.[1]

The ticket-scalper or speculator is not a creation of our own day; sometimes he was the lessee of the theater, for we find that, in 1616, Don Francisco Mejia, lessee of the *Doña Elvira* in Seville, exacted 20, 24, and even 32 reals for the *aposentos,* instead of 6 reals, and 2 reals for each *silla* instead of 24 maravedís.[2] In like manner, the youth who had charge of the *sillas* and *bancos* in *La Monteria* in 1633 charged 3 reals and even more, instead of one, the regular price.[3] And in 1637 Domingo Hernandez, who hired the lower *aposentos* in the same theater, compelled strangers to pay 20 and 24 reals, instead of 12.[4]

There were generally two outer doorkeepers or *cobradores;* one collected the money at the principal entrance and the other at the entrance for women. Two collections were made, one for admission and a second for the benefit of the hospitals,[5] besides the extra price paid for a seat, for this was not included in the entrance fee.

Two *alguaciles,* or peace officers, were also stationed, one at each door, and frequently also one in the women's gallery. Besides these there were persons to collect the extra charge for the *sillas* and *bancos,* and others in charge of the *aposentos* or rooms.

Green and dried fruits, water, sweets, *aloja* (a kind of

---

[1] Sanchez-Arjona, *Anales,* p. 262.

[2] *Ibid.,* p. 178.   [3] *Ibid.,* p. 283.   [4] *Ibid.,* p. 308.

[5] There are many references showing that two fees were collected: On March 26, 1614, Francisco Muñoz entered into an obligation with Alonso de Heredia, *autor de comedias,* to collect at both doors for him (*para cobrar á la puerta y traspuerta*). (Pérez Pastor, *Nuevos Datos,* p. 143.) And Cervantes, in the *"Adjunta al Parnaso,"* subjoined to his *Viaje del Parnaso* (1614), mentions the privileges sent by Apollo to the Spanish poets, and among them: *"Item,* that every comic poet who has brought out three successful comedias shall have the entry of the theaters without payment, unless it be the pittance for the poor at the second door, and even this, if need be, shall be excused him." (Edition of Madrid, 1784, p. 148.)

mead), and *barquillos* (thin rolled wafers) were sold among the audience.

The audiences were often unjust and noisy, and always hard to please. The *mosqueteros,* or infantry, as the rough and boisterous crowd who stood in the *patio* or pit, were called, constituted, as Ticknor says, the most formidable and disorderly part of the audience, and were especially feared by both author and actor, for upon their whims the success or failure of a comedia generally depended. Many are the complaints made, by even the greatest dramatists, of the injustice and turbulence of these spectators.

Lope de Vega often alludes to the *vulgo,* as he calls them, in a tone of bitter contempt, and Alarcon shows his utter despisal of the rabble by addressing them as *bestia fiera* (wild beasts) in the prologue to the first volume of his *Comedias* (1628): "To you I address myself, wild beasts, for to the noble it is unnecessary, for they speak for me better than I myself could do. Here are my comedias: treat them as is your wont; not as is just, but as is your pleasure, for they face you fearlessly and with contempt, and having passed the ordeal of your whistlings they can now readily pass that of your lurking-places. If they displease you I shall rejoice, for it will be a proof that they are good; if they please you, however, then the money they have cost you will be for me a sufficient revenge for this proof of their worthlessness." The theatrical manager Lorenzo Hurtado, in a *Loa* with which he began his representations in Madrid for the second time

In Seville, in 1620, 8 maravedís were collected for the benefit of the city at the second door of the *Corral de Doña Elvira* from each person who entered, and this continued to be the custom, for we read that in 1652 2 quartos (= 8 maravedís) were also collected at the second door of *La Monteria* for the same purpose. (Sanchez-Arjona, *Anales del Teatro en Sevilla,* pp. 213, 404.) In 1619 at the *Teatro de la Olivera* in Valencia the price of an *aposento* was 4 reals in Valencian money (= 5 reals 22 maravedís), which was afterward increased to 8 reals 16 maravedís. The share of the players was 8 dineros per person, and the entrance 6 dineros, so that the general admission was 14 dineros, which was paid at two doors, 8 at the first and 6 at the second door. (Lamarca, *El Teatro de Valencia,* p. 27.)

(1632–34?), addresses the *mosqueteros*, "who already have their whistles at their lips,"[1] and Roque de Figueroa, the friend of Lope de Vega, and one of the most celebrated theatrical directors of his time, tries to conciliate his audience in a *Loa*[2]. He speaks in turn to the spectators in the different parts of the theater: the *bancos* were back of the standing-place of the *mosqueteros* in the pit, the *gradas* were the rising seats on the sides, the *aposentos* were rooms whose windows extended around the three sides of the court-yard in different stories, the uppermost being the *desvanes*. These were occupied by persons of both sexes who could afford such a luxury, as Ticknor says, and who not unfrequently thought it one of so much consequence that they held it as an heirloom from generation to generation.[3] Even the court poet Calderon did not consider it beneath him to beg the indulgence of the *mosqueteros*.[4]

Nor were the women who attended the theater any

[1]   "A los mosqueteros,
Que en el pico de la lengua
Tienen ya los silbos puestos."
(*Entremeses de Quiñones de Benavente*, ed. Rosell,
Vol. I, Madrid, 1872, p. 32.)

[2] He addresses them as follows:

"Sabios y críticos bancos,
Gradas bien intencionadas,
Piadosas barandillas,
Doctos desvanes del alma,
Aposentos, que callando
Sabeis suplir nuestras faltas;
Infanteria española,
Porque ya es cosa muy rancia
El llamaros mosqueteros."
(*Ibid.*, p. 172.)

[3] *History of Spanish Literature*, Vol. II, p. 524. "Il y en a qui ont leur place aupres du Théâtre, qu'ils gardent de pere en fils comme un *Mayorazgo*, qui ne se peut vendre ni engager, tant ils ont de passion pour cela." (*Relation de l'Estat et Gouvernement d'Espagne* par François Bertaut, Cologne, 1666, p. 59.)

[4] At the end of Calderon's *El galan fantasma* (written in 1635 or earlier), Candil, the *gracioso*, thus addresses the *mosqueteros*:

"Yo, que pasé tantos sustos,
No quiero de nadie nada,

more orderly or charitable. Of course I do not refer here to the more respectable who occupied the boxes or *aposentos* and who generally went masked.[1] But the motley crowd that surged into the *cazuela* (stewing-pan), which men were not allowed to enter, was no less disorderly than the "infantry" of the *patio*, so that an *alguacil*, or peace officer, was always stationed in this gallery to keep them within bounds. Here no woman with any regard for her reputation entered unmasked.[2] Like the *mosqueteros*, these denizens of the *jaula*, or cage, as it was also called, pelted the actors with fruit, orange-peels, *pepinos* (cucumbers), or anything they found at hand, to show their disapproval, and generally came provided with rattles, whistles, or keys, which they used unsparingly.[3] Roque

> Sino de los Mosqueteros
> El perdon de nuestras faltas,
> Para que con esto fin
> Demos al *galan fantasma*."

[1] Guillen de Castro, *Los mal Casados de Valencia*, Act II. Malone notes that respectable women also wore masks in the English theaters. (*Historical Account of the English Stage*, p. 126.) The same custom prevailed in France: "Peut-être aussi dans les loges y avait-il quelques femmes honnêtes, mais trop curieuses, cachées sous le masque. On sait, en effet, que les dames ne sortaient jamais sans masque, sauf à le laisser attaché près de l'oreille, si elles ne le voulaient pas porter, comme font de bonnes dames de Paris, qui, encore qu'elles ne se masquent jamais dans la rue, craignant de s'échauffer ou pour quelque autre sujet, ont toujours le masque pendant, comme un volet près de la fenêtre, de peur que l'on n'ignore leur noblesse." (Rigal, *op. cit.*, p. 213, note, quoting *Maison des jeux*, Vol. I, p. 457.)

[2] In the interlude *De los Pareceres* by Benavente, one of the characters, Petronila, speaks of a lady whom she had seen at the entrance to the theater: "I could not speak to her," she says, "but watched her":

> "Que tapada se entraba en la cazuela."
> (*Entremeses*, ed. Rosell, Vol. II, p. 312.)

[3] In France ladies can hardly be said to have visited the Hôtel de Bourgogne (the only regular theater in Paris for nearly thirty years from the beginning of the seventeenth century) until Richelieu began to take an active interest in the theater, about 1635. Women did go to the theater, as Rigal says, "puisqu'il arrive à Bruscambille de leur adresser la parole; mais il ne le fait guère que pour leur dire des obscenités. C'étaient donc surtout des femmes perdues." He says further: "Les honnêtes femmes n'allaient point à l'Hôtel de Bourgogne et n'y pouvaient aller, effrayées par les insolents et par l'immoralité des spectacles; mais leur abstention même

de Figueroa, in the *Loa* above mentioned, addresses them:

> Damas que en aquesa jaula
> Nos dais con pitos y llaves
> Por la tarde alboreada,
> A serviros he venido,

thus showing the awe in which even the most famous players held these *mugercillas*. Indeed, Roque's prayer, begging the indulgence of his unruly auditors, is the best evidence of the character of this *vulgo*, before whom the works of the greatest dramatists of Spain were represented.

But despite the above description of the audience in Spanish theaters,[1] let us not imagine for one moment that these men and women were worse than we find them elsewhere in Europe at the public theaters. Indeed, the weight of the evidence here rather favors the Spaniard, as against other European nations. The plays that he saw were cleaner and on a higher moral plane than those which were represented before his contemporaries elsewhere. And this in spite of what we shall read hereafter concerning the immorality of the Spanish stage. An examination of the Elizabethan theater, or of the farces and comedies in France and Germany at this time, to say nothing of Italy,

---

était un mal et laissait le champ libre à l'immoralité comme aux insolences." (*Entremeses,* ed. Rosell, Vol. II, p. 214.)

[1] Suarez de Figueroa, in his *Passagero* (1617), says of these *mosqueteros:* "Dios os libre de la furia mosqueteril, entre quien si no agrada lo que se representa, no hay cosa segura, sea divina ó profana. Pues la plebe de negro no es menos peligrosa, desde sus bancos ó gradas, ni menos bastecida de instrumentos para el estorbo de la comedia, y su regodeo. Ay de aquella cuyo aplauso nace de carracas, cencerros, ginebras, silbatos, campanillas, capadores, tablillas de San Lázaro, y sobre todo de voces y silvos incesables. Todos estos generos de musica infernal resonaron no ha mucho en cierta farsa, llegando la desverguenza á pedir que saliesa á baylar el Poeta, á quien llamaban por su nombre" (fol. 104). Besides the instruments here mentioned by Suarez de Figueroa, which the *vulgo* brought to the theater for the purpose of creating a noise and disturbance, Gonzalez de Salas mentions the *castradores:* "Sabida cosa es, que las *Flautas Pastoricas* constaban antiguamente de aquella desigualdad de cañas, que hoi vemos imitada en los vulgares instrumentos, que la plebe llama grosseramente

whose theater was the most immoral in Europe, will soon convince one of the truth of this statement. The Spaniard was quick and vigorous in his disapproval of a play, and he made his dislike unmistakable, but he doubtless compares very favorably with his contemporaries in other countries.[1]

As already observed, the success or failure of a new comedia generally hung upon the judgment of this *populacho* in the pit. If they applauded and shouted *Victor!* it was a good augury, and the popularity of the play was assured; if they whistled and hissed, the comedia was doomed.[2] Bertaut relates the story of an author who went to one of these *mosqueteros* and offered him a hundred reals to be favorable to his play, which was about to be acted. But he replied haughtily that he would see whether the piece was good or not, and it was hissed.[3] Some years later, in 1679, Madame d'Aulnoy relates that the chief arbiter of the fate of a comedia in Madrid was a shoemaker, "who had acquired such absolute authority

Castradores. De estos usa hoi tambien el vulgo en los Teatros, para affligir, como con los Silvos, la no bien accepta Representacion." (*Nueva Idea de la Tragedia Antigua,* Madrid, 1778, Vol. I, p. 210.)

[1] An idea of the character of the rabble at the Hôtel de Bourgogne is furnished by the *Fantaisies de Bruscambille,* first printed in 1612. Bruscambille, irritated by the impatience of the mob, which is clamoring for the performance to begin, says: "A-t-on commencé? C'est pis qu'antan. L'un tousse, l'autre crache, l'autre pète, l'autre rit, l'autre gratte son cul," etc. Quoted by Rigal, *op. cit.,* p. 206, who remarks concerning the audience: "Et combien il était bruyant, agité, querelleur! La plus grande partie se trouvait au parterre, et là, debout . . . [elle] constituait pour les pièces et pour les acteurs le moins attentif et le plus irritable des juges." (*Ibid.,* p. 204.) "Ils ne cessent de parler, de siffler et de crier," etc. (*ibid.,* p. 208), and the players run the risk "d'être assommé à coups de pommes cuites." (*Ibid.*) Of the audiences at the Hôtel de Bourgogne during the first twenty or thirty years of the seventeenth century, Rigal says they were "en majorité turbulent, grossier et immoral." (*Ibid.,* p. 215.)

[2] James Mabbe, who was in Madrid in 1611–13, speaks of the "plaudits of the auditors in the theaters, crying, '*Vitor, Vitor,* . . . Pinedo or Fernandez,' while in the intervals he watched the Spaniards entertain the women they brought thither with good wines cooled with snow and sweetmeats." (*Celestina,* tr. by Mabbe, ed. H. Warner Allen, 1909, p. lxxviii.)

[3] *Relation de l'Estat et Gouvernement d'Espagne,* Cologne, 1666, p. 60.

in these matters, that authors were in the habit of going to him when they had finished a play, in order to procure his approval; they read their pieces to him, and the shoemaker, assuming a grave air, says a hundred impertinences, which they must endure. Finally, at the first representation, all eyes intently watch every move and gesture of this low fellow. The younger men, whatever be their quality, imitate him; if he yawns, they yawn; if he laughs, they laugh. Finally he gets impatient, draws forth a little whistle, places it to his lips, and immediately the whole house resounds with whistlings. The poor author is in despair, and all his pains are at the mercy of the good or ill humor of this scoundrel."[1]

Quick and unruly as the audiences were in showing their dislike of a play, they were equally noisy and demonstrative in manifesting their approval, which they did by crying *Victor!* Not infrequently dramatic authors—mostly second-rate ones—condescended, at the end of their plays, to ask the audience for a *victor*. Lope de Vega never stooped so low as this; at all events, I have not found a single instance in his comedias. His disciple, Montalvan, however, often sinned in this regard, as did also Moreto, and especially Francisco de Rojas. It was the custom of all playwrights—inaugurated, I believe, by Lope de Vega —at the conclusion of a comedia, to ask the auditors, who were generally addressed as "El ilustre Senado," to pardon the faults of the play. But these later dramatists often exercised considerable ingenuity in introducing the prayer for a *victor*. At the conclusion of Montalvan's *Cumplir con su Obligacion*, Mendoza says:

> To me then it falls to say it:
> Fulfil ye your obligation,
> And you all will have fulfilled it,
> If, as courteous as you are,
> You a *victor* in the bargain

[1] *Relation du Voyage d'Espagne,* La Haye, 1693, Part III, p. 21.

> Give, even if not for the Poet,
> For the wish he has to serve you.[1]

And Moreto ends his celebrated comedia *El Desden con el Desden* with the words:

> And with this and with a victor,
> Which most courteously and humbly
> The Wit begs, here the comedia
> *Scorn repaid with Scorn* concludeth.[2]

Rojas, in his *El más impropio Verdugo por la mas justa Venganza,* even carries his obligation for a *victor* beyond the grave:

> If you should at tip of tongue
> Or at hand applause have ready
> Or *victor* or other money,

[1] *Mendoza:* "A mí me toca el decirlo:
> *Cumplir con su Obligacion,*
> Y todos la havreis cumplido,
> Si como tan Cortesanos
> Nos dais de barato un vitor,
> Ya que no por el Poeta,
> Por el gusto de serviros."

So in *La mas constante Muger:*
> "Decid victor al deseo
> De quien vuestro esclavo es."

[2] "Y con esto, y con un vitor
> que pide humilde, y cortès
> el Ingenio, aqui se acaba
> *El Desden con el Desden.*"

In his comedia *Fingir y Amar* he asks for a *vitor* "if there be any at hand":
> "Un vitor si le hay a mano."

And in *La Confusion de un Jardin* he asks for it as a charity:
> "Dadle un vitor de limosna."

In his *El Parecido en la Corte* the actors call for a *victor* for him:
> "*Tacon:* Y con esto y con un vitor
> *Todos:* Para Moreto aqui tiene
> fin dichoso *el Parecido.*"

At the close of the comedia *Lo que son Mugeres,* Rojas asks for a *victor* because the play contains neither a death nor a marriage:
> "Y don Francisco de Rojas
> Un vitor sólo pretende

> In this life and in the other
> The poet will pay you for it.[1]

Many more examples might be cited, but we will conclude with this one by Solis, who, in his *El Doctor Carlino,* stoops to the groundlings, asking for a *victor* to bury his comedia:

> Here expireth the Comedia;
> If aught of success it merit,
> Give, to bury it, a *victor,*
> You, señores mosqueteros.[2]

We have seen the efforts that were made by the players to conciliate their audiences; these examples show quite conclusively that the playwrights feared them no less.

There were, quite naturally, in Spain, in these early days, not a few persons (and they have not decreased in our own time) who thought they were entitled to enter the theater without paying. As Ticknor says, it was deemed a distinction to have free access to the theater, and persons who cared little about the price of a ticket struggled hard to obtain it.[3] But it is safe to say that to the vast majority of those who tried to enter without paying, the gate-money was a matter of capital importance. These persons seem to have existed nowhere in such large

> Porque escribió esta comedia
> Sin casamiento y sin muerte."

Sin Honra no hay Amistad concludes with:

> "Dad un vitor de piedad
> Al que escribió la comedia."

> [1] "Si hubiere quien tenga á lengua,
> Como á mano algun aplauso,
> Un vitor ú otra moneda,
> En esta y en otra vida
> Se lo pagará el poeta."

> [2] "Y aqui espiró la Comedia;
> Si tuviere algun acierto,
> Dén para enterrarla un vitor
> Los señores mosqueteros."

[3] *History of Spanish Literature,* Vol. II, p. 525.

numbers as in Seville, where the *populacho* easily bore off
the palm for ruffianism,[1] a distinction which, I am told,
that city has maintained to the present day.   As a consequence, brawls and stabbing affrays at the doors of the
theaters were of frequent occurrence.

In 1615 Pedro Martinez de Asensio, to whom the city
of Seville had farmed out for 4000 reals annually the
charge of 8 maravedís which inured to the city from each
person entering the *corrales,* complained of the many persons who entered the *Doña Elvira* without paying, and
requested that those who enter by force be seized and
taken to the prison of the *Real Audiencia.*[2] In 1628 Luis
Candado, a well-known actor, was taking the money at the
door of *La Monteria* when one Juan de Heredia attempted to enter without paying.   It was charged that
Heredia took Candado's sword from him and threatened
him with it, though no harm was done, as others interfered.   Heredia tried to exculpate himself by declaring
that Candado had stooped to collect some coppers which
he had let fall, whereupon his (Candado's) sword was
pushed out from his belt, which sword Heredia grasped,
so that the owner of it might not injure himself.   Heredia
was fined 12 reals, "as an alms for some pious work, and
notified that henceforth he should pay at the door of the
theater."[3]   The spectacle of a *hidalgo* with a sword, gathering coppers, is certainly ludicrous.

By 1632 the number of persons who entered the *Coliseo*
without paying was so great that not enough money was
taken at the door to defray the expenses of the company.[4]

---

[1] Their reputation for never paying the entrance money when they could
possibly avoid it had reached every quarter of Spain. In the *Loa* to Turia's
La Fe pagada, printed in Valencia in 1616, we read:

> "Quien paga, y quien por honrado
> a lo de Sevilla se entra."

[2] Sanchez-Arjona, *Anales,* p. 164.

[3] *Ibid.,* p. 260.

[4] *Ibid.,* p. 281. In a *Bayle de Xácara* published about forty years after

In the following year, on January 5, a bloody affray took place at the door of *La Monteria*, when five or six young men in the dress of students forced their way through the first door and were met at the second by the *alguacil* with his "rod of justice," who declared that "on former occasions he had entreated them to pay on the day of a new comedia, since they did not pay on the other days." The ruffians withdrew, and arming themselves with swords, returned and attacked the *alguacil,* wounding him.[1]

In Madrid these brawls and stabbings at the theater doors seem to have been less frequent, though this may be due to the lack of exact information. That "deadheads" were equally plentiful, however, we may be quite sure. They stood around the doors of the theaters in the rain, drenched through, waiting for a chance to slip in without paying.[2]

Of the turbulent character of these audiences and of

this, we read that "only the *mosqueteros,* those who whistled down the comedias, paid their money":

> "En la comedia solo los mosqueteros
> los que siluan lo pagan con su dinero."
>   (*Migajas del Ingenio,* Zaragoza (no date), p. 30.)

And those who entered the theater *gratis* were the first to whistle:

> "Acabemos el bayle
> no nos le paguen
> con algun silvo fiero,
> que entre de balde."
> (*Bayle de la Entrada de la Comedia,* by Pedro Francisco Lanini,
>   *ibid.,* p. 18.)

[1] Sanchez-Arjona, *Anales,* p. 283. See also pp. 306 and 323. The latter case happened on June 4, 1638. Besides the public representations of the *autos* which were given, they were also performed this year in *La Monteria.* A waterman of Triana, when requested by the doorkeeper to pay, said that he never paid, and drawing a sword, wounded the *alguacil* who was standing at the door. On the following day a similar affray took place at the same theater, when the aggressor, "who was certainly a creole," in the words of the doorkeeper, "was one of those who did not pay, nor was he accustomed to do so." (*Ibid.,* p. 324.)

[2] In the *Jácara* sung by the company of Ortegón in Madrid, in 1635, Leonor sings:

> "En el corral de comedias
> Lloviendo á la puerta están

their ruffianly behavior within the theater there is other
and ample testimony. On the afternoon of November 10,
1639, in the theater *La Monteria* in Seville, a comedia was
performed, and after the *bayle* or dance at the end of the
first act had been executed by Jacinta Herbias, one Don
Pedro de Montalbo, a spectator who was studying for the
priesthood (*clerigo y estudiante*), cried out: "Bravo,
Jacinta!" to which Antonia Infante (who was playing the
first part to Jacinta's second) called from the stage:
"Bravo indeed, and welcome, for she deserves it." And
as some of those who were shouting exclaimed, "Bravo,
Jacinta, and down with Antonia!" one Don Lope de
Eslava arose and cried out, "Bravo, Antonia, and down
with Jacinta! and whoever says otherwise lies, like a
cuckold." Whereupon Don Pedro shouted, "You lie!"
On hearing which, Don Lope, blind with rage, drew his
sword, and rushing upon Don Pedro, mortally wounded
him. "Yet those were not wanting who asserted that an
old feud had existed between Don Pedro and Don Lope,
because the former had accused Doña Ana de Espinosa
[also an actress and wife of the actor Juan Roman] of
living with Don Lope."[1]

Another instance occurred in 1641. The students of
the college of Maese Rodrigo had been celebrating the
festival of the "Boy Bishop" (Obispillo),[2] and after creating a great tumult and scandal at the college gate, they
sallied forth upon the streets with "prohibited weapons,"
knocking down everybody they met on their way. In the
afternoon they went to the *Corral de la Monteria*, and

Mohadas y más mohadas,
Por colarse sin pagar."
(*Entremeses de Benavente*, ed. Rosell, Vol. I, p. 445.)

[1] Sanchez-Arjona, *Anales*, p. 304.
[2] "La farsa llamada del Obispillo" is as old as the fourteenth century.
(*España sagrada*, Tomo 45, trat. 88, cap. ii, p. 18, ed. of Madrid, 1832.
Wolf, *Studien*, p. 579.) See also, for the festival of the "Boy Bishop,"
Chambers, *The Medieval Stage*, Vol. I, pp. 336–371.

entering the *aposentos*, they caused the performance, which had already commenced, to be begun again. Not content with this, they started a fight on coming out, in which several persons were wounded.[1] Again, on Sunday, January 25, 1643, the comedia *San Cristóbal* was announced by posters to be played in the *Corral de la Monteria*, but the Inquisition had forbidden its performance until certain passages were expunged. The *autor* (director) came on the stage and announced this fact and offered to substitute another comedia. "The low and common people (*la gente baja y popular*), who had come because it was a feast-day and they were not working, and having congregated in great numbers because there were *apariencias*—a matter which the common people and the women enjoy more than the artistry, verses, and plot of the comedia—became turbulent and unruly because they wanted no other comedia than *San Cristóbal,* which they shouted amidst great tumult, and as this could not be represented without incurring the penalty of excommunication, they began to break benches and chairs, shattering them and destroying the curtains (*celosias*) of the *aposentos* and the whole theater, as well as the costumes of the players which they found in the green-room (*vestuario*)."[2] The company acting in *La Monteria* at this time was probably that of Manuel Alvarez Vallejo. ·And in 1645, while the company of Luis Lopez was representing in *La Monteria,* "there was another one of those scandals which were so frequent there. It appears that from the *cazuela,* where the women sit, somebody threw some lemon-peels (*cáscaras de limon*), which, falling upon the head of a man standing in the *patio,* he shouted: 'The devil take the ——. Why don't you look where you are throwing?' Whereupon a man who was close by replied: 'Why don't the cuckold look to what he says?' and at the

---

[1] Sanchez-Arjona, *Anales,* p. 349.
[2] *Ibid.,* p. 365.

same time dealt him a blow. At this the other drew a pistol, the discharge of which caused a great scandal."[1]

We have seen that from their very beginning the Spanish theaters had set aside a place exclusively for women. This gallery, called the *cazuela* (stewpan), *jaula de las mugeres*, or *corredor de las mugeres*, had a separate entrance and was provided with a doorkeeper, so that it might be wholly apart from the portion occupied by the men.[2]

Despite this arrangement of the theaters and the fact that an *alguacil* was always stationed at the women's entrance, the attempt to separate the men from the women was not always successful. In 1627 complaint was made in Seville "that the women occupied seats in the first and second rows of the *sillas* and *bancos* among the men, and likewise in other parts of the theater, from which great scandal results," etc.[3] And in 1651, in view of the continued disturbances in *La Monteria*, occasioned by permitting men and boys to enter the *cazuela* of the women, "against the expressed mandate," the lessee, one Juan de Bartanes, was notified to place at the entrance door,

---

[1] *Ibid.*, p. 374.

[2] The same precautions for separating men from women in the public theaters were observed in the Spanish colonies in South America. On April 17, 1630, an edict of the Viceroy of Peru, the Count of Chinchon, provided that men should not enter the *aposentos* of the women in the *Corral de las Comedias* of Lima; commanding that the said *aposentos* be separate, and that two entrances be constructed, one for men and the other for women, and imposing a penalty on all men who should be found in the galleries and *aposentos* reserved for women. It also provided that all representations cease before the bell for evening prayers (*oracion*), under the penalties provided therefor. At this time Antonio de Santoyo and his company, *Los Conformes*, were playing at the theater in Lima. (Pérez Pastor, *Nuevos Datos*, p. 219.) Even in the churches of Madrid separate entrances and exits were prescribed for men and women. James Mabbe (1611–13) "was duly shocked at the young men, who gathered about the church door to watch the women coming from their devotions, 'an ill custome, that is too much used in many great Cities, . . . especially in Madrid, where to prevent this Church-courting, the men are to goe in and out at one doore, and the women at another.'" (*Celestina*, translated by James Mabbe, edited by E. Warner Allen, London, 1909, p. lxxviii.)

[3] Sanchez-Arjona, *Anales*, p. 255.

"where the said women enter, new doorkeepers (*cobra-dores*) and satisfactory ones, so that in no circumstances men or boys be allowed to enter, under a penalty of 50 ducats, . . . and that the person in charge of the keys of the said *cazuelas* be notified not to permit any man or boy to enter, and he shall lock the door as soon as the comedia begins and not open it again until it be concluded, nor permit any one to be on the staircases," [1] etc. All of which did not keep Bernardo de Soto out of the "stewpan," for we read that on April 7, 1654, he, the said Bernardo, "ascended to the *cazuela* of the women in *La Monteria*, and getting under the seats, he began to raise the petticoats and touch the legs of those who were looking at the play, by which great scandal was occasioned; and the culprit was seized and sentenced to be banished from the city and ten leagues therefrom, for the term of two years, any infringement of this sentence to be expiated in one of the fortresses of Africa." [2]

While more or less force was sometimes used to enter the theaters without paying, peace, here as elsewhere, also had its victories, and other means were resorted to for viewing the comedia without the aid of reals and mara-vedís. As the Spanish theaters were open to the sky, people sometimes gathered on the surrounding housetops and looked at the performance. Complaint was made in this regard, in 1612, concerning the *Coliseo* in Seville, "which being uncovered, the neighbors ascended the roofs to view the representations, occasioning considerable loss and noise." [3]

Theatrical performances in Spain, as we have said above, were at first limited to Sundays and feast-days, but with the growing demand for these spectacles representations were authorized during the week, on Tuesdays and Thursdays, and sometimes they continued for fifteen or

---

[1] Sanchez-Arjona, *Anales*, p. 395.
[2] *Ibid.*, p. 408.   [3] *Ibid.*, p. 152.

twenty days before Shrovetide. On Ash Wednesday the
theaters were closed till Easter. But gradually the time
during which representations might be given was extended,
though all theaters were closed during Lent. It seems,
however, that even in very early times performances were
given on other than the prescribed days, for the Italian
Ganassa, who visited Seville with his company in 1575,
"having given, in the month of June, some performances
in the ancient *Corral de Don Juan,* so great was the number of spectators, especially of the common people, that
the city was petitioned to refuse a permit for these representations on account of the prejudice that resulted from
the fact that workingmen, in their eagerness to run after
this novelty, abandoned their employments; besides, the
great scarcity which prevailed in Seville did not admit of
such extraordinary expenditures."[1] We learn that in 1580
Ganassa obtained a license to perform two days in the
week, in addition to the feast-days, while Pedro de Saldaña
and Jerónimo Velazquez were permitted to represent only
on feast-days.[2] But that theatrical performances were not
long confined to these days we now have abundant
means of proving,[3] and in 1595 we find that the companies of Alonso de Cisneros and Gaspar de Porres were
to represent in Madrid from Lunes de Quasimodo (the
day following the first Sunday after Easter) till Corpus
Christi,[4] while in 1605 Baltasar Pinedo agreed to give
sixty performances in four months.[5] In 1639 Antonio de
Rueda agreed to give ninety performances on successive
days, except Saturdays, unless they be feast-days, in the
Corral de la Monteria at Seville,[6] but doubtless daily
representations (except on Saturday) had been given in
the theaters long before this time.

In general, no public representations took place on Sat-

[1] *Ibid.,* p. 49.   [2] *Ibid.,* p. 51.   [3] See Appendix A.
[4] Pérez Pastor, *Nuevos Datos,* p. 40.
[5] *Ibid.,* p. 89.   [6] *Ibid.,* p. 317.

urday, but as early as 1593 there is recorded an agreement by Gabriel Nuñez, *autor de comedias*, to go to Nava del Carnero by Sunday, August 1, "with the persons and baggage (*hato*) that may be necessary to represent, on the eve of the said Sunday, a comedia entitled *Los Comendadores* [by Lope de Vega], with its music and *entremeses*, and on the said Sunday another comedia *á lo divino* in the morning and one *á lo humano* in the afternoon, the latter to be *Los Enredos de Benetillo* [perhaps *Los Enredos de Benito* of Lope], or any other that may be demanded, with its music *de biola y guitarras.*" [1]

Representations were, of course, always given on Sunday. This day was much favored by both actors and *autores,* on account of the great crowd it drew, for which reason the comedias were always performed with greater savor. [2]

Besides the performances in the theaters of Madrid, the town council or *ayuntamiento* authorized public representations (*comedias publicas*) from time to time in the squares of the city, for which no fee was charged. In 1580 the Council of Madrid agreed to pay 300 ducats to each of the *autores* who were to represent comedias in the Plaza de San Salvador in honor of the safe delivery (*alumbramiento*) of the Queen, [3] and in 1620, on the occasion of the beatification of San Isidro, the patron saint of Madrid, the town council resolved to have comedias represented on the streets, ordered five stages to be erected for that purpose, and engaged five companies to give the per-

---

[1] Pérez Pastor, *Nuevos Datos,* pp. 36, 37.
[2] Rojas says:

> "Nosotros desseamos los domingos,
> Porque en domingo viene mucha gente,
> Y siempre las comedias en domingo
> Representamos todos con mas gusto."
> (*Viage entretenido,* Madrid, 1603, p. 575.)

In England plays on Sunday were forbidden by James I. in May, 1603. (Collier, *Shakespeare,* Vol. I, p. 167.)
[3] Pérez Pastor, *Nuevos Datos,* p. 12.

formances.[1] In Seville, in 1630, on the eve of the festival of the Conception of our Lady, public comedias and *bayles* were given by the companies of José de Salazar and Pedro de Ortegon,[2] and in 1631 the company of Damian Arias gave a public comedia in Seville, "paid for by the city," at the festival of Shrovetide. Each of these companies received 850 reals, which was the customary amount paid for a public comedia.[3]

The theaters were usually opened in September, and, in the absence of contagious diseases, continued (excepting the period of Lent) until about the middle of June. For example, on June 20, 1632, the *Corral de la Monteria* was closed on account of the heat (*por el calor*),[4] and in 1637 all representations in the *corrales* of Seville were forbidden, as the pest was then prevalent.[5]

The custom of issuing posters to announce the performance of a comedia was in early use in Spain, as we have seen. The distinction of first introducing them is generally awarded to Cosme de Oviedo of Granada, a well-known *autor de comedias*,[6] of whom we read as early as 1561, when he received seventy ducats for two cars which he brought out at the Corpus festival at Seville. A poster announcing a representation by the companies of Vallejo and Acacio on June 5, 1619, is still preserved in the Archivo del Ayuntamiento of Seville:

Vallejo i Acazio

Rpss.<small>tan</small> oi miercoles sus famosas fiestas

en doña el vira á las dos.

---

[1] Acuerdo de la Villa de Madrid de 6 Mayo 1620. "Acordóse que para las fiestas de S. Isidro haya comedias por las calles un dia de la octava y que se hagan cinco tablados 'para que representen cinco autores y se traigan de fuera los que faltaren' y que despues sirvan dichos tablados para las danzas." (Pérez Pastor, *Bull. Hispanique* (1907), p. 384; Rennert, *Life of Lope de Vega*, p. 277.)

[2] Sanchez-Arjona, *Anales*, p. 269.

[3] *Ibid.*, p. 271.   [4] *Ibid.*, p. 281.   [5] *Ibid.*, p. 306.

[6] "Cosme de Oviedo, aquel autor de Granada tan conocido, que fue el

It is about half a yard long and a foot wide, the upper line in Gothic characters, and done by hand, as most or all posters were, down to a much later time. This poster was put up at the corner of the Borceguineria, where such announcements were generally fixed, and a similar one at the *Doña Elvira*.[1]

Plays seem, however, to have been announced by public cry even as late as 1638, in which year Iñigo de Loaysa, a well-known actor, was murdered in the streets of Valencia while announcing the play for the following day.[2]   And in 1639 we find Agustin Romero, of the company of Francisco Velez de Guevara, combining with his duties as prompter those of posting placards, being engaged "para apuntar y hacer carteles."[3]

The most exclusive and costly seats in the Spanish thea-

primero que puso carteles." (Rojas, *Viage entretenido,* ed. 1603, p. 132; Sanchez-Arjona, *Anales,* p. 26.)
   [1] *Ibid.,* p. 200.   Sr. Paz y Melia, *Catálogo,* No. 2034, speaking of the MS. comedia *Los Mártires del Japon,* a copy made in Lisbon in 1637, says: "Contiene dos fragmentos de los carteles que antiguamente servían para anunciar las representaciones teatrales, análogos al que se conserva en el Archivo municipal de Sevilla."   This reference is evidently to the poster just mentioned above.   It is a great disappointment to learn that the two *fragmentos* mentioned by Sr. Paz, which are bound in with the play, are parts of two sheets of rough paper, upon one of which is written in red ink:

Jamas bista de . . .
Rep^{ta} Paz

while the other merely contains the word: Prim . . .
   [2] "Iñigo de Loaysa, de quien se dice que habiendo salido en Valencia á ofrecer anuncio para el dia siguiente, . . . le dieron un tajo en la garganta, de que murió degollado." (Sanchez-Arjona, p. 323.) There may be some confusion here with the actor Iñigo de Velasco, who was murdered in Valencia, December 1, 1643. (*Comedias de Calderon,* ed. Hartzenbusch, Vol. IV, p. 718.)
   [3] *Nuevos Datos,* p. 308. These play-bills or placards merely announced the names of the plays and the companies by which they were to be performed, and apparently did not contain a list of the characters, or the names of the actors by whom they were represented. The same custom obtained in England. While Spanish placards or posters, however, were done by hand, the "billes for players" in London were printed at least as early as 1587. "They were set up upon posts some certaine days before, to admonish the people to make resort to their theaters, that they may thereby be the better furnished, and the people prepared to fill their purses

ters were the *aposentos*[1] (stalls or boxes), which were occupied by the nobility and the rich. They were frequently rented by the year, the price varying from 100 to 150 ducats (a ducat = 11 reals) annually. Every one who made any pretension to being "upper-crust," we may be sure, had his *aposento,* just as nowadays such persons have their box at the opera. Among the distinguished personages occupying these favored places in Madrid in 1639 was the Florentine ambassador, who paid 100 ducats each for a yearly *aposento* in the *Corral del Príncipe* and the *Cruz.*[2]

The "ayuntamiento" or town council of the cities also generally possessed an *aposento* at the theater. In Madrid the "ayuntamiento" had one in each of the two theaters, for which 300 ducats were paid yearly.[3] Doubtless in most cities this was an "aposento grande con mayor adorno y autoridad que los demas aposentos que hay en la casa," as was the case in Valladolid in 1614.[4] Here those august dignitaries, the "Regidores," sat, who in those not over-scrupulous days guarded the destinies of the stage.

This privilege of the "Regidores" seems to have been abused by their sons, for on August 20, 1614, the town council of Madrid forbade the doorkeepers to allow anybody to enter the *aposentos* of these dignitaries in order to avoid the disorder caused by the fact that their sons used to visit these boxes and bring their friends, and because other persons also occupied them who had no right to do so.[5]

A curious fact noted by Pellicer is that "some gentlemen were in the habit of owing for their seats at the theater,"

with their treasures." (See Malone, *Historical Account of the English Stage,* p. 169.)

[1] The word is still used at the present day.
[2] *Nuevos Datos,* p. 314.
[3] Pérez Pastor, *Nuevos Datos,* pp. 122, 144.
[4] *Ibid.,* p. 155.   [5] *Ibid.,* p. 152.

i.e., they obtained seats on credit.   Thus, the books kept by the deputies show the following entry: "Sabado 18 de Mayo de 1602, debe el Corregidor un aposento.   El Regidor tres ventanas.   El Teniente Antonio Rodriguez un aposento.   El Príncipe de Marruecos una ventana."[1]

[1] *Tratado historico,* etc., Vol. I, p. 86.

CHAPTER VII

Women on the stage. In France, England, and Italy. Women on the Spanish stage. The companies of players. *Compañias reales.* *Compañias de parte.* Smaller companies. The *Entertaining Journey* of Rojas. The traveling of companies.

IT is probable that upon the Spanish stage women were originally impersonated by boys, as they were elsewhere in Europe during the greater part of the sixteenth century; a custom which lasted in England till after the Restoration. On the other hand, it is quite certain that, since the earliest times, women had taken part in public festivals and religious *autos,* as well as in the dances connected with them.[1] Concerning the French stage Bapst remarks: "It is to be observed that women, who at the close of the Middle Ages had begun to appear on the stage in pieces which contained nothing objectionable in the dialogue, no longer appeared at all upon the stage in the comedies or tragedies of the sixteenth century."[2]

Mantzius says: "As a rule, women did not appear upon the medieval stage, but children frequently did; they repre-

[1] The abuses mentioned by the author of a paper entitled *Abusos de Comedias y Tragedias,* quoted by Pellicer, and which is apparently without date, must refer to the earliest years of the Madrid *corrales.* "Women are gradually being introduced upon the stage in the place of boys, although the performances of boys of good appearance and rouged, attired as women, are held by some to be even a greater objection." The author also deplores the fact that separate places were not provided for men and women in the theaters, and that both sexes went in and out by the same door. (*Origen y Progresos,* etc., Vol. I, pp. 139, 140.) The latter complaint could only have been justified before 1582, when the *Corral de la Cruz* was built, which set apart a place for women, as we have seen above.
[2] *Essai sur l'histoire du Théâtre,* Paris, 1893, p. 146.

sented angels, young girls, or children's parts. . . . The more important female parts were performed by half grown-up youths, and particular care was taken to choose young men who were beardless and good-looking, and whose voices were not yet breaking. . . . On very rare occasions, nevertheless, women are seen to have acted in the Mysteries. Thus, besides the famous barber, Metz possessed another scenic celebrity in the person of an actress who even appeared in the same parts. We know, at all events, that she performed the part of St. Catherine, for the Chronicle says: 'And the "person" (*personnaige*) of St. Catherine was performed by a young girl, about eighteen years old, who was the daughter of Dediet the glazier, and she did her duty very well indeed, to the pleasure and delight of everybody.' . . . Though this case is not unique—at the Passion-play in Valenciennes, 1547, five young girls took part in the performance—we must take it for granted that female parts were only exceptionally acted by women. This is so much the more surprising, as women frequently appeared in the historical pantomimes and *tableaux vivants,* which the medieval towns habitually produced on festive occasions."[1]

The question which chiefly concerns us is the public theater, to which an admission fee was charged. And in regard to this M. Bapst further says: "Women did not appear, as a rule (d'une façon constante), upon a regular [French] theater until the second half of the seventeenth century. A single *comédienne de profession* is mentioned in the preceding century—Marie Fairet, wife of le Sieur Fairet, in 1545."[2] Again: "At the beginning of the six-

---

[1] *History of Theatrical Art,* Vol. II, p. 90.

[2] *Essai,* etc., p. 180. Creizenach, *Geschichte des neueren Dramas,* Vol. III, p. 70, gives the name as "Marie Ferré, die Frau des Marktschreiers Michel Fasset," and quotes the contract which has been preserved, wherein Marie Ferré agrees with "Anthoine de l'Espeyronnyère, joueur d'histoires," "à luy aider à joer chacun jour durant le dict temps tant et autant de foys que lui plaira en l'art de joueur d'enticailles de Rome, consistant en plusieurs ystoires moralles, farses et soubressaulx."

teenth century women appeared occasionally in Paris theaters, but always as representing the Queen—the parts of soubrette, nurse, and old women's rôles being always played by men. . . . In 1629 a troupe of French actors, containing women, went to London to act,[1] but before Richelieu began his reforms in the theater (about 1635), the coarseness [of the plays] excluded every respectable woman from the stage as well as from the audience." But women, in all probability, had been acting regularly in Paris for some years prior to this date. Indeed, we know that Marie Venier, wife of the comedian Mathieu le Febvre, called Laporte, had acted at least as early as 1610 "sur ce qu'on veut bien appeler le théâtre du Marais."[2]

In England it was not till September, 1656, that an English actress appeared upon the stage in the public theaters. This was Mrs. Coleman, wife of Coleman, the actor, and she played a kind of operatic part—Ianthe, in Davenant's *Siege of Rhodes*.[3] By this means the constant intercourse with France and Italy had produced a change in the public taste, so that, a little later, the royal license

[1] The fact is noted by Malone, *Historical Account of the English Stage,* ed. of Basil, 1800, pp. 130, 131: "1629.—November 4. For the allowing of the French company [with women actors] to play a farce at Blackfriars, £2." And Mantzius says that the London public was so unaccustomed to the appearance of women on the stage that the actresses belonging to this company were pelted with rotten apples when they appeared. (*History of Theatrical Art,* Vol. II, p. 280.) Again, Malone says: "in the office book of Philip Earl of Pembroke and Montgomery, I find a warrant for the payment of £10. to Josias Floridor for himself and the rest of the French players, for a tragedy by them acted before his Majesty in December last. Dated Jan. 8, 1635–6." For the scandal caused in London by two companies of French players who visited that city in 1629 and 1633, when the actresses were insulted and hissed off the stage, see Lotheissen, *Geschichte der französischen Literatur im XVII. Jahrhundert,* Wien, 1897, Bd. I, p. 494. Malone also quotes the following item: "£10. paid to John Navarro for himself and the rest of the company of Spanish players, for a play presented before his Majesty, Dec. 23, 1635." This John Navarro was Juan Navarro Oliver, who, with his wife, Jerónima de Olmedo, had belonged to the company of Cristóbal de Avendaño in 1632.

[2] Rigal, *Le Théâtre Français avant la Période classique,* Paris, 1901, pp. 55, 59.

[3] Sidney Lee says: "The first rôle that was professionally rendered by a

obtained by Davenant contained the following clause: "That whereas the women's parts in plays have hitherto been acted by men in the habits of women, at which some have taken offense, we do permit and give leave, for the time to come, that all women's parts be acted by women."[1]

While women appeared upon the public stage in Italy early in the second half of the sixteenth century, Nicoló Barbieri (Beltrame), a distinguished actor, in his pamphlet *La Suplica*,—a sort of apology for the dramatic profession, published at Bologna in 1636,— speaks of the custom, still prevalent in his day, of boys playing the rôles of women or young girls.[2]

The earliest Italian actress whose name has survived is mentioned by De Sommi, in his *Dialoghi in Materia di Rappresentazione scenica,* published in 1565 or 1566, in which he says: "Mirabile mi è sempre paruto e pare il recitare di una giovane donna romana, nominata *Flaminia,* la quale oltre all' essere di molto bella qualità ornata, talmente è giudicata rara in quella professione, che non credo che gli antichi vedessero nè si possi tra moderni veder meglio. . . . So che molti bei spiriti, invaghiti delle sue rare maniere gl' hanno fatto et Sonetti et Epigrammi, et molti altri componimenti in sua lode."[3]

Concerning Germany M. Bapst says: "To the actor Johannes Velten belongs the merit of having first definitely introduced women on the German stage, at the time that he translated the plays of Molière. In 1686 his troupe included three actresses: his wife, his sister, and Sarah von

woman in a public theater was that of Desdemona in *Othello,* apparently on December 8, 1660. The actress on the occasion is said to have been Mrs. Margaret Hughes, Prince Rupert's mistress." (*Shakespeare's Life and Work,* p. 188. See Malone, *Historical Account,* p. 141.)

[1] Mantzius, *History of Theatrical Art,* Vol. II, p. 280.

[2] *Ibid.,* p. 270.

[3] D'Ancona, *Origini del Teatro Italiano,* Vol. II, p. 413. These *Dialoghi dell' Ebreo* Leone de Somi, which are very interesting, may now be read in Rasi, *I Comici Italiani,* Firenze, 1897, Vol. I, p. 107. De Somi, a Mantuan, "fu autor comico, poeta e impresario di compagnie comiche," as is shown by a letter of his dated April 15, 1567. (*Ibid.,* p. 106.)

Bosberg. In 1690 his company contained, besides his daughter, two actresses by profession, named Richter and Moeller."[1]

It is certain, however, that women appeared upon the stage in Spain, in the public squares and *corrales,* at a very early date. It is quite probable that Mariana, the first wife of Lope de Rueda, acted in his little company of strolling players about the middle of the sixteenth century.[2] As already observed, women took part in the dances that always formed a part of the Corpus Christi celebrations, and also in the *autos,* as they were called, from very early times. A passage in the *Crónica de los Hechos del Condestable Miguel Lucas de Iranzo* proves that actresses appeared upon the stage in the ancient *momos* or *entremeses.*[3] It is also likely that women acted in the Italian company of Ganassa in Madrid (1579–83), and in the latter year we find an "obligation and agreement entered into between Miguel Vazquez and his wife Juana Vazquez, and Luis de Molina, *oficiales de comedias,* to work in the company of Juan Limos, *autor de comedias,* from this date [Madrid, March 15, 1583] until Shrovetide of 1584, receiving nine and a half reals for the three persons at the end of each performance, besides food, drink, lodging, and clean linen, and all expenses of travel."[4] In the following year an agreement was made by Agustin Solano, actor, residing in Madrid, "for himself and in the name of Roca Paula, his wife, being in the court [Madrid], with Tomás de la Fuente, *autor de comedias,* native of Toledo, to help him in all the *comedias* and *entremeses* which he may represent from this date [March 5, 1584] till Shrove-

---

[1] *Opus cit.,* p. 280. On the other hand, we are told that in Germany, as late as 1717, no women were allowed upon the stage. (*Shakespere Jahrbuch,* Vol. XXI, p. 236.)

[2] See above, pp. 11, 12.

[3] Fitzmaurice-Kelly, *Littérature Espagnole,* Paris, 1904, p. 178.

[4] Pérez Pastor, *Bulletin Hispanique,* 1906, p. 153. The term *oficial* instead of the more usual *representante* is used by Rojas, *Viage entretenido,* p. 53, where he speaks of "una compañia de tan buenos oficiales."

tide of 1585, receiving nine reals for each performance, besides four and a half reals for maintenance, in case the company should not provide it."[1] Roca Paula, being a married woman, could not make a binding contract without her husband's joining in it.

While these are the earliest instances that I have found recorded, it can hardly be doubted that women acted upon the stage at Madrid even prior to this time. Still, it appears that no license allowing women to act in the public theaters of the capital was granted before 1587. On November 17 of that year, Pedro Paez de Sotomayor, on behalf of his son-in-law, Alonso de Cisneros (*autor de comedias,* then absent from the city), presented a petition to the Corregidor of Madrid, setting forth that the Council of his Majesty had granted a license permitting married women to act upon the stage, and that, in pursuance of that license, women were then acting publicly in Madrid, and he requested the same license for his son-in-law, then in Seville, "so that it may be evident to the justices of the said city or of any other place where he may give representations." It recited another petition by the company called the *Confidentes Italianos,*[2] wherein these declare that they cannot perform the comedias which they have, without the women of their company, and pray for a license permitting these women to act. This latter petition had been granted "inasmuch as the women in the company are married women and their husbands are with them." It was especially provided, however, that they should not be permitted to appear in the habit or dress of men, and that "henceforth no boy be allowed to act attired as a woman."[3]

[1] Pérez Pastor, *Nuevos Datos,* p. 15. Ana de Velasco, wife of the actor Sebastian de Montemayor, was also a member of a company of players in Madrid, in 1584.

[2] The *Confidentes Italianos* were originally one of the companies of the Duke of Mantua. (Baschet, *Les Comédiens Italiens,* Paris, 1882, p. 23, and D'Ancona, *Origini del Teatro Italiano,* Vol. II, pp. 465 *et passim.*)

[3] Pérez Pastor, *Nuevos Datos,* pp. 19–23.

The Italian actresses to whom a license was especially granted were Angela Salomona and Angela Martinelli,[1] "married women whose husbands are members of the same company," and Silvia Roncagli (*la Francesquina*).[2] Appended to the petition of Pedro Paez de Sotomayor were the depositions of two witnesses who, "on the twenty-first day of the present month of November" (1587), had seen a comedia played by the Italians in the *Corral del Príncipe*, in which three women acted.[3]

About this time (1588), as already observed, the famous dance called the *zarabanda* was introduced upon the stage, to be followed by others hardly less wild and indecorous, and theatrical entertainments, always favored by the people, suddenly assumed a popularity that was unprecedented. Doubtless these "pestiferous" dances contributed in no small degree to the vogue which the theater now attained. But, as Pellicer remarks,[4] the growing popularity of theatrical representations and the consequent increase in the number of theaters and players throughout Spain, "the dances, songs, expensive costumes, and the acting, not only of women, but of women disguised as men, and the easy virtue of the theatrical profession, soon made the question of the continuance of theatrical representations a matter of grave controversy." A num-

---

[1] Concerning Angela Martinelli, wife of Drusiano Martinelli, one of the managers of this company *I Confidenti*, see above, pp. 45, 46.

[2] Referring to the latter, the decree states: "Si la Francesquina es la que yo vi en la posada del señor Cardenal, no la tengo por muchacho y ansi podrá representar." (Peréz Pastor, *Nuevos Datos*, p. 23.)

[3] Fr. Juan de Pineda, in the *Primera parte de los Treynta y cinco diálogos familiares de la Agricultura cristiana*, published at Salamanca in 1589, but the *Aprobación* of which is dated 1581, alludes to these Italian companies as "los extrangeros que sacan muchos millares de ducados de España cada un año," and mentions the subjects of some of the *farsas* played by them. Reproving the priesthood for visiting these plays, he says: "¡que no se os cubra la cara de vergüenza de que os vean autorizando y gozando de los cuentos de Medea y de Jason, y de Paris y Elena, y Eneas y Dido, y de Piramo y Tisbe." (Cotarelo y Mori, *Controversias, etc.*, p. 505.)

[4] *Tratado historico, etc.*, Vol. I, p. 119.

ber of eminent theologians took part in the discussion, and opinion was divided. Among those who favored the continuance of these spectacles was Fr. Alonso de Mendoza, an Augustinian and professor in the University of Salamanca, who declared, in 1587, "that the representation of comedias *as they are now represented in Spain* is not, of itself, a mortal sin, provided that lascivious songs and gestures be not introduced."[1]

The government accepted this view of the matter, with the effect of multiplying theaters and players,[2] adding to the number—already great—of *entremeses,* and introducing new dances, "and not the most decent ones," as Pellicer naïvely remarks. And in order to give the theater a certain air of piety and good repute, so many *comedias de santos* were written and acted that, as Rojas says:

> . . . al fin no quedó poeta
> En Sevilla, que no hiciese
> De algun santo su comedia.

It was even held that these plays were conducive to religion and good morals, and in a memorial to Philip II, in 1598, it was declared as a well-known fact that "several actors who had represented the lives of St. Francis and other saints, as well as some of the spectators, went straight from the playhouse to take the habit of St. Francis or of the saint represented, being stung by compunction."[3] On the other hand, the Jesuit Mariana cites the case of an actress who took the part of Magdalena in

---

[1] *Tratado historico,* etc., Vol. I, p. 120.

[2] The theaters of Madrid were, on the contrary, gradually reduced to the two principal playhouses in the Calle de la Cruz and in the Calle del Príncipe. Many other important cities, such as Seville, Valencia, Granada, and Saragossa, had permanent theaters, and no town was so small that it was not visited by strolling bands of players, so great had the craze for the theater become. By an order of June 22, 1600, Fleay tells us, only two playhouses were to be allowed in London, the *Globe* and the *Fortune.* (*Chronicle History of the English Stage,* Vol. I, p. 160.) This order was never observed.

[3] Pellicer, Vol. I, p. 122.

one of these *comedias de santos,* and of the actor who represented Christ, both of whom, he says, were notoriously immoral, "which was all the worse, inasmuch as they were famous players, and had often brought tears to the eyes of the spectators."[1]

Indeed, the "desenvoltura" of the actresses finally brought things to such a pass that on September 5, 1596, women were forbidden to appear upon the stage.[2] This prohibition, if ever enforced, was certainly of short duration.

Let us now turn to the companies of players as they were organized at this time. As early as 1586 a theatrical company contained thirteen or fourteen persons, besides the *autor* or director, for we find the company of the famous Nicolas de los Rios then consisting of that number, and even at the very height of the Spanish drama, from 1610 to 1640, the average number did not exceed from sixteen to twenty players.[3] As the number of characters to be represented in the comedia frequently exceeded the number of actors in the company, it was not

---

[1] *Ibid.,* p. 122.

[2] This instrument, preserved in the library of the Academy of History at Madrid, was first published by Schack, *Nachträge,* p. 29. It reads as follows: "Orden del Consejo à las Justicias del Reino.—'En el Consejo se tiene noticia que en las comedias y representaciones que se recitan en esta ciudad salen mugeres a representar, de que se siguen muchos inconvenientes, tendreys particular cuydado de que mugeres no representen en las dichas comedias, puniendoles las penas que os pareciere, aperciviendoles que haciendo lo contrario se executará en ellas.—de Madrid á cinco de Setiembre de mil e quinientos y noventa y seys años.'" It is also now reprinted in Pérez Pastor, *Nuevos Datos,* p. 44.

[3] More than half a century after this, theatrical companies in France were even much smaller. The company of Molière, when he appeared for the first time on the Paris stage after his return from the provinces, on October 24, 1658, consisted of the following nine persons: Joseph Béjart; Louis Béjart, his younger brother; Sr. du Parc, whose real name was René Berthelot, and stage-name Grosrené; Charles du Fresne; Sr. de Brie; Madeleine Béjart, sister of Joseph; Mlle. du Parc; Mlle. de Brie, whose stage-name was Catherine du Rosné; Geneviève Hervé, whose real name was Béjart, and who was a sister of Madeleine. Molière's company generally consisted of twelve to fifteen persons. The first appearance of the company in Paris was in Corneille's *Nicomède* and Molière's *Docteur*

unusual for a player to take two or even three parts.   In
many manuscripts of the comedias of Lope de Vega and
other early dramatists, the "reparto" (*dramatis personæ*)
shows this.   Indeed, Cervantes, at the close of his comedia *El Rufian dichoso,* calls attention to the fact that all
the female characters in the play can be taken by two
women.[1]   In the Elizabethan drama this was also frequently the case; so, in the Induction to Marston's *Antonio and Mellida* (1602), Piero asks Alberto what part
he acts.   He replies: "the necessity of the play forceth me
to act two parts."

Whether theatrical companies were licensed in Spain
prior to 1600, I do not know: it is probable, though I do
not find the fact noted anywhere.   By an ordinance of
1600, however, and again by a decree of 1603, the number
of licensed companies was limited, the latter decree naming
the eight heads of companies who received the license of
the King to represent comedias, which number was increased to twelve by a decree of 1615.[2]   The companies
authorized by these decrees were called *compañias reales*
or *de título.*   But at no time, despite these royal ordinances,
were the companies limited to those therein specified.
Numerous other companies soon sprang up, called *compañias de la legua,* which, acting without the King's
license, overran the whole peninsula.

Theatrical companies in Spain were of two kinds: those
in which the players worked for a salary paid them by the

Amoureux.   They played in the Salle des Gardes du vieux Louvre, on
Monday, Wednesday, Thursday, and Saturday.   After July 9, 1659, Molière and his company were allowed, on the payment of 1500 livres, to
play on Sunday, Tuesday, and Friday, which were the most fashionable
days and were called the *jours ordinaires.*   (*Registre de La Grange,* Paris,
1876, p. 3; Fischmann, *Molière als Schauspiel-direktor,* in *Ztft. für Fran-
zösische Sprache,* 1905.)

[1] "Hase de aduertir, que todas las figuras de muger desta Comedia, las
pueden hazer solas dos mugeres."   (*Ocho Comedias,* etc., Madrid, 1615,
fol. 112.)

[2] These decrees regulating theatrical companies will be considered in
Chapter X.

autor or manager, and those in which the players worked on shares. The latter were called *compañias de parte*. Such a company was organized in June, 1614, by the well-known *autor* and dramatist Andrés de Claramonte.[1] The agreement has been preserved, and is as follows:

Agreement and obligation of Andrés de Claramonte, one of the *autores de comedias* appointed by his Majesty, with Pedro Cerezo de Guevara, Francisco Mendoza, Juan Gasque, Miguel de Ayuso, for himself and for Luisa de Reinoso, his wife, Fernando Pérez and Maria de Montesinos, his wife, Maria Gabriela and Francisca Maria, her daughter, Sebastiana Vazquez, sister of the said Fernando Pérez, and Alonso Garcia, to form a company of players. And first that the said Andrés de Claramonte, Pedro Cerezo de Guevara, etc., . . . form a partnership company (*compañia de partes*) for the time and space that still remains of the present year, and which shall end at Shrovetide of the coming year, during which time the above-mentioned and each one of them bind themselves to go together in the form of a company and to play in all the towns of this kingdom and beyond during the said time, and to represent therein all the comedies and plays which the said Andrés de Claramonte possesses, by virtue of which the said Andrés de Claramonte binds himself to furnish (in order that they may be represented by the said company) as many as forty comedias and such others as the said company may require, besides the necessary *entremeses, letras,* and *bailes.*

Item: That the various rôles in the comedias shall be assigned amongst the members of the said company in such manner as shall seem most suitable to each in the opinion of the said company.

Item: During the said time the said members and each of them shall be bound, and by these presents are bound, to attend with all care and punctuality the rehearsals of all the comedias to be represented each day, at nine o'clock, at the house of the said Andrés de Claramonte, where rehearsals are ordinarily to take place, and shall not fail to be present at any one of the said rehearsals, under penalty of two reals to each one who shall not attend them in time and

---

[1] Claramonte, whose wife was Beatriz de Castro, died in the Calle del Niño, Madrid, on September 19, 1626. (Pérez Pastor, *Nuevos Datos,* p. 211.)

when he is called upon to speak; and if, being present at the said rehearsal, he shall leave it, and another should be obliged to speak for him, he shall pay likewise as a penalty one real every time that this happens. And the said fines and penalties are to be deposited with a certain person to be appointed, so that they may be distributed according to the will of the said company, in charities and pious works, masses, etc. The said fines to be paid on the same day by the member thus incurring them, out of the amount to be received by him on that day for acting and for maintenance (*de racion*).

Item: That during the said term there is to be a deposit chest with three keys, which chest is to remain in the custody of the said Maria Gabriela, the which keys the company will in due time deliver to the persons who may be agreed upon. Into this chest are to be put, from each performance that may be given, public as well as private, during the said time, twenty-five reals, which are always to remain deposited, and the chest is not to be opened until the said day of Shrovetide, which is the term when the said company ceases to be effective, in the said year one thousand six hundred and fifteen; and then the said chest is to be opened, and the money which may be deposited therein is to be divided amongst all the members of the said company conformably to what each one may be entitled to, according to this writing and which will be declared below.

Item: That from the proceeds of each of the comedias which may be represented are to be taken two reals, which the company may distribute in alms, masses, and pious works, together with the fines to be imposed upon the members for failing to be present at the rehearsals.

Item: If during the said time any member of the said company should fall sick, there is to be given to him the share which may belong to him in conformity with this writing—just as if he had really acted and taken part—as well for acting as for maintenance, and if he should remain behind sick in any place where the company should happen to be, he is to be paid the expense which he incurs for conveyance from that place to the place where the company may then be.

Item: That during the said time the said Andrés de Claramonte is to have and to take from what may proceed from all the said representations which may be given and from each one of them, public as well as private, on account of the labor of composition and study of them, six reals, and besides these six reals he is to have as his share (*de parte*) ten reals, and four reals for maintenance every day that there may be representations; . . . and the said Pedro Cerezo de Guevara also ten reals as his share and four reals for maintenance; . . . Juan Gasque four reals as his share and four reals for maintenance; Fernando Pérez and Maria de Montesinos, his wife, fourteen reals as their share, besides eight reals for maintenance; Maria Gabriela and Francisca Maria, her daughter, sixteen reals, besides four reals for maintenance; Miguel de Ayuso and Luisa de Reinoso, his wife, ten reals, besides seven reals for maintenance; and Alonso Garcia, four reals and three for maintenance.

Item: That if, during the said time, any member of the said company shall absent himself from it, he shall lose all that would have fallen to his share, as well of the amount that may be deposited in the said chest as of the costumes which the said company may have acquired during the said time, and shall lose fifty ducats besides, . . . which sum is to be shared amongst the other members of the said company who may remain therein.[1]

This agreement fairly represents all those made in similar cases. In another, executed on July 8, 1614, the various members are to meet at nine every morning, at the house of Pedro Bravo, for rehearsal. Here four reals are set aside from the proceeds of each performance until the amount reaches 400 reals, which are to be paid to Luis de Monzon for providing the costumes for the company.[2] A similar troupe, called *Los Conformes*, was organized by Juan de Vargas, Andres de Chavarria, Sebastian Gonzalez, and others in Madrid, in 1623. They were to go to the town of Leganés on October 14 and perform the comedia *La Morica garrida* of Juan de Villegas, with its *loa,* music, *entremes,* and *bayles,* for the sum of 400 reals.[3]

---

[1] Pérez Pastor, *Nuevos Datos,* pp. 145–148. Such a company was also formed in 1634 by Fernan Sanchez de Vargas and Juan de Malaguilla. (See *ibid.,* p. 235.)

[2] *Ibid.*

[3] *Ibid.,* p. 202. Other companies were *La Compañia española* in 1602

Besides the *compañias reales* and the *compañias de parte,*
there were many other kinds, ranging down the whole
gamut to the lone traveling mountebank. They can best
be described in the words of Agustin de Rojas Villandrando, whose *Viage entretenido,* first published at Madrid
in 1603, is one of the most interesting works that we
possess concerning the early Spanish stage. Rojas was
born in Madrid about 1575, and was in turn page, soldier,
scrivener in Granada (1599), and finally an actor. It was
in Seville, as he tells us, that he first saw a comedia acted,
and there he became a member of the company of Antonio
de Villegas, probably in 1600.[1] As he wrote his *Entertaining Journey* in 1602, his professional experience was
very limited, not extending over more than two or three
years. Many of his statements concerning the history of
the stage are therefore to be received with caution, but,
as he had been himself a strolling player, his description
of the various bands of actors which were then perambu-
lating the peninsula are, in the main, trustworthy, though
doubtless somewhat highly colored for effect.[2]

The *Viage entretenido,* it may be observed here, is in

(*Nuevos Datos,* p. 76) and *Los Andaluces* in 1605, the latter consisting of
Francisco Garcia de Toledo, Diego de Monserrate and his wife Mariana
Rodriguez, Juan de Ostos and his wife Maria de Herrera, Luis de Castro,
Cristóbal de Barrio, and Luis de Alvarez. (*Ibid.,* p. 89.) Such companies
formed the nearest parallel in Spain to the "sharers" of the Elizabethan
theater, as distinguished from the "hired men."

[1] Sanchez-Arjona, *Anales,* p. 105. Pérez Pastor, *Nuevos Datos,* pp. 351–
353, publishes an interesting document concerning Agustin de Rojas. It is
an agreement made in Valladolid on February 26, 1602, between Miguel
Ramirez, *autor de comedias,* and Agustin de Rojas, actor, in which the
latter agrees to act in all the comedias that may be produced as well in this
city [Valladolid] as in any other place where the said Miguel Ramirez
may be, as well in the theater as in any other part or spot that may be
designated during the said year, from the date of this writing [February
26, 1602] until Shrovetide of the coming year, 1603, and for which the
said Ramirez is to pay Rojas 2800 reals, and at the end of the year "a
doubloon for the washing of his linen," and shall furnish transportation
for Rojas, the latter binding himself to act with no other company during
the said time, etc.

[2] Among other works, Rojas was also the author of a comedia *El natural
desdichado,* which has been edited from the autograph in the Biblioteca

the form of a conversation between four persons: [Nicolas de los] Rios, [Miguel] Ramirez, [Agustin] Solano, and the author of the work, Agustin de Rojas, all actors, and the first two were, besides, famous *autores de comedias* or directors of companies. In the course of the conversation Rios had mentioned Cosme de Oviedo, "that well-known *autor* of Granada, who was the first to use posters" (p. 132). To which Solano adds: "And also the first to take a *gangarilla* through the towns on the coast." To the query of Ramirez, "What is a *gangarilla?*" Solano replies: "It is clear that you have not had much experience of the *farándula*, for you ask about such a well-known matter." To which Rios: "I have been an *autor* for more than thirty years, and this is the first time that it has come to my notice."

Solano: Well then, know that there are eight kinds of companies of actors, and all quite different; . . . there is the *bululu, ñaque, gangarilla, cambaleo, garnacha, boxiganga, farándula,* and the company. A *bululu* is a player who travels alone and afoot; he enters a village, goes to the curate, and tells him that he knows a comedia and a *loa* or two; he asks him to call the barber and sacristan, and he will recite it to them, so that they may give him something, that he may proceed on his way. These having assembled, he mounts upon a chest, and begins to recite, remarking as he goes on: "Now the lady enters and says so-and-so," and continues his acting while the curate passes around the hat, and having gathered four or five quartos, the curate adds a piece of bread and a bowl of soup, and with this he follows his star and continues his way. A *ñaque* consists of two men; they enact an *entremes* or portions of an *auto,* recite some *octavas* and two or three *loas;* they wear a beard of sheepskin (*zamarro*), play a drum, and charge an ochavo [= 2 maravedís], or in other kingdoms [parts of Spain] a dinerillo (that is what Rios and I used to do); they live contentedly, sleep in their clothes, go barefoot, are always hungry, rid themselves of their fleas amid the grain in summer and do not feel them on

Nacional, Madrid, and published by Sr. Paz y Melia in the *Revista de Archivos* for 1900.

account of the cold in winter. *Gangarilla* is a bigger company; here there are three or four men: one who can play the fool (*que sabe tocar una locura*) and a boy who plays the women's rôles. They represent the *auto* "The Lost Sheep," have beards and wigs (*cauellera*), borrow a woman's skirt and bonnet (which they sometimes forget to return), play two comic *entremeses,* charge each spectator a quarto [= 4 maravedís], and also accept a piece of bread, eggs, sardines, or any kind of odds and ends, which they put into a bag. They eat roast meat, sleep on the ground, drink their draught of wine, travel constantly, show in every farm-yard, and always have their arms crossed.

Rios: Why?

Solano: Because they never have a cloak to their backs. The *cambaleo* consists of a woman who sings and five men who lament; they have a comedia, two *autos,* three or four *entremeses,* a bundle of clothes which a spider could carry, and transport the woman now on their backs, now on a litter or hand-chair (*silla de manos*). They act in the farm-yards for a loaf of bread, a bunch of grapes, a stew of cabbage, and in the villages charge six maravedís, a piece of sausage, a task of flax, and anything else that happens along (not refusing the most worthless gift). They remain in one spot four to six days, hire a bed for the woman, and if any of the men be on good terms with the hostess, he gets a bundle of straw and a cover and sleeps in the kitchen, while in winter the straw-loft is his constant habitation. At noon they eat their beef-stew and each one six bowls of broth, all sitting at a table or sometimes on the bed. The woman distributes the food, shares out the bread and measures the watered wine, and each one wipes his hands wherever he can, for they have but one napkin amongst them, and the table-cloths are so shy that they do not cover the table by a foot. A *garnacha* consists of five or six men, a woman who plays first lady's rôles and a boy who plays the second; they carry a chest containing two smock-frocks, a coat, three pelisses, beards, wigs, and a woman's costume of taffeta (*tiritaña*). Their repertory consists of four comedias, three *autos* and as many *entremeses;* they carry the chest on a donkey's back and the woman, grumbling, on his rump, while the rest of the company follow afoot, driving the donkey. They remain eight days in a town, sleep four in a bed, eat a stew of beef and mutton, and some evenings a fricassee well seasoned. They get their wine in drams, their meat in ounces, their bread in pounds, and hunger by quarters [*arroba* = 11.5 kilos]. They give private perform-ances for a fried chicken, a boiled rabbit, four reals in money, two quarts of wine, and may be hired for a festival for twelve reals. In a *boxiganga* there are two women, a boy, and six or seven com-panions, and not seldom do they meet with vexations, for there is never lacking a fool, a bully, an impatient, an importunate, a sentimental, a jealous or a love-sick fellow, and having any one of these you can never travel with security, live contentedly, or even have much money. They are provided with six comedias, three or four *autos,* five *entremeses,* two chests—one containing the baggage of the company, the other the women's clothes. They hire four pack-mules—one for the chests, two for the women, and the other on which the men may alternate every quarter-league. They generally have two cloaks among the seven players, and with these they enter two by two, like the friars. Often, however, the mule-driver makes off with them, leaving the actors cloakless. Such players dine well; all sleep in four beds, perform by night and at festivals by day, and sup mostly on hash (*ensalada*), for, as they finish the comedia late, they always find a cold supper. While on the road they are fond of sleeping by the fireplaces, for perchance these may be hung with blood-puddings, chines, or sausages. These they enjoy with their eyes, touch with their fingers, and invite their friends, wrapping the sausages around their bodies, the blood-puddings around their thighs, and stowing away the chines, pigs' feet, chickens, and other trifles in holes in the yards or stables; and if they happen to be in a country inn, which is the safest, they mark the spot, so that they may know where the dead are buried. That sort of a *boxiganga* is dangerous, for it is more changeable than the moon and more unsafe than the border-land, unless it has a good head to rule it. The *farándula* is next to the company: it has three women, eight to ten comedias, two chests of luggage. The players travel on mules with drivers and sometimes in carts; visit the more important towns, dine separately wear good clothes, perform at Corpus festivals for 200 ducats, and live contentedly (that is, those who are not in love). . . . In the *companies* there is every kind of grub and trumpery; they know something of the seamy side and. also of good manners; there are very clever people among them, men much esteemed and persons well born, and even very respectable women (for where there are many there must be of all kinds). They take with them fifty comedias, three hundred quarters of luggage, sixteen persons who act, thirty who eat, one who takes the money at the door (and God knows what he steals). Some want mules, others coaches, some litters, others palfreys, and none there are who are satisfied with a cart, because they say that they have weak stomachs. Besides, there are generally many vexations. Their labor is excessive because of the great amount of study, the continuous rehearsals, and the varied tastes (though of this Rios and Ramirez know only too much), so that it is better to pass this in silence, for, in faith, much could be said on this subject.[1]

Despite the trivial details and the absence of much that would have been most desirable, this description of the various bands of strolling players by one of their number is so important that it could not be omitted here.

The traveling of theatrical companies at this time was necessarily slow. We have just seen from Rojas's description how the smaller bands of actors moved from place to place. The larger companies traveled with a little more convenience, still this was, after all, one of the greatest hardships they had to endure. We know the "strenuous life" some of them lead in our own day, when they leave the large cities and make "one-night stands" in the smaller towns, while the "barn-storming aggregations," which never remain more than a day or two in one place, suffer even greater trials. Yet one can easily imagine how much more laborious and toilsome must have been the life of an actor at this time, when the means of transportation were so primitive. Journeys which now, even on the Spanish railways, are traversed in a few hours, it then took as many days to accomplish.

Thus, in 1586, Nicolas de los Rios and Andrés de

---

[1] *Viage entretenido,* ed. of 1603, pp. 132–140. Other anecdotes illustrative of theatrical life in Spain may be found in Mateo Aleman's *Guzman de Alfarache,* Part II, Book I, chap. ii (ed. of Milan, 1615, p. 17), where a story is related concerning Cisneros and Manzanos, two well-known theatrical managers; also in the spurious second part of this work by Mateo

Vargas contracted to have their company, consisting of thirteen or fourteen persons and seventy quarters of baggage, transported from Madrid to Seville (a distance of about 270 miles) in thirteen days, at the rate of 38 reals for each person and 6 reals for each quarter of baggage.[1]

In 1610 certain carters of Illescas contracted with Alonso Riquelme to carry his company and their paraphernalia from that town to Aldea Gallega [near Lisbon, a distance of about 330 miles], at 70 reals for each person and 3 reals for each quarter of baggage, the carters agreeing to be in the said village within twenty-two days.[2] The costumes and properties were loaded on the backs of mules or upon carts, while the players also traveled in carts, or the larger companies in coaches. It appears from a document dated 1613, concerning the company of Antonio Granados, that a distinction was made between the *comediantes* and the *danzantes,* the former being carried in coaches and the latter in carts (*carros*).[3] Sometimes, in the case of distinguished players, another form of conveyance was especially stipulated, as in 1623, when the actor Juan Vazquez and Francisca de Torres, his wife, are to have three pack-animals (*tres caballerias iguales*), "for they are not to go upon the laden carts."[4]

How very expensive traveling was in these early days we also learn from an agreement made in 1630 by Francisco Moreno to furnish three mules (one with a saddle) for the journey which Antonia Manuela, wife of the *autor de comedias* Bartolomé Romero, made from Madrid to Seville, paying 100 reals for each mule and 100 reals to the mule-driver.[5] Sometimes, when a small town resolved to give a theatrical performance in connection with some church festival, it was especially stipulated that,

---

Lujan de Sayavedra, Book III, chapters vii and viii (*Bibl. de Autores Españoles,* Vol. III, pp. 418 ff.), where Guzman joins the company of Heredia.

[1] Pérez Pastor, *Nuevos Datos,* p. 17.
[2] *Ibid.,* p. 120. [3] *Ibid.,* p. 135. [4] *Ibid.,* p. 193. [5] *Ibid.,* p. 219.

in addition to the money, certain provisions were to be furnished to the actors, as when, in 1593, Gabriel Nuñez, *autor de comedias,* agreed to go to Navalcarnero (the little village where, more than half a century afterward, in 1649, Philip IV. married his second wife, Mariana of Austria) with his company to perform Lope de Vega's *Los Comendadores* and two other comedias for 300 reals, besides 24 *cuartales* [= 6 *fanegas* or about 10 bushels] of bread, 4 *arrobas* [=12 gallons] of white wine, 24 pounds of veal and 16 pounds of beef, a pig, a goose, two conies, and a hen, besides people to do the cooking, and free lodging.[1]

As early, at least, as 1602 some companies possessed such an extensive wardrobe that a particular person was charged with the care of it; with arrangements for traveling, etc. Thus we find Agustin Coronel, an actor, employed by Alonso Riquelme, *autor de comedias,* in March, 1602, to work in the company of the latter, "taking part in the comedias as well as in the *bayles,* and also to take care of the wardrobe and to arrange for the pack-animals and the traveling,"[2] etc.

Traveling in open carts in Spain in summer is not a very comfortable method of transportation, and at a later period we find covered carts especially provided for the players, as when, in 1633, five covered carts were furnished to the company of Fernan Sanchez de Vargas, to go from Madrid to the village of Parla.[3] In another case six carts, four of them covered, board, and lodging are to be provided for the company.[4] Sometimes a whole company traveled on mules, as in 1636, when Juan Rodriguez, an innkeeper, and Andres de Lobera, who hired out mules, agreed to furnish to Pedro de la Rosa, *autor de comedias,* thirty-three mules, with six drivers and a litter (for the

[1] Pérez Pastor, p. 37.
[2] *Ibid.,* p. 68.   [3] *Ibid.,* p. 233.   [4] *Ibid.,* p. 234.

autora Catalina de Nicolas, we presume), "to take the said *autor* and his company to the city of Segovia, the said *autor* paying 28 reals for each mule, including the drivers, and 50 reals for the litter." In this case the baggage was transported separately.[1] Indeed, Pedro de la Rosa seems to have furnished especial facilities for the traveling of his company, for on September 19, 1637, he provided "a coach with five mules to carry eight persons of his company from Madrid to Valencia for 660 reals."[2] And in 1638 the company of Luis Lopez, twenty in number, were conveyed in three "comfortable carts" (*carros bien acomodados*) from Guadalajara to Cuenca for 28 reals each.[3] A further conception of the expense of traveling may be formed from the fact that Antonio de Rueda, *autor de comedias*, in 1639 paid 850 reals each for four coaches to take his company from Madrid to Granada.[4]

Another hardship incident to the profession of acting was the unusual hour at which a performance was sometimes required to be given. In 1612 the company of Fernan Sanchez de Vargas was to take part in the Corpus festival in the town of Esquivias, and the agreement was that he should have his company in Esquivias on the Tuesday following Corpus at sunrise (*al salir del sol*), and on that day he was to represent in the morning the same *autos* that he had performed in Madrid, besides a comedia in the afternoon.[5] And in 1613 Pedro de Valdes was to have his company at Leganés on June 11 at six o'clock in the morning, to represent two *autos sacramentales* in the morning and a comedia in the afternoon, with all their *bayles* and *entremeses*.[6] Again, in March, 1617, Cristóbal de Leon, *autor de comedias*, agreed to represent two *autos*, with their *entremeses*, at the Corpus festival in Madrid, on Thursday, from two o'clock in the afternoon until twelve

---

[1] *Ibid.*, pp. 254-255. [2] *Ibid.*, p. 276. [3] *Ibid.*, p. 301.
[4] *Ibid.*, p. 316. [5] *Ibid.*, p. 127. [6] *Ibid.*, p. 134.

at night, and on Friday from six in the morning till noon, in such places as may be designated, for 600 ducats. "And if the court should be in Madrid, and it should be necessary to give more performances on Saturday, he is to receive the customary gratuity."[1] Indeed, the tribulations of the actor's life have probably not been overdrawn in the accounts that have come down to us. Rojas, who was for a time a *farandulero,* speaks with authority upon the subject, and to his narrative we now turn.

[1] Pérez Pastor, pp. 161, 162.

CHAPTER VIII

The actors. Their hardships. Alonso de Olmedo. Juan de Morales. Roque de Figueroa. Maria de Riquelme. *La Calderona.* Adventures of actors related in the *"Entertaining Journey."* The term *autor de comedias.* Relations of dramatist and manager. The stealing of plays. Honorarium of dramatists. Collaboration.

WHILE some conception of the hardships suffered by actors in Spain may be gained from what has been said in the previous chapter, we must turn once more to Agustin de Rojas for such a graphic description of the actor's trials and sufferings as we shall look for in vain elsewhere. Rojas speaks from experience, and let us hear what he says of the life of his fellow-players. "There is no negro in Spain or slave in Algiers but has a better life than the actor. A slave works all day, but he sleeps at night; he has only one or two masters to please, and when he does what he is commanded, he fulfils his duty. But actors are up at dawn and write and study from five o'clock till nine, and from nine till twelve they are constantly rehearsing. They dine and then go to the comedia; leave the theater at seven, and when they want rest they are called by the President of the Council, or the *alcaldes,* whom they must serve whenever it pleases them. I wonder how it is possible for them to study all their lives and be constantly on the road, for there is no labor that can equal theirs."[1] And Cervantes, who

[1] "Porque no hay negro en España,   El esclauo que es esclauo
   Ni esclavo en Argel se vende   quiero que trabaje siempre,
   Que no tenga mejor vida   por la mañana y la tarde,
   Que un farsante, si se aduierte   pero por la noche duerme.

doubtless knew them well, says this of actors: "Also I can say of them that in the sweat of their brows they gain their bread by insupportable toil, learning constantly by heart, leading a gipsy life perpetually from place to place, and from inn to tavern, staying awake to please others, for in other men's pleasure lies their profit; they have, besides, the merit that with their calling they deceive nobody, for continually they bring out their wares on the public square, submitting them to the judgment and inspection of everybody. The toil of the managers is incredible, and their anxiety extraordinary, and they need to gain much in order not to find themselves at the end of the year so embarrassed that it is needful for them to call a meeting of their creditors."[1]

But such recitals of the tribulations of the profession never did and never will deter others from joining their ranks. In all ages and in all countries[2] the mimic life of the stage has exercised a powerful attraction. And though no slave in Algiers, as Rojas says, had a harder lot than Spanish actors, their ranks were ever full, for generally they were a careless and shiftless lot, who took the days as they came, with little thought for the morrow. They

No tiene a quien contentar
  sino a un amo ò dos que tiene,
  y haziendo lo que le mandan
  ya cumple con lo que deue.
Pero estos representantes
  antes que Dios amanece,
  escriuiendo y estudiando,
  desde las cinco a las nueue.
Y de las nueue a las doze
  se estan ensayando siempre,
  comen, vanse a la comedia,
  y salen de alli a las siete.

Y quando han de descansar,
  los llaman al Presidente,
  los Oydores, los Alcaldes,
  los Fiscales, los Regentes,
Y a todos van a seruir
  a qualquier ora que quieren,
  que es esso ayre, yo me admiro
  como es possible que pueden
Estudiar toda su vida
  y andar caminando siempre,
  pues no ay trabajo en el mundo
  que puede ygualarse a este. . . ."
(*Viage entretenido*, pp. 368, 369.)

---

[1] *El Licenciado Vidriera*, in *Exemplary Novels*, translated by Maccoll, Glasgow, 1902, Vol. I, p. 191. See also Cervantes's comedia *Pedro de Urdemalas*, Act III, for a description of the qualifications of a good actor. (*Ocho Comedias*, etc., Madrid, 1615, fol. 217, verso.)

[2] In France the earliest contract with a professional actor that has been preserved is eloquent testimony to the wretched condition of wandering

were mostly drawn from the common people and were notorious for their loose manner of living, especially the women. To this statement, however, there were some notable exceptions, and occasionally we find a *hidalgo* or a person of the better class attracted to their number by the glamour of the stage. Among these was Alonso de Olmedo, afterward a distinguished actor and *autor de comedias*. He was born in Talavera de la Reina, the son of the *mayordomo* of the Count of Oropesa, and served the latter as a page. A theatrical company visiting his native town one day, he fell desperately in love with one of its members, Luisa de Robles. Olmedo joined the company in order to follow his *adorada,* but unfortunately the fair Luisa was married. However, fate decreed that her husband, Juan de la Abadia, should embark for Velez Malaga, when the vessel in which he sailed was attacked by Moors and sunk, and the captives taken to Barbary. Believing her husband dead, and presumably having no use for a dead husband, Luisa married Olmedo. Three years afterward, much to the surprise of both, probably, the husband, like another Enoch Arden, suddenly reappeared. Olmedo, much of whose former enthusiasm had doubtless cooled by this time—so we are told—with admirable resignation said to Luisa: "My dear, it is all over with our marriage; you take half of my wardrobe for your first husband, and half of the money and of the white linen for yourself, and good-by." And, as Sr. Sanchez-Arjona tells us, to console

players in that country. It antedates by a number of years the earliest Spanish document of a similar nature. It is dated 1545, and has already been referred to (p. 138). In it Marie Ferré (or Fairet) binds herself to perform in the troupe of Anthoine l'Espeyronnyère, in histories, farces, and somersaults, "en telle manière que chacun qui assistera prendra joyeuseté et recreation, pour gagner, amasser et lever deniers des personnes qui vouldront voir joer pour et au proffict dudict de l'Espeyronnyère," for which she is to receive, besides board and lodging, twelve livres Tournois [a very small sum], and if any one during the engagement should give her money or clothes, then "Gailharde, wife of the said l'Espeyronnyère, shall receive one half thereof." (Creizenach, *Geschichte des neueren Dramas*, Vol. III, p. 75.)

himself for his loss, he shortly afterward went to Zaragoza, where he married a daughter of the *mayordomo* of the Count of Sástago, named Jerónima [de Ornero], by whom he had six children.[1]

Thus runs the story. Unfortunately, however, facts have more recently come to light which cast some doubt upon the tale as just related. While it may be true in its main incidents, Luisa was certainly not the siren who first lured Olmedo upon the stage. In a petition to the town council of Seville in 1640,[2] Olmedo says that he had served the King at the Corpus festivals for forty years and that he had been director of a company for twenty-four years. This would place the beginning of his theatrical career in the year 1600, and his beginning as an *autor de comedias* in 1616. What we know of Luisa de Robles is briefly this: in June, 1618, she is described as the widow of Juan Labadia;[3] in September, 1623, she is called a single woman over twenty-five years old, and then belonged to Manuel Vallejo's company;[4] in 1624 she was in Antonio de Prado's company in Madrid, and in 1627 she and her husband, Juan de Labadia,[5] were in Manuel Simon's company in Seville. As Olmedo's wife Jerónima de Ornero and his daughter Maria were acting in his company in 1635, he playing old men's parts in his own company,[6] the episode related above must have taken place about 1618 or somewhat earlier. At this time, however, as we have seen, Olmedo had been upon the stage many years. Alonso de Olmedo was an *hidalgo,* and by a special decree of Philip IV., dated May 20, 1647, all the privileges of his rank were preserved to him, "although he had been an *autor de comedias.*" He died in 1651.

In 1630 Juan de Morales Medrano, one of the best-

---

[1] Sanchez-Arjona, *Anales del Teatro en Sevilla,* p. 223.
[2] *Ibid.,* p. 224.
[3] *Nuevos Datos,* p. 167.   [4] *Ibid.,* p. 201.
[5] The name is spelled in various ways; I have given it in each instance as I found it.   [6] Sanchez-Arjona, *Anales,* p. 297.

known actors and theatrical directors of his time, was sued for a debt of 1400 ducats, the balance of the purchase-money of a house in the Calle del Prado, as well as for the cost of improvements made on the said house. On notification to pay the debt under threat of arrest, he replied by claiming the privilege of *hidalguia,* having received a patent of nobility from the chancellery of Valladolid, by virtue of which "his person could not be taken for any debt unless it resulted from a crime, nor could his clothing or that of his wife, nor his arms or his horses, be attached, nor the other things which are reserved to *hijosdalgo.*"[1]

Roque de Figueroa was also a celebrated actor who had received a very careful education, and the story is related of him that on one occasion when a festival was to take place in the parish of San Sebastian in Madrid, an accident having happened to the preacher, Roque de Figueroa took off his sword, ascended the pulpit, and delivered an oration in Latin, much to the surprise of all present.[2]

Among actresses the famous Maria de Riquelme was no less noted for her beauty than for her virtuous and exemplary life. She was the wife of the *autor de comedias* Manuel Vallejo, upon whose death, in 1644, she abandoned the stage and devoted herself to religion, dying in Barcelona in 1656.[3]

Quite different had been the life of the celebrated Maria

[1] Pérez Pastor, *Nuevos Datos,* p. 239.
[2] Sanchez-Arjona, *Anales,* p. 254.
[3] Maria de Riquelme was the second wife of Manuel Vallejo, and must have married him after November 21, 1627, for on that date Francisca Maria, Vallejo's first wife, died. (See *Bulletin Hispanique* (1908), p. 255.) In April, 1631, Maria de Riquelme was in Vallejo's company and is called his wife. (Cotarelo, *Tirso,* p. 220.) She appeared as Casandra in Lope de Vega's *El Castigo sin Venganza* as it was performed before the King on February 3, 1632, by the company of Manuel Vallejo, who played the part of the Duke of Ferrara. (See my *Life of Lope de Vega,* Glasgow, 1904, pp. 340, n., *et passim.*) In a letter dated September 4, 1633, Lope de Vega says of her: "She is extraordinary in depicting passion in a way that imitates nobody, nor can any one be found to imitate her." (*Ibid.,* p. 350.) Caramuel says of her: "era tan impresionable por naturaleza, que, con asombro de todos, mudaba representando el color de su rostro, de-

Calderon, though it ended also in religious devotion. *La Calderona*, as she was called, was one of the many favorites of Philip the Fourth and the mother of his son Don John of Austria, born April 17, 1629. After a far from exemplary life she professed in the convent of Villahermoso, in the province of Guadalajara, where, "esteemed by the whole community, she was made abbess, and repenting of her past errors, there are those who declare she died in the odor of sanctity."[1]

The Spanish stage of this period, it is to be feared, could boast of few such exemplars of womanly virtue as Maria de Riquelme. But it would be most uncharitable to condemn all actresses on the evidence that we have concerning some of them. Still, in all probability, such incidents as the one related in a previous chapter concerning Jacinta Herbias and Ana de Espinosa were not rare. Indeed, as we shall see, the conditions of the Spanish stage, the publicity of the green-rooms, etc., rendered it almost impossible for a decent woman to remain upon the boards. Actors were mostly a shiftless lot recruited from the understrata of society, of whose free and easy lives we get many a glimpse in the work of Rojas, already cited. They were much addicted to gambling, and the following narrative, related

mostrando sus facciones la alegría, si su papel lo demandaba, ó la tristeza más profunda en los pasos patéticos, y figurando los afectos más opuestos en sus más rapidas transiciones de tal modo que era inimitable y única en este género de mímica." (Quoted by Sanchez-Arjona, *Anales*, p. 318.) It may be added that Maria de Riquelme's name does not occur among the players of Vallejo's company in 1643, when he represented *autos* in Seville. (*Ibid.*, p. 366.)

[1] Sanchez-Arjona, *Anales*, p. 286. See also an excellent work, Hume, *The Court of Philip IV.*, London, 1907, who characterizes Philip as: "Weak of will, tender of conscience, sensitive of soul. A rake without conviction, a voluptuary who sought sensuous pleasures from vicious habit long after they had ceased to be pleasures to him, and yet expiated them with agonies of remorse which made his soul a raging hell" (p. 171). Hume says: "It was in the *Corral de la Cruz* in 1627 that Philip first set eyes upon the girl whom one of Olivares's agents had sent from the country to act upon the Madrid stage. Her name was Maria Calderon, and at the time she appeared in the capital she was not more than sixteen years of age. She was no great beauty, but her grace and fascination were

by the actor Ramirez, occurs in the *Viage entretenido* (p. 141): "I recall a witty story which happened about four years ago to Alcaraz [a theatrical manager] concerning one of Cisneros's musicians, who, gambling with another actor in the green-room (*vestuario*), lost even the clothes on his back, so that he was left with nothing but his linen breeches. His turn came to sing in the third act. Snatching up quickly a cloak which did not belong to him and wrapping it about him under his arms, he sallied forth upon the stage with the greatest unconcern. Alcaraz, observing this shameless effrontery, determined that it should not go unpunished, and, taking a pin, fastened the cloak up as high as he could. The player, ignorant of what had happened, began to sing in this fashion, while the audience shouted. Nor did he learn the cause of the merriment until, withdrawing quite ashamed, he became aware of the joke that had been played upon him when he saw his whole shirt hanging out." Rios also tells the story of a companion of his in Antequera, who, one night, had lost everything he had, so that he was obliged to remain in bed until a suit of clothes was sent him with which to go to the theater, and that night he had to go home again and remain in bed.[1]

---

supreme, and her voice was so sweet and her speech so captivating that Madrid fell in love with her at once." (*Ibid.*, p. 208.) *La Calderona* did not, however, retire from the stage on the birth of her son Don John of Austria. What we know of her stage life is this: In March, 1623, she was the wife of Pablo Sarmiento and both were acting in the company of Juan Bautista Valenciano. (*Bull. Hispanique* (1908), p. 248.) In 1624 she appeared in Lope de Vega's *El Poder en el Discreto,* and in 1626 she played the part of Fenis in Lope's *Amor con vista.* When she was again married we do not know, but in 1632 her husband was Tomas de Rojas, and in this year she received 1050 reals for acting in two comedias and two *autos* in the village of Pinto, besides transportation for herself, her husband and maid, lodging and eight reals maintenance for every day she was on the journey. (Pérez Pastor, *Nuevos Datos,* p. 226.) She took part in the Corpus festival of the same year at Seville, leaving the company of Juan Jerónimo Valenciano, of which she was then a member, for this purpose. (Sanchez-Arjona, *Anales,* p. 285.) We do not know when she retired from the stage.

[1] *Viage entretenido,* p. 143.

A number of ludicrous adventures of actors are related by the same author, of which one may find a place here:

We left Valencia on account of a misfortune that befell us— Solano and I—one on foot and without a cloak, and the other walking and with only his doublet. We gave them to a boy who got lost in the town, and we were left gentlemen of the road. At night we arrived at a village, worn out and with only eight quartos between us. Without supper (*sin las assaduras*), we went to an inn to ask for lodging, but they told us that they could not provide for us, nor could a lodging be found anywhere, because a fair was being held. Seeing the little chance there was of our finding a lodging, I resorted to a stratagem. I went to another inn and represented myself as a West Indian merchant (for you see I resemble one in the face). The hostess asked whether we had any pack-animals. I replied that we came in a cart and that, while it was coming with our goods, she should prepare two beds for us and some supper. She did so, and I went to the *alcalde* of the village and told him that a company of players had arrived, on their way through, and asked his permission to give a play. He inquired whether it was a religious play, to which I answered in the affirmative. Permission being granted, I returned to the inn and advised Solano to review the *auto* of "Cain and Abel," and then go to a certain place to collect the money, for we were going to play that evening. Meanwhile I went to hunt up a drum, made a beard out of a piece of sheepskin, and went through the whole village proclaiming our comedia. As there were many people in the place, we had a large audience. This done, I put by the drum, took off my beard, returned to the hostess, and told her that my goods were coming and asked her for the key of my room, as I wanted to lock them up. To her question what they were, I replied spices (*especeria*). She gave me the key, and hastening to the room, I stripped the sheets from the bed, took down some old gilt leather hangings and two or three old cloths, and in order that she might not see me descend the stairs, I made up a bundle, threw it out of the window, and came down the stair like a flash. As I reached the yard, the host called me and said: "Mr. Indian, do you want to see a comedia by some strolling players who arrived a short time ago? It is a very good one." I answered, "Yes," and hurried out to hunt up the bundle of clothes with which we were to play the farce, anxious lest the host should see it; but, though I searched everywhere, I could not find it. Seeing the misfortune which faced me, and that my back might suffer for it, I ran to the place (*hermita*) where Solano was busy taking the money and told him what had happened. He stopped "gathering," and we left with what he had collected. Consider now the plight of all these people! Some without merchants or bedclothes, the others deceived and without a comedia! That night we traveled but little and that on the by-paths. In the morning we took account of our finances and found we had three and a half reals, all in small coppers. As you see, we were now rich, but not a little timid, when, about a league off, we discovered a hut, and, arriving there, we were received with wine in a gourd, milk in a trough, and bread in a saddle-bag. We breakfasted and left that night for another town, where we directly took steps to get something to eat. I requested permission [to perform], sought out two bed-sheets, proclaimed the eclogue through the streets, procured a guitar, invited the hostess, and told Solano to collect the money. Finally, the house being full, I came out to sing the ballad, *Afuera, afuera, aparta, aparta.*[1] Having finished a couplet, I could go no further, and the audience gazed in astonishment. Then Solano began a *loa* with which he made some amends for the lack of music. I wrapped one of the sheets about me and began my part, but when Solano appeared as God the Father, with a candle in his hand and likewise enveloped in a sheet, open in the middle, and besmeared all around his beard with grape-skins, I thought I should die for laughter, while the poor public (*vulgo*) wondered what had happened to him. This being over, I appeared as a fool and recited my *entremes,* then continued with the *auto,* and the point arrived when I was to kill the unhappy Abel; but I had forgotten the knife with which I was to cut his throat, so, tearing off my false beard, I cut his throat with *it.* Hereupon the mob arose and shouted. I begged them to pardon our shortcomings, as the company had not yet arrived. At last, with all the people in an uproar, the host came in and told us that we had better get out, and thus avoid a sound drubbing. Upon this good advice we put distance between us, and that same night we left with more than

[1] A Moorish ballad printed in the *Romancero General*, Madrid, 1604, fol. 25.

five reals which we had taken in. After we had spent this money and had sold what few effects we had, eating often only the fungi which we gathered on the road, sleeping on the ground, walking barefoot (not on account of the mud, but because we had no shoes), helping the mule-drivers to load their animals or fetching water for them, and living more than four days on turnips, we arrived timidly one night at an inn, where four drivers, who were stopping for the night, gave us twenty maravedís and a blood-pudding (morcilla) to play a comedia for them. After this hardship and misery we reached the end of our journey, Solano in doublet, without *ropilla*[1] (which he had pawned at a tavern), and I bare-legged and shirtless; with a large straw hat full of air-holes, dirty linen breeches, and jacket torn and threadbare. Thus ragged, I determined to enter the service of a pastry-cook, but Solano being a shrewd fellow, did not take to any work, and this was the state of things when, one day, we heard a drum beat and a boy announced the excellent comedia *Los Amigos trocados,* to be performed that night in the town hall. When I heard this my eyes began to open. We spoke to the boy, and, recognizing us, he dropped the drum and began to dance for joy. We asked him whether he had any small coin about him, and he took out what he had, which was tied up in the end of his shirt. We bought some bread and cheese and a slice of codfish, and after our repast he took us to the *autor* (who was Martinazos). I don't know whether it grieved him to see us so ragged, but finally he embraced us, and after we had related all our hardships to him, we dined, and he bade us rid ourselves of our fleas, so that they might not cling to the costumes, for we were to act in the comedia. That night, in fact, we took part, and the next day he made an agreement with us to act in his company, each one to receive three quartillos [= three fourths of a real] for each representation. He now gave me a part to study in the comedia "The Resurrection of Lazarus," and to Solano the rôle of the resurrected saint. Every time the comedia was played the *autor* took off a garment in the dressing-room and loaned it to Solano, charging him especially to let no fleas get into it. When the play was ended he returned to the dressing-room, took off the costume, and donned his old clothes. To me he gave stock-

---

[1] A close-fitting unbuttoned tunic reaching to the thighs, with open sleeves hanging from the shoulder. (Hume, *Philip IV.,* p. 447.)

ings, shoes, a hat with plumes, and a long silk coat (*sayo*), beneath which I wore my linen breeches (which had been washed in the meanwhile), and thus, as I am such a handsome fellow, I came on the stage like a gewgaw (*brinquiño*) with my broad beaming face. We continued this happy life for more than four weeks, eating little, traveling much, with the theatrical baggage on our backs, and without ever making the acquaintance of a bed. Going in this way from one village to another, it happened to rain a good deal one night, so, on the next day, the director told us—as it was only a short league to where we were going—to make a litter of our hands and carry his wife, while he and the other two men would carry the baggage of the company, the boy taking the drum and the other odds and ends. The woman being quite satisfied, we made a litter with our hands, and she wearing a beard,[1] we began our journey. In this way we reached our destination, completely worn out, foot-sore and covered with mud; indeed, we were half dead, for we were serving as pack-mules. Arrived in the village, the director immediately requested permission to play, and we acted the farce of "Lazarus." My friend and I put on our borrowed clothes, but when we arrived at the passage concerning the sepulcher, the director, who took the part of Christ, said several times to Lazarus, "Arise, Lazarus! *surge! surge!*" and seeing that he did not arise, he approached the sepulcher, believing that he had fallen asleep. He found, however, that Lazarus had arisen, body and soul, without leaving a trace of the clothes behind. Not finding the saint, the people were aroused, and it seeming that a miracle had taken place, the director was much astonished. Seeing the fix we were in, and that Solano had left without informing me, I took the road to Zaragoza, without, however, finding any trace of Solano, nor the director of his clothes, nor the spectators of Lazarus, who, they doubtless thought, had ascended to heaven. I then joined a good company and gave up that toilsome life.[2]

As already observed, the earliest theatrical managers in Spain also frequently wrote the pieces played by their companies, hence the name *autor,* which was originally applied

---

[1] Rojas explains that a beard and sometimes a small mask was worn as a protection to the complexion.

[2] *Viage entretenido*, Madrid, 1603, pp. 91–101.

to them and which afterward merely designated the chief
or director of a company, whether he wrote plays or not.
A manager who could not write comedias for his company
naturally cast about him for some one who could provide
them, and hence at an early period we find men traveling
with companies of players whose office it was to furnish
comedias.   In France at this time we find Alexandre
Hardy, and in England many playwrights wrote for Henslowe's and other companies.   Sometimes these dramatists
were also professional actors; but of this class Spain has
no names among its actor-authors that will even remotely
compare with Shakespeare or Molière.[1]   Its greatest
dramatists were churchmen, not players.   Indeed, among
the great Spanish dramatic authors only one, Alarcon, was
not a member of the priesthood.   Of actors who were also
playwrights the best-known names in Spain are Lope de
Rueda, Juan de Villegas, and Andres de Claramonte.[2]
In 1589, when Lope de Vega had been writing for the
public stage at least three or four years, we find Alonso del
Castillo, an actor, making an agreement with Gaspar de
Porres, a theatrical manager, to work in the company of
the latter from December 1, 1589, till Shrovetide of 1591,
"and the said Alonso del Castillo is to furnish to the said
Gaspar de Porres nine comedias composed by him, and
amongst them he is to give him the comedia *Las Escuelas*

---

[1] "Son nom de théâtre [Molière] paraît pour la première fois dans l'acte
du 28 Juin, 1644, par lequel Daniel Mallet, danseur de Rouen, s'engage
à servir la troupe 'tant en comédie que ballets,'" etc. (Soulié, *Recherches
sur Molière,* Paris, 1863, p. 38.) It is possible that Molière may have seen
the performances of the company of Spanish players headed by Pedro de la
Rosa, which made a tour through France in 1643, and which visited Paris
in that year. (Sanchez-Arjona, *Anales,* p. 329.) Rosa again returned to
Paris in 1674. Sebastian de Prado was also in the French capital with his
company in 1660, on the occasion of the marriage of Louis XIV. to Maria
Teresa, daughter of Philip IV. (*Ibid.,* p. 342.) Molière certainly saw
the latter company, for in the *Registre de La Grange,* p. 22, after
"Dimanche 11me Juillet, 1660," we read: "Il vint en ces tems vne Troupe
de Comediens Espagnolz qui joua 3 fois à Bourbon: vne fois à demye pist,
la seconde fois à vn escu, et la 3me fois fist vn four."

[2] Alonso de la Vega, a contemporary of Lope de Rueda, and also an

de Athenas, which he is now writing, and he is to give them to no other person, until the four years be past which begin with Shrovetide of 1591. He is to receive five and a half reals for acting and maintenance every day that he may be in the company before he has delivered the said comedia. On account of the said comedias and representations Gaspar de Porres will give him food and drink and clean linen or two and a half reals per day, and is to furnish him transportation and besides 3200 reals," paying 200 reals on account in cash.[1]

This remuneration for acting was by no means liberal. Castillo could certainly not live extravagantly even in those days on two and a half reals per day, the usual smallest allowance being three reals, and when we consider that Solano, an actor, in 1595 received 3000 reals per year, it is likely that Castillo's histrionic ability was not of a very high order. Unfortunately, we are unable to judge of his merits as a playwright, as neither his *Escuelas de Athenas* nor any other play of his has survived, so far as I know. On the other hand, 3200 reals for nine comedias by an author of no more reputation than Castillo was rather liberal, when we remember that Lope de Vega, some years after this, received only 500 reals for a comedia.

It is probable that the more important theatrical companies always contained some one capable of patching up or remodeling a play to suit the exigencies of the occasion, and while but few cases are cited of Spanish

actor, was the author of three plays, which were first published at Valencia in 1566. On the title-page he is called "illustre poeta y gracioso representante." He was a Sevillan by birth and took part in the Corpus festival in that city in 1560. His plays have been republished by Sr. Menéndez y Pelayo, Dresden, 1905. Andres de la Vega, a well-known *autor de comedias* more than half a century later, was the author of a comedia entitled *San Carlos,* a manuscript of which, dated at Madrid, March 21, 1642, is now in the Biblioteca Nacional. (Paz y Melia, *Catálogo de Comedias manuscritas,* No. 3010.)

[1] Pérez Pastor, *Nuevos Datos,* p. 25. Lope de Vega had written a number of comedias for Gaspar de Porres prior to this time. See my *Life of Lope de Vega,* p. 38.

actors who could also perform this function, we learn that
Pedro de Pernia, an actor in the company of Roque de
Figueroa, could, in case of accident, furnish twelve to
sixteen columns on short notice.[1]

As regards the relations between the dramatists and the
managers of companies, it depended entirely upon whether
the author was one of the well-known and recognized playwrights or whether he was an obscure poet struggling for
recognition. In the former case there was frequently great
rivalry among the *autores de comedias* to secure the latest
plays. Lope de Vega, because of some real or fancied
affront, had at one time (1614) refused to write any comedias for Hernan Sanchez de Vargas, one of the best-known
actors and *autores* of the time, while he greatly favored
Alonso de Riquelme, whom he then provided with comedias. Sanchez even appealed to Lope's patron, the Duke
of Sessa, to aid him in conciliating Lope, while the latter
persisted in his refusal, alleging that Sanchez had all the
poets of Andalusia, including Luis Velez de Guevara, to
write for him, while no poet would furnish comedias to
Riquelme, on account of the latter's friendship for Lope.[2]
On the other hand, the nascent, struggling poet was frequently treated with great severity by the actors and was
often subjected to the greatest indignities by both managers
and players. Cervantes, who knew the theater well and
who would doubtless have preferred to be one of the
playwrights idolized by the mob, than be the author of

[1] In an *entremes* written by Quiñones de Benavente and performed in
Madrid by the company of Figueroa in 1628 (?), we read:

"(*Sale Pernia.*)
¿No es Pernia éste que sale,
Que representa, que bayla,
Que hace versos, que remedia,
Si sucede una desgracia,
Doce ó diez y seis colunas
De la noche á la mañana?"
(*Entremeses*, ed. Rosell, Madrid, 1872, Vol. I, p. 167.)

See also the story related by Quevedo, *Vida del gran Tacaño*, cap. xxii.
[2] Rennert, *Life of Lope de Vega*, Glasgow, 1904, p. 222.

Don Quixote, tells a story of one of these poetasters in the *Coloquio de los Perros:* "Gradually we arrived at the house of a manager of plays, who, as far as I recollect, was called Angulo the Bad, to distinguish him from another Angulo, not a manager but an actor, the best comedian that plays then had and now have. All the company was assembled to hear the play of my master, . . . and, in the middle of the first act, one by one and two by two they all went out and departed, except the manager and me, who served for listeners. The play was such that, although I was an ass in the matter of poetry, it seemed to me that Satan himself had composed it for the total ruin of the said poet, who was already beginning to feel uneasy as he saw the solitude in which his audience had left him, and it was no wonder that his prophetic soul told him within of the calamity that was threatening him, which was the return of all the actors, who were more than twelve, and who, without uttering a word, laid hold of my poet; and if it had not been that the authority of the manager, full of entreaties and protests, interfered, without doubt they would have blanketed him. I was in consternation at the result, the manager disgusted, the players cheerful, and the poet fretful. With much patience, although his face was somewhat contorted, he took his play and put it in his bosom, while, muttering, he remarked, 'It is not good to cast pearls before swine,' and without saying a word more he quietly went off." [1]

But if the better-known playwrights were not subjected to personal insult, they nevertheless frequently suffered in their reputations at the hands of unscrupulous theatrical directors. Even the greatest of them all, Lope de Vega, frequently complains of his treatment by them. In the dedication of his comedia *Los Muertos vivos* [2] to the

---

[1] *Exemplary Novels,* translated by N. Maccoll, Glasgow, 1902, Vol. II, p. 202. See also Castillo Solórzano, *Aventuras del Bachiller Trapaza,* chap. xv, ed. of Madrid, 1905 (La Enciclopedia Moderna), pp. 234 ff., and *La Garduña de Sevilla,* near the end.

[2] Printed in Part XVII of his *Comedias,* Madrid, 1621.

dramatic poet Salucio del Poyo, Lope expresses himself concerning the dishonest practices of theatrical managers. After alluding in very flattering phrases to the fame acquired by Poyo, he says that this is, in another sense, a misfortune for the dramatist, "as, on account of the good reputation which you have in this capital, the theatrical managers, when they have any comedia whatever with the author of which they are not satisfied, adorn their placards with your name, and since most of these comedias, being written by some ignorant fellow, are detestable, you would lose much reputation among those who know, if the injury and its discovery did not reach those who esteem you at the same time." He adds that "a poor comedia, after it has run the gauntlet of villages, servants, and men who live by stealing them and adding to them, is so disfigured as to be scarcely recognizable."[1]

But the dramatist had other difficulties to contend with besides the unscrupulousness of theatrical directors; I allude to the dishonest practices of booksellers who issued pirated editions of the comedias, to the great detriment of the poet's reputation.[2] That the playwright suffered any financial loss through these fraudulent versions issued by the booksellers is not very likely, for the plays were sold by their authors to the managers of companies, except perhaps in the rare cases of playwrights like Andres de Claramonte and Juan de Villegas, who were also actors and

---

[1] *Life of Lope de Vega*, pp. 293, 294. See also the Prologue to Lope's Part XVII (*ibid.*, p. 291), in which he complains bitterly of the tricks and deceptions of booksellers and theatrical managers.

[2] Lope de Vega, as is well known, complained of the piratical booksellers in his *Peregrino* (1604) and lastly in his *Dorotea* (1632). (See my *Life of Lope de Vega*, pp. 156, 344.) So Montalvan in the *Prologo* to the first volume of his *Comedias*, Madrid, 1635, is especially bitter against the booksellers of Seville, "*donde no ay libro ageno que no se imprima,*" and says that they cut the comedias down to four *pliegos* although eight may be necessary, and that they issue from the press full of errors, barbarisms, lies, and nonsense. Calderon also frequently deplores their practices. It is a curious fact that a comedia of Lope, *Sin Secreto no ay Amor,* circulated as a *suelta* under the name of Montalvan, a disciple of Lope.

directed their own companies. Having bought a play
from its author, it was of course to the interest of the purchasing manager to prevent its appearing in print and thus
becoming common property. Besides, plays were often
acquired surreptitiously by some individual possessing a
good memory, who visited the theater and noted down what
he could, filling in the rest from memory or *de su cosecha,*
and then disposing of them to some bookseller or theatrical
manager. Lope de Vega alludes with bitterness to the
pirated versions of his plays as early as 1603, in the Prologue to *El Peregrino en su Patria,* and frequently thereafter, notably in 1620 in the Prologue to Part XIII of his
Comedias. He says: " . . . To this must be added the
stealing of comedias by those whom the vulgar call, the one
Memorilla, and the other *Gran Memoria,* who, with the
few verses which they learn, mingle an infinity of their own
barbarous lines, whereby they earn a living, selling them
to the villages and to distant theatrical managers; base
people these, without a calling, and many of whom have
been jail-birds. I should like to rid myself of the care of
publishing these plays, but I cannot, for they print them
with my name while they are the work of the pseudo-poets
of whom I have spoken. Receive then, Reader, this Part,
corrected as well as it was possible to do it, and with my
good will, for the only interest it has is that you may read
these comedias with less errors, and that you may not
believe that there is any one in the world who can note
down a comedia from memory, on seeing it represented;
and if there were such a person I should praise him and
esteem him as standing alone with this power, even though
he should lack understanding, for seldom are they found
together, as philosophers declare and as experience con-
firms."[1]

A curious instance of this filching of plays, of which he
was an eye-witness, is related by Suarez de Figueroa:

[1] *Life of Lope de Vega,* p. 272.

"There is at present in Madrid a young man of remarkable memory, named Luis Remirez de Arellano, a native of Villaescusa de Haro and the son of noble parents. This person takes from memory an entire comedia on hearing it three times, without the slightest variation either in plot or verses. The first day he devotes to the general disposition of the plot, the second to the variety of the composition, and the third to the exactness of the verses. In this manner he commits to memory any comedia he desires. He thus noted down in particular *La Dama Boba, El Principe perfeto,* and *La Arcadia* [all comedias by Lope de Vega], besides others. Being present on one occasion, listening to *El Galan de la Membrilla* [also by Lope], which was being represented by the company of Sanchez, the latter began to interrupt the argument and cut short the speeches so obviously that, being questioned as to the cause of this hastening and mutilation of the play, he replied publicly that some one was present in the audience (and he pointed him out) who in three days took down from memory any comedia, and that he recited the comedia thus badly for fear that he might wrongfully get possession of it. Hereupon there was great excitement among the auditors, who requested that the play be stopped until Luis Remirez left the theater."[1]

[1] *Plaza universal de todas Ciencias y Artes,* Perpiñan, 1630, pp. 254, 255. Espinel had mentioned this Remirez years before, in his *Marcos de Obregon,* ed. of Barcelona, 1618, fol. 240, where he says: "There, is a young man in Madrid named Luys Remirez, who, on seeing any comedia represented, can go home and write down the whole of it without missing a letter or mistaking a verse." This Luis Ramirez was also a poet. Montalvan says of him: "Luis Ramirez, Poeta elegante, vizarro, y conceptuoso con muchisimo estremo, y de tan rara y prodigiosa memoria, que de oir una o dos vezes una comedia, la repite toda entera, cosa que no se ha contado jamas de ningun antiguo, ni moderno." (*Para Todos,* Madrid, 1645, Prologue; see also *ibid.,* fol. 273, verso. On the stealing of Montalvan's plays, see *ibid.,* Prologue.) Malone, *Historical Account of the English Stage,* Basil, 1801, p. 156, remarks: "It was a common practice to carry table-books to the theater, and either from curiosity, or enmity to the author, or some other motive, to write down passages of the play that was represented; and there is reason to believe that the imperfect and mutilated

As to the *honorarium* received by dramatic poets, it of course varied greatly, depending upon the popularity and reputation of the writer. Moreover, about the middle of the seventeenth century comedias commanded a much higher price than was paid for them at the beginning of that period. This, however, is doubtless due in no small measure to the great depreciation in the value of money during the reign of Philip the Fourth. In 1601 Lope de Vega, then the undisputed ruler of the Spanish stage, received 500 reals for his comedia *La hermosa Alfreda,* and we may assume that this was the customary sum paid to the most prominent playwrights at this time and for some years thereafter, while the average sum received by Lope for an *auto* was 300 reals.[1] In 1625 Pedro de Valdes, a theatrical manager, paid 460 reals for Guillen de Castro's *Las Maravillas de Babilonia,*[2] in 1627 Andres de la Vega sold to Hernan Sanchez de Vargas eight comedias for 3600 reals,[3] and in 1633 the dramatist Don Rodrigo de Herrera sold to Juan Martinez, theatrical manager, his comedia *Castigar por Defender* for 700 reals "vellon,"[4] and the same poet, in his last will and testament, dated at Madrid, December 14, 1657, declared that 600 reals were

---

copies of one or two of Shakespeare's dramas, which are yet extant, were taken down by the ear or in shorthand during the exhibition."

[1] As we shall see hereafter, four *autos sacramentales* were represented annually in Madrid at the festival of Corpus Christi. Lope's services were also greatly in demand for this species of dramatic composition, and in 1608 he wrote the four *autos* represented at Madrid in that year. They were: *El Adulterio de la Esposa, El Caballero del Fenix, Los Casamientos de Joseph,* and *La Niñez de Cristo.* (Pérez Pastor, *Bull. Hispanique* (1907), p. 374.) In 1611 Lope de Vega received 1200 reals for the four *autos* which he wrote for the Corpus festival at Seville of that year. (Sanchez-Arjona, *Anales,* p. 149.) Calderon, Spain's religious poet *par excellence,* received much larger sums after the middle of the seventeenth century for his *autos.* (See below, pp. 320, 321.)

[2] Pérez Pastor, *Nuevos Datos,* p. 209.

[3] *Ibid.,* p. 213. It is probable that in these instances a larger sum had been paid for these comedias originally, inasmuch as when these sales took place the plays had already been acted upon the stage, and it was the *new* comedia which was always in greatest demand.

[4] *Ibid.,* p. 232.

still due him for his comedia *Lo Cauteloso de un Guante y Confusion de un Papel,* for which he had received 200 reals on account, as 800 reals was the sum that he had received for the other comedias he had written.[1]

Concerning the honorarium received by English playwrights in the time of Shakespeare, it seems to have been greater than the sums paid Spanish poets, when the relative reputations of the writers are considered. Malone says: "The customary price of the copy of a play in the time of Shakespeare appears to have been twenty nobles or six pounds thirteen shillings and fourpence."[2] In some cases it seems that the poet received the profits of the second or third performance of his play. The same writer says: "From D'Avenant, indeed, we learn that in the latter part of the reign of Queen Elizabeth the poet had his benefit on the second day. As it was the general practice in the time of Shakespeare to sell the copy of the play to the theater, I imagine, in such cases, an author derived no other advantage from his piece than what arose from the sale of it. Sometimes, however, he found it more beneficial to retain the copyright in his own hands; and when he did so, I suppose he had a benefit. It is certain that the giving authors the profits of the third exhibition of their play, which seems to have been the usual mode during a great part of the seventeenth century, was an established custom in the year 1612, for Dekker, in the prologue to one of his comedies, printed in that year, speaks of the poet's *third day.*"[3] He further adds: "When an author sold his piece

---

[1] Pérez Pastor, *Bibliografía Madrileña,* Part III, Madrid, 1907, p. 386.

[2] *Historical Account of the English Stage,* Basil, 1800, p. 178.

[3] *Ibid.,* pp. 172, 173. *Henslowe's Diary* gives the most authentic information concerning the sums received by playwrights for their pieces. In 1598 Michael Drayton received £6 for the play of *William Longsword.* The entry is as follows: "I receued forty shillings of m[r] Phillip Hinslowe in part of vi[ll] for the playe of Willm longsword to be deliu[r]d p[r]sent w[th] 2 or three dayes the xxi[th] of January | 1598 |. Mih Drayton." (*Henslowe's Diary,* ed. Greg, Part I, 1904, p. 59.) In 1598 Anthony Munday received £5 for *Robin Hood:* "Layd owt unto antony monday the 15 of febreary 1598 for a playe boocke called the firste parte of Robyne hoode, v[ll]."

to the sharers or proprietors of a theater, it could not be performed by any other company, and remained for several years unpublished; when that was not the case, he printed it for sale, to which many seem to have been in-

(*Ibid.*, p. 83.) The same amount was paid for the second part of *Robin Hood*, which seems to have been written by Munday, Chettle, and Shaw (*ibid.*, p. 84), while Drayton, Dekker, and Chettle received £4 5s. for "the famos wares of henry the fyrste & the prynce of walles" (*ibid.*, p. 85), though a payment on account may have been previously made. Again, in 1598, Drayton, Dekker, Chettle, and Wilson received £6 "for the boocke of goodwine & his iii sonnes" (*ibid.*, p. 85), and Richard Hathwaye received £5 for "his boocke of kynge arthore" (*ibid.*, pp. 86, 87). In 1599 Dekker received £6 for his *History of Fortunatus* (*ibid.*, pp. 114, 115), and in 1601 he was paid the same sum for *Kynge Sebastian of portyngall*, while in 1602 Thomas Haywood received £6 for *A Woman killed with Kindness* (*ibid.*, p. 189), so that £6 seems to have been the usual price for a play at the beginning of the seventeenth century. The following lucid statement of the matter is given by Greg (*Henslowe's Diary*, II, p. 126): "For the earlier period, that is, down to 1597, we entirely lack evidence upon the subject, and in the absence of any reasonable basis, conjecture would be worse than useless. From the end of 1597 onward, we have, on the contrary, very full evidence, which shows that the sums paid to authors were gradually rising. This was only part of the general rise in prices during this period, due to the steady depreciation of money consequent upon the continued influx of the precious metals from the New World. The earliest play for which we have complete records is *Mother Redcap*, for which Drayton and Munday received £6 in full. This appears to have been the usual sum, though it is probable that in some cases not more than £5 was given, as for each part of *Robin Hood*. The first part of *Black Baldman* was bought for £7, but for Part II the authors only got the usual sum of £6. This continued the standard for a long time, with occasional variations of £5 on the one hand and £7 on the other. We suddenly find Chapman receiving £8.10 for his *World runs on Wheels*, though this may possibly include a payment for another piece. Chapman appears, however, to have commanded prices rather above the average, and Dekker and Jonson received £8 for *Page of Plymouth*. Prices now begin to fluctuate considerably. Day and Haughton only get £5 for *Cox of Collumpton* and *Thomas Merry*, respectively, but the authors of *Sir John Oldcastle* get £7 for each part, besides a bonus of 10s. on the occasion of the first performance, and Wilson £8 for *2 Henry Richmond*, a play of which the first part is not recorded. The highest price entered [in the *Diary*] also appears about this time, namely, the £10 paid for *Patient Grissel* (Dekker). It is, however, pretty certain that, though the company authorized the expenditure of sums amounting to this total, the authors did not really get them, but only £6 most likely. The prices drop again, moreover, to something between £5 and £7 till about May, 1602, when £8 begins to be a not infrequent price. This sum was obtained by the six or more playwrights concerned in *Cæsar's Fall* and the three who sufficed to compose *Merry as may be* for court. The prices paid by Worcester's men are exactly the same, and it may be said

duced from an apprehension that an imperfect copy might be issued from the press without their consent."[1]

It may be observed that the custom then prevalent in England, of two or three or even more authors collaborating in the production of a play, was also common in Spain. Mira de Mescua claims to have been the first to introduce this practice among his fellow-playwrights:

> Porque soy el que ha inventado
> El componer de consuno.[2]

That three poets should collaborate in writing a comedia, each undertaking an act, was not infrequent; in the comedia *La Luna Africana*,[3] eight "ingenios" took a hand, while *La Conquista de Toledo y Rey Don Alfonso el VI.* was written by eight wits in three hours,[4] and it took no less than nine poets to write *Algunas Hazañas de las muchas de Don Garcia Hurtado de Mendoza, Marques de Cañete*.[5] They were: Mira de Amescua, the Conde del Basto, Luis de Belmonte, Juan Ruiz de Alarcon, Luis Velez de Guevara, Fernando de Ludeña, Jacinto de Herrera, Diego de Villegas, and Guillen de Castro, any one of whom alone (with the exception, perhaps, of the Conde del Basto) could doubtless have written a better play.

throughout the standard price remains £6, but that while in the earlier period £5 is not uncommon, toward the end payments of £7 and even £8 became comparatively frequent. A decade later prices had risen greatly. A third-rate poet like Daborne, evidently deep in Henslowe's toils, gets £10 to £20 a play, and is constantly asserting in his correspondence that he can get £25 elsewhere."

[1] *Historical Account of the English Stage*, p. 175.

[2] *Comedias de D. Juan Ruiz de Alarcon y Mendoza*, ed. Hartzenbusch, p. xxxiii (*Bib. de Aut. Esp.*, Tomo XX).

[3] Paz y Melia, *Catálogo*, No: 1929.

[4] *Ibid.*, No. 684.

[5] Published in *Comedias de Alarcon*, ed. Hartzenbusch, pp. 489 ff.

CHAPTER IX

The salaries of actors in the sixteenth and seventeenth centuries. Managers turn actors. *Corrales* in various cities. Valencia as a theatrical center. It is visited by players from Madrid. Sums received by managers for the performance of a comedia. For *autos sacramentales*. Receipts of a representation. The rental of the *corrales*.

ACTORS were generally engaged by the managers of companies for a period of one or two years, beginning at Shrovetide or Ash Wednesday. They were paid every evening, as soon as the play was over, unless there was an express agreement to the contrary. In the comedia *El mejor Representante: San Ginés,* by Cancer, Rosete, and Martinez de Meneses, we read:

> Know that every night the player
> Gets the wages which he earneth;
> This the *autor* pays, if even
> In the chest there be no money.[1]

The salaries of actors varied greatly, of course, according to their skill and proficiency, or the power they possessed of attracting an audience. Thanks to the investigations of that indefatigable scholar, Dr. Cristóbal Pérez Pastor, to whom we owe nearly everything that has been added to our knowledge of the old Madrid stage during

---

[1] "Un representante cobra
Cada noche lo que gana,
Y el Autor paga, aunque
No ay dinero en la caxa."
(*Comedias Escogidas,* Vol. XXIX, 1668, p. 199.)

the last half-century, we now possess a mass of material concerning the actors of the latter part of the sixteenth and the whole seventeenth century which is of the greatest interest and importance. Among the documents collected in his various publications are many contracts and agreements between managers and actors which give us all desirable information in regard to the salaries received by players. As we know little or nothing concerning the relative merits of the vast majority of these more than eighteen hundred actors, it would be useless to specify any save those who occupied the most prominent positions in their profession or whose names are best known in the annals of the Spanish stage.

It is interesting, however, to give the earliest case cited by Dr. Pérez Pastor, under the year 1574, a time when neither the *Corral de la Cruz* nor the *Corral del Príncipe* had yet been established in Madrid. On May 17, 1574, Juan de Sigura, an actor, agreed to work in the company of Jerónimo Velazquez, "from to-day until Shrovetide of 1575, for the sum of 100 ducats [= 1100 reals], and besides he is to receive food, drink, and lodging, and to have his clothes washed, and is to be conveyed on horseback, whenever necessary. And if the said Sigura should absent himself from the company during the said time, the *autor* [Velazquez] may seek another actor in the place of the said Sigura, and the latter shall pay the costs and besides a ducat for every *auto* or comedia which he may miss."[1]

In May, 1595, Agustin Solano, a well-known actor and one of the interlocutors in the *Viage entretenido* of Rojas (1603), agrees to work in the company of Gaspar de Porres for two years, from Shrovetide to Shrovetide, acting such parts as may be assigned to him, and to receive 3000 reals per year.[2]

Generally, besides the amount to be received for acting,

[1] *Nuevos Datos*, p. 334.   [2] *Ibid.*, p. 42.

an additional sum was stipulated for the maintenance of
the player, and in earlier times it was also expressly stated
that the player was to be provided with clean linen, as
when, in 1595, Jusephe Gonzalez, actor, and his wife
Luisa Benzon are to receive, in addition to their wage,
"one doubloon each year to wash their clothes, as is customary, and as other managers give, besides mules and a
cart for them and their baggage, when they leave the
court."[1]

Minors were frequently bound out to the managers of
companies for a term of years, as when Francisco Ortiz,
in May, 1600, was placed with Gaspar de Porres for four
years, "to serve him and help him in his farces and *autos*
in everything which may be required, as well in private as
in public representations, and the said Gaspar de Porres is
to clothe, feed, and shoe him, and furnish whatever else
may be necessary, and to take care of him in his illness,
and to provide lodging and clean clothes, and to furnish
transportation when the company leaves Madrid, for
which, at the end of the said time, he [Ortiz] is to receive
90 ducats."[2] This is probably the Francisco Ortiz whom
we find in 1617 as manager of a company.[3]

A list of some of the more prominent players and their
salaries here follows:

On February 26, 1602, Agustin de Rojas (author of the
Viage entretenido) agrees to act in the company of Miguel
Ramirez (an interlocutor in the *Entertaining Journey*)
from that date until Shrovetide, 1603, for 2800 reals.[4]

In March, 1604, Miguel Ruiz and his wife, the celebrated Baltasara de los Reyes (called *la Baltasara*),
agreed to act in the company of Gaspar de Porres for one
year, receiving 16 reals for each performance and 6 reals
daily for maintenance, besides traveling expenses.[5]

In September, 1604, Juan de Angulo is engaged to act

[1] *Ibid.*, p. 39.   [2] *Ibid.*, p. 53.   [3] *Ibid.*, p. 161.
[4] *Ibid.*, p. 351.   [5] *Ibid.*, p. 84.

in the company of Antonio Granado for one year, receiving 5 reals daily for each representation and 3 reals for maintenance.[1]

1606: Juan Catalan and his wife Mariana de Guevara were engaged by Alonso Riquelme for one year from Shrovetide to Shrovetide, "to sing, act, and help in the *entremeses*," receiving 15 reals for each performance, besides 6 reals daily for maintenance, while Agustin Coronel is to receive from the same *autor* 7 reals for each representation, besides 4 reals daily for maintenance. Diego Lopez Basurto, a famous comic actor (*gracioso*), joined the same company, receiving 9 reals for each performance and 3 reals daily for maintenance.[2]

1610: Luis Alvarez and his wife Mariana de Herbias agreed to act in the company of Alonso Riquelme for one year from Shrovetide, 1610. "To Mariana Herbias are to be assigned all the parts formerly played by Lucia de Salcedo, for she takes the latter's place, and in the new comedias she is to share the principal rôles with another actress. They are to receive 22 reals for each representation and 10 reals daily for maintenance."[3]

1611: Pedro Llorente and his wife Maria de Morales agreed to act in the company of Tomas Fernandez de Cabredo for one year, receiving 20 reals for each performance, 8 reals for maintenance, besides traveling expenses for the couple and a servant.[4]

1614: Luis Quiñones engaged for one year to sing either solos or accompanied, in the troupe of Pedro de Valdes, receiving 14 reals for each representation, 6½ reals for maintenance, and 300 reals for Corpus. Also

---

[1] *Nuevos Datos,* p. 355. This was probably the "Angulo, *el malo*," who afterward became director of a company and who is mentioned by Cervantes. See *Don Quixote,* ed. Clemencin, Vol. IV, p. 190, and also *Nuevos Datos,* p. 169, where Juan de Angulo and Bernarda Gonzalez, his wife, received (in 1619) 12 reals for each performance and 6 reals daily for maintenance, besides "the customary amount for the Corpus festival" and transportation.

[2] *Ibid.,* p. 93.   [3] *Ibid.,* p. 116.   [4] *Ibid.,* p. 126.

Juan de Villanueva, to receive 10 reals for each performance and 4 for maintenance.[1] Juan de Graxales and his wife
Catalina de Peralta agreed to act in the company of Alonso
de Villalba; they are to receive 22 reals for each representation, 8 reals for maintenance, and 22 ducats for the
octave of Corpus, besides traveling expenses and costumes.[2]

1619: Francisco de Castro is to receive from Tomas
Fernandez, besides his pay, transportation for himself and
wife, and if the latter do not accompany him, she is to
receive several pairs of silk stockings.[3] Alonso Fernandez
de Guardo and his wife Ana Cabello agreed to act in the
company of Fernan Sanchez de Vargas for one year, "giving to the said Ana Cabello the first parts, of which she
may not be deprived, for this is the especial agreement."
They received 24 reals for each performance, 10 reals for
maintenance, and 400 reals for the Corpus festival, and
traveling expenses for the couple and servant. Bartolomé
de Robles and his wife Mariana de Guevara are to go
with Maria Lopez to represent four comedias in the town
of Buendia, receiving food and lodging and 1080 reals;
700 for the married couple and 380 for Maria Lopez.[4]
Pedro Garcia de Salinas (a famous comic actor) and his
wife Jerónima de Valcazar are to act for two years in the
company of Sanchez, beginning at Shrovetide, 1619;
Salinas to play the part of *gracioso,* and Jerónima second
women's rôles, receiving 24 reals for each representation
and 8 reals for maintenance, besides traveling expenses and
costumes.[5]

1620: Andres de la Vega and his wife, the famous
Maria de Cordoba, called *Amarilis,* agreed to act in the
company of Tomas Fernandez during the year 1621, receiving 36 reals for each representation and 14 reals for
maintenance, besides 600 reals for the Corpus festival and
four riding-animals for traveling.[6]

[1] *Ibid.,* p. 138.   [2] *Ibid.,* p. 141.   [3] *Ibid.,* p. 169.
[4] *Ibid.,* p. 171.   [5] *Ibid.,* p. 172.   [6] *Ibid.,* p. 187.

1623 : Juan de Villegas, actor (and also a playwright of distinction), agreed to act in the company of Manuel Vallejo, receiving 22 reals for each representation and 8 reals for maintenance.[1] In the company of Domingo Balbin in this year Roque de Figueroa (afterward a famous director) and his wife Maria de Olivares received 22 reals daily, besides 11 reals for maintenance. Juan de Bezon, a well-known *gracioso,* and his wife Ana Maria (*la Bezona*) received, in the company of Hernan Sanchez, 27 reals daily, 13 reals for maintenance, besides 700 reals for the Corpus festival and three riding-animals for traveling.[2] Bartolomé Romero and his wife Antonia Manuela, in the company of Juan Bautista Valenciano, received 24 reals for each representation and 14 reals daily for maintenance.

1632 : In December Maria Calderon (*la Calderona,* mother of Don John of Austria, born in 1629) agreed to go to the town of Pinto to act in two *autos* and two comedias on Corpus Christi and the following day, for which she received 1050 reals, besides traveling expenses for herself, her husband Tomas de Rojas, and a maid, and lodging and 8 reals daily while going and returning.[3]

1633 : Maria de Cordoba is to act, sing, and dance in two comedias at Daganzo, furnishing the necessary costumes. The two comedias are to be selected from the following: *No hay Dicha ni Desdicha hasta la Muerte* (by Mescua? Rojas Zorrilla?) ; *Amar como se ha de Amar* (Lope) ; *El Milagro por los Celos* (Lope) ; *Sufrir mas por querer mas* (Villaizan) ; *El Mariscal de Biron* (Montalvan) ; *La Puente de Mantible* (Calderon) ; *La Dicha del Forastero* (Lope) ; and *El Examen de Maridos* (Alarcon). She is to receive 800 reals, board and traveling expenses for herself and maid. In 1639 the same actress received 1000 reals for four comedias at Valdemoro.[4] It will be seen that players generally received an extra sum

[1] *Nuevos Datos,* p. 192.   [2] *Ibid.,* p. 203.
[3] *Ibid.,* p. 226.   [4] *Ibid.,* pp. 226, 302.

for the Corpus festival, and about this time the custom came into vogue of also giving additional sums for other festivals.

1634: In the company of Pedro de la Rosa in this year Francisco de Velasco, who played first young men's rôles (*primera parte de galanes*), and his wife Ana Fajardo, who was to play any part that might be assigned to her, received 19 reals for each performance, 4 reals for maintenance daily, and 400 reals for the Corpus festival, besides three riding-animals, while Cosme Perez (called *Juan Rana*), the greatest comic actor (*gracioso*) of his time, received 20 reals for each performance, 10 reals for maintenance, and 550 reals for Corpus, besides three riding-animals. Players of old men's rôles generally received very small pay; Pedro Sanchez Baquero, who played first old men's parts in this company ("primera parte de" *barba*), getting but 5 reals daily and 5 reals for maintenance, with one riding-animal and baggage carried.[1] Musicians seem to have been well paid, for in March, 1633, Alonso Gomez Camacho agreed with the director Sanchez to take part in the Corpus festival and its octave, playing the violin, dancing, and directing the music for 500 reals.[2]

1637: Maria de Quiñones played the principal parts in the company of Tomas Fernandez, receiving 16 reals for each representation, 9 reals for maintenance, and 500 reals for the Corpus festival, besides three riding-animals.[3]

1638: Pedro Manuel de Castilla, of the company of Antonio de Rueda, and one of the most celebrated *galanes* of his time, received 20 reals daily, 10 reals for maintenance, and 500 reals for Corpus, while Diego Osorio, a famous *gracioso*, received 15 reals, besides 8 reals daily for maintenance and 350 reals for Corpus.[4]

1639: Mariana de los Reyes played first parts in the company of Andres de la Vega, receiving 100 ducats

[1] *Ibid.*, p. 245.   [2] *Ibid.*, p. 232.   [3] *Ibid.*, p. 258.   [4] *Ibid.*, p. 301.

(= 1100 reals) for the Corpus festival, 11 ducats each
for the festivals in August and September, and 7 ducats
for each of the other festivals; besides, "a trunk full of
clothes which she had pawned is to be released, she to pay
the amount due and to be allowed 5 reals daily for maintenance when the company travels."[1] In this year the company of Antonio de Rueda contained, among others, Pedro
de Ascanio and his wife Antonia Infante; the former was
to act, dance, and sing, the latter to play third parts and
to sing and dance the principal part in the *saynetes*, they
receiving 30 reals daily and 500 reals for Corpus. This
is the earliest mention of the word *saynete* (in the sense
of a short interlude) that I have found. In the same
company Doña Jacinta de Herbias y Flores, widow, was
engaged to act second parts, dance, and sing, receiving 21
reals daily, besides 440 reals for Corpus.[2]

These data are more than sufficient to show the remuneration received by actors and actresses in Spain during the most flourishing period of the drama.[3] If, for the
purpose of comparison, we convert these sums into English money, and reckon that a real at the close of the six-

[1] *Nuevos Datos*, p. 302.

[2] *Ibid.*, p. 304. These are the actresses who figure in the episode related
on p. 127.

[3] Concerning the pay of English actors Malone says: "It is not easy to
ascertain what were the emoluments of a successful actor in the time of
Shakespeare. They had not then annual benefits, as at present. The clear
emoluments of the theater, after deducting the nightly expenses for lights,
men occasionally hired for the evening, etc., which in Shakespeare's house
was but forty-five shillings, were divided into shares, of which part belonged to the proprietors, who were called housekeepers, and the remainder was divided among the actors, according to their rank and
merit." (*Historical Account*, p. 188.) "About twenty pounds was a considerable receipt at the Blackfriars and Globe theater on any one day."
(*Ibid.*, p. 194.) He further says that Hart, the celebrated tragedian, after
the Restoration had but three pounds per week as an *actor*, but he had
besides six shillings and three pence every day on which there was a
performance at the King's theater, making in all about one hundred and
forty-six pounds for a season of thirty weeks. (*Ibid.*, p. 198.) It appears
that English actors were also frequently hired at Shrovetide. Of the
actors in the pay of Henslowe, we find a contract with Thomas Downton,
who on January 25, 1599, "ded hire as his couenante servante for ii yers

teenth century was equivalent to sixpence,[1] we shall see
that their pay was large in comparison with other voca-
tions, and was probably much higher than the sums received by English players of the same period, who were not
shareholders. The 3000 reals per year received by Agustin Solano in 1595 was the equivalent of about £75, while
Agustin de Rojas in 1602 received 2800 reals, or about
£70, per annum. Where the player was paid a certain sum
for each representation, which was the almost universal
rule, as we have seen, it is much more difficult to calculate
the total sum, for representations were not given every
day and never on Saturdays, and the length of the theatrical season varied, though it was generally from thirty to
thirty-two weeks in a year. Still, how liberally Spain, as
poor as she was in 1632, was willing to pay for theatrical
exhibitions may be seen in the case of the great actress
Maria Calderon, who received 1050 reals for four performances on two days, besides all expenses paid, the
equivalent of over £26, and Maria de Cordoba in the following year received 800 reals (= £20) for two representations. Even larger sums were received by players in

to beg[a]yne at shrofe tewesday next & he to geue him viii s. a wecke as
long as they playe & after they lye stylle one fortnyght then to geue him
hallfe wages." (*Henslowe's Diary*, ed. Greg, p. 40.) And in a memorandum of July 27, 1597, we read: "I heayred Thomas hearne with ii
pence for to searve me ii yeares in the qualetie of playenge for fyve
shellynges a weacke for one yeare & vi s. viii d. for the other yeare which
he hath covenanted hime seallfe to searue me & not to departe from my companey tyll this ii yeares be eanded." (*Ibid.*, p. 201.) See also the agreement of Henslowe with "John Helle the clowne" "to contenew with me
at my howsse in playinge tylle strafe tyd next after the date aboue
written" (August 3, 1597), etc., and the contract with William Borne,
ibid., p. 203. Here from Shrovetide to Shrovetide was also frequently the
term of the contract. Soulié, *Récherches sur Molière*, Paris, 1863, p. 61,
prints two contracts with actors of a much later period (1664), in which
the players are obliged to be "dans la ville d'Abbeville en Picardie avec
leurs hardes, bagages et paquets pour commencer la représentation des
pièces qui seront convenues entre eux du jour des fêtes de Pâques prochain
jusqu'au mercredi des Cendres aussi prochain." One of the actors agrees to
play the comic rôles and "travailler aux décorations desdites pièces pour
les peintures qu'il y conviendra faire."

[1] Minsheu's *Spanish Dictionary*, London, 1599, *ad verb.*

the succeeding years, though perhaps, on account of the great depreciation in the value of money, the actual value was no greater.

During this whole period which we have been considering the manager of every theatrical company, or *autor de comedias* as he was called, was invariably also an actor. The cases are therefore very frequent in which we find an *autor* one year becoming a member of another's company in the next, and in the succeeding year reappearing at the head of a company, according as fortune was favorable or adverse to him.

There is an early and interesting example in 1602, when Jerónimo Lopez de Sustaya, *autor de comedias,* and his wife Isabel Rodriguez agreed with Antonio Granado, also an *autor de comedias,* to act in the latter's company for two years, receiving 6 reals daily for maintenance and 5300 reals yearly, to be paid every four months. However, Jerónimo Lopez is to give Granado "the comedias which he may have, and among them the following four: *San Reymundo, Los Caballeros nuevos, La Fuensanta de Cordoba,* and *El Trato de la Aldea,*" all of which he declared that "he had bought from the poets who had written them, paying his money for them, so that the said Antonio Granado may use them as to him may seem best."[1] In like manner Francisco de Sotomayor, who had been director of a company in 1631, and his wife Vicenta Lopez joined the company of Roque de Figueroa in 1632, as we learn from a *Loa* by Benavente:

> *Bezon:* Who are you?
> *Sotomayor:* Sotomayor,
> Who, an authorized director,
> Have this year become a player,
> Since to me players are lacking.[2]

---

[1] Pérez Pastor, *Nuevos Datos,* p. 64.
[2] *Entremeses,* edited by Rosell, Vol. I, p. 231. So in 1638 Pedro Manuel de Castilla and Tomas de Heredia, who had been directors of companies in

With the establishment of fixed *corrales* in Madrid, as already observed, the taste for theatrical representations grew rapidly until it became a passion with all classes, high and low. Every large city possessed a theater, while every town and hamlet, be it never so poor, looked forward with eagerness to the advent of a company of strolling players, whose visits seem to have been looked upon as the crowning event of the year, and for whose representations, especially those upon some festival, large sums of money were expended. We have already described the *corrales* of Madrid and Seville, but Valencia, Granada,[1] Valladolid, and Salamanca must have had theaters at a very early date. It has been already remarked that the importance of Valencia as a theatrical center has generally been exaggerated. While a *corral* certainly existed in that city as early as 1583 or 1584, there is no evidence of any unusual dramatic activity in Valencia before the arrival of Lope de Vega in that city in 1588. In this year Lope was tried for criminally libeling Jerónimo Velazquez, a theatrical director, and several members of his family. He was convicted and sentenced to banishment for two years from the kingdom of Castile, and for eight years from the court (Madrid) and five leagues therefrom. The first two years of his banishment, till 1590, he expiated in Valencia, whither he went with his wife and family. That Lope was very active in writing for the stage during this period is evinced by the testimony

the preceding year, belonged to the company of Rueda and Ascanio. (*Ibid.,* pp. 368, 369.)

[1] According to Pedraza, *Historia ecclesiastica de· Granada,* quoted by Schack, *Nachträge,* p. 18, Granada possessed a permanent theater a few years after the conquest by Ferdinand the Catholic in 1492. Representations took place in the *Casa de Carbon* on the Darro, until the *Coliseo* was erected in the Puerta del Rastro, called now the Puerta Real. "It was arranged in the form most suited for this purpose, with *aposentos* divided for men and women, and a *patio* surrounded by *gradas,* protected from the sun and rain, but open to the sky in the center, as was the Amphitheater at Rome." Of the *Coliseo* in the Puerta Real, Pedraza says: "El Coliseo donde se representan las comedias es un famoso teatro:

of Gaspar de Porres, a theatrical manager, who testified at
the trial for libel that he received comedias from Lope
every two months, and Porres's testimony is supplemented
by that of Quiros, another *autor de comedias*.[1] It is to
Lope's sojourn in Valencia in 1588–90 that the powerful
impulse which the drama received in that city is wholly
due. He was the founder of the Valencian School, for we
hear nothing of it before Lope visited Valencia, and that
the latter city was always dependent upon Madrid in
theatrical matters is shown by abundant evidence. After
the capital, as already observed, the most important theatrical center was Seville, yet the *corrales* of Seville were
also frequently visited by the large theatrical companies
of Madrid. Concerning the establishment of fixed *corrales* in the other principal cities, there are no data
at hand, so far as I know, but they certainly possessed
them before the close of the sixteenth century. In
the *Archivo Historico Nacional* there is a petition, dated
1602, to establish a theater in the "Cárcel vieja"
in Cordoba,[2] but it is probable that a *corral* existed
there prior to this date. In 1606 the company of Juan
de Morales Medrano inaugurated the playhouse (*casa
de comedias*) in Zamora,[3] and in the same year they
appeared in Segovia, though it seems doubtful whether
there was then a fixed theater in the latter city.[4] In 1608
Alonso de Riquelme took his company to Toledo, to remain thirty days, the lessee of the *casa de comedias* in
Toledo, Juan Gallegos, agreeing to pay 50 ducats (= 550

apenas la fama del Romano le quita el primer lugar. Es un patio quadrado con dos pares de corredores que estriban sobre colunas de marmol
pardo, y debaxo gradas para el residuo del pueblo. Está cubierto el
teatro de un cielo bolado, la entrada ornada de una portada de marmol
blanco y pardo con un escudo de las armas de Granada."
    [1] *Life of Lope de Vega*, pp. 38–40.
    [2] *Nuevos Datos*, p. 79.
    [3] Sanchez-Arjona, *Anales*, p. 125. But see *ibid.*, p. 109, note, from which
it appears that there was a *casa de comedias* in Zamora in 1599.
    [4] *Nuevos Datos*, p. 96.

reals) daily "for the whole company."[1] At least as early as 1584 Valencia was visited by a company of players from Madrid, when Alonso de Cisneros represented there for three months, prior to November 6 of that year.[2] In this same year, apparently, for the account is not clear, "N. Velazquez," whom I take to be Jerónimo Velazquez, had also performed in Valencia,[3] while Rodrigo and Francisco Osorio were in the same city in 1588,[4] Bartolomé Lopez de Quiros in 1588 or 1589, and Juan de Vergara in 1594–95. In 1601 Gaspar de Porres took his troupe there from Toledo,[5] and in 1619 we find a theatrical manager, Hernan Sanchez de Vargas, who had always been connected with companies organized in Madrid, where he resided from the beginning of his career, taking up his residence in Valencia.[6] In 1623 Cristóbal de Avendaño and Maria Candau, his wife, took their company to Valencia for fifty representations, and he again visited the city with his company in 1631, being guaranteed a subsidy (*ayuda de costa*) of 140 reals of plate double for each representation.[7] In April, 1628, Juan Jerónimo Almella or Amella took his company to Valencia for sixty performances,[8] and in 1635 Sebastian Gonzalez and his wife Maria Manuela went to Valencia to give one hundred and forty performances, receiving 140 reals for each

[1] *Ibid.*, p. 110.
[2] Lamarca, *El Teatro de Valencia*, Valencia, 1840, p. 18.
[3] *Ibid.*, p. 19.
[4] Cotarelo, *Lope de Rueda*, p. 30; *Life of Lope de Vega*, p. 39.
[5] *Nuevos Datos*, p. 59. [6] *Ibid.*, p. 186. [7] *Ibid.*, pp. 195, 220.
[8] A melancholy record of the disastrous sojourn of Amella's company at Valencia in this year has recently been published by Henri Mérimée (*Bulletin Hispanique* (1906), p. 377); the company came to grief in June, when Amella's wardrobe and comedias were seized by one Jerónimo Alfonso, *clavarius* of the General Hospital of Valencia, for money advanced to and expended in behalf of Amella. The document, dated June 14, 1628, declares that "Ego hieronimus Alfonso, etc. . . . conffiteor et in veritate recognosco me habere in commandam et purum depositum a vobis Hieronymo Amella, fabularum Aucthore, et domna Emanuela Henrriques, vidua, valentiæ commorantibus, presentibus, acceptantibus, et vestris pro tuhitione et securitate quantitatum per me vobis et pro vobis solutarum, prestitarum et bistractarum raupas et fabulas siue comedias infrascriptas

performance,[1] while in 1637 Pedro de la Rosa gave fifty representations in the same city,[2] followed by Bartolomé Romero in the next year, who likewise gave fifty representations, "the amount for each comedia to be no less than 150 reals plate."[3]

Not only all the large cities of Spain, but the theaters of Lisbon also, drew upon the companies of the capital. Of Madrid companies visiting Lisbon I have found no earlier record than 1610, though we may be quite certain that this was not their first advent in the Portuguese capital. In that year the company of Alonso Riquelme and Pedro de Villanueva went to Lisbon,[4] to be followed in 1615 by Pedro de Valdes and Jerónima de Burgos,[5] and by Cristóbal Ortiz de Villazan in 1619, who agreed with the Royal Hospital of All Saints of Lisbon to go to the latter city and perform during the months of October and November, "producing new comedias, *bailes*, and *entremeses*." Doña Catalina de Carvajal is named as the owner of the *casa de comedias* of Lisbon, and in the same year Pedro Cebrian is to bring his company from Madrid and to act there for three months, beginning on December 1, 1619.[6] In 1639 Bartolomé Romero's company visited Lisbon, and in the same year they were followed by Pedro Ascanio and Antonio de Rueda,[7] while Romero again represented in Lisbon from November, 1640, till Shrovetide of 1641.[8]

We have several times had occasion, in the course of these pages, to mention the sums received by a director and his company for a theatrical performance. This sum, of course, not only varied greatly at different periods, being

---

et inmediate sequentes." A list of Amella's theatrical costumes follows, as well as of the comedias that constituted the repertory of his company. This list of comedias, no less than seventy-two in number, is important, as it appears to contain several which are otherwise unknown.

[1] *Nuevos Datos*, p. 242.
[2] *Ibid.*, p. 261. [3] *Ibid.*, p. 292. [4] *Ibid.*, p. 122.
[5] *Ibid.*, p. 158. [6] *Ibid.*, p. 178. [7] *Ibid.*, pp. 289, 290.
[8] *Ibid.*, p. 323.

much larger as we advance further into the seventeenth century, but at one and the same period it depended upon the size and excellence of the company. A few examples, in addition to those already cited, may follow here.

In 1593 Gabriel Nuñez and Andres de Naxera, *autores de comedias,* agreed to go to the village of Villaverde and represent a comedia "á lo divino" and one "á lo humano," with their *entremeses,* receiving 20 ducats (= 220 reals), besides traveling expenses, lodging, "and somebody to do their cooking";[1] and in 1602 the company of Luis de Castro went to Salvanés to represent an *auto* in the morning and a comedia in the afternoon, for which they received 900 reals, "besides twelve beds for the nights they may spend there, a *fanega* of wheat baked into bread, and three carts to take them from Torrejón to Salvanés."[2] It is very probable that these were companies of the poorer kind, but at a much later time, in 1634, we find that one of the most famous directors, Hernan Sanchez de Vargas, played three comedias at the town of Villarubia de Ocaña, receiving 2000 reals, besides a sheep, eight hens, a *fanega* of baked bread, and three *arrobas* (= about twelve gallons) of wine.[3]

Generally the director's compensation was in money only. In 1601 Pedro Jimenez de Valenzuela and Gabriel Vaca took their company to the town of Barco and performed four comedias, with their *entremeses,* at a festival, receiving 3450 reals.[4] This seems to be a large sum and doubtless included all traveling and other expenses. In the following year Pedro Rodriguez, Diego de Rojas, and Gaspar de los Reyes, managers of the company called *La Compañia Española,* performed in the same town two comedias "á lo divino": *El Castigo en la Vanagloria* and *Los Mártires Japones,* with two *entremeses* each, and two comedias "á lo humano": *El Conde Alarcos* and *El Cerco*

[1] *Ibid.,* p. 37.   [2] *Ibid.,* p. 69.   [3] *Ibid.,* p. 237.
[4] *Ibid.,* p. 55.

de Córdoba, with two *entremeses* each, music and *baile,* for
3630 reals; no transportation was furnished, but the "mayordomos" of the village were to provide fifteen pounds of
trout.[1]　In 1605 Gaspar de Porres and his company represented on three consecutive days, also in Barco de Avila,
the following four comedias: *La próspera Fortuna de Rui
Lopez de Avalos* (by Salustio del Poyo); *La adversa
Fortuna de Rui Lopez de Avalos* (also by Poyo); *La Condesa Matilda* (Lope de Vega); and either of the "comedias
divinas": *El Lego del Carmen* or *El Hermano Francisco,*
and an *entremes* with each comedia, for 4200 reals.[2]　In
1612 the company of Tomas Fernandez went to Torrijos,
and on June 26 and 27 represented three comedias, with
their *bailes* and *entremeses,* for 1400 reals and lodging for
sixteen persons, besides six or eight carts "to take his company to the said town and afterward to Toledo."[3]　In 1614
Juan de Morales Medrano agreed to go to Torrijos with
his company and give two representations, a comedia "á lo
divino" in the morning and one "á lo humano" in the afternoon, with their *bailes* and *entremeses,* for 1250 reals;
the comedia to be *La Honra hurtada,* "which must not
have been represented in any of the surrounding towns."[4]
In 1619 Tomas Fernandez received 2300 reals for four
comedias performed on July 6 and 7.[5]　In 1623 Juan de
Vargas and the company called *Los Conformes* represented
in Leganés the comedia *La Morica garrida* of Juan de
Villegas, with its music, *entremeses,* and *bailes,* for 450
reals.[6]　In 1634 Hernan Sanchez de Vargas gave four
comedias in two days at Santa Cruz de la Zarza for 2500
reals,[7] and on the following day, Sunday, June 18, at
Villarubia de Ocaña he represented two comedias, and one
on the succeeding day in the morning, for 2000 reals.[8]　In
1636 Pedro de la Rosa and his company received 1500

[1] *Nuevos Datos,* p. 75.　[2] *Ibid.,* p. 90.　[3] *Ibid.,* p. 130.
[4] *Ibid.,* p. 143.　[5] *Ibid.,* p. 183.　[6] *Ibid.,* p. 202.
[7] *Ibid.,* p. 236.　[8] *Ibid.,* p. 236.

reals for representing two comedias at Torrejon de Ardoz,[1] and we find that down to about 1640, this was the usual amount received for performing a comedia, i.e., about 750 reals. Toward the middle of the century this sum rose and gradually increased till 1660, after which time no data are available. In 1648 Antonio Garcia de Prado gave four representations in the town of Brihuela, for which he received 4900 reals,[2] and in 1655 Alonso de la Paz, *autor de comedias,* represented Calderon's comedia *Santa Maria Egipciaca* and two others at the town of Torija for 2850 reals and lodging for his company,[3] while in 1659 Diego Osorio and his company performed three comedias and an *auto* in the villa de Sonseca for 4000 reals;[4] indeed, in the previous year this same director had received an even larger sum, the largest, in fact, of which I find any record, when he represented an *auto* and the comedia *La Dama Corregidor,* by Sebastian de Villaviciosa and Juan de Zabaleta, at Colmenar Viejo on June 23, receiving 5200 reals, besides traveling expenses, food, and lodging.[5]

It seems that about this time the wretched condition to which Philip the Fourth had reduced his country, which was now entirely exhausted, and the universal poverty and destitution of the common people, due perhaps no less to the contempt for honest labor than to oppressive taxation, also affected the theater in no small degree. The King continued to give great and expensive festivals and comedias at the palace, besides spending large sums on the yearly *autos* at the Corpus festival, although he was practically bankrupt. Still, there can hardly be a doubt that the theater was no longer in the flourishing condition in which it was prior to the middle of the seventeenth century. Theatrical companies seemed to be quite as much

---

[1] This village recently achieved notoriety through the dastardly attack made upon the life of Alfonso XIII. and his bride in Madrid on June 1, 1906. The assassin was killed in Torrejon.

[2] Pérez Pastor, *Calderon Documentos,* Part I, p. 159.

[3] *Ibid.,* p. 226.   [4] *Ibid.,* p. 262.   [5] *Ibid.,* p. 256.

dependent upon the King for support as they were upon the populace. Philip the Fourth interfered with the playhouses in the most arbitrary manner, suddenly commanding actors and actresses or whole companies to appear at the palace for his own private festivals or comedias, without notice to the public. A comedia would be advertised and the theater filled with spectators, when a command would be received from the King that certain actors or actresses in the play were to appear at the palace. As an instance we may cite the declaration (on February 28, 1658) of the *autor de comedias* Francisco Garcia, called *Pupilo*, who says that "there will be no representation to-day of *La Adúltera penitente*, because at eight o'clock this morning, by order of the Marquis of Eliche, they took him [Garcia] to the Buen Retiro to rehearse the comedia which he is to represent before his Majesty on Shrove Tuesday, the title of which is *Afectos de Odio y Amor* [by Calderon]. . . . And they likewise took away Isabel de Galvez, Maria de Escamilla, and Manuela de Escamilla to rehearse another comedia entitled *El Embustero*, which is to be represented before his Majesty." And the same Francisco Garcia declared on March 4 that "yesterday, being about to represent the comedia *La Adúltera penitente*, and there being many people in the *corral*, at about two o'clock in the afternoon there came an order from the Marquis of Eliche, and they took away Isabel de Galvez and Maria and Manuela de Escamilla and others of his company to the comedia which is to be rehearsed in the Zarzuela for representation before his Majesty."[1] A like instance occurred in the previous year, when Francisco Garcia did not perform on February 10, and the *Teatro de la Cruz* was closed, "because they had taken the women of his company to represent the comedia of *Lazarillo* before his Majesty."[2]

---

[1] Pérez Pastor, *Calderon Documentos*, Part I, pp. 253, 254.
[2] *Ibid.*, p. 244.

An instance of the waning popularity of the theater may be seen in the fact that on Friday, April 30, 1660, Vallejo represented in *la Cruz* Juan de Zabaleta's comedia *No Amar la mayor Fineza,* "never before seen or performed," and which we are told was a failure "on account of the few people who were in the theater, the lessees taking but 294 reals." "On Saturday, May 1, Vallejo did not represent, because there was not a soul in the theater," while on Sunday, May 2, Vallejo again represented Zabaleta's comedia, when the lessees had but 203 reals. On Thursday, May 17, Vallejo represented Montalban's *Los Amantes de Teruel* in the *Teatro del Príncipe;* "the whole receipts were given to him, and in all there were but 116 reals for the poor company."[1]

Where long engagements were made the lessee of the theater generally guaranteed to the director of the company a certain amount daily as an *ayuda de costa,* besides which he received a share of the receipts. In one instance, in 1623, when the company of Cristóbal de Avendaño gave fifty representations in Valencia, he received 40 ducats [= 440 reals] for each performance, besides an advance payment of 1000 ducats.[2] The largest sum recorded as having been received by an *autor de comedias* is 1000 reals for each of sixty performances at the *Coliseo* in Seville, which was paid to Hernan Sanchez de Vargas in 1619.[3] If the company was inferior the remuneration of the manager was, of course, correspondingly low, as when Juan de Peñalosa in 1636 represented the two famous comedias *Casa con dos Puertas mala es de guardar,* by Calderon, and *Nunca mucho costó poco,* by Lope de Vega, for 100 reals, besides traveling expenses.[4] A company must surely have been in desperate straits to act for such a small sum.

---

[1] *Ibid.,* pp. 275, 276.
[2] *Nuevos Datos,* p. 195.
[3] *Ibid.,* p. 177.   [4] *Ibid.,* p. 256.

For the production of the *autos sacramentales* at the festival of Corpus Christi a much larger amount was paid to the managers of companies than was paid for the performance of a comedia. This was not only on account of the length of the festival, but also because of the greater expense which had to be incurred for costumes and other accessories, though the *carros* were at the expense of the municipality. As early as 1599 (and doubtless there were earlier instances) it is expressly stipulated in the agreements made with *autores de comedias* for the representation of *autos* that no other company except the one so chosen shall have the right to perform in Madrid from Easter until Corpus.[1]

In 1578 Alonso de Cisneros represented three *autos* in Madrid, for which he received 3300 reals, besides 275 reals for drawing the carts from place to place.[2] In 1592 Gaspar de Porres received 600 ducats [= 6600 reals] for representing the *autos* entitled *Job* and *Santa Catalina* at the Corpus festival at Madrid in that year.[3] In 1606 the four *autos* were represented in Madrid by the companies of Juan de Morales Medrano and Baltasar Pinedo, each representing two *autos*, for which each director received 650 ducats.[4] In 1609 the companies of Domingo Balbin and Alonso de Heredia performed two *autos* each at Corpus in Madrid for 600 ducats,[5] and in 1610 Alonso Riquelme agreed to represent two *autos* at the festival of Corpus of that year "on Thursday and Friday until twelve o'clock at night in such places as may be designated, re-

---

[1] "5 Abril 1599.—Obligacion de Gaspar de Porres, autor de comedias (fiador Jerónimo Lopez) de hacer dos autos para la fiesta del Corpus con sus entremeses, con condicion de que desde resurreccion hasta el Corpus no han de traer a esta Villa otra compañia sino es la suya." (Pérez Pastor, *Nuevos Datos*, p. 49.) And in 1627, when Roque de Figueroa and Andres de la Vega represented *autos* in Madrid, we read: "Es declaracion que no se ha de permitir trabajar a otro autor en Madrid desde fin de Cuaresma hasta pasado el Corpus." (*Bull. Hisp.* (1908), p. 254.)

[2] *Nuevos Datos*, p. 11.   [3] *Ibid.*, p. 31.   [4] *Bull. Hisp.* (1907), p. 372.
[5] *Nuevos Datos*, p. 112.

ceiving for the said *autos* with their *entremeses* 600 ducats."[1] The same sum was received by Hernan Sanchez de Vargas for representing the other two *autos* in this year. In fact, 600 ducats was the amount paid to every theatrical director for representing two *autos* at Corpus in Madrid down to the year 1637. In 1615 the *autos* at Madrid were given by the companies of Pedro de Valdes and Hernan Sanchez de Vargas, and it was stipulated that "before Corpus no other company was to represent in Madrid except these two,"[2] and in 1617, when Cristóbal de Leon performed them, it was agreed that he should represent two *autos* at Corpus on Thursday "from two in the afternoon till twelve at night and on Friday from six in the morning until noon, in such places as may be assigned to him,"[3] while when Pedro de Valdes represented the *autos* in 1621, he was to give them on Thursday from two in the afternoon till twelve at night and on Friday from six in the morning until midnight.[4] In 1632 they were performed by Manuel Vallejo's company, who received 600 ducats "for the two days, and if they should represent on the Saturday after Corpus he is to receive 1000 reals, or 100 ducats, and besides an 100 ducats gratuity, obliging himself to pay the half of the 100 ducats which he receives to the *ganapanes* who draw the carts."[5] In 1637 the companies of Pedro de la Rosa and Tomas Fernandez Cabredo received 800 ducats each for the Corpus festival at Madrid,[6] and the same sum was paid to Rueda and Ascanio in 1638, and to Bartolomé Romero for two *autos* in 1640.[7] This latter document is dated March 14, 1640. On the other hand, a document dated March 12, 1640, states that Bartolomé Romero was to receive 950 ducats "for half the festival of Corpus," i.e., for two *autos*, the other two *autos* being given

[1] *Ibid.*, p. 117. [2] *Ibid.*, p. 156. [3] *Ibid.*, p. 161.
[4] *Ibid.*, p. 188. [5] *Ibid.*, p. 224. [6] *Ibid.*, pp. 266, 269.
[7] *Ibid.*, p. 322

by the companies of Luis Lopez de Sustaete and Damian
Arias de Peñafiel "under the same conditions."[1] In 1645
each company received 925 ducats for two *autos*,[2] and in
1655 the companies of Diego Osorio and Francisca Verdugo, widow of Riquelme, each represented two *autos* at
Madrid, receiving 10,750 reals, or about 975 ducats.[3]

After 1658 only two *autos* were represented each year
in Madrid at Corpus. In 1660 they were entitled *La Paz
universal* (*El Lirio y la Azucena*) and *El Diablo mudo*,
both written by Calderon, and they were acted by the companies of Diego Osorio and Jerónimo Vallejo, who received 950 ducats each, which amount was paid until the
death of Philip the Fourth.[4]

Concerning the receipts of a theatrical performance,
something has already been said.[5] About 1575, before
either of the permanent theaters of Madrid were built,
the profits of a representation in one of the *corrales* were
from 140 or 160 to 200 reals. This was the sum received
by the hospitals to which the *corrales* belonged, exclusive
of the share of the *autor de comedias* and his company.[6]
On February 8, 1580, when Juan Granados was representing in one of the *corrales* of Madrid, he contributed
his share of the profits of the performance toward defraying the expenses of the new *Corral de la Cruz*. This
share amounted to 200 reals *vellon*.[7] And Alonso de
Cisneros, not to be outdone in generosity by his rival,
contributed the proceeds of a performance on October 19,
1580, to the same purpose. His share, which was the
money paid at the door (*entrada*), was 233 reals, while

---

[1] Pérez Pastor, *Calderon Documentos*, Vol. I, p. 121.
[2] *Ibid.*, p. 126.   [3] *Ibid.*, p. 238.
[4] *Ibid.*, p. 269 *et passim*.
[5] See above, pp. 31, 41, 56.
[6] Pellicer, *Histrionismo*, I, p. 56.
[7] *Ibid.*, p. 60. According to Pérez Pastor, it was Cisneros who represented on that day in the *Cruz*, "y dió para ayuda de costa del corral 200
reales que le correspondian de su aprovechamiento como autor." (*Bulletin Hispanique* (1906), p. 77.)

the deputies of the brotherhoods received 174 reals.[1] It thus appears that at this time the total receipts of a performance varied from about 350 to 450 reals *vellon*. About three years after this, in 1583, "on some occasions" the hospitals realized as much as 300 reals as their share of a single performance.[2] On February 10, 1586, Jerónimo Velazquez gave a representation to which women only were admitted,[3] which realized 760 reals, the charge being one real for each person. From a representation given on August 10, 1603, the share of the brotherhoods was 282 reals.[4]

The theaters of Seville furnish interesting information upon this point. We learn that from April 3, 1611, to February 4, 1614, five hundred and twenty-six representations of comedias were given in that city: two hundred and sixty-eight in *Doña Elvira* and two hundred and fifty-eight in the *Coliseo*. During this period of nearly three years the city received as its share of the takings of the theaters 53,346 reals, or a little over 101 reals for each representation.[5] As the city's portion consisted of eight maravedís from each person who entered the theater, we find that the average attendance at these popular theaters during this period, when the drama was at its height, was about 431. We have seen above (p. 56) that in 1622 in Seville the average number of persons who paid an admission to the theater was 350. Indeed, the renting of the *corrales* in Seville seems frequently to have been a losing speculation for the lessees, and as early as 1619

---

[1] "Valió el aprovechamiento de la entrada de la puerta, que pertenecia al dicho Cisneros, 233 reales . . . y para las Cofradias hubo aquel dia de entramos tablados (*gradas*), corredor (*de las mugeres*), y ventanas (*aposentos*) 174 reales." (Pellicer, I, p. 61.) That Cisneros represented on October 18 is confirmed by Pérez Pastor, *Bull. Hisp.* (1906), p. 77.

[2] *Ibid.*, p. 76.

[3] See above, p. 43.

[4] "De las mugeres = 97 rs.; de los hombres = 119 rs.; de las ventanas = 48 rs.; de las celosias y sillas = 18 rs., = 282 reals." (Pellicer, *Histrionismo*, I, p. 85.)

[5] Sanchez-Arjona, *Anales*, p. 147.

we find that "comedias have reached such a point in this city [Seville], that very few people come to see them, and all *autores* or managers of companies who visit the city leave it in debt and ruined."[1]

As regards the rental paid for the *corrales,* we have, for the early period at least, some definite information. On May 5, 1568, Jerónimo Velazquez began to represent in one of the *corrales* of Madrid and paid 6 reals for each day that he gave a performance.[2] In 1574 the Italian, Ganassa, paid 10 reals per day for the rent of the *Corral de la Pacheca,*[3] and in 1583 Antonio Vazquez and Juan de Avila, who performed in the *Corral del Príncipe,* also paid a daily rental of 10 reals.[4] It seems that for the year 1579 the sum of 6000 maravedís was paid for the rental of the *Corral de Puente.*[5]

For a number of years following 1583 we have no information, but it appears that even prior to 1600 the brotherhoods had sublet various privileges. In 1602 the *bancos* and *ventanas* of the two Madrid theaters were let to Alonso and Juan Estebanez. Afterward, instead of a partial renting, the deputies of the brotherhoods determined upon a total rental. This began in 1615, according to Pellicer, when the two *corrales* were rented to Juan de Escobedo for two years for 27,000 ducats, and at the expiration of this lease, in 1617, to Matias Gonzalez for four years for 105,000 ducats, and in 1621 to Luis Monzon, Gabriel de la Torre, and Gabriel Gonzalez, also for the term of four years, for 106,500 ducats, beginning on St. John's day of that year and ending in 1625. The two theaters were then leased to Francisco de Alegria from 1629 to 1633, for 115,400 ducats, and for the four following years to Juan de la Serna y Haro for 100,700

---

[1] Sanchez-Arjona, *Anales,* p. 197.
[2] Pellicer, I, p. 48.   [3] *Ibid.,* p. 54.   [4] *Ibid.,* p. 69.
[5] *Bulletin Hispanique* (1906), p. 77. This sum is almost incredibly small, less than 200 reals, while there were at least fifty representations in the *corral* during that year. (*Ibid.,* pp. 73–75.)

ducats.[1] These amounts are very large compared with
the rentals of the Seville theaters. In 1585 the rent of
the *Huerta de la Alcoba* was 450 ducats yearly. In 1611
that of the *Coliseo* was 2250 ducats, which was reduced
to 2000 ducats in 1622, though even at this figure it was
a losing enterprise for the lessee, as it was shown to be
worth only about 1600 ducats.[2] That the leasing of the
Madrid theaters was not always profitable is shown by the
fact that, on the death of Francisco ·de Alegria (see
above), his widow, Doña Juana Gonzalez Carpio, declared in a petition that her husband had not only left her
without means to support herself and her four children,
but that he had also dissipated a large part of her dowry.[3]

[1] Pellicer, *Histrionismo*, I, pp. 96, 97, who gives the conditions of Luis
Monzon's lease, *ibid.*, pp. 98 ff. I do not understand the statements in
Pérez Pastor, *Nuevos Datos*, pp. 82, 111, 123, 129, 134, 141, and 158. The
latter, for instance, reads: "Arrendamiento de los corrales de comedias
de la Cruz y del Príncipe, desde Carnestolendas de 1615 á Carnestolendas
de 1616, hecho por Cristóbal Lopez en 900 ducados por tercios [i.e., in
three payments]. Madrid, 7 Abril 1615." The amount of the rent, moreover, is so low that the persons mentioned were probably sublessees of
some privilege; in 1609 the sum specified is only 400 ducats. (*Ibid.*, p. 111.)
[2] Sanchez-Arjona, *Anales*, pp. 72, 148, 222.
[3] Pellicer, I, p. 98.

CHAPTER X

Character of the actors and actresses. Decrees regulating theatrical performances. The opposition of churchmen. Decrees of 1598, 1600, 1603, 1608, and 1615 for the reformation of comedias.

DESPITE the hardships endured by companies of strolling players, they seem never to have had any difficulty in recruiting their ranks. Looked at askance in every town and hamlet, and often threatened at the village gates as perverters of the public morals and promoters of idleness, there were still, at all times, many to whom this life made a strong appeal. Though under the ban of the church and denied civil rights for centuries, the followers of Thespis have continued to flourish and increase, so potent has been the glamour of the stage and so alluring the love of a wandering life. Even amid the trials and tribulations so graphically described by Agustin de Rojas, their numbers in Spain steadily multiplied, and with the increase in numbers the growing license of the stage kept pace. We have already mentioned the lascivious dances, like the "pestiferous *Zarabanda*," the *Chacona, Escarraman,* and others which, making their appearance about 1588, became one of the most powerful attractions of the comedia. Urged on by the applause of the dreaded *mosquetero* and of the dissolute "noble," these dances were carried to a point which sorely tried the conservers of the public morals, which latter were by no means exalted in that not over-scrupulous age.

The dissoluteness of the actresses, who were frequently disguised as men upon the stage, and the dangerous influence of these performances upon a people among whom the craze for theatrical representations had become universal, caused a few eminent theologians, in 1587, to step into the breach and attempt to stem the tide that was sweeping everything before it. They failed, as we have seen, for the indecent songs and dances, which the government made a feeble effort to suppress, were succeeded by others not more decorous, and the result was that in 1596 women were forbidden "to act in the said comedias."[1] Whether this prohibition was ever enforced, however, is open to serious doubt; at all events, the death of Princess Catharine, Duchess of Savoy and sister of Philip the Third, on November 6, 1597, offered an opportunity for putting a stop to the comedia, and the King accordingly commanded the theaters of Madrid to be closed.

The churchmen and other opponents of the theater took advantage of this suspension of theatrical representations to renew the question of suppressing them permanently. The King submitted the matter to a council of three theologians, who, after prolonged discussion, finally decided against the theaters, and the King concurring in this "consulta theologica,"[2] a royal rescript was issued on May 2, 1598, declaring that thenceforth no comedias should be represented. Among other evils attrib-

---

[1] See above, p. 145.

[2] The following is the text of this *consulta,* as given by Schack, and which is contained in a MS. in the Royal Academy of History: "Consulta que hizieron a S. M. el Rey D. Felipe II Garcia de Loaysa, Fray Diego de Yepes y Fray Gaspar de Cordoba sobre las Comedias." After recommending the complete suppression of the comedia, they say: "Destas representaciones y comedias se sigue otro gravisimo daño y es que la gente se da al ocio, deleytes y regalo, y se divierte de la milicia, y con los bailes deshonestos que cada dia inventan estos faranduleros y con las fiestas, banquetes y comedias se haze la gente de España muelle y afeminada e inhabil para las cosas de travajo y guerra.— . . . Pues siendo esto asi y teniendo V. Mgd. tan precisa necesidad de hazer guerra a los enemigos de la fé y apercebirnos para ella, bien se vee quan mal aparejo es para las armas el uso tan ordinario de las comedias que aora se representan en España. Y a juizio de personas prudentes, si el Turco o xarife o Rey de Inglaterra quisieran buscar una invencion eficaz para arruinarnos y destruirnos, no la hallaran mejor que la destos faranduleros, pues a guisa

utable to comedias, according to this *consulta,* was "that they fostered habits of idleness and pleasure-seeking in the people and turned their minds from warlike pursuits; that the banquets, festivals, and comedias were rendering the Spanish people effeminate and unfit for the hardships of war, and that the King, being obliged to wage war against the enemies of the faith, was ill prepared, as a result of the comedias as they are now represented in Spain. That, in the judgment of prudent persons, if the Turk or the King of England wished to seek an efficient device to ruin and destroy the Spanish nation, he could find none better than that of these players," etc.

This recommendation of the council of theologians was followed, as just stated, by a royal decree prohibiting the representation of comedias. Pérez Pastor states that the King called this *consulta* of theologians at the instance of D. Pedro de Castro, Archbishop of Granada, who had represented to his Majesty the harm resulting from these representations. This is borne out by the only text of the decree of May 2, 1598, directed to the Corregidor of Granada, which has only lately been discovered.[1] That this prohibition was not intended to be permanent is evinced

de unos mañosos ladrones abrazando matan y atosigan con el sabor y gusto de lo que representan, y hazen mugeriles y floxos los corazones de nuestros Españoles, para que no sigan la guerra o sean inutiles para los trabajos y exercicios della." (*Geschichte der dramatischen Literatur und Kunst in Spanien,* Vol. III, *Nachträge,* pp. 28, 29.)

[1] *Bibliografía Madrileña,* Part I, Madrid, 1891, p. 308. The text of this royal provision is: "Don Phelipe, por la gracia de Dios, etc . . . . A vos el nuestro Corregidor de la ciudad de Granada: Sepades que Nos fuimos informados que en nuestros reinos hay muchos hombres y mugeres que andan en Compañias y tienen por oficio representar comedias y no tienen otro alguno de que sustentarse, de que se siguen inconvenientes de gran consideracion. Y visto por los de nuestro Consejo fué acordado que debiamos mandar dar esta nuestra Carta para vos en la dicha razon. E Nos tuvimoslo por bien; por lo qual os mandamos que, por ahora, no consintais, ni deis lugar que en esa Ciudad ni su tierra, las dichas Compañias representen en los lugares publicos destinados para ello, ni en casas particulares, ni en otra parte alguna; y no fagades ende al so pena de la nuestra merced. Dada en la Villa de Madrid, en 2 de Mayo de 1598." (Cotarelo y Mori, *Controversias,* p. 620.)

by its very words. It commands that the Corregidor of
Granada "for the present ("por ahora") shall not consent
or permit in the said city or its neighborhood the said companies to represent in the public places destined for that
purpose, nor in private houses, nor in any other place
whatever."

This decree was doubtless intended primarily to apply
to Madrid,[1] though I have been unable to find the text
which refers to the theaters of the capital. The theaters
of Madrid were, however, closed, but only for a short
time, for in the course of the same year in which the
decree was issued, the city sent a petition to the King
requesting its revocation, which petition has been preserved. In this *Memorial* the various reasons are
set forth why comedias should again be permitted in
Madrid, stating among other things that if excesses
exist in the comedias, they can readily be removed;
that comedias had been represented in the time of the
King and of his predecessors, and that they were permitted and favored in all well-instituted commonwealths;
that the comedia is "an example, notice, portrait,
mirror, model, doctrine, and warning of life, whereby
prudent and docile men may restrain their passions, flee
vices, elevate their thoughts, and learn virtues by demonstration, for all these are to be found in the comedia,
whence it follows that more may be apprehended by the

---

[1] It is very probable that the closing of the theaters in Madrid in 1598
was also due, in no small degree, to the prevalence of the pest in that
city. This is shown by the following work published in Madrid in that
year: *Breve Tratado de Peste, con sus causas, señales y curacion: y de lo
que al presente corre en esta villa de Madrid, y sus contornos.* Compuesto
por el Doctor Antonio Perez Medico y Cirujano de su Magestad. . . . En
Madrid, Por Luis Sanchez. Año MDXCVIII. In his dedication he states
that he had undertaken to attend "assi a la formacion de la casa y hospital, para recoger los que por esta villa huuiese tocados deste mal, como á
la cura dellos, dando noticia á V. m. y al señor Corregidor don Rodrigo
del Aguila, dos veces en la semana, de lo que passa," etc. (Pérez Pastor,
Bibliografía Madrileña, Part I, p. 312.) Pérez Pastor (*ibid.*, p. 308)
terms it *"mal de secas* que en la época se padecía en Madrid."

eyes than may be taught by the understanding. There is represented the happy end of the just king, the reward of virtue, the importance of prudence," etc. That those who visit the comedia may be reduced to two classes: the idle and vicious, and the virtuous and occupied, and the comedia does not make the former worse nor the latter less good (*menos buenos*), for to the one it serves as a bridle and restraint upon their vices, and to the others as a spur to virtue and labor, of which both will be deprived if comedias be suppressed entirely. The most urgent reason assigned is that three or four of the largest hospitals of the city are supported by the comedia, the General Hospital receiving in each year more than 8000 ducats. Another reason is that, comedias in Spain being always written in verse, the actor is thereby prevented from interpolating anything he chooses; he is obliged to speak what the poet has written, etc. Lastly and strangely enough, it recites that comedias had not been prohibited elsewhere "in these kingdoms."[1]

It is probable that this protest was originated by the directors of the hospitals of Madrid, who thus saw the chief source of their income cut off. Still, this *Memorial* was unavailing for the moment, though the King seems to have been willing that the theaters should be reopened, and an edict had been prepared to that effect, but his confessor, Fray Diego de Yepes, opposed it so strenuously that the order was revoked.[2]

Finding the King on their side, the overseers of the hospitals, we may feel sure, did not relax their efforts to secure the repeal of a law which stifled them out of exis-

---

[1] *Memorial de la Villa de Madrid pidiendo al Rey Felipe II. que se abriesen los teatros, cerrados por la muerte de la Infanta Dª Catalina, Duquesa de Saboya*, Madrid, 1598. Printed in full in Pérez Pastor, *Bibliografía Madrileña*, Part I, p. 304.

[2] This information is furnished by Cabrera, *Relaciones,* etc., p. 5, where we find the following entry: "Madrid, 16 de Enero 1599. Habiase proveido á instancia de los hospitales, que se representasen comedias, por la mucha necesidad que padecian los pobres sin el socorro que desto les

tence. Accordingly, we find that on March 10, 1599, the town council of Madrid resolved to send Sr. Gregorio de Paz to Valencia, where the King then was, to present to his Majesty, on the part of the city, a memorial begging permission to have the city decked in the customary manner for the reception of the Queen, and also that the King be pleased to permit comedias and public representations.[1] So strongly did this petition move Philip the Third that he overruled the objections of his confessor, and on April 17, 1599, comedias were again allowed to be played in the theaters of the kingdom.[2]

On the following day Philip the Third was betrothed to the Archduchess Margaret at Valencia, and during these festivities an allegorical *auto* by Lope de Vega, entitled *Las Bodas del Alma con el Amor divino*,[3] was represented in one of the public squares of Valencia.

With this decree, however, the opponents of the theater, among whom the most influential was Don Pedro de Castro, Archbishop of Granada, were not satisfied. They insisted upon the evil effects of the plays, and especially of the dances then in vogue upon the stage. Accordingly, in April, 1600, a council, consisting of four of the King's Council, four theologians, and Fray Gaspar de Cordoba,

venia, pero el Confesor de S. M. lo ha resistido de manera que se ha mandado revocar la orden dada."

[1] "Acuerdo de 10 de Marzo de 1599:—Que el Sr. Gregorio de Paz vaya á la ciudad de Valencia á llevar á S. M. de parte desta Villa un memorial suplicandole dé licencia á esta Villa para que para el recibimiento de la Reyna nuestra señora se pueda vestir como es acostumbrado y para que se sirva dar licencia para que haya comedias y representaciones públicas. —Acuerdos del Ayuntamiento de Madrid, t⁰ 24, f⁰ 16." Sr. Pérez Pastor adds: "En este año se dejó (sesión de 8 de Enero) para después el nombrar las comisiones de Autos, danzas y toros." (*Nuevos Datos*, p. 49.)

[2] "Madrid, á 17 de Abril 1599:—Tambien se ha dado licencia para que de aqui adelante se hagan comedias en los teatros como las solia haber, las quales dizen que se comenzarán á representar desde el lunes." (Cabrera, *Relaciones*, etc., p. 18.)

[3] Published in his *Peregrino en su Patria*, Seville, 1604, fols. 86–108. The memorial of Alonso de Cisneros printed by Pérez Pastor, *Nuevos Datos*, p. 348, requesting that he be allowed to meet the new Queen with his company and to perform on the way, doubtless refers to this event.

the King's confessor, was called[1] to determine what restrictions were to be imposed upon the theater, or rather to formulate the conditions under which comedias might be represented. The opinion of the theologians was that "the comedias, as they had been represented up to that time and as they were then performed in the theaters, with the sayings, actions, gestures, *bailes,* and vulgar and lascivious dances, were unlawful and that it is a mortal sin to represent them." They resolved that the conditions under which comedias might be represented were the following: (1) That the subject-matter of the comedia be not evil or licentious, and that all immodest dances, sayings, and gestures be eliminated, as well from the comedias as from the *entremeses.* (2) That the many companies of players be reduced to four, which companies alone shall be licensed to represent comedias. (3) That women should not in any circumstances be permitted on the stage, nor should monks or prelates visit the theaters; and if boys play female characters, wearing women's attire, they must not appear rouged and must bear themselves with due modesty. (4) That no representations shall take place in Lent, nor on the Sundays in Advent, nor on the first day of the three *Pasquas;* nor may any company remain in any town more than one month in each year, nor may two companies play at the same time, and in the said month they may play only three days in each week—on Sunday and on two other days—which should

---

[1] Pellicer, *Histrionismo,* Vol. I, p. 151. Cotarelo y Mori, *Controversias,* p. 208, says it was the Duke of Lerma who was favorable to the continuance of the comedia and who desired this commission to be appointed, the text of which, directed to one of the King's Council, the Licentiate Bohorques, is as follows: "Su Magestad ha mandado que quatro de su Consejo se junten con quatro teólogos en el aposento del P. Confesor [Fr. Gaspar de Cordoba] para conferir y ajustar la forma en que se pueden permitir las comedias. Uno de los señalados es Vm. y el P. Confesor avisará el dia en que se hubiese de hacer la junta. De Casa, 19 de Abril de 1600." This Council, Sr. Cotarelo says, could not agree, and it was finally increased to include eleven theologians who formulated the *dictamen.*

be feast-days, when there are any. (5) That in churches and convents only plays of a purely devotional character be allowed. Further conditions were that the men should be separated from the women and should enter by different doors; that no plays should be acted in the universities of Alcalá or Salamanca, except during vacation; that all comedias and *entremeses,* before being acted in public, shall be played before a number of learned persons, among them at least one theologian; that a judge be appointed to enforce the penalties against those who break these conditions; and, finally, that a license to perform should be granted for one year only "como para prueba y experiencia de su observancia."[1]

This *dictamen* of Fray Gaspar de Cordoba and his ten colleagues was referred to the King's Council, who issued it in the same year, though modified in several particulars. After reciting in substance the opinion of the theologians that there should be nothing improper in the comedias nor in the songs and dances, concurring in the seasons and times fixed by them, and adding that on the days that comedias are given the doors of the theater shall not be opened until two o'clock, "so that the people may not miss the Mass, and for other reasons," the document proceeds as follows: "And since they [the theologians] likewise say that women shall not act because their freedom (*desenvoltura*) in such public acts incites to evil, and that if, in the place of women, boys appear on the stage in female attire, they shall not appear rouged or in any unseemly make-up (*compostura*), it appears to this Council that it is much less improper that women should act than that boys should appear in female attire, even though they be not rouged nor made up, provided that the said women do not appear in the habit or dress of men and be accompanied by their husbands or fathers, and not otherwise.

[1] Pellicer, *Histrionismo,* Vol. I, p. 151. This *dictamen* is now reprinted in Cotarelo y Mori, *Controversias,* p. 208.

"As regards the opinion of the churchmen that there shall be only four companies of players in the kingdoms and that none of them may remain in any one place longer than a month, and that they may not perform in any one place more than four months in any whole year, and that two companies may not play at the same time in one place nor act more than three days in any week, Sundays and feast-days included, it appears that that portion which refers to the number of companies and to the days on which they may represent ought to be at the disposal of the Council, as it has always been, so that the Council may decree as it seems proper," etc.[1]

That the recommendation of the theologians that there should be but four companies of players was disregarded, is further shown by the following *autores de comedias*, whom I find mentioned between February, 1600, and April 26, 1603; Melchor de Villalba, Gabriel de la Torre, Gaspar de Porres, Juan de Villalba, Baltasar Pinedo, Diego Lopez de Alcaraz, Pedro Jimenez de Valenzuela, Gabriel Vaca, Antonio de Villegas, Miguel Ramirez, Juan de Tapia, Luis de Castro, Alonso de Paniagua, Jerónimo Lopez de Sustaya, Alonso Riquelme, Pedro Rodriguez, Melchor de Leon, Diego de Rojas, Gaspar de los Reyes,

---

[1] Cotarelo y Mori, *Controversias sobre la Licitud del Teatro*, pp. 163, 164. The resolution of this Council as given by Cabrera de Cordoba varies only slightly from the above, stating that permission is granted to represent *comedias de historias*, but that they must not contain acts of religion or of the saints. The passage in Cabrera, *Relaciones*, p. 59, under date of February 4, 1600, is: "Solamente se ha tomado resolucion que puedan representarse comedias en los teatros de aqui adelante, lo qual estaba prohibido por evitar el escándalo y mal exemplo que en ellas habia; pero porque los hospitales no pierdan el provecho que se les sigue, sin lo qual se padecia mucha en la cura de los pobres, y estaban para cerrarse los hospitales porque no bastaban las limosnas, se da licencia para se representar comedias de historias, y que no se mezclen actos de religion ni de santos; y que las mugeres que representaren no se pongan en habito de hombre, sino trayendo vaqueros largos, y que sean casadas con los mismos que representaren, y que fuera de alli los unos ni los otros no puedan andar vestidos de seda ni con guarnicion de ella ni de oro, sobre lo qual ha habido junta de teólogos, canonistas y juristas, para tomar esta resolucion."

Juan de Morales Medrano, and Gabriel Nuñez, no less than twenty-one heads of companies.

By a royal rescript dated April 26, 1603, the number of theatrical companies was limited to eight.[1] The text of this decree is as follows: "For very good and sufficient considerations his Majesty has commanded that within these kingdoms there may be only eight companies of players and the same number of *autores* or managers of them, as follows: Gaspar de Porres, Nicolas de los Rios, Baltasar de Pinedo, Melchor de Leon, Antonio Granados, Diego Lopez de Alcaraz, Antonio de Villegas, and Juan de Morales, and that no other company may represent within these kingdoms, and that you take notice of this, so that you may fulfil and execute it inviolably within your district and jurisdiction; and if any other company should represent, you shall proceed against the manager and the actors and punish them with due rigor; and you shall not in any manner permit companies to represent in the monasteries of friars or in the convents of nuns, nor shall there be any representations during Lent, even though they be in the sacred manner; all of which you will guard and fulfil,"[2] etc.

[1] It appears that such a craze for theatrical performances had seized all classes by this time, especially artisans, that an attempt was made by the authorities to check it in the year preceding this decree. In 1602 the Alcaldes de Casa y Corte caused it to be proclaimed publicly that no workman or tradesman of any occupation whatever, nor their masters, visit the comedia on work-days, under a penalty of two years of banishment and a fine of 2000 maravedís. (Pérez Pastor, *Bulletin Hispanique* (1907), p. 367.) See also below, p. 220, note 2.

[2] This decree of April 26, 1603, is as follows: "Por muy justas causas y consideraciones a mandado su Magestad que en todos estos reynos no pueda auer sino ocho compañias de representantes de comedias y otros tantos autores de ellos, que son Gaspar de Porres, Nicolas de los Rios, Baltasar de Pinedo, Melchor de Leon, Antonio Granados, Diego Lopez de Alcaraz, Antonio de Villegas y Juan de Morales, y que ninguna otra compañia represente en ellos; de lo qual se adbierte a Vm. para que ansi lo haga cumplir y executar ynviolablemente en todo su distrito y jurisdiccion, y si otra qualquiera compañia representase, procederá contra el autor della y representantes, y los castigará con el rigor necessario y en ninguna manera permita que en ningun tiempo del año se representen comedias en monasterio de frayles ni monjas, ni que en el de la quaresma

The article of this decree restricting the number of *autores de comedias* to eight seems not to have been observed, for, in addition to the eight enumerated above, I find the following directors of companies between 1603 and 1615: Alonso de Riquelme (especially designated as "de su Magestad"), Antonio Ramos, Domingo Balbin, Alonso de Heredia, Hernan Sanchez de Vargas, Alonso de Villalba, Tomas Fernandez de Cabredo, Cristóbal Ramirez, Pedro de Valdes (called "de su Magestad," February 2, 1614), Pedro Llorente, Andres de Claramonte ("de los nombrados por su Magestad," March 28, 1614).

In 1608 an order for the government and regulation of the theaters of Madrid was issued by the licentiate Juan de Tejada, of his Majesty's Council, to whom was committed the protection and government of the General Hospital of the capital, and of the other hospitals which shared in the profits of the theaters. This order is so important and is so clearly the basis of the subsequent decree of 1615 for the regulation of the theaters, that I copy it here. It shows, among other interesting things, that women were not confined to seats in the *cazuela*, but that, besides the *aposentos*, they also occupied the *gradas* and *tarimas*. These regulations are as follows: "(1) That before a manager may enter this court [Madrid] with his company, he must first obtain a license from that officer of the Council who is the protector of the said hospitals, and without this he may not enter. (2) That before *Pascua de Resurreccion* of each year the managers of companies shall give to the Council an account of the company they have, declaring that the persons whom they bring are married and to whom they are married, and the same before representing in this court, under penalty of 20,000 maravedís for the hospitals and punishment

aya representaciones dellas, aunque sea a lo divino; todo lo qual hará guardar y cumplir. Porque de lo contrario se tendrá su Magestad por deservido. De Valladolid á 26 de Abril de 1603 años." (Schack, *Nachträge*, p. 30, and now reprinted in Cotarelo, *Controversias*, p. 621.)

besides. (3) That the manager who shall happen to be
in this court shall select his theater for the first week,
which begins on Monday, otherwise he is estopped; and
if three *autores* should happen to be here, they shall
divide, each one representing two days successively (*de
arreo*), in such manner that in twelve days each one is to
represent eight comedias, four in each of the theaters.
(4) That two days before the representation of a comedia, *entremes,* or song, the said comedia, etc., is to be
taken to the officer of the Council for examination, and
until the necessary license be procured, the comedia, etc.,
is not to be assigned to the players for study, under
penalty of twenty ducats and other punishment; and no
woman shall appear to dance or act in male attire, under
the same penalty. (5) That the doors of the theaters shall
not be opened until twelve o'clock, noon, and representations shall begin during the six months from October 1
at two o'clock, and during the other six months at four
in the afternoon, so that the performance may end one
hour before nightfall; and the commissioners and *alguaciles* shall take particular heed that this be complied with.
(6) That it be clearly indicated on the posters what
comedias are to be represented each day, and he who for
good cause shall fail to do so shall give an account of it
to the officer of the Council, under the said penalty.
(7) That the brotherhood of the *Pasion* and of the
Soledad shall each year name two Commissioners, satisfactory persons, rich and unoccupied, who shall take their
turn by weeks in each theater, and before naming the
whole number they shall furnish the list to the officer of
the Council, so that he may attend, if he so desire. (8)
That the said Commissioners appoint responsible and
trustworthy persons to receive the profits, who shall allow
nobody to enter without paying the required sum, and
they shall not leave the doors until at least the first act is
over, and having done so, they shall hand over the money

to the proper person for distribution. (9) That only the four Commissioners, the person with the book, and the money-takers (*cobradores*) shall enter without paying either for entrance or for a seat, and no other person, either because he is an *alguacil*, scrivener, brother (*cofrade*), or deputy, nor for any other cause, and of this the *alguaciles* shall take particular heed, so that there may be no disputes on this account, and if there be, they shall arrest the person, etc. (10) That the said Commissioner shall, during his week, at ten o'clock in summer and at eleven in winter, come every day to the theater to which he has been designated, to assign (*repartir*) the benches and *aposentos*, preferring titled persons and the nobility who may have sent to request them. (11) That they allow no man to enter or remain in the *gradas* or *tarimas* of the women, nor allow any woman to enter at the men's entrance, nor permit any one to enter the dressing-room or elsewhere unless he be a player, and if any one shall do so, the *alguaciles* shall put him in prison and shall duly report it, so that the person may be punished; and no friar shall likewise be permitted to enter the *corrales* to see the comedias, as hereinbefore commanded. (12) That no man be permitted to enter the *aposentos* especially designated for women, unless he be known to be the husband, father, son, or brother, etc. (13) That no *banco* or *aposento* be given without payment for it, but the Commissioners may give two *bancos* only every day in each theater, during the week in which they serve, to accommodate the money-takers and such others as are necessary, and no *aposento* may be given to anybody, although it be vacant. (14) That none of the said Commissioners may depute another in his place; if for good reasons he be unable to attend, he shall notify his companion. (15) That four Commissioners shall consult concerning any repairs to the theater, etc. (16) That that officer of the

Council who is protector of the hospitals shall name each year a Commissioner of the said hospitals, who shall keep the books of the profits of the said comedias and share the same among the said hospitals as agreed upon. (17) That the said *Comissario de libro* shall, on each day that a comedia is given, go to the treasury of the theater at three o'clock, and count what has been received from the seats, *bancos*, and *aposentos*, as well as the quartos taken at the doors, and shall divide it in the manner required, etc. (18) That of the five quartos [= 20 maravedís] which are received at the entrance from each man and woman, the manager shall take three, and the General Hospital one, and the other hospital of the capital and that of Anton Martin each one half a quarto; and of the money which results from the *asientos, bancos, aposentos, ventanas,* and *celosias,* the General Hospital shall receive the one fourth part, that of the *Niños expositos* another fourth part and one eighth of it, and the rest to go to the *Hospital de la Pasion,* as heretofore determined, etc. (19) That of the money which proceeds from the *ventanas, celosias,* and other things of which the General Hospital does not receive the quarto entrance money, one fifth be given to the said hospital, and the remainder be divided as profits from the *asientos* and *aposentos.* (20) That a separate account be kept of the moneys resulting from the renting of the *corrales,* the coach-house, and the six reals which each *autor* gives for each representation for repairs, and of the other things that cannot be divided each day, and that care be taken that these sums be collected, etc. . . . (26) That eight days before the close of the year the Commissioners shall announce the leasing of the *corrales* for the following year, etc. . . . (29) That the lessee shall not receive for each *aposento* more than twelve reals, nor for each *banco* more than one real, under penalty, etc. . . . (31) That no curtains or hangings may be put in the *aposentos,* nor benches in the *patio,* unless they be fastened to the walls."[1]

On October 3, 1611, Doña Margarita of Austria, wife of Philip the Third, died, after having given birth to a son on September 22, and the theaters were closed in consequence. This was a blow not only to the players, but also to the playwrights. Thus deprived of his immediate source of income, we find Lope de Vega complaining of his ill luck in a letter of October 6–8, to his patron, the Duke of Sessa: "I have bidden good-by to the Muses on account of the absence of comedias; I shall feel their loss, for, after all, they were a help in the frequent illness that my little family suffers." Again, speaking of the same subject, he says: "Only the comedia has felt the misfortune," and adds: "with due discretion they are already trying to resuscitate the play for the good of the hospitals."[2]

What the result of the recommendation of D. Juan de Tejada was we do not know, but on April 8, 1615, the Council issued another decree for the "Reformation of Comedias," which does not differ materially from the decree of 1603, except that it declares that there shall be twelve *autores de comedias,* instead of eight, and names them, and reënacts the recommendation of D. Juan de Tejada (of 1608) in many of its provisions. It declares that there shall be no more than twelve companies of players, to be named by the Council, who shall have a certificate of their appointment signed by Juan Gallo de Andrade, secretary of the Cámara del Consejo. That the Council appoints the following twelve *autores:* Alonso

---

[1] Cotarelo y Mori, *Controversias,* pp. 622–625. In this year (1608) we find an "Auto de los Alcaldes de Casa y Corte" forbidding all men from stopping at the door of the theater where women enter or leave the house, under a penalty of 200 ducats and banishment for four years from the court and five leagues therefrom. Madrid, May 6, 1608. (*Bull. Hispanique* (1907), p. 374.)

[2] Rennert, *Life of Lope de Vega,* p. 198. Two years after this, on October 19, 1613, writing from Lerma to his patron, the Duke of Sessa, Lope de

Riquelme, Fernan Sanchez, Tomas Fernandez, Pedro de Valdes, Diego Lopez de Alcaraz, Pedro Cebriano, Pedro Llorente, Juan de Morales, Juan Acacio, Antonio Granados, Alonso de Heredia, and Andres de Claramonte, who, and no others, may conduct companies for the space of two years next following the eighth day of April, and they shall have in their companies persons of good lives and habits, and shall each year furnish an account of them to the person whom the Council may designate, and the same shall be done by those who may be named *autores* hereafter, every two years.

That the directors and married actors be accompanied by their wives.

That they shall not wear costumes against the pragmatics of the realm, except upon the stage or wherever they may represent.

That the actresses shall appear only in decent women's attire and shall not represent in underskirt (*faldellin*) only, but shall at least wear over it a gown or loose overskirt (*baquero ó basquiña suelta enfaldada*), and they shall not act in male attire nor assume the rôles of men, nor shall men or youths represent women on the stage. It prohibits all lascivious or immodest songs, dances, or gestures, and permits only such as may be in conformity with the old dances and *bailes,* and especially forbids all the *bailes de escarramanes, chaconas, zarabandas, carreterías,* and all similar dances, concerning which it commands that the *autores* may not make use of them in any manner whatsoever, under the penalties declared, nor may they invent other new and similar ones bearing different names.   And all songs and dances must be approved by the Council, even those which are permissible.

Vega says that he had received word from Madrid that women had been forbidden to visit the comedia. His words are: "De Madrid me han escrito que por pregon publico se ha prohibido que las mugeres no vayan á la comedia, no sé que se murmura aqui acerca de la causa." (Schack, *Nachträge,* p. 34.)   I find no mention elsewhere of such a prohibition.

It provides further that in each theater of Madrid an especially appointed *alguacil* shall be present (besides Juan Alicante, *alguacil de la casa y corte de S. M.*), and the other two *alguaciles* during the time for which they may be appointed, each to remain in the theater to which he may be designated, and all are to take precautions that there be no noise, uproar, or scandal; that the men be kept separated from the women, both in the seats and in the entrances and exits, to avoid all unseemly acts; and they shall permit nobody except the players to enter the dressing-rooms. They are further to see to it that the auditors leave the theater before dark and that the theaters be not opened until noon.

That the *autores* and their companies shall not represent in private houses in Madrid without the license of the Council, nor shall they admit anybody to their rehearsals.

That no comedias whatever be represented from Ash Wednesday until the first Sunday after Easter, nor on the Sundays in Advent, nor on the first days of the *Pascuas.* That all comedias, *entremeses, bailes,* dances, and songs, before they are handed over to the actors to be studied, shall be taken to the censor appointed by the Council, who shall pass upon them and shall give a license, signed by him, permitting their representation, and without this license they may not be performed.

That no two companies may be in one place at the same time except in the court [Madrid] and in Seville, nor may they be more than two months in one place in any year.

That no performance be given in any church or monastery unless the comedia be purely one of devotion.

That the *autores* or players who fail to observe the above-mentioned declarations be punished in the following manner: For the first offense a fine of 200 ducats, to be devoted to charitable works; for the second the double of this fine and banishment from the kingdom for two years, and for the third infraction two years in the galleys. The decree is signed by Juan Gallo de Andrade.[1]

We have seen that by the above decree of 1615 only twelve *autores de comedias,* or directors of companies, were permitted to give theatrical performances, and that these *autores* were to exercise this privilege for two years only, except by special reappointment. Among the *autores de comedias* between 1615 and 1640 who were especially designated as "appointed by his Majesty," I have found the following, though there were doubtless others: Cristóbal Ortiz de Villazan (1619); Manuel Vallejo (1623); Juan Bautista Valenciano (1623); Juan Martinez (1624); Bartolomé Romero (1637); Pedro de la Rosa (1637); Luis Bernardo de Bovadilla (1637); Andres de la Vega (1638); Juan Roman (1638); Francisco Velez de Guevara (1639); Francisco Alvarez de Vitoria (1639); Pedro de Cobaleda (1639).

Of *autores de comedias* not designated as appointed by the King, the following names occur between 1615 and 1640: Cristóbal de Leon, Pedro Cerezo de Guevara, Francisco Mudarra, Francisco Ortiz, Juan Catalan, Alonso de Olmedo y Tofiño, Cristóbal de Avendaño, Jerónimo Sanchez, Antonio de Prado, Juan Jerónimo Almella, Roque de Figueroa, Juan Vazquez (*El Pollo*), Lorenzo Hurtado de la Cámara, Francisco Lopez, Juan Bautista Espinola or Espinosa, Sebastiano Gonzalez, Juan de Malaguilla, Juan Peñalosa, Francisco Solano, Segundo de Morales, Juan Rodriguez de Antriago, Damian Arias de Peñafiel, Pedro de Linares, Pedro de Ascanio, Antonio de Rueda, Gabriel de Espinosa, Damian de Espinosa, Luis Lopez de Sustaete, Francisco Garcia, and Pedro Manuel de Castilla (*Mudarra*).

For some time prior to 1615, however, the question of

---

[1] Cotarelo y Mori, *Controversias,* etc., pp. 626, 627. This decree had previously been published in part by Sepúlveda, *El Corral de la Pacheca,* p. 41.

completely suppressing the comedias must have been again discussed, for on February 25, 1615, a resolution was adopted by the town council or *ayuntamiento* of Madrid, which reads: "Having heard that there is a question of prohibiting comedias, and that in lieu of the profits which the hospitals derive from the comedias certain excises and imposts are to be levied, . . . it has been shown by experience that it is less dangerous to have comedias than to suppress them, for those who go to see them are thus prevented from having recourse to other things of greater danger and prejudice to them; . . . it is therefore resolved that the council entreat his Majesty that comedias may be permitted as heretofore, and that the proceeds resulting therefrom be devoted to the hospitals," etc.[1]

The comedia, it seems, had not been flourishing as heretofore, and in the previous year (1614) there had been a general complaint on the part of the overseers of the charities dependent upon the theaters, in which they were supported by the *autores,* that the income from the comedia had been greatly diminished on account of the decreased attendance at the theaters. The reasons assigned were various: "because the price of admission had been raised; because the *bancos* and *aposentos* had been farmed out, and further restrictions had been made as to the entrance of women into the theaters, and, finally, because there are no good *autores* nor any dances by women."[2]

The representation of comedias was continued under the restrictions prescribed by the decree of 1615, but Pellicer says that they were not so popular, "having lost the salt and attraction of the picaresque dances, of which the youth of both sexes are so fond."

This condition of things was not destined to continue long. As one may readily imagine, the managers of the

---

[1] Pérez Pastor, *Nuevos Datos,* p. 359.
[2] Pellicer, *Histrionismo,* Vol. II, pp. 159, 160.

theaters were not slow to give the public what it asked, and gradually, one after another, every restriction that had been placed upon the theaters was disregarded.[1] Besides the twelve privileged companies of players (*compañías reales* or *de título*) numerous other companies soon sprang up (*compañías de la legua*, as they were called), which overran the peninsula and apparently took no pains to avoid the capital. According to Pellicer, there were no less than forty, their total membership amounting to over one thousand persons.[2]

Indeed, a writer quoted by Ticknor declares that in 1636 there were as many as three hundred companies of

[1] Other measures respecting the theaters were enacted in succeeding years. In 1624 churchmen were prohibited from visiting the theaters or bull-fights: Acuerdo de la Junta de Reformacion. "En 24 de Marzo 1624 acordó la Junta que los religiosos no fueran á las comedias ni á los toros." (Pérez Pastor, *Bull. Hisp.* (1908), p. 250.) In the following year an attempt was even made to prevent the printing of comedias: Acuerdo de la Junta de Reformacion. "Y porque se ha reconocido el daño de imprimir libros de comedias, novelas ni otros deste genero por el que blandamente hacen a las costumbres de la juventud, se consulte a su M^d ordene al Consejo que en ningun manera se de licencia para imprimirlos." In the margin is the following note: "Hablose sobre deste punto a 7 de Marzo [1625] con el s^r Conde Duque, y parecio á S. Exª que el Presidente mi señor dé su oficio lo hiciesen, y que su S^a podria mandar asi." (*Ibid.*, p. 251.) In the same year it was again declared that the men should be separated from the women in the theaters and that the companies of players be reduced from forty to twelve: Acuerdo de la Junta de Reformacion: "En la Junta de 29 de Junio 1625 se acordó que hubiese separacion de hombres y mugeres en los corrales de comedias, que las compañias de 40 se reduzcan à 12." (*Ibid.*) And in December, 1625, it was recommended that representations in Madrid be given in only one theater: Acuerdo de la Junta de Reformacion. "En 11 de Diciembre de 1625 acordó la Junta que en la corte se representase en un solo corral cada dia." (*Ibid.*, p. 252.) While on January 11, 1626, it was declared that but one comedia should be represented each day in Madrid. (*Ibid.*, p. 252.) The two latter decrees were certainly never observed.

[2] Cervantes, *Don Quixote*, Madrid, 1797–98, Vol. IV, p. 110, note. Pellicer's information is probably derived from a memorial presented to Philip IV. by one Santiago Ortiz. The date of this instrument has been fixed in 1639, though this is uncertain. Ortiz says that, in spite of the decree of the Council that there should be no more than eight (*sic*) companies, there were now more than forty. "Vieronse en poco tiempo discurrir con desvergüenza grande por el reino 40 compañias, en que se ocupaban mil ó pocas menos personas de ambos sexos, gente bagabunda, de vida licenciosa y casi toda de costumbres estragadas, etc. A este gente perdida suelen agregarse hombres facinerosos, clerigos y frailes apóstatas

players in Spain.[1] That this number is greatly exaggerated does not admit of a doubt. It is probable that there were not more than twenty companies of standing in Spain in 1636. Of smaller strolling bands we have no information, but there were doubtless many, as there had been for years. Still, the theater was undoubtedly on the wane.

In some parts of Spain, indeed, theatrical representations were not tolerated at all, as in Navarre, and "come-

y fugitivos, que se acogen como asilo de estas compañias para poder andar libres y desconocidos á la sombra de ellas. Maridos que sólo sirven de excusa á sus mugeres, y mugeres que sólo sirven de excusa á sus maridos, falsos ó verdaderos, y que con sus desenvolturas y bufonerias encantan á los viejos y á los mozos . . . hallan valedores para todo, y nunca sus delitos pueden refrenarse con algunas penas." (Sanchez-Arjona, *Anales del Teatro en Sevilla*, p. 282.) Pellicer states that Santiago Ortiz, the author of this memorial, was an actor, but Cotarelo y Mori, *Controversias*, p. 541, shows quite conclusively that this is an error and that he was probably "algun religioso austero," and fixes the date of the memorial in 1649.

[1] *History of Spanish Literature*, Boston, 1888, Vol. II, p. 518, note 9. The writer alluded to by Ticknor under the title "Pantoja, *Sobre Comedias*," is really Simon Lopez, to whom reference has already been made. "Pantoja" was the name of a lady who had expressed scruples concerning the legality of comedias, to which the work of Simon Lopez was a reply. (Cotarelo, *Controversias*, p. 399, note.)

The following statement from Leon Pinelo's *Anales* is not without interest, and is, besides, a flat contradiction of the assertion of "Pantoja." After describing the funeral of Lope de Vega in 1635, Pinelo says, under the year 1636: "En este insigne Ingenio [Lope] tuvieron principio las comedias en la forma que hasta oy permanezen, y con su muerte han ydo descaeziendo, de modo que el Doctor Montalvan en el año de 1632 pone setenta y siete Poetas de que refiere los nombres, y los mas escrivian comedias: oy no podremos señalar quatro que se apliquen a esta ocupazion, y asi se van despoblando los Teatros y desaciendo las Compañias de la farsa." (Schack, *Nachträge*, p. 36.) Still, one is curious to know whom Pinelo had in mind when he says that "not four poets can be named nowadays who devote themselves to writing plays." In 1636 Guillen de Castro was dead, but Calderon was then at the height of his fame, and Mira de Mescua, Alarcon, Rojas, Velez de Guevara, Montalban, Moreto, and Tirso de Molina were still among the living, though perhaps the latter had then practically ceased writing for the stage. That the companies of players were not *all* disbanded in 1636 is shown by the fact that among the principal *autores* who had companies in that year or shortly thereafter are the following: Pedro de la Rosa, Manuel Vallejo, Hernan Sanchez de Vargas, Tomas Fernandez de Cabredo, Bartolomé Romero, Luis Bernardo de Bovadilla, Alonso de Olmedo, Antonio

dians who entered that kingdom were severely punished,"
as Crespi de Borja writes in 1649.[1] The same writer also
says that comedias were at this time not often acted in
Valencia, Segorve, Játiva, and other places. And as early
as 1620 an anonymous writer says: "In other cities like
Plasencia, Burgos, León, Toro, Zamora, Cuenca, Ocaña,
and others, actors are rarely seen, unless it be to represent
some festival."[2] Two years later, in 1622, the mayordomo of the hospitals of the city of Vitoria proposed that
a theater be erected in the city to provide a revenue for the
hospitals, and to this the town council assented. But the
hijosdalgo of the city and the natives of the surrounding
country objected to a theater, declaring that the inhabi-
tants were very industrious and that they would become
worthless and their business and employments would suffer; moreover, a portion of the site that had been chosen
would, from its darkness, afford lurking-places for thieves
and vagabonds. The structure was begun, though it
remained unfinished and was never used as a theater.[3]
That for some time prior to 1634 there had been no comedias represented in Murcia, we learn from a letter of
Francisco de Cascales to Lope de Vega.[4] And in 1694

de Prado, Roque de Figueroa, Andres de la Vega, Luis Lopez de Sustaete,
Antonio de Rueda, and others.

Since writing the above I have found that the statement of Pinelo,
though under the year 1636, was not actually written until 1658. It may
have been correct at the latter date. See *Comedias de Moreto,* edited by
D. Luis Fernández Guerra, p. xii (*Bibl. de Autores Españoles*).

[1] "En Navarra no sólo no las [i.e., comedias] hay, pero son castigados
gravemente los comediantes si entran en ella." He further says, speaking
of comedias: "en las ciudades donde no las hay continuas, como en Valencia, Játiva, Segorve y otros lugares del reino, donde nunca ó raras
veces las hay, no se ven ni se hacen mayores delitos cuando faltan estas
comedias." (Quoted by Cotarelo y Mori, *Controversias,* p. 194.) This
is a rather startling statement, if true, for it shows the early decline of
the comedia in a city—Valencia—which was one of the great theatrical
centers at the beginning of the seventeenth century.

[2] Cotarelo y Mori, *Controversias,* p. 229.
[3] Pérez Pastor, *Nuevos Datos,* p. 190.
[4] *Cartas filologicas,* Murcia, 1634: "Muchos dias ha, Señor, que no tene-

comedias were banished from the city of Cordoba and its
theater was ordered to be torn down by the city council.[1]

mos en Murcia comedias; ello·deve ser porque aqui han dado en perseguir
la representacion, predicando contra ella, como si fuera alguna secta ó
gravisimo crimen." (Edition of 1779, p. 127.) I do not know the date of
this letter, but it was written after 1621. See also Schack, *Nachträge*, p. 61.
[1] *Controversias*, p. 209.

CHAPTER XI

Private representations before the King. Philip the Third. Philip
the Fourth. The latter's fondness for the theater. Representations in 1622. Festivals at Aranjuez. The "Buen Retiro."
Lope's *Selva sin Amor*. Dramatic spectacles by Calderon. Decree of 1641 regulating plays. The theaters closed in 1646 and
again in 1682.

ON March 31, 1621, the theaters of Madrid were closed
on account of the death of Philip the Third, and all comedias were suspended until July 28 of that year.[1]   The *autos*
were represented on Corpus Christi as usual, and in Madrid they were performed by the companies of Pedro de
Valdes and Cristóbal de Avendaño, who were the only
autores permitted to act in Madrid "from the day the
license should be given until Corpus."[2]   During the *autos*
of this year we are told that not a castanet was heard, out
of respect for the late King.   At Seville they were presented by the companies of Hernan. Sanchez de Vargas
and Juan Bautista Valenciano.[3]

Upon the opening of the *corrales* of Madrid, on July
28, 1621, the first comedia to be performed was Lope de
Vega's *Dios haze Reyes*, which was represented by the
company of Diego Lopez de Alcaraz.[4]

[1] Pellicer, Vol. I, p. 161. It is probable that this prohibition also extended
to Seville. Fernandez-Guerra (*Alarcon*, p. 351) states that the theaters
were closed only till May 9, 1621.

[2] Pérez Pastor, *Nuevos Datos*, p. 188.

[3] Sanchez-Arjona, *Anales*, p. 217.

[4] Pellicer, *Histrionismo*, Vol. I, p. 161, says: "Comenzó Alcazar por una
comedia de Lope de Vega," etc. This is evidently a mistake for Alcaraz,
since we know that the latter, who had been an *autor de comedias* since
the last decade of the sixteenth century, was in Madrid in 1621 and the

Of the kings of Spain during the period with which we are concerned, Philip the Second seems to have lent no support to the theater nor to have favored it in any material way. Indeed, nothing could have been more opposed to his gloomy religious character, and while Philip the Third inherited much of the somberness of his father's nature, which toward the close of his life developed into a like religious fanaticism, he seems not to have been averse to the stage and even had a theater built in the palace for private representations, though this was probably due more to the interest and delight which the Queen took in such performances. As Schack has observed, it results from the *Relaciones* of Cabrera that as early as the beginning of the seventeenth century comedias were represented in the royal palace or Alcázar, which stood upon the spot where the royal palace stands to-day, i.e., in the west end of Madrid, while the Buen Retiro is situated in the east end of the city, and that Philip the Third, besides the stage which appears to have been in one of the royal saloons, also caused a theater to be built in the *Casas del Tesoro,* near the palace.[1]

Many private representations of comedias before the court doubtless took place in the years preceding the building of this theater, of which a few are recorded. These were all given at the instance of the Queen. On January 30, 1603, the Queen commanded that 1500 reals be paid to Nicolas de los Rios for five comedias acted in her presence at Valladolid during that month, and on

beginning of 1622. (*Nuevos Datos,* p. 189.) The name "Alcazar" had misled Chorley into supposing that the Alcázar theater (i.e., in the Royal Palace) was meant. See my *Life of Lope de Vega,* p. 489. Lope's play contains no *gracioso,* and Chorley says that it is to be presumed that Lope purposely refrained from introducing a comic character, as the period of mourning for the King's death was not yet over.

[1] *Nachträge,* p. 26. The passage in Cabrera is as follows, under the date, Madrid á 20 de Enero 1607: "Hase hecho en el segundo patio de las casas del Tesoro un teatro donde vean sus Magestades las comedias, como se representan al pueblo en los corrales que estan deputados para ello, porque puedan gozar mejor de ellas que quando se les representa en

July 14, 1603, he received 600 reals for two co?
one of which he represented at Burgos in June, ?
at Valladolid, where the court then was, on July 13, 1603.
Again, on August 25 of the same year Juan de Morales
Medrano received 600 reals for two comedias played
before the Queen in August, while Antonio de Villegas
was paid 1200 reals for four comedias acted in the
Queen's presence in Valladolid in September, 1603.[1] On
October 20, 1604, the Queen commanded that 2000 reals
be paid to Gaspar de Porres on account of the comedias
represented before her during this year in Valladolid, and
1600 reals, the balance due him, on November 23, for
twelve comedias acted between August and the end of
November, i.e., 3600 reals for the twelve comedias.[2]

The *autos sacramentales* made a stronger appeal to
Philip the Third than comedias, and were often represented in private before the royal family. In 1609 Balbin
and Heredia represented *autos* before the King in the
Escorial,[3] and in June, 1613, Alonso de Riquelme and his
players proceeded to San Lorenzo el Real to repeat before the King the *autos sacramentales* which he had represented at Corpus of that year in Madrid. For this
private representation Riquelme was to have received
3100 reals, "but 200 reals were deducted as a fine, because
he did not furnish new costumes, in accordance with the
agreement which he had made."[4]

With the accession to the throne of Philip the Fourth,
in 1621, at the age of sixteen[5] (he was born April 8, 1605),

su sala, y asi han hecho alrededor galerias y ventanas donde esté la gente
de Palacio, y sus Magestades iran alli de su Camara por el pasadizo que
está hecho, y las veran por unas celosias." (*Relaciones de las Cosas
sucedidas en la Corte de España desde el año 1599 hasta 1614,* por Luis
Cabrera de Cordoba. Edited by D. Pascual de Gayangos. Madrid, 1857,
p. 298.)

[1] Pérez Pastor, in *Bull. Hispanique* (1907), p. 368.
[2] *Ibid.,* p. 369.　　　[3] *Ibid.,* p. 375.
[4] *Nuevos Datos,* p. 135.
[5] Philip III. died March 30, 1621, so that, in fact, the new King was not
quite sixteen.

a more favorable period for the drama was inaugurated. He was a generous patron of art and literature and was especially an ardent admirer of the theater. As Schack has said: "His name is indissolubly linked with the great artists and poets who glorified his reign. Under his protection the greatest Spanish painters, led by Velazquez, were united at Madrid to a school which will compare favorably with that of any other country."

With Philip the Fourth the theater was a ruling passion, in which perhaps his inordinate weakness for the *comediantas* played no less a part than his admiration for the comedia. He not only greatly encouraged dramatists,[1] but is said to have himself written a number of plays, among which *Dar la Vida por su Dama* has been persistently ascribed to him, though it is now conceded that this comedia was written by Antonio Coello.

Philip's taste for these spectacles was developed at a very early age, and in 1614, being then nine years old, he appeared as Cupid in a representation given by the prince and princesses before the King and Queen and ladies of the court, the little Count of Puñonrostro impersonating Venus. The movement of the car in which Cupid came upon the stage made him ill, however, and "he vomited twice, though no other mishap befell him, and they say that he played his part exceedingly well," as the chronicler gravely informs us.[2]

[1] So we are told by all writers on the Spanish drama, but if we except Calderon, Bocangel (an insignificant playwright), and D. Jerónimo de Villayzan, whose career was a very short one, I cannot recall another instance in which this king gave any substantial aid to a dramatist. Alarcon, it is true, held an unimportant appointment with a high-sounding title, but this was not bestowed upon him by Philip. Nearly all the other dramatists were priests, who depended upon the church for their subsistence. The greatest of them all was sorely neglected by Philip; the only royal favor that Lope de Vega ever received was a pension in Galicia of 250 ducats annually, granted to him a few years before his death. The King's promise to provide for Lope's son-in-law was never kept. (*Life of Lope de Vega*, pp. 376, 415. But see above, p. 37, note 2.)

[2] "De Madrid 8 de Marzo 1614: El jueves de la semana pasada, el

A minute account of another festival in which this princeling took part has since been published by the Marques de la Fuensanta del Valle and D. José Sancho Rayon from a manuscript in possession of the editors. It took place at Lerma on November 3, 1614, and the comedia represented was Lope de Vega's *El Premio de la Hermosura,* though from the description here given the play must have differed considerably from the version as now printed in Lope's *Comedias,* Part XVI, Madrid, 1621. The subject of the comedia, we are told, was taken from Lope's epic *La Hermosura de Angélica:* the costumes, stage machinery, and decorations are described in detail, and a list of characters, with the names of those who impersonated them. Here, too, the little prince represented Cupid, and besides "he threw out the *Loa.*"[1]

It would be very interesting to know the titles of the comedias thus privately represented before the King and Queen in the first decades of the seventeenth century. Lists of such plays have been published for the year 1622 and for subsequent years, and doubtless the Archives of the palace will reveal others prior to these dates.[2] Beginning on October 5, 1622, the private performances given in the apartments of the Queen on Sundays, Thursdays, and feast-days during that year, as first published by Schack (*Nachträge,* p. 66), were as follows:

Príncipe Nuestro Señor con los meninos representaron una comedia delante del Rey y sus Altezas y las damas, sin entrar otro ninguno; representó el Príncipe al dios Cupido, y de salir en un carro se mareó y tuvo dos vómitos, pero no se le siguió otro mal; y dicen lo hizo bonisimamente, y el condecito de Puño en Rostro hizo la diosa Venus, y los otros los demas personages, y ha habido algunos á quien ha parecido que no se habia de permitir que representase su Alteza, aunque la poca edad le disculpa; al cual se le ha muerto el enano Bonami, que él queria mucho, y lo merecia porque era mucho de estimar," etc. (Cabrera, *Relaciones,* p. 547.)

[1] *Comedias inéditas de Frey Lope Felix de Vega Carpio.* Tomo I, Madrid, 1873, p. 479.

[2] In September, 1622, Cristóbal Ortiz de Villazan had also representado three comedias in the private apartments of the Queen. (*Bull. Hisp.* (1908), p. 247.)

COMEDIAS REPRESENTADAS EN OCTUBRE:

Autores.

Pedro de Valdes.
> *Los Celos en el Caballo* (Ximénez de Enciso).
> *La despreciada Querida* (Juan Bautista de Ville-gas).
> *La Pérdida de España* (D. Juan de Velasco y Guzman?). It also bears the alternative title *La más injusta Venganza.*

"For these three comedias 900 reals were paid, or 300 reals each, at the command of the Queen, on the petition of Jerónima de Burgos, wife of the said *autor*, for prior to this only 200 reals had been paid for the representation of a comedia."

Alonso de Olmedo.
> *Ganar Amigos* (Alarcon).
> *Rodamonte Aragonés* (Juan Bautista de Villegas). It also bears the alternative title *El valiente Luci-doro.* See Paz y Melia, *Catálogo*, No. 3399.
> *Poderosa es la Ocasion*(?). Repre-sented twice.
> *Como se engañan los Ojos* (Juan Bautista de Villegas).

Cristóbal de Avendaño.
> *El Labrador venturoso* (Lope de Vega).
> *El Infante de Aragon* (Andrés de Claramonte).
> *El Rey Angel.* Perhaps this is *El Rey Angel de Sicilia*, by Juan Antonio de Mojica. See Paz y Melia, *Catálogo*, No. 2901.

The above three comedias were represented in October and November.

Cristóbal de Avendaño.

> *Cautela contra Cautela* (Tirso de Molina and Alarcon).
>
> *La Pérdida del Rey D. Sebastian* (?). Perhaps this is *El Rey Don Sebastian y Portugues más heroico,* by Juan Bautista de Villegas. See Paz y Melia, *Catálogo,* No. 2904.
>
> *Lo que puede la Traicion* (?).
>
> *El Marido de su Hermana* (Juan Bautista de Villegas).
>
> *El Martir de Madrid* (Mira de Mescua). See Paz y Melia, *Catálogo,* No. 2029.
>
> *El Labrador venturoso* (Lope de Vega).

Cristóbal de Avendaño.

> *El Labrador venturoso* (Lope de Vega).
>
> *San Bruno* (?).
>
> *La Caida de Faeton* (?). See Paz y Melia, *Catálogo,* No. 1225.

Cristóbal de Avendaño.

> *Ir y quedarse* (?).
>
> *Quien no se aventura* (Guillen de Castro).
>
> *El Príncipe ignorante* (?). Perhaps Lope's *El Príncipe inocente,* mentioned in his *Peregrino en su Patria* (1604).
>
> *Mas merece quien mas ama* (Antonio Hurtado de Mendoza). Acted twice.
>
> *Las Victorias del Marques de Cañete* (written by nine *Ingenios*). See Barrera, *Catálogo,* p. 31. Acted in conjunction with the company of Valdes.
>
> *Trances de Amor* (?). Calderon wrote a play *Lances de Amor y Fortuna,* published in 1636.

Juan de Morales Medrano.
{
El Niño del Senado (?).

La Conquista de Jerusalen (?). See Paz y Melia, *Catálogo*, No. 1508. Twice represented.

Celos engendran Amor (?).

Las Pobrezas de Reynaldos (Lope de Vega).

La Vengadora de las Mugeres (Lope de Vega).

El Vencedor vencido en el Torneo. Perhaps this is *El Vencedor vencido*, by D. Juan de Ochoa of Seville. See Paz y Melia, *Catálogo*, No. 3428.

La milagrosa Eleccion de Pio V. (Moreto).
}

[Manuel] Vallejo.
{
La Judit Española (?).

La Romera de Santiago (Tirso de Molina).

Las Pruebas de la Lealtad (?).

Las Burlas de Pedro de Urdemalas (Lope de Vega?). See my *Life of Lope de Vega*, p. 524.

La Selva de Amor (?). It cannot be *Selva de Amor y Celos*, by Francisco de Rojas, who was not born till 1607. Perhaps it is Lope's *Selvas y Bosques de Amor*.
}

Pedro de Valdes.
{
[Amor], Pleito y Desafio (Lope de Vega).

Los Celos en el Caballo (Ximénez de Enciso). Represented twice.

D. Sancho el Malo (?).

Las Azañas del Marques de Cañete (by nine *Ingenios*). Represented by Valdes and Avendaño. See above.

La despreciada Querida (Juan Bautista de Villegas).
}

The whole number of comedias represented in the apartments of the Queen from October 5, 1622, to February 8, 1623, was forty-five.

Another very important list of comedias represented before Philip the Fourth between 1623 and 1654 was published many years ago by Sr. Cruzada Villaamil.[1] It consists of about three hundred titles, beginning with five comedias performed by the company of Juan Bautista de Villegas, and including one (*Como se engañan los Ojos*) which he himself had written. The latest play in the list is Calderon's *La Hija del Aire*, acted by the company of Adrian Lopez in November, 1653. For each of these representations the King paid 200 reals.

Of the private representations of comedias just mentioned, those which took place in the autumn of 1622 and in the early months of 1623, to the young Queen, Isabel of Bourbon (elder daughter of Henry the Fourth, the great Béarnais, and first wife of Philip the Fourth), were given in her private apartments in the Alcázar, then the royal residence in Madrid. She died on October 6, 1644. In appears that, before these performances were given, Philip the Fourth desired to erect a theater in the palace, and accordingly commanded that one should be built "near the game of *pelota*." Objection was made to the King's plan by the Council, and whether it was ever carried out in the form proposed I do not know.[2] That representations continued to be given in the Alcázar, however, for some

---

[1] In *El Averiguador*, Tomo I, Madrid, 1871. The great scarcity of this publication induced me to reprint the list in the *Modern Language Review*, Cambridge, England, Vol. II, 1907, with additions, under the title "Notes on the Chronology of the Spanish Drama." It will be seen that the King was less liberal than the Queen in his expenditures for this favorite amusement.

[2] "31 Agosto 1622.—Habiendo entendido que su magestad quiere hacer en Palacio un corral de comedias, se acordó que para el primero Ayuntamiento se llame á la villa para tratar dello y se llame al Sr. Luis Hurtado particularmente para saber dél, como veedor de las obras de su magestad, lo que en esto hay.

"Acordóse (2 Septiembre 1622) que se llame á la Villa para el lunes á

years, is certain. The King, prior to this, and until the completion of the sumptuous palace, the Buen Retiro, in 1632, had festal performances given in the royal gardens at Aranjuez, where an immense stage was constructed by the Italian architect Cesare Fontana, the theater being one of great magnificence. Here a splendid festival was presented on the King's seventeenth birthday, April 8, 1622. Don Juan de Tarsis, Count of Villamediana, was the author of the comedia, *La Gloria de Niquea y Descripcion de Aranjuez,* which was presented on that occasion.[1]

In 1631, on a large tract of land adjoining the royal monastery and convent of San Jerónimo, Philip began the erection of a new royal residence, the Buen Retiro, "a fantastic palace of pleasure and pastime which was to

fin de tratar del nuevo corral de comedias que su magestad es servido y manda que se haga junto al juego de pelota. En 5 de Septiembre se acordó hablar al Presidente del Consejo exponiendole los daños que la Villa tendria con la instalacion del nuevo corral de comedias, pues no podria dar á los hospitales los 60,000 (ducados) anuales que les da." (Libros de Acuerdos del Ayuntamiento de Madrid. Pérez Pastor, *Nuevos Datos,* p. 191.)

[1] *Obras de Don Juan de Tarsis, Conde de Villamediana y Correo Mayor de Su Magestad,* Çaragoça, por Juan de Lanaja y Quartanet, Inpresor del Reino de Aragon y de la Universidad, Año 1629, pp. 1–54. Mr. Martin Hume gives the following account of this festival: "In the following spring of 1622 there was a great series of festivals at Aranjuez, where the court was then in residence, to celebrate Philip's seventeenth birthday. Already the glamour of the stage had seized upon Philip and his wife, and one of the attractions of the rejoicings was the representation, in a temporary theater of canvas erected amidst the trees on the 'island garden,' and beautifully adorned, of a comedy in verse by Count of Villa Mediana, dedicated to the Queen. The comedy was called *La Gloria de Niquea,* and Isabel herself was to personate the goddess of beauty. It was night, and the flimsy structure of silk and canvas was brilliantly lit with wax lights when all the court had assembled to see the show; the young King and his two brothers and sister being seated in front of the stage, and the Queen in the retiring-room behind the scenes. The prologue had been finished successfully, and the audience were awaiting the withdrawing of the curtain that screened the stage, when a piercing shriek went up from the back, and a moment afterward a long tongue of flame licked up half the drapery before the stage, and immediately the whole place was ablaze. Panic seized upon the splendid mob, and there was a rush to escape. The King succeeded in fighting his way out with diffi-

obscure utterly the groves, gardens, and ancient palaces of the Pardo and the Casa de Campo, which had been the delight of Philip the Second and Philip the Third."[1] The palace was surrounded by extensive gardens, groves, and artificial lakes, and contained a magnificent theater. On a portion of the site occupied by the Buen Retiro had formerly stood an aviary with a collection of poultry, belonging to the Countess of Olivares,[2] husband of the King's favorite, the Count-Duke of Olivares, to whose ideas the palace owed its origin and who was the leading spirit in its erection and completion. As the palace and its gardens were not finished until October, 1632, the festival, which was one of the greatest magnificence, given to the royal couple by the Count-Duke on St. John's eve, 1631, took place in the gardens of the Duke of Maqueda and D. Luis

culty, and made his way to the back of the stage in search of his wife. In the densely wooded gardens that surrounded the blazing structure he sought for a time in vain, but at last found that Villa Mediana had been before him, and that the half-fainting figure of the Queen was lying in the Count's arms. Whatever may have been the truth of the matter, this, at all events, made a delightful *bonne bouche* for the scandalmongers, who hated Villa Mediana for his atrabilious gibes, and it soon became noised abroad that the Count had planned the whole affair, and had purposely set fire to the theater that he might gain the credit of having clasped her in his arms, if but for a moment." (*The Court of Philip IV.*, p. 58.) Four months after this, in August, 1622, Villa Mediana was murdered in Madrid, while returning home in his coach, soon after dark. An account of the above-mentioned festival at Aranjuez, and a description of the magnificent theater erected there by the skill of Capitan Julio Cesar Fontana, together with a descriptive poem entitled *Relacion de la Fiesta de Aranjuez en Verso*, by Don Antonio de Mendoza, will be found in that author's works, entitled *El Fenix Castellano*, etc., Lisboa, 1690, pp. 426 ff.

[1] Mesonero Romanos, *El Antiguo Madrid*, Madrid, 1881, Vol. II, p. 163; Hume, *The Court of Philip IV.*, p. 238.

[2] Hence the term *gallinero* sometimes applied to the palace, but generally, it seems, to the theater, for we read frequently of comedias represented in the *gallinero* of the Buen Retiro. Madame d'Aulnoy's description is as follows: "Le Buen Retiro est une maison Royale à l'une des portes de la Ville. Le Comte-Duc y fit faire d'abord une petite maison qu'il nomma *Gallinero,* pour mettre des poulets fort rares qu'on lui avait données; & comme il alloit les voir assez souvent, la situation de ce lieu qui est sur le penchant d'une colline, & dont la vue est tres agreable, l'engagea d'entreprendre un bâtiment considerable. . . . La

Mendez de Carrion, which adjoined each other. During this festival two comedias were represented: *Quien mas miente medra mas,* written by Don Francisco de Quevedo and D. Antonio de Mendoza, and performed by the company of Vallejo, and Lope de Vega's sprightly comedy *La Noche de San Juan,* represented by the company of Cristóbal de Avendaño.[1]

In October, 1632, the completion of the Buen Retiro was celebrated with a festival of great splendor, beginning with a cane tourney in which the King and the Count-Duke took part, followed by other sports and entertainments. It was celebrated by Lope de Vega in a poem entitled *A la primera Fiesta del Palacio nuevo.*[2] A play for the solemnity of swearing fealty to the infant prince Baltasar, written by the Prince of Esquilache, and acted at the palace in this year, is mentioned by Ticknor, as well as two other plays acted on the same occasion—one by Antonio de Mendoza and the other by Lopez de Enciso.[3]

From this time forth representations in the theater of the Buen Retiro were of frequent occurrence, and, according to Pellicer, in 1640 people began to visit them in the same manner as they did those in the *Corral de la Cruz* and in the *Príncipe.*[4]

Salle pour les Comedies est d'un beau dessin, fort grande, toute ornée de sculpture & de dorure. L'on peut être quinze dans chaque loge sans s'incommoder. Elles ont toutes des jalousies, & celle où se met le Roi est fort dorée. Il n'y a ni Orchestre ni Amphitheatre. On s'assit dans le parterre sur des bancs." (*Relation du Voyage d'Espagne,* La Haye, 1693, Vol. III, p. 6.)

[1] Pellicer, *Histrionismo,* Vol. II, pp. 167 ff., and Hume, *The Court of Philip IV.,* p. 231.

[2] Published in his *Vega del Parnaso,* Madrid, 1637, fol. 61, v. Besides the magnificent theater which the King had built in the palace of Buen Retiro, spectacles were also represented upon the pond in the gardens. See below.

[3] *History of Spanish Literature,* Vol. III, p. 48, note.

[4] *Avisos de Pellicer,* 7 Febrero 1640. "El Rey nuestro Señor con toda su casa y la Señora Princesa de Cariñan está desde el dia de San Blas en el Buen Retiro, donde ha de tenerse hasta la Quaresma. Hase em-

Among the festal performances before the royal family in the palace, it may not be without interest to mention Lope de Vega's pastoral eclogue *La Selva sin Amor*, which was sung before his Majesty sometime prior to November 22, 1629. This, as Ticknor says, was the first attempt to introduce dramatic performances with music. The eclogue was wholly sung, and, as Lope himself says, "it was a thing new in Spain." It was played with a showy apparatus of scenery and stage machinery prepared by Cosme Lotti, an Italian architect.[1] It was to the latter's great skill, moreover, that the success of many of the sumptuous court representations given by the king were in no small measure due. Among them may be mentioned: *"Circe.* A Dramatic Spectacle which was represented on the great pond of the Retiro, the invention of Cosme Lotti, at the request of her most excellent Ladyship the Countess of Olivares, Duchess of San Lucar la Mayor, on the night

pezado á representar en el teatro de las comedias que se ha fabricado dentro y concurre la gente en la misma forma que á los de la Cruz y del Príncipe, celebrándose para los Hospitales y autores de la Farsa. Es obra grande." (Schack, *Nachträge,* p. 72.) *"Los Bandos de Verona,* de D. Francisco de Rojas, estrenóse el 4 de Febrero de 1640, representandola la compañia de Bartolomé Romero, y fué la primera comedia que se hizo en el coliseo del Buen Retiro, asistiendo gente que pagó la entrada como en los demás corrales" (Bib. Nac., MS. V–48), quoted by Julio Monreal, *Cuadros viejos,* Madrid, 1878, p. 124, note.

[1] *History of Spanish Literature,* Vol. II, p. 508. He says further that "the earliest of the full-length plays that was ever sung was Calderon's *La Purpura de la Rosa,* which was produced before the court in 1660, on occasion of the marriage of Louis the Fourteenth with the Infanta Maria Theresa—a compliment to the distinguished personages of France who had come to Spain in honor of that great solemnity, and whom it was thought no more than gallant to amuse with something like the operas of Quinault and Lulli, which were then the most admired entertainments at the court of France." Unfortunately a slight matter of chronology interferes at this point. While Quinault and Lulli collaborated for fourteen years, producing on an average an opera a year, the earliest, *La Fête de l'Amour et de Bacchus,* was not brought out until 1672, just twelve years after Calderon's *La Purpura de la Rosa.* In Pérez Pastor, *Calderon Documentos,* Tomo I, p. 277, we read of a "fiesta (comedia) toda cantada, de D. Pedro Calderon de la Barca, que se habia de hacer el domingo 28 deste mes [Noviembre 1660] a los años del Príncipe, Nuestro Señor." This was, doubtless, *La Purpura de la Rosa.* Lope de Vega's dedi-

of St. John [June 24, 1634?].[1] Also Calderon's *El mayor Encanto Amor*, "a *fiesta* which was represented before his Majesty on St. John's eve in the year 1635, on the pond of the royal palace of the Buen Retiro," and *Los tres mayores Prodigios*, a festival also produced in the Retiro on the St. John's eve of the following year. These plays were given in the open air, and in the latter case the three acts were represented on separate stages, beside one another, each act by a different company of players: the first act on the stage on the right hand by Tomas Fernandez, the second act on the left by Pedro de la Rosa, and the

cation of the *Selva sin Amor* to the Almirante de Castilla is so important for the history of the stage of the time that I give the most interesting parts of it: "No aviendo visto V. Excelencia esta Egloga, que se representó cantada a sus Magestades y Altezas, cosa nueua en España, me pareció imprimirla, para que desta suerte, con menos cuydado la imaginasse V. Excelencia, etc. . . . La maquina del Teatro hizo Cosme Lotti ingeniero Florentin, por quien su Magestad embió a Italia, para que assistiesse a su seruicio en jardines, fuentes, y otras cosas, en que tiene raro y excelente ingenio. . . . La primera vista del Teatro, en aviendo corrido la tienda que le cubria [it will be observed that here there was an outer curtain], fue un Mar en perspectiua, que descubria á los ojos (tanto puede el Arte) muchas leguas de agua hasta la Ribera opuesta, en cuyo puerto se vian la ciudad, y el Faro con algunas Naues, que haziendo salva disparauan, a quien tambien de los Castillos respondian. Vianse assimismo algunos pezes, que fluctuauan, segun el mouimiento de las ondas, que con la misma inconstancia, que si fueran verdaderas, se inquietauan, todo con luz artificial, sin que se viesse ninguna, y siendo las que formauan aquel fingido dia mas de trezientas. Aqui Venus en un carro que tirauan dos Cisnes, habló con el Amor su hijo, que por lo alto de la maquina rebolaua. Los instrumentos ocupauan la primera parte del Teatro, siu ser vistos, a cuya armonia cantauan las figuras los versos, haziendo en la misma composicion de la Musica, las admiraciones, las quexas, los amores, las iras, y los demas afectos. Para el discurso de los Pastores se disparecio el Teatro maritimo, sin que este mouimiento, con ser tan grande, le pudiesse penetrar la vista, transformandose el Mar en una selva, que significaua el soto de Mançanares, con la puente, por quien passauan en perspectiua quantas cosas pudieron ser imitadas de las que entran y salen en la Corte: y assimismo se vian la casa del campo y el Palacio, con quanto desde aquella parte podia determinar la vista, . . ." etc. (*Laurel de Apolo*, Madrid, 1630, fol. 103.)

[1] Pellicer, *Histrionismo*, Vol. II, p. 146. A translation of this curious document will be found in: *Love the greatest Enchantment, The Sorceries of Sin, The Devotion of the Cross*, from the Spanish of Calderon, by Denis Florence Mac-Carthy, London, 1861, p. 5.

third upon the middle stage by the company of Antonio de Prado.[1]

These private representations before the King by the various theatrical companies which happened to be in Madrid were of very frequent occurrence. Certain actors or actresses whom the King especially desired were called from other cities, and sometimes entire companies were thus commanded by the King for these private func-

[1] Calderon, *Comedias,* Part II, Madrid, 1637. My copy is of the second edition, Madrid, 1641, where the play begins on fol. 257. It is preceded by a *Loa.* These plays were produced upon a floating theater "which the wasteful extravagance of the Count-Duke of Olivares had erected on the artificial waters in the gardens of the Buen Retiro." In the concluding verses of the play Calderon says that "the water was very happy on this gracious night." Ticknor, however, states that "a storm of wind scattered the vessels, the royal party, and a supper that was also among the floating arrangements of the occasion, prepared by Cosme Lotti, the Florentine architect," though the play was successfully acted several times during the month. He fixes the date as June 12, 1639, which, however, was certainly not its first representation. (*History of Spanish Literature,* Vol. II, p. 481, note.) Ticknor's source of information was probably the *Anales de Madrid* of Antonio Leon Pinelo, who, under the year 1640, says: "La noche de San Juan hubo en el Retiro muchos festines, y entre ellos una Comedia representada sobre el Estanque grande con maquinas, tramoyas, luces y toldos: todo fundado sobre las barcas. Estando representando, se levantó un torbellino de viento tan furioso, que lo desbarató todo, y algunas personas peligraron de golpes y caidas." (Quoted by Pellicer, *Histrionismo,* Vol. I, p. 193. See the very interesting note on St. John's eve, in *Don Quixote,* ed. Clemencin, Vol. VI, pp. 259 ff.) A number of these *particulares,* as private performances were called, belonging to a somewhat later period, are mentioned by Schack, *Nachträge,* pp. 73, 74, among them being the comedia of Antonio de Solis, *Psiquis y Cupido,* which was produced in the Buen Retiro on a scale of great magnificence, the machinery for it being especially constructed by the Italian engineer Maria Antonozzi. It appears that, beginning on October 29, 1661, the theatrical representations in the palace were in charge of the Marquis of Heliche, while those in the Buen Retiro were under the superintendence of the Duke of Medina de las Torres. (*Ibid.,* p. 74, and see especially Pérez Pastor, *Calderon Documentos,* Vol. I, and the *Poesías de Solis,* Madrid, 1692, *passim.*) Concerning the sums of money expended by Philip IV. on these private representations, Barrionuevo tells us that a comedia sometimes cost the King as much as 50,000 ducats. Under date of January 23, 1655, he writes: "Vendrá el Rey, Sabado, 30 de éste, derecho á Palacio, que no va al Retiro, como solia, por estarle preparando una Comedia en él, de tramoyas, que dicen costará más de 50,000 ducados; que por acá no se trata sino de pasar alegremente esta pobre vida, dé donde diere y quede lo que quedare." (*Avisos,* Vol. I, p. 213.) The same writer also chronicles the following: "Miercoles 17 de éste [Enero de 1657] se

tions,[1] though they had been announced to appear in the public theaters, which were frequently closed on that account.[2]

Among the dramatists of the time an especial favorite of the King was Don Jerónimo de Villayzan y Garcés. It is said that Philip used to go incognito to the *Corral de la Cruz* to see Villayzan's comedias acted, entering his box by a passage from the Plazuela del Angel. It was, moreover, the common report at the time that Villayzan aided the King in his dramatic labors.[3] Certain it is that before January, 1623, when Villayzan was not yet nineteen years of age, one of his comedias, *Transformaciones de Amor,* was represented privately before the King by the company

hizo en la Zarzuela la comedia grande que el de Liche tenia dispuesta para el festejo de los Reyes. Costó 16,000 ducados, que pagó de su orden el Conde de Pezuela. . . . Todas las tramoyas y aparatos se han traido del Retiro, al nuevo coliseo que se ha hecho en la ermita de San Pablo, para tornarla á hacer este Carnaval. . . . Dió Liche á D. Pedro Calderon 200 doblones por la comedia," etc. (*Avisos,* Vol. III, p. 176.)

[1] See above, p. 198.

[2] "Madrid, 20 Diciembre 1656.—Petición de los arrendadores de los corrales contra Pedro de la Rosa, que no representó en los dias 15 y 16 de Diciembre porque, segun confiesa, estuvo estudiando y ensayando la fiesta de los años de la Reina, que se ha de hacer el 22 del presente mes. Tampoco representó el dia 18, aunque tenía puesto carteles para hacer la comedia *El Conde Lucanor* [atribuida á Calderon]. (Pérez Pastor, *Calderon Documentos,* Vol. I, p. 243.) Again, we read in a notarial certificate dated Madrid, February 24, 1657: "Y ansimismo doy fee vi cerrados los corrales el lunes de Carnestolendas, doze de dicho mes, por haber ido al Retiro las compañias de Pedro de la Rosa y Diego Osorio á hacer la fiesta de la Zarzuela conducidos por el alguacil de corte Joseph Caballero y vi conducir las dichas compañias, y este dia no representó Francisco Garcia por haberle llevado las mugeres al ensayo de la comedia de Don Pedro Calderon, que se hizo el martes siguiente a Su Magestad." (*Ibid.,* p. 244. See also pp. 277, 280, *et passim.*) It appears that the King did not always go to the theater for the sole purpose of seeing the play. The following curious bit of news is chronicled by Barrionuevo under date of February 27, 1656: "S. M. ha mandado no vayan mañana á la Comedia sino solas mujeres, sin guarda-infantes, porque quepan más, y se dice la quiere ver con la Reina en las celosías, y que tienen algunas ratoneras con más de 100 ratones cebados en ellas para soltarlos en lo mejor de la fiesta, asi en cazuela como en patio, que si sucede, será mucho de ver, y entretenimiento para SS. MM." (*Avisos,* Vol. II, p. 308.)

[3] Barrera, *Catálogo bibliográfico y biografico del Teatro antiguo español,* p. 491.

of Juan Bautista de Villegas.[1] Another, *Sufrir mas por Querer mas*, was acted before the King some time prior to November, 1632, and again on October 17, 1637, and it pleased the King so greatly that he commanded that it should not at that time be represented elsewhere.[2] Still another of his comedias, *Ofender con las Finezas*, was played before the King by the company of Manuel Vallejo on February 5, 1632, and again on November 13, 1633.[3] Villayzan died at the early age of twenty-nine, in 1633, in which year his friend Lope de Vega published an elegy on his death.[4]

During the first twenty years of the reign of Philip the Fourth, comedias continued to be represented, presumably, in accordance with the restrictions prescribed by the decree of 1615. That this decree was a dead letter is evinced by the fact that a new series of regulations for the theater was issued in 1641, at the instance of D. Antonio de Contreras, "of the Council and Chamber of his Majesty." These regulations, however, did not differ in any essential particular from those of 1615; indeed, most of the articles were a literal repetition of the previous decree. Here and there slight changes were made, as, for instance, no woman above the age of twelve years shall be allowed to act unless she be married, nor shall any manager permit her to be in his company, if she be unmarried; also that no person, whatever be his quality or condition, be allowed to enter the retiring-room of the players, under penalty of 20,000

---

[1] See my "Notes on the Chronology of the Spanish Drama," in *Modern Language Review*," Vol. III (1907).

[2] Barrera, *Catálogo*, p. 492. The play must have been originally represented before the King some time prior to 1632, for in November of that year it belonged to the repertory of Andres de la Vega, a theatrical manager. (Pérez Pastor, *Nuevos Datos*, p. 226.)

[3] *Modern Language Review*, Vol. III (1907), p. 48.

[4] *Elegia a la Muerte de D. Gerónimo de Villaizan*, por su amigo Frey Lope Felix de Vega Carpio.—En Madrid por Francisco Martínez, año 1633. See Gallardo, *Ensayo de una Biblioteca española*, Tomo IV, p. 977.

maravedís for the first offense, and for a second infraction under such penalty as the *Consejo Protector* may declare. A like penalty is provided in the case of men found in the entrances or exits of the women.[1]

According to an *Aviso* dated March 1, 1644,[2] the chief subject of gossip in Madrid at that time was the restrictions and regulations imposed upon comedias and players by D. Antonio de Contreras. Provisions are, however, alluded to which are not contained in the above-mentioned decree of 1641, among them that "henceforth no comedia which is the author's own invention may be represented,[3] but only histories or the lives of saints," and that no actor or actress may appear upon the stage in costumes of gold or *telas*. Moreover, a new comedia, never seen before, may be represented only every eight days, and "the *Señores* may not visit any actress more than twice."[4]

On the death of the Queen, Isabel of Bourbon, first wife of Philip the Fourth, on October 6, 1644, the theaters were again closed. How long this interruption lasted in Madrid, I do not know. In Seville, at all events, representations were given in 1645, for in May of that year the companies of Luis Lopez and Lorenzo Hurtado de la Cámara were acting in that city.[5] The *autos* were regu-

---

[1] This regulation of 1641 was first published by Sepúlveda, *El Corral de la Pacheca*, pp. 556 ff. It is now reprinted in full in Cotarelo y Mori, *Controversias*, pp. 632, 633.

[2] In a MS. Cod. 12 of the National Library. Pellicer, *Histrionismo*, Vol. I, p. 220.

[3] This provision, Pellicer states, was intended to prohibit the writing of "comedias de amores y de galanteos, las quales se llamaban *Comedias de capa y espada.*"

[4] How this last regulation was to be enforced against the *Señores* we are not told, but as very few of the provisions of these theatrical ordinances seem ever to have been observed, this one, which allowed the *Señores* but two visits to an actress, was quite gratuitous. Still, as this provision doubtless concerned a very large class, it offered the more timid admirers a loophole of escape in the very remote contingency of their being apprehended on a second visit.

[5] Sanchez-Arjona, *Anales*, p. 374.

larly presented in Madrid in 1645, Calderon receiving 300 ducats *vellon* for writing them.[1]

Once more, on October 9, 1646, the theaters were closed on account of the death of Prince Baltasar. This again raised the question of whether comedias should be permitted, and, according to Pellicer, a council of theologians again submitted some regulations—"bastante difusas"—to the King, recommending that *for the present* comedias be suspended, beginning with "Pasqua de Flores." They explain what they mean by "for the present," alleging, among other reasons, "until God may be pleased to put an end to the wars with Portugal in which Castile is now engaged." Among the conditions recommended by them were: "That the companies should be reduced to the number of six or eight, and that the *compañias de la legua,* which are composed of *gente perdida,* who travel through the smaller towns, should be prohibited; that the comedias to be represented relate to some proper and moral subject or concern the life or death of some exemplary person or some noble deed, and that they should be without intermixture of any love-affair, and that, in order to attain this end, nearly all the comedias that had been represented down to that time should be prohibited, especially those of Lope de Vega, which had worked such harm in the customs of the people." They provided, further, that no comedia may be represented without previously obtaining a license; that the costumes of the players be reformed, especially the *guardainfantes* (very wide hoop-skirts (of the women and the décolleté gowns[2]

[1] Pérez Pastor, *Calderon Documentos,* Vol. I, p. 126.

[2] Pellicer (*Histrionismo,* Vol. I, p. 218, note) says: "Esta moda llamada el *Degollado* continuó con el nombre de el *Escotado,* porque consistia en usar las mugeres unos jubones escotados, que daban lugar á descubrir la garganta, la espalda y los pechos, cuyo escandaloso uso, despues de haber dado copioso materia á los Teologos moralistas, dió motivo á un Real Decreto, que le prohibió, permitiendole solamente á las mugeres públicas."

and strange head-dresses; that players be permitted to wear only one costume in any one play, except where the change is exacted by the comedia, nor shall women wear men's attire, and their skirts, moreover, must reach to the feet, etc. Dances also were regulated; only married women were allowed to act or dance, only players were permitted to enter the green-rooms, and comedias were to be begun at two o'clock in winter and at three in summer, so that the play may be over before dark.[1]

There is much uncertainty concerning the date on which comedias were again allowed to be represented upon the public stage at Madrid after the death of Prince Baltasar. It appears there had been no plays acted in the theaters of Seville and Madrid, at all events, even for some time prior to the Prince's death,—since Shrovetide, 1646.[2]

We know that the *autos* were represented in Madrid as usual in 1648, for Calderon wrote them and received 300 ducats for them;[3] the theaters of Seville were also open in this year,[4] though there had been no representations during the preceding year, as we have just seen, nor were any *autos* presented in Seville in 1648, the theaters not resuming until September 15, when the company of Esteban Nuñez began forty performances in the *Coliseo*. The pest was prevalent in Andalucia during the years 1646–49, the theaters being finally closed in the latter year on account of the havoc wrought by the contagion, though representations were resumed in Seville in 1650.[5]

Sometime during the period 1646–47 a number of

[1] Pellicer, *Histrionismo*, Vol. I, pp. 217–220.

[2] "En el manuscrito de *Noticias y casos memorables de la ciudad de Sevilla*, que procedente de la biblioteca del señor Conde del Aguila se conserva en el Ayuntamiento, se dice:—1646. Este año prohibió el Consejo las comedias; á lo menos en Sevilla y Madrid no las hubo desde Carnestolendas." (Sanchez-Arjona, *Anales*, p. 379.)

[3] *Calderon Documentos*, Vol. I, p. 163.

[4] Sanchez-Arjona, *Anales*, p. 380.

[5] *Ibid.*, pp. 383–386.

autores de comedias petitioned the King for permission
to again represent comedias, alleging various reasons and
requesting the King to command that comedias be freed
of all indecent or objectionable features, etc.[1]

According to Pellicer, the cities that were most in-
sistent upon the reopening of the theaters were Zaragoza
and Valencia. Already in 1650 and 1651, he continues,
comedias were again being acted in the King's palace[2] in
Madrid, and in the other chief cities of Castile, and now
this permission was extended to Zaragoza. With this
example before it, the city of Valencia renewed its peti-

[1] "Peticion hecha en Cortes a S. M. para que no se prohiban las Comedias:—Por algunos autores de Comedias se a significado al Reyno = El
Reyno haviendo reconocido que la mayor parte de lo que se saca de las
comedias se convierte en diferentes obras pias como son Hospitales . . .
y importar en cada un año mas de 80 mil ducados y ser evidente que
zesando el uso dellas, las çiudades an de eligir otros medios para
suplirlos (por ser tan preziso y nezessario no faltar a cosa tan meneste-
rosa) y que estos recarguen sobre los muchos que estan impuestos y que
los pobres bengan a ser gravados en ellos, quando eran exemptos de lo
que se sacava de las comedias y que cada uno lo pagava voluntariamente, y
generalmente ser los más acomodados y·llegarse asta aver sido de general
desconsuelo para todos el que se aya mandado zesen las comedias porque
como ordinariamente no tenian otro divertimiento y que en lo aparente
siempre se a tenido por licito y no perjudicial ni dañoso a la Republica,
pues a averlo sido en tantos años como ha que se introdujeron asi en
estos Reynos como en todos los de Europa, se hubiera rresuelto zesasen, y
por ser un tiempo en que todos se hallan con tantos rrogos y afliçiones, les
es mas sensible el que les falte este entretenimiento; por cuyas rraçones
suplica el Reyno a V. Md. se sirva de mandar se continuen y hagan las
dichas comedias dando orden se reforme la parte que tuvieren de pro-
fanidad ó indeçencia ó que mirasen a dar mal exemplo y que las justicias
pongan particular cuidado en que se escusen las disensiones y alborotos,
que suelen ofrecerse entre la gente oçiosa y mal entretenida con que
pareze se rrepararán los daños que de hazerse las comedias se an experi-
mentado rresultan; y porque las personas de quien se componen no se
dividan ni ausenten destos Reynos en caso que V. Md. tenga por bien
de condezender con esta suplica, convendrá que con toda brevedad se
tome rresolucion a ella porque de dilatarse sea muy dificil el bolverse a
juntar este genero de gente. V. Md. mandará lo que mas convenga," etc.
(*Archivo general Central,* entre los papeles correspondientes á los años
1646-1647. *Revista de Archivos* (1883), pp. 179, 180.)

[2] Two years before, in 1648, Antonio de Prado had represented eleven
comedias privately before the King and Queen, and the company of
Juana de Espinosa had performed eight before March, 1647. (*El Averiguador,* Tomo I (1871), p. 170.)

tion and induced the Council to consult the King on February 15, 1651. To this *consulta* the King replied with a decree permitting "*comedias de historias*, as they are represented in Madrid," to be performed in Valencia also.[1]

The first comedia represented in Madrid when the theaters were reopened was *Santa Maria Magdalena*.[2] That theatrical companies, however, were acting in other parts of Spain prior to 1650 is a well-attested fact. In 1649, during the journey of the new Queen, Doña Mariana de Austria, from Vienna, the company of Roque de Figueroa represented a comedy before the King on one of the royal vessels lying at Tarragona.[3]

Another royal order, chiefly concerning the abuses that had gradually been introduced in the matter of women's costumes on the public stage, and which the decree of 1646 had been intended to remedy, was issued on January 1, 1653.[4] On the death of Philip the Fourth (September 17, 1665), the theaters were once more closed, and a

[1] "En esta Corte se ha ido tolerando el que haya Comedias de historias, y en la forma que el Consejo tendra entendido; y si este año se permitieren, podrá correr en Valencia lo mismo, precediendo su examen y moderacion al exemplo de lo que se hiciese aqui; pues el conceder á los pueblos algun licito desahogo parece preciso." (Pellicer, *Histrionismo*, Tomo I, p. 223.)

[2] *Loc. cit.*, p. 223. A number of comedias bearing this title have survived, and it is impossible to determine which one is here meant. The thirst for novelty would preclude Lope's play, which was written before 1618. The comedia so entitled by Luis Velez de Guevara (who died in 1644) is of unknown date. It may be Jacinto Maluenda's *La Magdalena*. See Paz y Melia, *Catálogo*, No. 704.

[3] "Mientras los esclavos hizieron aguada, entretuvo S. M. el tiempo, oyendo una comedia que Roque de Figueroa, Autor dellas, representó en la Antepopa de la Real con su Compañia, que entonces acaso se hallava en Tarragona." (*Real Viage de la Reyna N. S. Doña Mariana de Austria desde la Corte de Viena hasta estos sus Reynos de España*, Madrid, 1649, quoted by Schack, *Nachträge*, p. 73.)

[4] This decree was first published by Schack (*Nachträge*, p. 80) from a MS. in the Royal Academy of History at Madrid. It is as follows: "Quando permiti que volviesen las comedias (que se avian suspendido por los desordenes y relaxacion de trages y representaciones que se avian esperimentado) fué con orden preciso que eso se executase con atencion muy particular a la reformacion de los trages y a la decencia de las

decree was issued by the Queen, Doña Mariana of Austria, on September 22, 1665, prohibiting the representation of comedias throughout the kingdom, and declaring "that they shall cease entirely until the King, my son, shall be of an age to enjoy them."[1] The theaters remained closed, however, but little more than a year, when the city of Madrid, on November 17, 1666, petitioned the Queen Regent that they be reopened. The question was again referred to the Council, who threshed the whole matter over once more, with the inevitable result that a decree was issued, on November 30, again permitting the representation of comedias,[2] which were continued until July 14, 1682, when the theaters were again closed on account of the pest.

representaciones que se havrá de obserbar, de suerte que no hubiese, ni en lo uno ni en lo otro, cosa alguna que ofendiese la publica honestidad. Y porque he entendido que en esto se falta gravemente en las partes donde se representa y que los trages no son con la moderacion y ajustamiento que se deve, os ordeno que embieis ordenes á la Corona en todo aprieto (de suerte que se observen precisa y indispensablemente) que ninguna muger pueda salir al teatro en havito de hombre, y que si huviere de ser preciso para la representacion que hagan estos papeles, sea con trage tan ajustado y modesto, que de ninguna manera se les descubran las piernas ni los pies, sino que esto esté siempre cubierto con los vestidos ó trages, que ordinariamente usan, o con alguna sotana, de manera que solo se diferenzie el trage de la cintura arriba imponiendoles las penas que os pareciere y disponiendo que inviolablemente se executen en las que contravinieren al cumplimiento de la orden referida.—Rubricado de la real mano de S. M.—Madrid, a 1º de Enero de 1653.—Al Vicecanciller de Aragon." This decree is also now printed in Cotarelo, *Controversias*, p. 635.

[1] "El sentimiento á que ha obligado la falta del Rey nuestro Señor, pide que prohiba generalmente en todos estos Reynos el representar Comedias, y asi mando se den luego por el Consejo las ordenes necesarias para que cesen enteramente, hasta que el Rey mi hijo tenga edad para gustar de ellas." (Pellicer, *Histrionismo*, Vol. I, p. 270.)

[2] *Ibid.*, pp. 271–274.

CHAPTER XII

The "Partidas" of Alfonso the Learned concerning secular plays.
The church and the theater. Public players declared infamous.
Opposition of the clergy to the theater. It is mostly due to the
players. Character of the actresses.

THE fact that the modern theater had its origin in the
liturgical services of the early Christian church naturally
induced that body, as the great conservator of public
morals, to keep a watchful eye on the growing popularity
and development of the religious celebrations and representations, which finally culminated in the profane theater.

The *Partidas* of Alfonso the Learned, written between
1252 and 1257, had already declared what part the clergy
might take in these representations, namely: "that religious persons (*clerigos*) may not be actors in the farcical
plays (*juegos de escarnios*),[1] so that people come to
see them, how they are acted. And if other persons represent them, the clergy shall not come to see them, for
much clownishness and lewdness are committed in them.
Nor shall these things be done in the church; rather do
we declare that those who do these things shall be driven
from the church in disgrace, for the church of God is intended for prayers and not for lewd plays. But the clergy
may represent such matters as the birth of our Lord Jesus
Christ, in which is shown how the angel descended to the

---

[1] Ticknor, *History of Spanish Literature*, Vol. I, p. 269, translates *juegos
de escarnios* = buffoon plays; Wolf translates "Spottspiele." See also the
note in Ticknor, *ibid*. Doubtless rude farces with their accompaniment of
horse-play are meant.

shepherds and told them of the birth of Christ. And likewise of his appearance and how the three Magi came to adore him; and of his resurrection, which shows how he was crucified and arose on the third day. Such things as these, which move men to do good and to have devotion in the faith, may be represented, and, besides, so that men may remember that just as here the things have, in truth, happened. But these things must be done with decorum and with great devotion, and in the large cities, where there are archbishops and bishops, and by their authority or that of their representatives, and they must not be performed in villages or in mean places, nor for the purpose of gaining money."[1]

Dramatic representations continued to flourish in the churches, but, through the laxity of the clergy, the abuses increased to such an extent that the council of Aranda, in 1473, enacted a decree, similar to the law just mentioned, to regulate these performances, and strongly condemning "the abuses which had crept into the festivals of the birth of Christ, that of St. Stephen, St. John, the feast of the Innocents," etc., and forbidding other festivals in which theatrical plays, masks, monsters, shows, and many de-

---

[1] "Los clerigos . . . no deben ser facedores de juegos de escarnios porque los vengan á ver gentes, como se facen. E si otros omes los ficieren, non deben los clerigos hi venir, porque facen hi muchas villanias e desaposturas. Ni deben otrosi estas cosas facer en las eglesias: antes decimos que los deben echar de ellas deshonradamente á los que lo ficieren: ca la eglesia de Dios es fecha para orar e non para facer escarnios en ella. . . . Pero representacion hay que pueden los clerigos facer, asi como de la nacencia de nuestro Señor Jesucristo en que muestra como el angel vino á los pastores, e como les dijo como era Jesu Cristo nacido. E otrosi de su aparicion como los tres reyes magos le vinieron á adorar. E de su resurreccion que muestra que fué crucificado e resucitó al tercero dia: tales cosas como estas que mueven al ome á facer bien e á haber devocion en la fe, pueden las facer, e demas, porque los omes hayan remembranza que segun aquellas fueron las otras fechas de verdad. Mas esto deben facer apuestamente e con muy grand devocion e en las cibdades grandes donde oviere arzobispos ó obispos, e con su mandado de ellos ó de los otros que tovieren sus veces, e non lo deben facer en las aldeas, nin en los lugares viles, nin por ganar dinero con ellas." (*Partida* I, tit. vi, leg. 34.)

vices and lewd figures are brought into the churches, thus creating a tumult; besides, it forbade "all derisive speeches or the recitation of lewd verses, which interfere with the divine offices and make the people unmindful of their devotions," etc. However, decorous and devout representations which move people to devotion are not prohibited.[1]

Those persons who, outside the church, made a living by playing in the public squares—the singers and players of instruments (*juglares*) and mimic players (*remedadores*)—had been declared infamous by the *Partidas* of Alfonso X.,[2] and the church declared them without civil rights, a stigma under which all public players rested in France until 1642,[3] while their ecclesiastical rehabilita-

---

[1] "Quia quaedam tam in metropolitanis quam in cathedralibus et aliis ecclesiis nostrae provinciae consuetudo inolevit et videlicet in festis Nativitatis Domini nostri Jesu Christi, et sanctorum Stephani, Ioannis et Innocentium aliisque certis diebus festivis, etiam in solemnitatibus missarum novarum (dum divina aguntur) ludi theatrales, larvae, monstra, spectacula, nec non quam plurima inhonesta et diversa figmenta in ecclesiis introducuntur, tumultuationes quoque et turpia carmina et derisorii sermones dicuntur, adeo quod divinum officium impediunt et populum reddunt indevotum: nos hanc corruptelam sacro approbante consilio, revocantes hujusmodi larvas, ludos, monstra, spectacula, figmenta, tumultuationes fieri, carmina quoque turpia et sermones illicitos dici, tam in metropolitanis quam cathedralibus ceterisque nostrae provinciae ecclesiis dum divina celebrantur praesentium serie omnino prohibemus: statuentes nihilominus, ut clerici, qui praemissa ludibria et inhonesta figmenta officiis divinis immiscuerint aut immisceri permiserint, se in praefatis metropolitanis seu cathedralibus ecclesiis beneficiati exstiterint, ex ipso per mensem portitionibus suis mulctentur: si vero in parochialibus fuerint beneficiati triginta et si non fuerint quindecim regalium poenam incurrant fabricis ecclesiarum et tertio synodali aequaliter applicandam. Per hoc tamen honestas representationes et devota quae populum ad devotionem movent, tam in praefatis diebus quam in aliis non intendimus prohibere." (Quoted by Schack, *Geschichte der dramatischen Lit. u. Kunst in Spanien*, Vol. I, p. 136.)

[2] "Otrosi [son infamados] los que son juglares e los remedadores e los facedores de los zaharrones que publicamente andan por el pueblo ó cantan ó facen juegos por precio, esto es porque se envilecen ante otros por aquel precio que les dan. Mas los que tañeren estrumentos ó cantasen por facer solaz á si mesmos, ó por facer placer á sus amigos ó dar solaz á los reyes ó á los otros señores, non serian por ende enfamados." (*Partida* VII, tit. vi, leg. 4.)

[3] "Die Kirche erklärt ihn (den Jongleur) für infam, für ehr- und

tion was only effected by the great Revolution, and in Spain to this day an actor who dies in his profession cannot be buried in soil consecrated by the church.

Speaking of the actor's profession in England, Collier says: "It was a profession in bad repute before Elizabeth came to the throne, and long afterward; and poverty, peculiar circumstances of position, or a strong passion for theatrical performances, could alone have induced an individual to attach himself to it."[1] In 1572 a statute was enacted in England declaring that common players in interludes, etc., not belonging to a baron or higher personage, or not having a license from two justices of the peace, should be dealt with as rogues and vagabonds.[2]

The church, as Cotarelo says, "put an end to pagan spectacles; but the church itself, in the obscurity of the Middle Ages, gave origin and birth to the modern drama. At first forming part of the liturgy, in alternating chants, dialogues, and choruses, with some sort of scenic apparatus; then amplifying and complicating these true representations with events in the life of Jesus Christ, of his saints, or of the heroes of the Old Testament, and afterward by permitting, within or without the churches, these embryonic dramas to be enacted in the vulgar tongue, with great apparatus, and with music, songs, and other popular pastimes, the church greatly facilitated their growth. And when, on account of the abuses which this

rechtlos, und unter dem Einflusse des kanonischen Rechts spricht ihm auch das bürgerliche Gesetz die Handlungsfähigkeit ab. Diese Infamierung hat in Frankreich die Jahrhunderte überdauert: jene Schauspieler, welche in 1637 Corneilles *Cid* kreirten, waren noch bürgerlich und kirchlich ehrlos. Erst 1642 hob eine königliche Verfügung die bürgerliche Infamierung auf. Die kirchliche Rehabilitierung hat dem französischen Schauspieler erst die grosze Revolution gebracht. Erst sie hat diesem tausendjährigen Zweikampf zwischen Kirche und Spielmann ein Ende gemacht." (Morf, *Aus Dichtung u. Sprache der Romanen*, p. 153.)

[1] *Memoirs of the Principal Actors in the Plays of Shakespear*, London, Shakspeare Soc., 1846, p. 3.

[2] Fleay, *A Chronicle History of the London Stage*, London, 1890, p. 44.

tolerance necessarily produced, it closed its doors to every profane element, we see the modern theater created."[1]

While the church, "ever vigilant for the decorum of its ceremonies," as the same writer says, "tried to extirpate every kind of excess and evil practice," we know that its success was only partial. Moreover, at the beginning of the sixteenth century this vigilance of the church, at its fountain-head at all events, had very much relaxed, so far as dramatic representations are concerned. Alexander VI. and his court were certainly not inclined to guard the stage or protect it from abuse because of any moral or religious scruples they may have had. It is questionable, indeed, whether the stage had ever sunk to a lower depth than it did under their august patronage.[2]

Nevertheless, the actor remained under the ban of the church, and this lasted in some countries, as we have seen, until late in the eighteenth century: the great Molière was denied the rights of sepulture by the Catholic Church and was buried at night, like a criminal.

---

[1] *Controversias*, etc., p. 9.

[2] At the court of Alexander VI., besides the *commedie*, other spectacles were prepared for the delectation of these noble personages, as "lo spettacolo de' cavalli e cavalle in amore, goduto dal Papa e da Madonna Lucrezia *cum magnu risu et delectatione*, da una finestra del palagio" (D'Ancona, *Origini del Teatro Italiano*, Vol. II, p. 71, note), and the "ballo delle meretrici," etc. And we mention only in passing the comedy *La Calandra*, by Cardinal Bibbiena—performed before *sua santa* at Rome in 1514—in order to record a matter which concerns us much more nearly. Cardinals and pontifical secretaries were not ashamed to travel in the company of prostitutes and to entertain them at their tables. On the evening of August 10, 1513, the Marquis Federico Gonzaga, being only twelve years old, supped at the house of the Cardinal of Mantua, his uncle, with the Cardinal d'Aragona, Cardinal Sauli, Cardinal Cornaro, several bishops and noblemen, and the courtesan Albina; on the preceding Thursday he had been at the house of the Cardinal of Arborea, where there was recited, in Spanish, a comedia of Juan de la Enzina, and where were gathered together *piu putane spagnole che omini italiani*. (Graf, *Attraverso il Cinquecento*, Roma, 1888, p. 265. See also D'Ancona, *Origini*, Vol. II, p. 82.) The play by Enzina was probably *Placida y Victoriano*, which, according to Moratin, was printed in Rome in 1514. It is evident that the "vigilance," at this time, must have originated elsewhere than at Rome.

In Spain, as late as 1789, two members of the theatrical profession, Cristóbal Garrigó and Antonia Lopez Antolin, were refused the "sacrament of marriage" by the church, because they were actors, "their profession of acting making them unworthy of the sacraments, they being *ipso facto* infamous and public sinners";[1] and in the following year communion (*la comunion pascal*) was refused to the actor (*primer galan*) Antonio Cabañas and to his son. In Spain, to this day, as already remarked, an actor who dies in his profession cannot be buried in soil consecrated by the church, because, as Sr. Cotarelo says, "ecclesiastical sepulture is due only to those who die in the communion of the church, and because the rituals, not excluding the Roman, prohibit it to public sinners, which actors are."[2]

It is doubtful, however, whether, except in rare cases, the sacraments of the Catholic Church were refused to a player. In 1590 Fray Manuel Rodriguez, in his *Obras morales en Romance,* says: "The priests are obliged to deny communion to actors, as they are defined in the Council of Basle, because they are public sinners. And observe that we do not speak here of the actors of farces and comedias, because they are not public sinners, but we speak of such players who publicly teach others to do evil things, such as those who do publicly things that pertain to the magic arts, tumblers," etc.[3]

This is substantially repeated by Fr. Alonso de Vega in

---

[1] "El cura, entendiendo que eran de oficio cómico, se negó á conferirles el sacramento del matrimonio, representando al señor gobernador del obispado que su ejercicio de representantes los hacia indignos de los sacramentos, siendo por él infames y pecadores publicos." (Cotarelo y Mori, *Controversias,* etc., p. 400.)

[2] "Los cómicos que mueren en el oficio no pueden ser enterrados en sagrado, porque la sepultura eclesiastica sólo se debe á los que mueren en la comunion de la Iglesia, y porque los rituales, sin excluir el romano, la prohiben á los pecadores públicos, cuales son los cómicos. Ni vale alegar la costumbre contraria, porque como dice Inocente III.: *Consuetudo, quae canonicis oviat instituis, nullius debet esse momenti."* (*Controversias,* etc., p. 405.)   [3] *Ibid.,* p. 525.

1609, who says: "Priests are obliged to deny communion to actors who teach others publicly to do evil things, etc.; . . . but players do not sin in practising their profession, for it is not unlawful in itself."[1]   Indeed, in 1598, D. Pedro Vaca de Castro, Archbishop of Granada and Seville, who had opposed the representation of comedias as "a fountain of great evil," inquired very particularly concerning players as to whether "they fulfil the precepts of the church, especially those of confession and holy communion."[2]   And in 1614 it was the opinion of Francisco Ortiz, who wrote an *Apologia en defensa de las Comedias que se representan en España,* that the sacraments should be given to actors, because the prohibitory canons refer only to the Roman *mimes,* not to modern *autos.*[3]

None of these prohibitions of the church was observed in the sixteenth and seventeenth centuries, so far as we can judge by such records of the marriages and deaths of players as have come down to us.   In 1596, for example, Ana Ortiz requests that she be buried in the parish of Santa Cruz, in the tomb of her husband, Pedro Paez de Sotomayor (an *autor de comedias*), "who is buried near the altar of San Cosme and San Damian."[4]   And on the death of Pedro Llorente, an *autor de comedias,* on January 30, 1621, we read: "He received the holy sacraments at the hands of the licentiate Corralan, and requested in his will that twelve masses for his soul (*misas de alma*) and three hundred ordinary ones be said."[5]   In like manner Cristóbal Ortiz de Villazan, an *autor de comedias,* on his death, on July 1, 1626, received the holy sacraments, and Jerónima de Burgos, who died on March 27, 1641, and whose life had been far from exemplary, received the holy sacraments and was buried by the Brotherhood of Our Lady of the Novena.[6]

[1] *Controversias,* etc., p. 584.   [2] *Ibid.,* p. 578.   [3] *Ibid.,* p. 491.
[4] Pérez Pastor, *Nuevos Datos,* p. 44.   [5] *Ibid.,* p. 360.
[6] *Ibid.,* p. 327. The only exception that I have found is the following,

During the long conflict in Spain between the theater and the church, besides the many opponents of the theater —who, almost without exception, flayed the actors without mercy—there were also a few clerical defenders of the histrionic art. These controversies have been collected with great diligence by Sr. Cotarelo y Mori, in the large volume from which we have frequently quoted, and while many are mere diatribes against the comedia and the players, not infrequently, as it seems, by men who had never seen a comedia performed—to judge by the general terms in which their arguments are framed—others contain observations which are not without interest in our present purpose. One of the earliest defenders of the stage was Diego de Cabranes, in his *Armadura espiritual*, the privilege of which is dated 1525. His opinion is that fineries (*atavios*) for the representation of farces for recreation only are not unlawful. His work is of importance as a proof of the early date at which farces were acted in public.

In 1559 Fray Francisco de Alcocer, in his *Tratado del Juego*, says: "The representation of farces and inventions is another kind of play which, when they are stories from the sacred scriptures (*sagrada escritura*), or concerning other devout things, and are performed by persons who represent them with the grace which such matters require, is a good and honest pastime and conducive to devotion. And one should always take care that the persons who represent the plays should likewise understand what they are representing, and that they should be so skilful in what they do and should know so well what they

---

and it happens to be the case of a famous *autor de comedias:* "29 Marzo 1610. Partida de defuncion de Nicolas de los Rios.—En Madrid, en veinte y nueve de Marzo de 1610 años murió de aplopegía (*sic*) en la calle de las guertas, Nicolas de los Rios, autor de comedias, casado con Inés de Lara. No recibió el viático ni textó, enterróle su muxer en San Sebastian en orden de quarenta reales." (Archivo parroquial de San Sebastian. Pérez Pastor, *Nuevos Datos*, p. 118.)

say that the people present be edified and moved to devotion. This is often lacking, and the actors are sometimes so vulgar and act so badly that it rather provokes to laughter, although they should not be condemned on this account, provided their intention be good. Other historical farces there are, and also those invented by their authors, which, provided there be nothing unseemly (*deshonesto*) in them which is provocative of sin, are not to be condemned, while those farces which are lewd and immoral should not be represented."[1] This, it will be remembered, was in the period of Lope de Rueda.

On the other hand, the opponents of the comedia among theological writers are legion. One of the most important as well as one of the earliest is Fr. Juan de Pineda, the editor of the famous *Paso honroso defendido por Suero de Quiñones*. His *Dialogos de la Agricultura* were written in 1581, just prior to the time of Lope de Vega's first attempts at writing for the public stage. He says: "Turning now to our own actors, inciters to evil lives, I should like to know what law of reason can give consent to them or what king should permit them, and especially those foreigners [the Italians] who carry away many thousands of ducats from Spain every year." That these actors employed their mother tongue, we learn from one of the interlocutors in the dialogue, who says that he went several times to the comedia, "especially to that of the Italians, who better understood the expression of the emotions," and that he took his wife with him, "she being a person of almost as good sense as I am, and who even understands Italian." "What could married men say, who take or send their wives and daughters to such spectacles, even if they should not return home at night?"[2]

Pedro de Ribadeneira, a Jesuit priest, in his *Tratado*

---

[1] Cotarelo y Mori, *Controversias*, p. 55.
[2] *Controversias*, p. 505.

de la Tribulacion (1589), is most bitter in his denunciation of actresses. "The low women (*mugercillas*) who ordinarily act are beautiful, lewd, and have bartered their virtue, and with gestures and movements of the whole body, and with voices bland and suave, with beautiful costumes, like the sirens they charm and transform men into beasts and lure them the more easily to destruction, as they themselves are more wicked and lost to every sense of virtue."[1]

And not only theologians opposed the comedia, but no less a person than Lupercio Leonardo de Argensola, who had himself written three tragedies, *La Isabela, La Alexandra* (so much praised by Cervantes), and *La Filis,* which is now lost. Why Argensola should oppose the comedia, it is not easy to say. Perhaps he was piqued at the failure of his tragedies, which are very mediocre and extremely sanguinary productions, to judge by the two which have survived. At all events, Lupercio's brother, Bartolomé, who was a priest as well as poet, never expressed any opposition to the stage of his day. In 1598 Lupercio addressed a memorial to Philip II. in which he vehemently protested against the comedia as then acted, which was the comedia of Lope de Vega. Speaking of actresses, he says: "The lure which the devil used was their singing, dancing, and exquisite costumes, and the various personages whom they represented every day, attiring themselves as queens, goddesses, shepherdesses, and as men; and the representation of the most pure Queen of the Angels has been profaned by them. And so true is this, that in presenting a comedia of the life of Our Lady in this capital, the actor who played the part of St. Joseph was living in concubinage with the woman who represented Our Lady, and this was so notorious that many were scandalized and laughed when they heard the words which the most pure Virgin replied to the angel's

[1] *Ibid.,* p. 523.

question: *Quomodo fiet istud,* etc. And in this same comedia, arriving at the mystery of the birth of Our Saviour, this same actor who played the part of Joseph reproved the woman in a low voice because she was looking, as he thought, at a man of whom he was jealous, calling her by a most vile name which is wont to be applied to evil women."[1] Argensola likewise speaks of the scandal of these actors wearing priestly vestments at the festival of Corpus, and, "what is worse than all, to see the wounds of Our Saviour painted on those hands which a short time before were occupied in playing cards or the guitar."

Fray José de Jesus Maria, writing in 1600, says: "The comedias as they are represented nowadays are most indecent and prejudicial to all classes of people, because they nearly all treat of lascivious things or dishonest love-affairs."[2] He says further: "What pleasure or what edification can it give to the spectator to see (as I have seen in this capital) an actor embrace and kiss publicly in the theater the very wife of the *autor de comedias?*"[3] He alludes to the gross impropriety of having common players perform the *autos* of Corpus Christi, saying: "If there be anything in Spain which offends strangers and pious natures at this festival, it is to see vile men (*sucios*) and infamous, accustomed all their lives to representing obscene and hideous things (*cosas torpes y feas*), representing mysteries so lofty and ineffable; and that the woman who represents the lewdness (*torpezas*) of Venus, as well in comedias as in her private life, should represent the purity of the Sovereign Virgin in an act so divine and solemn." (*Ibid.*)

One of the most distinguished among the opponents of the theater was the historian Padre Juan de Mariana. He had denounced it as early as 1599 in the treatise *De Rege,* and again in his *De Spectaculis,* ten years later. In his work *Contra los Juegos publicos,* a translation

---

[1] *Controversias,* p. 67.   [2] *Ibid.,* p. 370.   [3] *Ibid.,* p. 377.

which, it is said, he himself made of his *De Spectaculis*, with amplifications, he opposes the theater with great vehemence.[1] He would particularly exclude all players from taking part in religious festivals in the churches or in the public *autos* at Corpus, and expresses his horror at having heard the most gross and indecent *entremeses* recited in churches, and dwells upon the great prejudice to religion and morals that low-lived players should represent the lives of saints, etc. All actors should be banished from public and church festivals, from which also, in his opinion, all dances should be eliminated.[2]

Again, in the *Diálogos de las Comedias* (1620), by an anonymous writer, we read: "An actress appears upon the stage to represent a Magdalen or the Mother of God, and an actor to represent the Saviour, and the first thing you see is that the greater part of the audience recognizes this woman as a prostitute (*ramera*) and the man as a bully. Could there be a greater indecency in the

[1] It is not certain that Mariana himself translated the *De Spectaculis* into Spanish. Cirot, in his excellent work, *Mariana, Historien*, Paris, 1905, nowhere says so. Gallardo, *Ensayo*, Vol. II, Index of MSS. at the end, p. 100, mentions the "Tratado *De Spectaculis*, traducido en castellano por él mismo (Q. 41)." See below, p. 294. Mariana died in 1623.

[2] "Pretendo empero que los faranduleros se deben de todo punto desterrar de las fiestas del pueblo cristiano y de los templos. . . . Pues ¿con qué cara los cristianos faranduleros tomados de la plaza y de los mesones los meten en los templos para que por ellos se augmente la sagrada alegria de las fiestas? . . . Pero dirás por ventura que en los templos no tratan de cosas torpes, sino que representan historias sagradas tomadas ó de los libros divinos, ó de las historias de los sanctos, lo cual pluguiese á Dios fuese verdad, y no antes para mover al pueblo á risa tratasen de cosas torpisimas. Y es cosa muy grave no poder negar lo que confesar es grande vergüenza; sabemos muchas veces en los templos sanctisimos, principalmente en los entremeses, que son á manera de coros, recitarse adulterios, amores torpes y otras deshonestidades, de manera que cualquier hombre honesto está obligado á huir tales espectáculos y fiestas si quiere mirar por el decoro de su persona y por su vergüenza; y ¿creerémos con todo esto que las cosas que huyen los hombres modestos son agradables á los sanctos? Yo antes creeria que todos estos juegos se debrian desterrar de los templos sanctisimos como estiercol y burla de la religion, principalmente cuando se hacen por públicos faranduleros, porque siendo su vida torpe, parece que con su misma afrenta afean antes la religion . . . y ¿sufrirémos que una muger deshonesta represente á la

world? Having finished this part, the same actress appears in an *entremes*, representing an innkeeper's wife or a prostitute, simply by putting on a bonnet or tucking up a skirt, and then comes out in a wicked *baile* and dances and sings a *carrateria* which they call 'The Clothes Laundry,' in which all the unseemly occurrences in a laundry are represented; and he who played the part of the Saviour in a beard takes it off and comes out and sings or dances or performs the *baile* of 'There goes Molly' (*Allá va Marica*). Does this not show the greatest indecency and mockery of our faith?"[1] The same *Diálogo* tells us that "actors are the filth and scum of the world (*la horrura y hez del mundo*), and very rarely are good people found among them"; that "very often they can neither read nor write, and they are wicked people who have an aversion to work," etc., but "by dint of industry and perseverance, here and there one becomes eminent, like Cisneros, Leoncillo, Granados, Morales, Villegas, Rios, and others."

The shafts of Fray Jerónimo de la Cruz, in his *Iob evangelico stoyco ilustrado* (1638), are directed not so much at the players as at the comedias—at their plots and subject-matter. "In the comedia is represented, with the brilliant colors which the devil knows how to give to idle thoughts and a wanton heart, how the married woman may betray her husband: it [the comedia] facilitates the deed and diminishes fidelity with the example it sets before

virgen Maria ó Sancta Catalina, y un hombre infame se vista de las personas de san Agustin y san Antonio? . . . creeria yo que por la misma razon se deben echar dellos [los templos] las danzas, que conforme á la costumbre de España, con gran ruido y estruendo, moviendo los pies y manos al son del tamboril por hombres enmascarados se hacen; porque ¿ de qué otra cosa sirven sino de perturbar á los que rezan y oran y á los que cantan en comun?" Mariana, *Contra los Juegos publicos*, chap. vii, pp. 422, 423 (*Bibl. de Autores Españoles*, Vol. XXXI), and see also chap. xii of the same work, which is devoted wholly to the *bayle y cantar llamado Zarabanda*. (*Ibid.*, p. 433.) The latter chapter, Pellicer says, was added in the Spanish translation. (*Histrionismo*, Vol. I, p. 128, note.)

[1] *Ibid.*, p. 218.

one of how others have done so. It incites the maiden to thoughts which she knows not, and to desires which she does not understand. It furnishes a means to outwit the severity of the father and the precaution of the mother. It teaches her to receive secret letters, to reply to them, and what she has to do in any conjecture to attain an end: to feign in public and to lose her fears in secret; to make false keys, to seek hidden doors and windows; not to fear the darkness of the night nor the dangers of the house. To the young it teaches liberties, boldness, and insolence; the plausible excuse, the bland speech, the deceptive sigh," etc.[1]

Especially was the opposition most bitter to the representation of religious and sacred comedias (*comedias á lo divino*) and to the *autos sacramentales,* when performed by the actors of the public theaters, for here the characters of saints and of the Virgin Mary were frequently assumed by players whose lives were notoriously immoral.[2] In addition to the instances already given, many more could be cited from the work of Sr. Cotarelo, but enough has been adduced to show the nature and extent of the opposition to plays of this character.

Amid the great mass of controversy upon the question

---

[1] *Ibid.,* p. 203.

[2] See above, the excerpt from Mariana. Nearly two hundred years later, in 1789, Don Simon Lopez, speaking of the *comedias de santos,* says: "What matters it that the comedia be on a sacred subject, if those who represent it be consummate rogues? What matters it if the life of the saint, which is the theme of the comedia, be good, if in the very same narration are mingled a hundred evil things; if there be interjected *sainetes, tonadillas,* obscene witticisms, and low innuendos to please the taste of the audience and to attract them, with the object of gaining more money? Because the rascally actors know very well that if all were devout and Christian the crowds would soon be lacking." He cites as an example the priest Montalvan's *Santa Maria Egipciaca* (*La Gitana de Menfis*). This, which is a *comedia de santos,* he says is wholly a tissue of lies, perjuries, blasphemies, false testimony, jealousies, suspicions, gallantries, solicitations, low puns, vile allusions, and inciting gestures. "In it are depicted murder, robbery, and revenge. In it at every step the names of God, Jesus, and Mary are profaned. In it miracles, prayers, sanctity, and penitence are ridiculed. In it wickedness and effrontery

of the lawfulness of the comedia which has been collected by Sr. Cotarelo, the voices of the defenders of the theater make but a feeble outcry, which is drowned and over-whelmed by their opponents.[1] There can be little doubt that the latter had good grounds for their protests, due not so much to the plays themselves as to the character of the players, for the Spanish comedia, especially as it is represented by three of its greatest writers, Lope de Vega, Alarcon, and Calderon, compares very favorably, as regards its moral tone, with the contemporary plays of England, Italy, or France,[2] as we have already re-marked.

Indeed, it is almost certain that the strong feeling against the comedia, which found its expression in the utterances of the theologians and the various decrees of the government concerning the regulation of the stage, was mostly due to the excesses of the players themselves. As a body they seem to have been anything but respecta-

are lauded, and procurers and go-betweens are introduced. In it a public woman is deified, giving her the divine name of Mary. And even more: in it an actor who a short time before took the part of a gay gallant is seen transformed into a hermit in a religious habit, imitating all the most sacred ceremonies," etc. All this, he says, was seen in the public theater of Murcia on August 16, 1789, performed on a Sunday by the company of Francisco Baus. (Cotarelo, *Controversias,* p. 410.)

[1] Among the later defenders of the stage was the well-known dramatist Francisco Bances Cándamo, in an inedited work formerly in the possession of Don Pascual de Gayangos, entitled *Teatro de los Teatros de los pasados y presentes Siglos: Historia escénica griega, romana y castellana.* Sr. Gayangos gives a long excerpt from this work in his Spanish transla-tion of Ticknor's *History.* Tomo III, pp. 454 ff.

[2] Even taking the Spanish dramatists of a lesser order—among whose works occasionally we find plays unsurpassed by the best—it may be said that there is little, on the whole, which calls for our censure, when com-pared with the rest of the drama of the time. Nowhere, for example, so far as my reading goes, do we meet with the brutality and utter lack of a sense of decency that is only too often exhibited in the Elizabethan drama. Its relatively high moral plane is, indeed, one of the distinguish-ing marks of the Spanish national drama. Only one offender need be named here, and he, unfortunately, one of the greatest dramatists of them all, and a priest, besides, like many of his fellow-playwrights: Tirso de Molina. He seems to have been constitutionally incapacitated from allow-ing a play to leave his hands without a slight smudge, at all events. In

ble, being mostly from the lower walks of life, though there were not a few exceptions, as we have seen. In the vast army of players which Spain produced in little more than half a century—nearly two thousand names are known to us—many became famous. A number are highly praised by Lope de Vega, among them Alonso de Cisneros, Agustin Solano, Melchor de Villalba, Nicolas de los Rios, Antonio de Villegas, Luis de Vergara, Baltasar Pinedo, Juan de Morales Medrano, Sanchez de Vargas, Alonso de Olmedo, and others. Damian Arias de Peñafiel was universally regarded as the greatest Spanish actor of his time. Of him Caramuel says: "Arias possesses a clear, pure voice, a tenacious memory, and vivacious manner, and in whatever he said it seemed that the Graces were revealed in every movement of his tongue and Apollo in every gesture. The most famous orators came to hear him in order to acquire perfection of diction and gesture. At Madrid one day Arias came upon the stage reading a letter; for a long time he held the audience in suspense; he was filled with emotion at every line, and finally, aroused with fury, he tore the letter to shreds and began to declaim his lines with great vehemence, and though he was praised by all, he won greater admiration on that day by his action than by his speech."[1]

fact, on account of "the evil example and tendency of his profane comedias," the Junta de Reformacion, in 1625, urged his banishment to one of the most remote monasteries of his order and that he be excommunicated *latae sententiae,* "so that he may write no more comedias or profane verses." Acuerdo de la Junta de Reformacion: "Tratóse del escandalo que causa un *fraile mercenario que se llama Mº Tellez por otro nombre Tirso,* con comedias que hace profanas y de malos incentivos y exemplos y por ser caso notorio se acordó que se consulte a Su Magestad mande que el Pe confesor diga al Nuncio le eche de aqui a uno de los Monasterios mas remotos de su Religion y le imponga excomunion latæ sententiæ para que no haga comedias ni otro ningun genero de versos profanos y que esto sea luego." (Pérez Pastor, *Bull. Hisp.* (1908), p. 250.)

[1] "Arias habet vocem claram et puram, memoriam firmam et actionem vivacem, et quidquid ipse diceret in singulis linguae motibus Charites et in singulis manuum videbatur habere Apollines. Ad eum audiendum

Of comic actors, Cosme Perez, called *Juan Rana,* was without a peer in his day. Among the celebrated actresses who were deceased in 1615, Suarez de Figueroa[1] mentions Ana de Velasco, Mariana Paez, Mariana Ortiz, Mariana Vaca, and Jerónima de Salzedo. Of those living at that date he mentions Juana de Villalba, Mariflores, Michaela de Luxan [the *amiga* of Lope de Vega], Ana Muñoz, Jusepa Vaca, Jerónima de Burgos, Polonia Perez, Maria de los Angeles, and Maria de Morales. Of these actresses perhaps the widest celebrity was gained by Jusepa Vaca, wife of Juan de Morales Medrano. She was much favored by Lope de Vega, who wrote for her—"la gallarda Jusepa Vaca," as he calls her—the comedia *Las Almenas de Toro.* Michaela de Luxan was the mother of four of Lope's children: Mariana and Angelilla, of whom we know nothing, Marcela, who became a nun, and the son Lope Felix.[2] Jerónima de Burgos, wife of the actor Pedro de Valdes, also enjoyed the friendship of the great dramatist for years, and for her he wrote the comedia *La Dama boba* in 1613, though when he fell out with her he was unkind enough to accuse her of having once sold hot rolls in Valladolid. Of Maria de los Angeles, wife of Jerónimo Sanchez, actor, Lope, in a letter written in May, 1614, in a fit of ill will, says that she was brought up in the *Rastro* of Toledo, among the tripevenders (*mondongueras*). Several other actresses acquired great renown at a somewhat later date, among them Maria de Cordoba y de la Vega (*Amarilis*),[3] Ma-

confluebant excellentissimi concionatores, ut dictionis et actionis perfectionem addiscerent. Matriti semel Arias sibi legens epistulam in theatrum ingressus, longo tempore habuit Auditores suspensos, ad singulas lineas percellebatur, et demum furore percitus laceravit epistulam et incepit exclamare vehementissima carmina. Et tametsi laudaretur ab omnibus, majorem illa die agendo quam loquendo admirationem extorsit." (*Rhythmica,* editio altera, Campaniae, 1668, p. 706, quoted by Schack, *Nachträge,* p. 64.)

[1] *Plaza Universal,* ed. of 1630, p. 336.
[2] See my *Life of Lope de Vega, passim.*
[3] Caramuél says of her: "Sub idem tempus [1624] Amaryllis (sic eam

ria Calderon (*La Calderona*), the favorite of Philip the Fourth, and mother of his son, Don John of Austria, and Maria de Riquelme, who shines with especial splendor in this fragile company, as a woman of unblemished reputation and an actress of singular gifts and attainments.[1] "She possessed great beauty and was of so lively an imagination that, to the astonishment of all, she could entirely change the color of her countenance while speaking. At the narration of some happy incident her face was suffused with a rosy tint, but if an unfortunate circumstance intervened, she suddenly became deathly pale; and in this she was alone and inimitable."[2]

These and some others "enjoyed, no doubt," as Ticknor says, "that ephemeral, but brilliant, reputation which is generally the best reward of the best of their class; and enjoyed it to as high a degree, perhaps, as any persons that have appeared on the stage in more modern times."[3]

While it is true that the comedia was endangered by the loose and vicious lives of the players, the temptations to which the latter were subjected were, on the other hand, so great that their conduct need cause us little surprise. This is especially true after the accession to the throne of Philip the Fourth. The court of that monarch was, without doubt, one of the most dissolute in Europe. From his early years he had shown an extreme fondness

vocabant) inter Comicas floruit, quae erat prodigiosa in sua arte. Eloquebatur, canebat, musicis instrumentis ludebat, tripudiabat, et nihil erat, quod cum laude et applausu non faceret." (Schack, *Nachträge*, p. 64.)

[1] See above, pp. 163, 164.

[2] "Paucis post annis theatra adsurgebat Riquelmae, adolescenti pulchrae, apprehensiva tam forti praeditae, ut inter loquendum vultus colorem cum omnium admiratione mutaret: nam, si in theatro fausta et felicia narrarentur, roseo colore suffusa auscultabat; si autem aliqua infausta circumstantia intercurreret, illico pallida reddebatur. Et in hoc erat unica, quam nemo valeret imitari." (Caramuel, quoted by Schack.)   A contemporary Italian actress, Virginia Andreini (1583–1628), is also said to have possessed this power of changing the color of her face at will. (Rasi, *I Comici Italiani*, Vol. I, p. 147.)

[3] *History of Spanish Literature*, Vol. II, p. 519.

for the stage and especially for actresses.[1] Few could withstand the all-powerful influences of this royal rake, and his idle and dissolute courtiers eagerly followed the example set by their master. Only a woman of extraordinary strength of character could avoid falling a victim to this horde of inveterate debauchés. They wrangled and fought for the favors of the frail *comediantes*. We need not be surprised at the words of Madame d'Aulnoy, who, writing some years later than the period which chiefly occupies us (but in which, in all probability, matters had little changed), says: "One can say that actresses are worshiped at this court. There is not one who is not the mistress of some great lord and for whom quarrels have not taken place and men have not been killed. I do not know what may be the attraction of their speech, but in truth they are the ugliest carcasses in the world. They are frightfully extravagant, and one would rather let a whole family perish of hunger than permit one of these beggarly comédiennes to lack the most superfluous thing."[2]

[1] Sepúlveda has truly said: "Don Felipe IV fué rey, poeta y galan enamoradísimo, un tanto calavera al uso de los Lindos, . . . romantico en sus inclinaciones y novelesco en sus aventuras. A no haber nacido rey hubiera sido histrión." (*El Corral de la Pacheca*, p. 261.)

[2] *Relation du Voyage d'Espagne*, La Haye, 1693, Tome III, p. 23. This statement of Madame d'Aulnoy's is supported by the testimony of an anonymous writer of a much earlier date (1620), who says: " . . . pues sin ser muy viejo he visto tantos caballeros y señores perdidos por estas mugercillas comediantes: uno que se va con una; otro que lleva á otra á sus lugares; uno que les da las galas y trata como á reina; otro que la pone casa y estrado y gasta con ella, aunque lo quite de su muger e hijos, y él ande tratandose infamemente; otro que con publicidad celebró en iglesia publica el baptizo de un hijo de una destas farsantas, colgando la iglesia y haciendo un excesivo gasto con musica de capilla y con convite. No hay compañia destas que lleve consigo cebados de la desenvoltura muchos destos grandes peces ó cuervos que se van tras la carne muerta. Sabemos por nuestros pecados todos tanto destos infortunios que es una de las mayores infamias de nuestra nacion. Oimos decir que el otro señor salió desterrado por la otra *Amarilis;* otro por la otra *Maritardia ó Maricandado,* que le dieron un faldellin que costó mil ducados, un vestido que costó dos mil, una joya de diamantes rica; y todo esto se escribe y gacetea en otros reinos y se pierda mucha honra, y aun se desacredita la cristiandad." (Cota-

The utter lack of privacy in the dressing-rooms of the theaters, which were used indiscriminately by both sexes, could not fail to have a most demoralizing influence. Here the actresses received the visits of nobles and other idle and dissolute hangers-on, for whom the rear entrance of a theater has ever had a powerful attraction.[1] The fact that they consorted with nobles and grandees and received their protection inspired in these actresses an insolence and effrontery that sorely tried the respectable portion of the community. An honest woman ventured with diffidence upon the public streets, especially upon those which had become the recognized walks of these favored creatures.[2] Their unseemly conduct contributed in no small degree to the general demoralization which a love of idleness, a contempt for honest labor, and an inordinate desire for ostentatious extravagance were rapidly spreading through all classes of the capital. The *Avisos* or news-letters of various writers of this period show only too plainly the havoc which idleness and immorality had made in all ranks of society.

relo, *Controversias*, p. 215.) This statement has an additional interest from the fact that the actresses here mentioned, *Amarilis* (Maria de Córdoba y la Vega), *Maritardia* (or Maria Tardia, wife of Cebrian Dominguez), and *Maricandado* (Maria Candau, wife of Cristóbal de Avendaño), were at this time at the height of their theatrical careers.

[1] The same conditions prevailed in France as late as 1639. "En 1639 encore, les comédiens, hommes et femmes, n'avaient pour s'habiller et se déshabiller au théâtre qu'une seule chambre: encore y fallait-il recevoir les importuns, qu'il eût été imprudent d'éconduire." (Rigal, *l. c.*, p. 167.)

[2] Their favorite resort in Madrid was the *Mentidero de los Representantes*, or Liars' Walk of the Players—a small square with trees, situated in the Calle del Leon, between the Calle de las Huertas and the Calle del Prado, in the immediate neighborhood of which most of the actors and actresses lived, and which they visited daily to discuss their engagements and other matters of interest to the theatrical world. "Formerly the Calle del Leon, beginning at the Calle del Prado and continuing to the Calle de Francos and Calle de Cantarranas, was somewhat wider than at present and formed a small square surrounded by trees, called the *Mentidero de los Representantes*." (Schack, *Nachträge*, p. 63.) It was within a few yards of the house, situated in the Calle de Francos, between the Calle del Leon and the Calle del Niño, which Lope de Vega occupied for a quarter of a century (1610–35) and in which he died.

But while players were frequently on terms of intimacy with the nobility, they were nevertheless often treated in a manner which showed that the grandee had by no means lost the lofty conception he had always entertained of himself as the representative of the absoluteness of divine right. An instance occurred on February 8, 1637. Don Juan Pacheco, eldest son of the Marquis of Cerralbo, wanted Tomas Fernandez, a well-known *autor de comedias*, to give a new comedia on the day of San Blas, to celebrate the recovery from a quartan fever of a daughter of the Marquis of Cadreita, whom Don Juan at that time was courting (*galanteaba*). As Fernandez refused to do this, the nobleman hired an assassin to stab him, and while this stabbing was going on, we are told that Don Juan was walking up and down in the cemetery of San Sebastian, awaiting the outcome. "That is the way these rascals (*picaros*) ought to be treated," he remarked, an action, as the chronicler quietly observes, "which appeared wrong to nearly all, because, besides the fact that there were few people in the theaters on that day, the

Lope's house was in the very heart of the players' quarter and may be seen on the map of 1656. It is not without interest to note that on July 13, 1674, the celebrated actress Mariana Romero, bought from Luis de Usátegui, son-in-law of Lope de Vega, the house in the Calle de Francos in which Lope died in 1635. On a plan of Madrid published in 1800, the street is still called the Calle de Francos, though its name has since been changed to the Calle de Cervantes. It seems that in the latter half of the seventeenth century the *Mentidero* was shifted to the Calle de Cantarranas.

> "Calle de Cantarranas
> y Mentidero
> para los Comediantes
> todo es lo mismo."
> (*Loa para la compañia de Felix Pascual*, in *Migaxas del Ingenio*, Zaragosa (no date), fol. 33, v.)

There was another *Mentidero* in Madrid, "Las Gradas de San Felipe, Conuento de San Agustin, que es el mentidero de los soldados, de adonde salen las nueuas primero que los sucessos." (Guevara, *Diablo Cojuelo*, Tranco III. See also Mesonero Romanos, *El Antiguo Madrid*, 1881, Vol. I, p. 261, and Vol. II, p. 44; and Sepúlveda, *Madrid viejo*, Madrid, 1887, pp. 1 and 335.) Clemencin says: "En tiempos antiguos la Puerta de Guadalajara era, como ahora la del Sol, el sitio adonde concurria la

lessees were interested in them [the actors] as well as the General Hospital."[1]

Nowhere else can the reader gain a more vivid conception of life in the Spanish capital during the golden age of the drama than in these *Avisos* and *Anales*, the forerunners of the modern newspaper. They reveal an extraordinary condition of moral obliquity among all classes, but especially among the nobility, headed by the weak, profligate, and very pious King—*El Catolico Monarca, Felipe IV.*, as he was called, and one of whose proudest titles was "Defender of the Faith." It would have been a miracle indeed if the stage had been able to resist this general contamination.[2]

---

gente ociosa, y el mentidero de Madrid. Después se trasladó á las gradas de San Felipe." (*Don Quixote*, ed. Clemencin, Part II, chap. xlviii, Vol. V, p. 465.)

[1] *La Corte y Monarquia de España en los Años 1636 y 1637*, edited by Ant. Rodriguez Villa, Madrid, 1886, p. 90.

[2] The license permitted in the public processions during carnival seems almost incredible. See *ibid.*, pp. 107–110. On this occasion, as usual, the festival concluded with a *famosa comedia* which was represented in the *salon* of the King. "And these *fiestas* ordinarily not being free from unfortunate incidents which happen on such occasions, so in this one there was much rowdyism; many were beaten and wounded, and a soldier of the guard was stabbed." (*Ibid.*, p. 110.)

CHAPTER XIII

The term *comedia* defined. The various kinds of comedias. The licensing of comedias. The representation of a comedia. *Loas, Entremeses, Jácaras, Sainetes, Mogigangas.*

THE term *comedia* as used by Spanish dramatists is not the equivalent of our word "comedy." "Since the time of Lope de Vega every play in three acts or *jornadas* and in verse is called a *comedia*. Both these requisites were essential to a *comedia*. Of the conception of comedy as we have received it from the ancients, and of its meaning as opposed to tragedy, we must free ourselves entirely. The Spanish comedia is a species which embraces these differences and in which they are resolved. Here both these elements mutually interpenetrate one another and are transfused, i.e., romantic dramas result, which are neither comedies nor tragedies, but combine both; or either element may predominate, in which case pieces are produced which, according to our current conception, are sometimes comedies, sometimes tragedies, but which nevertheless do not cease to be *comedias* in the Spanish sense. In other words, the *comedia* may have either a tragic or comic effect, but it is not confined to either."[1]

As Morel-Fatio has clearly and briefly defined it: "La *comedia* désigne une action dramatique quelconque, sans égard pour les effets qu'elle doit produire dans l'âme du

[1] *Geschichte der dramatischen Literatur und Kunst in Spanien,* Vol. II, p. 74. Ricardo de Turia, in the "Apologetico de las Comedias españolas," says: Ninguna Comedia de quantas se representan en España lo es, sino Tragicomedia, que es un mixto formado de lo Comico y lo Tragico, etc. He further says that Spaniards want their comedias "abivado con saynetes de bayles y danzas que mezclan en ellas." *Norte de la Poesia española,* etc. Valencia, 1616.

spectateur, mais une action dramatique telle seulement que les Espagnols l'ont conçue; la *comedia* est le drame espagnol et n'est que cela." The same author says that *comedia* is identical with our "play" or the German *Schauspiel.* "Les drames les plus noirs de Calderon sont encore des *comedias.*"[1]

Attempts have frequently been made to define more clearly the various kinds of comedias, but it cannot be said, that, upon the whole, they have resulted satisfactorily. The earliest of these essays was made by a dramatist who was the first to write comedias in Spain in the manner which, as afterward perfected by Lope de Vega, became the comedia *par excellence.* I allude to Bartolomé de Torres Naharro, whose volume of plays, under the title *Propaladia,* was first published at Naples in 1517. He divides comedias into two classes: *Comedias a noticia,* or such as treat of events which have actually happened, and *Comedias a fantasia,* or such the action of which is the pure invention of the author.[2]

Suarez de Figueroa, who possessed an intimate knowledge of the theater of his time, writing in 1617, distinguishes two kinds of comedias: (1) *Comedias de cuerpo* and (2) *Comedias de Ingenio* or *de Capa y Espada.* The latter division he does not define; of the former he says: "*Comedias de cuerpo* (if we except those about the kings of Hungary or princes of Transylvania) are such as treat of the life of some saint and which employ all kinds of machinery and stage artifices to attract the rabble."[3] These are generally called *comedias de santos.*

---

[1] *La Comedia espagnole du XVIIe Siècle,* par Alfred Morel-Fatio, Paris, 1885, pp. 10, 13.
[2] "Cuanto a los generos de comedias: a mi parece que bastarian dos para en nuestra lengua castellana. Comedia a noticia y comedia a fantasia. A noticia se entiende: de cosa nota y vista en realidad de verdad: como son *Soldadesca y Tinellaria* [two of his plays]: a fantasia, de cosa fantastica o fingida que tenga color de verdad aunque no lo sea, como son *Serafina, Ymenea,*" etc.
[3] *El Passagero,* Madrid, 1617, Alivio III, fol. 104. *Comedias de cuerpo,*

Comedias de Capa y Espada have been defined as plays
that are based upon events and occurrences in ordinary
daily life and in which no higher personages intervene
than noblemen or gentlemen, and which are acted in the
ordinary costume of the time. They derived their name
from this costume, the cloak and sword, the dress of the
higher ranks of society in Spain; only the subordinate
characters, the servants and peasants, were represented in
the costume of the lower classes.[1] They generally required little or no scenery for their representation.
Schack says, moreover, that the distinguishing characteristics of the *Comedia de Capa y Espada* are based entirely
upon external circumstances (*äuszerliche Umstände*) and
that it is erroneous to introduce into the definition any
inner motive of the action. They have been defined as
dramas of intrigue, but they may just as well, in certain
instances, be denominated dramas of character.[2] It is
indeed futile to attempt, in this general division of the
comedia, to draw any sharp dividing line. On the other
hand, those comedias the action of which is not laid in
ordinary domestic life, and in which kings and princes
intervene, and which required a greater display of scenery
or costume and machinery, were called *Comedias de Teatro, de ruido,* or *de cuerpo.* To this class belonged historical or mythological dramas, those based upon legends

Figueroa says, are excellently suited to beginners, for, however worthless
they may turn out, the audience will not dare to hiss them, out of respect
for the saint. They are, moreover, the easiest to write, for he states that
he knew a tailor in Toledo who had composed several of these plays
which had been represented fifteen or twenty times. This man could
neither read nor write, but made his verses on the street and would request an apothecary, or any other shopkeeper in whose shop he happened
to be, to write his verses down upon scraps of paper.

[1] Schack, *op. cit.,* Vol. II, p. 96.
[2] The dramatist Francisco Bances Cándamo, in an inedited work already
cited (p. 266, note 1), ascribes the invention of *Comedias de Capa y Espada*
to Don Diego [Ximénez] de Enciso: "Este empezó las que llaman de
capa y espada: siguiéronle despues D. Pedro Rosete, D. Francisco de
Rojas, D. Pedro Calderon de la Barca," etc. (Ticknor, *History of Spanish
Literature,* tr. by Gayangos, Tome II, p. 553.)

or the lives of saints, etc., in which the scene of action was laid in some remote country or period. But here again it is useless to attempt any sharp distinction, which, as a matter of fact, the dramatists themselves never attempted. Let us now turn to the representation of a comedia. Before a theatrical performance could be given in any town or municipality, a license had to be obtained, and sometimes, before this was granted, a gratuitous representation of the comedia had to be given to the authorities.[1] Moreover, every time a comedia was represented, a special license was necessary, which was written upon the manuscript used by the players. Among the early manuscripts of Lope de Vega containing such licenses are *El Leal Criado*, dated at Alba, June 24, 1594, which contains, among others, a license to Luis de Vergara to represent it in Granada, dated October 30, 1595.[2]

[1] This "représentation spéciale et gratuite" was also frequently exacted in France, as in the case of Roland Guibert and his company before they were permitted to act in Amiens in 1559. (Rigal, *Le Théâtre Français avant la période classique*, Paris, 1901, p. 17.) Likewise the English comedians who traveled through Germany in the latter part of the sixteenth and in the seventeenth century were frequently obliged to give a trial performance before receiving a license to act; to this performance the wives and children of the members of the Council were admitted free. This occurred, for instance, in Frankfort in 1592. A list of the plays to be given also had to be furnished to the city authorities, as was done at Ulm in 1603 and 1609. Plays were announced by drums and trumpets, the company parading the streets. In 1613 the players went through Nürnberg with two drums and four trumpets, stopping in the squares, though in this year they were forbidden to halt in the Hay Market. In those cities in which the public theater belonged to the municipality, a lease was entered into between the manager of the company and the civil authorities. In Regensburg in 1613, Spencer, who is said to have taken in 500 gulden at the first representation, had to pay a weekly rental of 22 florins. That these visits of the English players were profitable is shown by the fact that for eight representations in Nürnberg, from July 15 to July 31, 1628, the receipts were 661 florins 7 kreutzers and 2 pfennigs, and the number of spectators varied from 2665 to 515, though this latter case was the only one in which the number fell below one thousand. (Creizenach, *Die Schauspiele der Englischen Komödianten*, Berlin and Stuttgart (no date), p. xx *et passim*.) The fee for licensing a play for performance in England at the close of the sixteenth and in the early seventeenth century was invariably seven shillings. *Henslowe's Diary*, ed. Greg, Vol. II, 1908, p. 115.

[2] This play contains another license dated at Granada, November 4, 1603,

Representations in the Madrid theaters, as already observed, began at two in the afternoon during the six months beginning with October 1, and at four during the remaining six months. The fee paid at the door entitled the person to admission only—to the run of the house. He could stand in the *patio* or pit with the *mosqueteros* or groundlings, as they were called in the Elizabethan theater; but if he wanted a seat, an extra sum must be paid. Those who desired seats naturally came early, especially if a new comedia was to be given, and at one time they must have resorted to the theater so early in the day that this matter required regulation by the government, and the theaters were not allowed to open their doors before noon.[1]

While waiting for the musicians with guitars and harps to appear, the sellers of fruit, confections, *aloja* (a kind of mead), *barquillos* (a thin rolled wafer), etc., were busy passing around among the spectators.[2] The unruly and

showing that a new license had to be obtained every time the piece was performed. Other early plays by Lope containing licenses are *Laura perseguida*, dated at Alba, October 12, 1594; *El Blason de los Chaves*, dated at Chinchon, August 20, 1599; and *Carlos V. en Francia*, Toledo, November 20, 1604. These licenses are all printed in *Comedias Escogidas de Lope de Vega*, ed. Hartzenbusch, Vol. IV, pp. xvi, xvii (*Bibl. de Autores Esp.*).

[1] Quevedo, *Vida del gran Tacaño*, Cap. XXII, says that when a new comedia was played, it was necessary to send at twelve o'clock for a seat: "Era menester enviar á tomar lugar á las doce, como para Comedia nueva." The nobility, who were favored by government regulation in the choice of seats, used to send their servants to secure them.

[2] A vivid picture of the interior of a Spanish theater at this time is given in the comedia *La Baltasara*, "Comedia famosa," the first act of which was written by Luis Vélez de Guevara, the second by Don Antonio Coello, and the third by Don Francisco de Roxas. The first act represents the interior of the *Corral de la Olivera* in Valencia. A bill-poster appears, who pastes up a placard announcing the performance of "la gran comedia del *Saladino*" by the licentiate Poyo, to be given by the company of Heredia. The dialogue is carried on by spectators in the theater. Presently the fruit-sellers appear (they are designated by numbers); the stage direction is: *Los compañeros repartidos por el patio, dizen:*

"1. Avellanas.
   2. Piñanes mondados. 3. Peros de Aragon.
   4. Turron. 5. Membrillos.

boisterous audience signified its impatience by hissing, whistling upon keys, shouting, and noises of every conceivable kind. Presently the musicians could be heard *templando los instrumentos;* the hour for beginning the performance had at last arrived, and the musicians appeared upon the stage and sang a ballad or *seguidilla,* after which some member of the company entered to *echar la loa,* i.e., "throw out the loa" or compliment, as it was called in technical phrase.[1]

Loas occur in two forms, either (1) as monologues, bearing generally but a very imperfect relation to the following play and frequently no relation whatever, or (2) as short, slight dramatic sketches which may be prefaced to any comedia, like the *loas* of Rojas Villandrando or Quiñones de Benavente; sometimes the *loa* directs the mind of the auditor to what is to follow, as the *loas* to Calderon's *autos,* or much more rarely it may be essential to the comprehension of the play which it precedes, as in the *loa* to Calderon's *Los tres mayores Prodigios.*

6. Suplicaciones, barquillos.
7. Agua de Anis, Cavalleros.
8. Aloja de nieve fria.
9. Datiles de Berberia.

Vejete: Qué confusion, qué locura!
Viuda: Todo esto hermosura causa,
   Que es de la naturaleza
   La variedad lo mejor.
Vejete: Los moços de la comedia
   Vienen ya con sus guitarras,
   Con harpas, y con diversas
   Galas que el Abril embidia," etc.
   (*Comedias Escogidas,* Vol. I, Madrid, 1652.)

The date of this play is not known. Baltasara de los Reyes, in whose honor it was written, was a famous actress and the wife of Miguel Ruiz, actor, who is also one of the characters in the play. Both were acting in the company of Gaspar de Porres in 1604, in that of Melchor de Leon in 1607, and in that of Pedro de Valdes in 1614. The play was composed after she had retired from the stage, which she is said to have done at the height of her success, to enter a hermitage dedicated to St. John the Baptist, near Cartagena. It is probable that *La Baltasara* was written about 1630, when the memory of the actress was still fresh in the minds of theater-goers.

[1] Caramuel says: "Hodie Prologus Comoediis Hispanis praemittitur et

Originally the *loa* was recited for the purpose of gaining the good will and attention of the audience, which, we are told, could be done in four ways: "(1) By commending the plot, story, poet, or the *autor* who represented the play. (2) By censuring or upbraiding the fault-finder or giving thanks to the kindly disposed auditors. (3) The third manner is argumentative, in which is declared the history or fable which is to be represented, and this, justly, is little used in Spain, because it deprives the listener of much of the pleasure of the comedia to know beforehand the outcome of the story to be represented. (4) The fourth is called mixed; it is styled *introito* because it appears at the beginning, *faraute* because it explains the argument, and now they call it *loa* because in it the comedia or the audience or the festivity during which it is given is praised; . . . but all is directed to the one end: to gain the good will and attention of the audience."[1]

vocatur *Loa,* quia profunditur in Auditorum laudes: et recitare prologum est *echar la loa,* quasi laudes non tam dicantur quam in Auditores profundantur." (*Rhythmica* (1668), quoted by Schack, *Nachträge,* p. 26.)

[1] "La *loa* o prologo de la comedia, que otros llaman introito o faraute, a mi opinion no es parte de la comedia, sino distinto y apartado, y asi diré aora lo que del se puede dezir. Al principio de cada comedia sale un personage a procurar y captar la benevolencia y atençion del auditorio, y esto haze en una de quarto maneras comendativamente, encomendando la fabula, historia, poeta o autor que la representa. El segundo modo es relativo en el qual se zayere y vitupera el murmurador o se rinde gracias a los benevolos oyentes. El tercero modo es argumentativo, en el qual se declara la historia o fabula que se representa, y este con razon en España es poco usado, por quitar mucho gusto a la comedia, sabiendose antes que se represente el sucesso de la historia. Llamase el quarto modo misto por particular de los tres ya dichos, llamaronle introito por entrar al principio: faraute por declarar el argumento, y aora le llaman loa por loar en el la comedia, el auditorio o festividad en que se hace. Mas ya le podremos asi llamar, porque han dado los poetas en alabar alguna cosa como el silencio, un numero, lo negro, lo pequeño y otras cosas en que se quieren señalar y mostrar sus ingenios, aunque todo deve ir ordenado al fin que yo dixe, que es captar la benevolencia y atencion del auditorio." (*Cisne de Apolo, de las excelencias y dignidad y todo lo que al Arte poetico y versificatorio pertenece. Los metodos y estylos que en sus obras deve seguir el poeta.* Por Luys Alfonso de Carvallo, Clerigo. Medina del Campo, 1602, p. 124. Schack, *Nachträge,* p. 23.) This is essentially what Alonso Lopez Pinciano had said some years before, in his *Philosophia Antigua,* Madrid,

This peculiarly Spanish form of prologue is a development of the *introito*, in vogue as early as the time of Torres Naharro, whose *Propaladia* was first published in 1517. Here, however, the *introito* was merely a sort of argument of the play that follows. Likewise each of the later pieces of Lope de Rueda, the *Colloquio de Camila, Colloquio de Timbria*, etc., is prefaced by an *introito* or *argumento*, a brief résumé of the following play. This is also the case in his comedias, which are accompanied by short prefatory notes, spoken generally by Lope de Rueda himself, for they are called *Introito que hace el Autor*. But the later *loas*, beginning with those of Lope de Vega, rarely have any connection whatever with the comedia which follows. Generally they are merely the relation of some trivial incident, nearly always in a playful, humorous vein, and conclude with an appeal to the good will and attention of the audience.[1] Lope de Vega must have written a great many of these slight pieces, nearly all of which have disappeared. They are generally in the *romance* or ballad measure, sometimes in *redondillas*, and vary in length from a little more than a hundred lines to three or four times that number.

Among the best known *loas* are those written by Agustin de Rojas and printed in his *Entertaining Journey;* they

1596, p. 413. He calls the *loa* "prologo": "Ay un prologo, que es dicho comendatiuo: porque en el o la fabula, o el autor es alabado. Y ay prologo relatiuo, adonde el Poeta da gracias al pueblo, o habla contra algun aduersario. Ay le tambien argumentatiuo, que es el que diximos daua luz, por lo passado a lo porvenir. Y ay prologo de todos mezclado, que no tiene nombre y se podria llamar prologo misto."

[1] The first volume of Lope de Vega's *Comedias*, Valladolid, 1604, contains eleven *loas*. Some doubt has been cast upon the authorship of these *loas*. The fact, however, that they were printed at this early date rather favors their authenticity, as no other writer of *loas* was prominent at this time, excepting Rojas. Indeed, some of them, notably the one beginning *Vemos con lobregas nubes* and the seventh, *Quien dize que las mugeres,* seem like Lope's in his best vein. There are also five *loas* in the spurious Part III (1612) of Lope's *Comedias* and four in Part VII, Barcelona, 1617, and in the *Fiestas del Santissimo Sacramento*, Çaragoça, 1644. See below.

embrace both monologues and small dramatic sketches in which a whole company took part. It is hard to see wherein these longer *loas*, performed by several actors or by a whole company, differed from the *entremeses*. Rojas's *loas* are upon every conceivable subject; one is in praise of Seville, the city in which the company was about to perform,[1] while another extols the company of Antonio de Villegas.[2] The most famous of them all is the *Loa en Alabanza de la Comedia*,[3] to which reference has already been made. Having passed in review the most distinguished dramatists, the *loa* concludes:

> Who with these is not acquainted?
> Who, whom fame of them not reacheth?
> Who in wonderment beholds not
> Their rare wit and sounding phrases?
> And allowing that 't is true,
> 'T is not strange that I should venture
> In their name now to entreat you
> That, because of the great rev'rence
> Which to their rare works is owing,
> While their plays are represented,
> You may pardon the shortcomings
> Of the players who perform them.[4]

And so nearly all of them conclude with a similar appeal. To give a conception of the diversity of subjects

[1] *El Viage entretenido*, Madrid, 1603, pp. 9–20.
[2] *Ibid.*, pp. 48–55.   [3] *Ibid.*, pp. 118–132.

[4] "Quien a todos no conoce?
> quien a su fama no llega?
> quien no se admira de ver
> sus ingenios y elocuencia?
> Supuesto que esto es assi,
> no es mucho que yo me atreva
> a pediros en su nombre,
> que por la gran reuerencia
> Que se les deue a sus obras,
> mientras se hazen sus comedias,
> que las faltas perdoneys
> de los que las representan."
> (*Ibid.*, pp. 131, 132.)

treated by Rojas in his *loas,* we may add that there is one
in praise of thieves;[1] in praise of Tuesday ("el soberano
dia Martes") ;[2] on beautiful teeth ("colmillos y mueles")
and how to preserve them;[3] one extolling the swine
("puerco"), which is very witty, and ends:

> And if long have been my praises
> Of an animal so lovely,
> May he who should be one pardon
> Me, and therefore not feel shameful.[4]

Rojas well describes the *loa* in one which he wrote in
praise of Sunday, and in it he tells us, moreover, that even
in his day every conceivable subject had been exhausted
and that it was impossible to write what had not already
been written:

> So many and so varied are the dramas,
> So great, indeed, the multitude of ballads,
> So varied, too, the subjects of the *loas*
> That have been written hitherto, I wonder
> How one can write what 's not already written,
> Or we say what has not been said already.
> Some make their farces of involved inventions,
> Others of stories fabulous and fictions,
> Loas that sing the praises of the letters,
> Of plants and animals and varied colors.
> One what is black, the other white extolleth,
> Silence this one, humility that other,
> And many more which I fail to remember.
> And 't is a labor now as ill requited,
> This writing loas, as in times now distant
> It by all men was held in estimation, etc.[5]

[1] *Ibid.,* p. 681.   [2] *Ibid.,* p. 597.
[3] *Ibid.,* p. 377.   [4] *Ibid.,* p. 693.

[5] "Son tantas y tan varias las comedias,
   tanta la muchedumbre de romances,
   y tan grande el discurso de las loas,
   que hasta agora se han hecho, que me espanto

He declares that *loas* were written:

> In both the ancient comedy and modern
> To gain the list'ner's ear and kindly favor, . . .
> To sing the praises of its gallant spirits,
> And to exalt its wits in their due measure.

Rojas excelled in writing these slight pieces; his are among the very best that have come down to us, and it is interesting to know that he was the member of the company who not only wrote the *loas*, but who also invariably recited them.

To about the same period or a little later belongs the well-known collection of *loas* and *entremeses* of Luis Quiñones de Benavente, first published under the title *Joco Seria, Burlas Veras*, etc., Madrid, 1645. In these several actors always take part and sometimes the entire company for which they were written. A number of them serve as a kind of introduction of the company to the audience; the peculiarities of the actors are hit off, their ability is praised, and the new comedias which the company brings are mentioned; like all these compositions, they are written in a jovial, humorous vein, intended to put the audience in good spirits.[1]

> que nadie pueda hazer mas de lo hecho,
> ni nosotros dezir mas de lo dicho.
> Unos hazen las farsas de marañas,
> otros de historias fabulas, ficciones,
> las loas de alabanças de las letras,
> de plantas, animales, de colores,
> uno alaua lo negro, otro lo blanco,
> este el silencio, la humildad el otro,
> sin otras muchas, de que no me acuerdo.
> Y es trabajo tan mal agradecido,
> esto de loas, como en otro tiempo
> fue de todos los hombres estimado," etc.
>   (*El Viage entretenido*, Madrid, 1603, pp. 569, 570.)

[1] They have been republished by Don Cayetano Rosell, *Entremeses, Loas y Jácaras, escritas por el Licenciado Luis Quiñones de Benavente*, Madrid, 1872, 1874, 2 vols. Many of them are of especial importance as furnishing interesting information concerning some of the most prominent players of the time.

It appears that the *loa* had lost much of its vogue before the end of the second decade of the seventeenth century. Indeed, according to Suarez de Figueroa, *loas* had already ceased to be recited in 1617. He says: "In the farces which are ordinarily represented they have already discontinued that part called the *loa,* and from the slight purpose which it served and the fact that it was wholly foreign to the subject-matter of the play, it was certainly an advantage to suppress it."[1] It is difficult to reconcile Figueroa's statement, however, with the known fact that *loas* continued to accompany the comedia, though not with the frequency of former years, long after the date mentioned; indeed, some of Quiñones de Benavente's *loas* were written twenty years after this.

These *loas,* as already stated, from being simple recitals by a single member of the company, gradually became short, humorous pieces which did not differ essentially from the *entremeses* or short interludes which always accompanied the comedia, except that they were wholly without plot and consisted merely of dialogue held together by the loosest thread. They were generally accompanied by music and singing. Some were sung in part, as the *loa* with which Antonio de Rueda and Pedro Ascanio began to represent in Madrid in 1638.[2] Here the *loa* opens with Borja, an actor, who enters with a harp, followed by Maria de Heredia, both singing. The scene upon the stage at the beginning of another *loa* with which Tomas Fernandez began at Madrid in 1636 is indicated at the opening: "Enter the whole company two by two, with hands joined, dancing to the sound of instru-

---

[1] "En las farsas que comunmente se representan, han quitado ya esta parte que llaman Loa. Y segun de lo poco que servia, y quan fuera de proposito era su tenor, anduvieron acertados. Salia un farandulero, y despues de pintar largamente una nave con borrasca, ó la disposicion de un exercito, su acometer y pelear, concluia con pedir atencion y silencio, sin inferirse por ningun caso de lo uno lo otro." (*El Passagero,* Madrid, 1617, fol. 109.)

[2] *Entremeses,* etc., *de Quiñones de Benavente,* ed. Rosell, Vol. I, p. 366.

ments and bearing torches; making a reverence, they sing. Juanico, the son of Bernardo, is to be on the stage before the *loa* begins, playing with two other boys, and as soon as his father enters he is to tell him (Juanico) to keep quiet."[1]

The *loa* with which Roque de Figueroa's company returned to Madrid in 1633(?) appears to have been wholly·sung, except the *autor's* introductory dialogue with the actor Bezon. It is entitled *"Loa segunda que cantó Roque de Figueroa,"* etc.[2]

The *loa* being concluded, the first act or *jornada*[3] of the comedia followed, though, as Ticknor says, "in some instances a dance was interposed, and sometimes even a ballad followed this, so importunate was the audience for what was lightest and most amusing." After the first act an *entremes* followed, and perhaps another *bayle* or dance.

The name *entremeses* (French *entremets*, a side-dish), applied to festal pieces accompanied by singing, is found

---

[1] *Entremeses,* etc., *de Quiñones de Benavente,* ed. Rosell, Vol. I, p. 288.

[2] *Ibid.,* p. 224. In a *loa* represented by Lorenzo Hurtado in Madrid (1632(?) or 1635(?)) the direction is given at the opening: "Enter Bernardo without singing, to throw out the *loa*."

[3] While the term *jornada* instead of *act* had been commonly employed in the religious plays of the Middle Ages, which often lasted several days, and was also used by Torres Naharro as early as 1517, that word is not found in the manuscripts of Lope de Vega, who always uses *Acto* instead, and this seems to have been the custom of Tirso de Molina, to judge from the only autograph of his, *La Tercera de la Sancta Juana* (1613), that I have seen. That the term *jornada,* however, was well known at the beginning of the seventeenth century, is shown by the definition of Luys Alfonso de Carvallo: *"Jornada es nombre Italiano, quiere decir cosa de un dia, porque giorno significa al dia. Y tomase por la distincion y mudança que se hace en la comedia de cosas sucedidas en diferentes tiempos y dias, como si queriendo representar la vida de un Santo hiciesemos de la niñez una jornada, de la edad perfecta otra, y otra de la vejez."* (*Cisne de Apolo,* etc., Medina del Campo, 1602, quoted by Schack, *Nachträge,* p. 23.) *Jornada* seems to have been reintroduced into current usage by Calderon and his school. Virués, *Obras trágicas,* etc., Madrid, 1609, uses both terms. Caramuel says: "Actus est id, quod hodie vocamus *jornada:* et jam praescripsit consuetudo, ut Comoedia nonnisi tres actus habeat et duabus horis repraesentetur." (Schack, *Nachträge,* p. 26.)

as early as 1412 in the Archives of Valencia, and, as we have seen,[1] Lamarca claims a Valencian origin for these *entremesos*, as they were called.[2] It is very probable that *entremeses*, originally perhaps of a quasi-religious character, formed a part of the great church festivals from the earliest times. But these short pieces were gradually stripped of any religious significance they may have had, and finally every short farce or interlude was called an *entremes*. Such pieces, especially designated as *entremeses*, were brought out at festivals by the great Constable Don Alvaro de Luna.[3] Lope de Vega, in his *Arte nuevo de hacer Comedias*, speaking of Lope de Rueda, says that "from him has remained the custom of calling

[1] Introduction, p. xi.

[2] Wolf speaks of "jene Festschaustücke mit Gesang, die, wie bei den Nordfranzosen *Entremets*, damals auch in Spanien *'Entramesos'* oder *Entremeses* genannt wurden" (Studien, p. 585), and discussing the sixteenth-century MSS. of *Autos* and *Farsas*, since published by Rouanet (see above, p. 7, note 2), he remarks concerning the *Entremes de las Esteras*, contained therein: "Dass dieses Stück schon zu den *Entremeses* in der spätern allgemein üblich gewordenen Bedeutung dieses Gattungsnamens gehört habe, wird aus dem Personenverzeichniss (*figuras*) wahrscheinlich; denn es treten darin auf: *'Melchora, Antona, un bobo, un lacayo, un bachiller, el amo de las mozas.'* Hier hätten wir also das älteste Document für den Gebrauch von *'Entremes'* in dieser Bedetung." (*Ibid.*, p. 598, note.) An *entremes* belonging to the middle of the sixteenth century, written by Sebastian de Horozco of Toledo, is now printed in his *Cancionero*, Seville, 1874, pp. 167 ff. It is entitled: "Un Entremes que hizo el auctor á ruego de una Monja parienta suya evangelista para representarse como se representó en un Monasterio de esta Cibdad (Toledo) dia de Sant Ju⁰ Evangelista." "Introduzense quatro personas.— Un villano que viene á comprar al alcaná [antigua calle de Toledo donde se conservaban las tiendas á la usanza morisca] ciertas cosas para dar a una zagala;—y un Pregonero que entra pregonando, una moça de veinte años perdida;—y un Fraile que pide para las animas del purgatorio, á quien los otros cuelgan porque los combide, porque dizen que se llama fray Ju⁰ evangelista;—y un Buñolero que pregona buñuelos calientes. Comen los buñuelos y despues mantean al fraile sobre la paga. Y vanse todos a beber a una taberna y asi se acaba."

[3] Ticknor, Vol. I, p. 271, note. "Fué muy inventivo é mucho dado á fallar invenciones, é sacar entremeses en fiestas," etc. *Cronica de D. Alvaro de Luna, Madrid*, 1784, p. 182. As Ticknor remarks: "It is not to be supposed that these were like the gay farces that have since been passed under the same name, but there can be little doubt that they were poetical and were exhibited." Don Alvaro was executed in 1453.

the old comedias *entremeses*."[1] *Entremeses*, the editor
of Quiñones de Benavente observes, were for the purpose of avoiding the tedium between the acts, for without them "la mejor comedia tiene hoy el peligro de
los desaires que padece entre jornada y jornada." "And
so," he continues, "a manager who had a poor comedia,
by putting in two *entremeses* of this kind, gave it crutches
to prevent it from falling, and he who had a good one
put wings to it, to raise it still higher."[2]

Lope de Vega, alluding to his youthful efforts in writing
comedias, says:

> And some I wrote at eleven years and at twelve,
> Each of four acts as well as of four sheets,
> For each act was contained within a sheet,
> And in the spaces three that came between,
> Three little *entremeses* then were made,
> Though now there 's scarce one, and a *bayle* too,[3] etc.

Of these *entremeses* Lope certainly wrote a great many;
whether those printed in the volumes of his *Comedias*
are really his, it is impossible to decide, nor can the
entremeses contained in the *Fiestas del Santissimo Sacramento*, Zaragoza, 1644, be ascribed to him with cer-
tainty.[4] They are of varying length and character, some
being dramatic, some lyrical.

[1] Edition of Milan, 1611, p. 363. Ticknor rightly traces the *entremeses*
of Lope de Vega back to Lope de Rueda, whose short farces were of the
same nature, while into his longer pieces Rueda introduced *pasos* or passages, which might be detached from them and used as *entremeses*. They
were short and lively dialogues in prose without plot "and merely intended to amuse an idle audience for a few moments." *History of Spanish
Literature*, Vol. II, p. 63. Timoneda published an *entremes* in 1565, which
Barrera says is "la mas antigua obra de teatro asi denominada." *Catálogo*, p. 393.

[2] *Entremeses*, etc., *de Quiñones de Benavente*, ed. Rosell, Vol. I, p. xx.
"Entremes apud Hispanos est Comoedia brevis, in quâ Actores ingeniose
nugantur." Caramuel, *Rhythmica, Campaniae*, 1668, quoted by Schack,
Nachträge, p. 26.

[3] *Arte nuevo de hacer Comedias*, Madrid, 1609, fol. 206.

[4] Of the various editions of Part I of Lope's *Comedias* which I possess,

Many collections of *entremeses* were published in the seventeenth century; the earliest and one of the best is that by Luis Quiñones de Benavente, so often mentioned

those of Valladolid, 1604; Amberes, 1607, and Milan, 1619, contain the *loas* only, while that of Valladolid, 1609, contains both the *loas* and *entremeses*, the latter at the end of the volume. The title is: *Primera Parte de Entremeses de las Comedias de Lope de Vega.* As but few copies of this first part contain these *entremeses*, I give a list of them: (1) *Entremes primero de Melisendra.* It is divided into two *jornadas* and is preceded by a "loa muy graciosa"; the *entremes* is in verse and occupies nine pages; it is, in fact, a burlesque comedy. (2) *Entremes segundo del Padre engañado.* (3) *Entremes tercero del Capeador.* (4) *Entremes quarto del Doctor Simple.* (5) *Entremes quinto de Pedro Hernandez y el Corregidor.* (6) *Entremes sexto de los Alimentos.* (7) *Entremes septimo de los Negros de Santo Thome.* (8) *Entremes octauo del Indiano.* (9) *Entremes noveno de la Cuna.* (10) *Entremes decimo de los Ladrones engañados.* (11) *Entremes undecimo de la Dama fingida.* (12) *Entremes duodecimo de la Endemoniada.* All these except the first are in prose. The so-called third part of Lope's *Comedias* —*Tercera Parte de las Comedias de Lope de Vega, y otros Autores, con sus Loas y Entremeses,* etc., Madrid, En casa de Miguel Serrano de Vargas, Año 1613—contains the following *entremeses:* (1) *Entremes famoso del Sacristan Soguijo,* (2) *Entremes famoso de los Romanos* (should be *los Romances*), (3) *Entremes famoso de los Huebos,* and these *loas:* En Alabança de la Espada, De las Calidades de las Mugeres, La Batalla Nabal, De las Letras del a. b. c., Del suntuoso Escurial. These *entremeses* are very witty, especially the second, the subject being a peasant who has been driven mad by reading the *Romancero.* Part VII of Lope's *Comedias,* Barcelona, 1617, also contains three *entremeses: Los Habladores, La Carcel de Sevilla,* and *El Hospital de los Podridos,* which are, however, now generally ascribed to Cervantes. It should be stated that Lope expressly denies the authorship of the *loas* and *entremeses* contained in the volumes which preceded Part IX of his *Comedias.* In the prologue to Part XV, Madrid, 1621, he alludes to them as those "loas y entremeses que el no imaginó en su vida," while the *entremeses* in Part VIII are expressly declared in the volume itself to be the work of Francisco de Avila and of Barrionuevo. The fact, however, that Lope denies his authorship should not be taken too seriously. He also asserted that all the volumes of his *Comedias* preceding Part IX were published without his knowledge, though for some of the volumes, at least, this can be disproved. (See my *Life of Lope de Vega,* p. 253.) Concerning the rare volume, of which I possess a copy, entitled *Fiestas del Santissimo Sacramento,* which also contains *loas* and *entremeses* attributed to Lope, a word may be said here. Menéndez y Pelayo writes: "Es cierto que las loas y los entremeses no son de Lope, á lo menos en su totalidad, pero tampoco el colector los dió por tales, limitandose á decir que *se habian representado en la Corte* con los autos." (*Lope de Vega,* ed. Spanish Academy, Vol II, p. 2.) Of these Sr. Menéndez ascribes without qualification to Benavente: *La Muestra de los Carros, Los Organos,* and *El Remediador;* he states that *La Hechizera*

in these pages.[1] Among these a number were wholly sung, while others were partly sung and partly recited. Among the former, called *Entremeses cantados*, like that of *La Puente Segoviana*, *La Guardainfante*, and others, some are so short that it could have taken but a few minutes to perform them. Others are dramatic in character and contain the liveliest dialogue in the language of the *barrios bajos*.

Generally two *entremeses* accompanied a comedia,[2] though sometimes even three were played, one following

may be by Lope and that the *loa en Morisco* is also probably Lope's, because the Moor who recites it is named Ametillo, who was a slave of Lope's friend Gaspar de Barrionuevo in Seville in 1603. (See also *Life of Lope de Vega*, pp. 112, 113.) It seems that some objection might be made to the ascription of *La Muestra de los Carros* to Benavente. It does not appear in the latter's *Joco Seria*, published in 1645 (the year following the appearance of the *Fiestas del Santissimo Sacramento*), and was not again printed, to my knowledge, until 1658, in the *Teatro poetico*, at Zaragoza. Moreover, its general style and the reference to the actress *la Bezona* seem more in the manner of Lope. *Los Organos*, ascribed above to Benavente, was written by Braones. (See below, p. 295, note 2.) For an excellent account of the *entremeses*, see *Intermèdes espagnols du XVIIᵉ Siècle*, par Leo Rouanet, Paris, 1897. Cervantes excelled all others in this species of composition.

[1] A list of the various collections of *entremeses* will be found in the preliminary pages of Rosell's edition, though I miss the following: *Migaxas del Ingenio, y Apacible Entretenimiento, en varios Entremeses, Bayles, y Loas, escogidas de los mejores Ingenios de Españ* . . . Impresso por Diego Dormer Impressor de la Ciudad, y del Hospital Real, y General de nuestra Señora de Gracia, de la Ciudad de Zaragoça. A Costa de Juan Martinez de Ribera Martel, Mercader de Libros. iv + 96 fols. 16mo. It bears no date, but was probably printed between 1670 and 1675. It contains two *entremeses* by Benavente (*Los Escuderos y el Lacayo* and *El Desengaño*), one by Monteser, and a *loa* by Zaualeta; all the rest are by Lanini. I am indebted to my colleague, Dr. Crawford, for the use of this little book, which is excessively rare. For a description of this collection, see *Modern Language Notes*, 1907, p. 52. Since the above was written this volume has been republished (Madrid, 1909) with excellent notes by Cotarelo y Mori.

[2] In some instances, however, only one *entremes* is specified to be represented with a comedia, as in August, 1603, when Nicolas de los Rios represented at Fuenlabrada an *auto* with two *entremeses* and a comedia with its *entremes*, music, and bayle. (*Nuevos Datos*, p. 81.) In 1604 Gaspar de Porres represented in Esquivias an *auto* with three *entremeses* and a comedia with three other *entremeses*. (*Ibid.*, p. 87. See also *ibid.*, pp. 90, 98.) It will be noticed that these were all representations in small towns.

the *loa,* and the play always concluded with a *bayle* or dance:

Y al fin con un baylecito
yua la gente contenta.[1]

Besides the *entremeses* and *bayles,* short pieces called *jácaras* were also sung between the acts of a comedia. Pellicer describes these *jácaras cantadas* as ballads set to music.[2]

The volume of *loas* and *entremeses* written by Benavente also contains six *jácaras.* Some were sung by a single actress, as the *Jácara de Doña Isabel, la Ladrona, que azotaron y cortaron las orejas en Madrid,* sung by Francisca Paula, which contains two hundred odd verses written in ballad measure; others were sung by several members of the company, not only upon the stage, but, to add zest to them, they were sung from different parts of the theater, for, as Pellicer says, the public "was crazy about them" (era perdido por ellas). In the *jácara* that was sung by the company of Bartolomé Romero (1637–1643(?)), Tomas, the *gracioso,* stood upon the stage, Juliana in the *cazuela* or women's gallery, Maria de Valcazar in the uppermost gallery (en lo alto del teatro), Pedro Real in the *gradas,* Pedro de Valcazar in the *grada segunda,* and Ines in the *desvan.*[3] In another *jácara,* sung by the same company, Maria de Valcazar appeared in the *patio,* or pit, on horseback.[4]

[1] Rojas, *Viage Entretenido,* ed. 1603, p. 126.

[2] "*Jácaras cantadas,* que eran los Romances puestos en musica." (*Histrionismo,* I, p. 164.) Ticknor defines them as "roistering ballads, in the dialect of the rogues, which took their name from the bullies who sang them, and were at one time rivals for favor with the regular *entremeses.*" (Vol. II, p. 533.)

[3] *Entremeses de Benavente,* ed. Rosell, Vol. I, p. 220.

[4] *Ibid.,* p. 286. The *Diccionario de Autoridades* thus defines the *Xacara:* "Composicion Poetica, que se forma en el que llaman Romance, y regularmente se refiere en ella algun sucesso particular, ò extraño. Usase mucho el cantarla entre los que llaman Xaques, de donde pudo tomar el nombre. . . . Xaque en la Germania significa el Rufian."

The requests for *jácaras* generally came from the occupants of the pit or *patio*, and in case the audience did not demand them, a player was sometimes stationed in the *patio*, who called for a *jácara*, as in the one which Francisca Paula sang in the company of Bartolomé Romero (in 1638(?) or 1640(?)), where we read: "Pide en el patio jácara un representante."[1]   In the *jácara* which Antonia Infanta sang in the company of Alonso de Olmedo (in 1636 or 1637), the stage direction is: *Dan voces en el patio pidiendo jácaras, y sale Antonia Infanta, y dice representando:*

> *Antonia:* Entendamonos, señores,
> ¡Cuerpo de diez con sus vidas,
> De catorce con sus almas,
> Y de veinte con su grita!
> ¿Regodeo cada hora?
> ¿Perejil cada comida?
> ¿Sainete cada bocado?
> ¿Novedad cada visita?
> Medraremos en corcova.
> ¿Jacarita cada dia?[2] etc.

The piece concluding with the players singing:

> Jácara nos pedistes,
> Ya os la servimos;
> Y si pidierais ciento,
> Fuera lo mismo.

And in a *jácara*, also sung in the company of Romero, the *gracioso* Tomas begins:

> ¡Que tanta jácara quieres,
> Patio mal contentadizo!
> Ayer ¿ no te la cantamos
> Por todo cuanto distrito
> Tiene este pobre corral?

[1] *Entremeses de Benavente*, ed. Rosell, Vol. I, p. 162.
[2] *Ibid.*, p. 90.

Pues si no quedó resquicio
Por donde no se cantasen,
¿Qué habemos de hacer contigo?
Las novedades no duran
Por los siglos de los siglos.
¿Por donde ó qué han de cantar
Que no esté ya hecho ó dicho?[1]

One can readily imagine the confusion and uproar caused in the theaters by the turbulent mob of *mosqueteros* shouting for *jácaras*. Indeed, it finally became an intolerable nuisance in Seville, and in 1648 the city authorities threatened all such disturbers with fine and imprisonment.[2]

These slight pieces, overflowing with mirth and exuberant spirits, rarely consumed more than ten or fifteen minutes. They find their modern congeners in the *Tonadilla*.

Sainete, a word meaning a delicacy or relish, came into vogue as the appellation of a one-act farce toward the middle of the seventeenth century. The term *sainete*, it is true, is found in Mariana's treatise *Contra los Juegos públicos*, which originally appeared in Latin, in 1609,

---

[1] *Ibid.,* p. 284, and see p. 443, the *jácara* that was sung in Ortegon's company in 1635.

[2] "En la ciudad de Sevilla, a diez y nueve días del mes de noviembre de mil y seiscientos y cuarenta y ocho años, el Sr. D. Antonio de Mendoza, Marques de San Miguel, . . . Teniente de Alcaide destos Alcázares Reales de Sevilla, dijo que por cuanto en el corral de *La Monteria* ha habido y hay mucho ruido, alboroto y quistiones por causa de pedir á los representantes bailes y jácaras y otras cosas fuera de la representacion, mandó se pregone en el dicho corral de *La Monteria* que ninguna persona de cualquier estado y calidad que sea no inquiete ni alborote las comedias que se representan en la dicha *Monteria* pidiendo jácaras ni bailes ni otras palabras, sino que dejen representar á su voluntad lo que quisiere el autor y su compañia; pena que el que contraviniere á ello, si la persona fuese ordinaria, de vergüenza pública y dos años de servicio de *mamora*, y las demás personas dé cien mil maravedís y dos años de un presidio: y asi lo mandó.—*El Marques de San Miguel.*" (Sanchez-Arjona, *Anales del Teatro en Sevilla,* p. 381. See also the excellent work of E. Mérimée, *La Vie et les Oeuvres de Francisco de Quevedo,* Paris, 1885, pp. 386 ff.)

under the title *De Spectaculis*.[1] However, the chapter of the Spanish translation (xii) containing the word is said to be a later addition.[2] It occurs in the *jácara* sung in Olmedo's company in Madrid, in 1636, as the quotation above shows; but here the word is used in its ordinary meaning, not as a theatrical term. The earliest mention of the word in its present sense, that I have found, is in 1639, when Antonia Infante was engaged to play the "primera parte del *saynete*," in the company of Antonio de Rueda.[3] The *sainete* did not differ in any essential particular from the *entremes*. It was slightly longer and commonly contained more characters than the majority of the *entremeses*, but it was of the same general type.[4]

Vera Tassis, in his "Life of Calderon" prefixed to the first volume of the *Comedias*, says that Calderon wrote "cien Saynetes varios," but none has apparently been preserved. Hartzenbusch[5] has published a number of *en-*

---

[1] The word *saynete* occurs in a ballad printed in the *Romancero General*, ed. of 1604, fol. 497, beginning:

"Mancebito de buen rostro

.   .   .   .

No se come ya tan rancio
que aun las de catorze enfadan,
y les piden por saynete [i.e., as a relish]
la Chacona, y Çarauanda."

Doubtless from such association as this the word acquired its later meaning. The above ballad is contained in the "Parte Trezena" of the *Romancero*, which, according to Wolf, *Studien*, p. 349, is merely a reprint of the second part of the *Manojuelo de Romances* of Gabriel Laso de la Vega, Zaragoza, 1603.

[2] See above, p. 264, end of note.   [3] *Nuevos Datos*, p. 304.

[4] Schack says: "Nichts Anderes als solche Entremeses unter verändertem Titel sind denn im Grunde auch die sogenannten *Sainetes*, die seit der Mitte des 17, Jahrhunderts häufig vorkommen. Man pflegt ihren Unterschied von jenen dahin zu bestimmen, dasz sie mit Musik und kleinem Ballet begleitet und von complicierter Handlung seien; allein ohne ausreichenden Grund, denn Gesang und Tanz bildet gewöhnlich auch den Schlusz der Entremeses, und was den dramatischen Plan anlangt, so hält das Sainete es hiermit ebenso nach Belieben wie die ältere Art des Zwischenspiels." (*Geschichte der dramatischen Literatur und Kunst in Spanien*, Bd. II, p. 108. See also Rouanet, *Intermèdes Espagnols du XVIIe Siècle*, p. 39.)

[5] *Comedias de Calderon*, Vol. IV, at the end.

tremeses, two *mogigangas,* and two *jácaras entremesadas*
which have been ascribed to Calderon, but their authorship is doubtful. It is probable that Vera Tassis applied
the term then most current to the *entremeses* which Calderon had written, for toward the close of Calderon's life
the *sainete* became very popular. Among the expenses
for the Corpus festival at Madrid in 1675, we find 150
ducados (= 1650 reals) paid for four *sainetes* written by
Don Manuel de Leon Marchante, who seems to have
been the most successful writer of this species of dramatic
composition at that time.[1] He continued to write *sainetes*
for this festival till the death of Calderon in 1681, when,
for the composition of two *sainetes* and for finishing an
auto which Calderon had left unfinished, he received 1000
reals vellon.[2] It was not till after the middle of the
eighteenth century that the *sainete* reached the height of
its popularity at the hands of Ramon de la Cruz.

The *mogiganga* (masquerade, mummery) "contains a
greater number of episodic personages than the *entremes;*
it is sometimes intermingled with dances."[3] As it be-

---

[1] Pérez Pastor, *Calderon Documentos,* Vol. I, p. 342.

[2] *Ibid.,* p. 372. In 1656 Moreto wrote *loas* and *sainetes* for the Corpus
festival at Seville. During the next decade Alonso Martin de Braones
was a well-known writer of *sainetes* and *mogigangas* in the same city.
He wrote the *entremes* entitled *Los Organos,* which has been ascribed to
Lope de Vega. (Sanchez-Arjona, *Anales,* pp. 411, 439.)

[3] Rouanet, *l. c.,* p. 39. In *Don Quixote* (Part II, chap. xi) a company of
players is met upon the road, one of whom, we are told, "venia vestido
de boxiganga con muchos cascabeles," etc. A *boxiganga,* Rojas tells us,
was a small company of strolling players, who, as Clemencin observes:
"en algunas ocasiones se vestirian ó disfrazarian con vestidos ridículos
para divertir á los expectadores; esto seria *vestir de boxiganga.* De esta
palabra hubo de derivarse la de *mogiganga* [cf. *vimen—bimbre, mimbre*],
que no se encuentra entonces y sí despues en significacion de fiesta en que
concurren varias personas disfrazadas con trages ridículos." Andres del
Castillo entitled the six short novels which he published in 1641 *La
Mogiganga del Gusto* (The Masquerade of Taste). They have been
republished by Sr. Cotarelo (Madrid, 1908). Toward the close of Calderon's career we read of *sainetes* and *mogigangas* as regular accompaniments of the *autos* at Corpus. Thus in 1680 Don Manuel de Leon
Marchante received 1600 reals for the *entremeses* and *mogigangas* at
Corpus in Madrid, and in 1681 Francisco de la Calle was paid 1500 *reals*

longs to the latter half of the seventeenth and especially to the eighteenth century, it falls without the limits of this work.[1]

vellon for a *saynete* and *mogiganga*. (Pérez Pastor, *Calderon Documentos*, Vol. I, pp. 368, 372.)

[1] The earliest use of *mogiganga* in its present sense, that has come to my notice, is in 1659.—"Mande V. m. dar . . . a Pedro de la Rosa, autor de comedias, por si y su compañia 8400 reales . . . los 7700 en que se concertaron los dos autos que se an de hacer, con los entremeses, bayles y mojigangas . . . y los 700 reales para el vestuario de entremeses y mojigangas.—29 Mayo, 1659." Martí y Monsó, *Estudios historico-artisticos*, Zaragoza, 1902(?), p. 567.

CHAPTER XIV

The representation of *autos sacramentales*. Description of the *autos* at Madrid. The *carros*. Abuse of the representation of *autos*. Protests of churchmen. Sums paid for the representation of *autos*. *Autos* in the theaters. Great expense of these festivals.

THE *autos sacramentales*[1] were performed at the instance of the municipalities of the various cities and towns at the festival of Corpus Christi. As Ticknor says, they were in the height of their success in the age of Lope de Vega and in that immediately following, and had become an important part of the religious ceremonies arranged for the solemn sacramental festival to which they were devoted, not only in Madrid, but throughout Spain, the

[1] The meaning of this term has been given above (Chapter I). This is not the place for an esthetic appreciation of the *autos sacramentales*. For this the reader is referred to the works of Schack, Ticknor, Gonzalez Pedroso, and others. Ticknor's criticism (Vol. II, p. 293, note) "that, at all periods, from first to last, the proper *autos* were rude, gross, and indecent" is much too severe and too sweeping. There are doubtless passages in some of these *autos* which seem irreverent to a Protestant, and of one, *La Araucana,* by Lope de Vega, so orthodox a Catholic as Sr. Menéndez y Pelayo has remarked: "Muy robusta debia de ser la fe del pueblo que toleró farsa tan irreverente y brutal," and to enjoy many of these productions they must be viewed "con los ojos de la Fé," to use Lope's own words. *La Puente del Mundo,* cited by Ticknor, is hardly a fair specimen of Lope's *autos.* It is an absurdly extravagant and irreverent production, as Menéndez y Pelayo admits, and is nothing more than a parody *a lo divino* of *La Puente de Mantible,* an episode of the French poem *Fierabras* (Academy's edition of Lope de Vega, Vol. II, p. lxxvi). What finally led to the suppression of the *autos sacramentales* by Charles III., in 1765, was, in all probability, not because of the *autos* themselves, but of the inevitable accompaniments of the *auto:* the procession and the *loas, entremeses,* and *bayles.* These frequently degenerated into a spirit of irreverence and brutality that is shocking. We need only cite as an instance that the very *auto* just mentioned, *La Puente del*

theaters being closed while they were represented.[1] From the earliest times they seem to have been accompanied by dancing, and since the time of Lope by a *loa* and an *entremes*.[2] These *autos* were acted upon movable cars (*carros*) which passed through the city to the various stations where the representation was to take place, and hence this was called *La Fiesta de los Carros*.[3] Preceding these cars, strange figures were paraded in the procession —the *Tarasca*,[4] a sort of serpent surmounted by a figure portraying the "Woman of Babylon," and huge figures representing Moorish or negro giants, called *Gigantones*, etc.[5]

The theatrical managers whose companies were to represent the *autos* were selected by the "comisarios" ap-

---

Mundo, is preceded by a *Loa del Escarraman*, of which Sr. Menéndez y Pelayo says: "Incredible as it may seem, this is a paraphrase *a lo divino* of the famous *jácara* of Quevedo, *Carta de Escarramán á la Mendez*," Escarramán having been a notorious bully of Seville who served ten years in the galleys for his crimes.

Juan de Mariana, in his treatise *Contra los Juegos públicos* (chap. xii), says that the *Zarabanda*, the most indecent of these *bayles*, was danced in the representations of the *autos* at Corpus Christi and also in the nunneries. (See above, p. 71, note 4.)

[1] Vol. II, p. 293.

[2] See above, pp. 67 ff., and Pérez Pastor, *Nuevos Datos*, p. 117.

[3] In 1586 Jerónimo Velazquez represented three *autos* at Corpus, in Madrid, the painter Rui Lopez de Avalos agreeing to paint three triumphal cars, "las verjas donde se ha de poner el S. Sacramento y los carros donde se han de representar los autos de este año." Pérez Pastor, *Bulletin Hispanique*, 1906, p. 366. See also below, p. 310.

[4] Benavente describes it as half serpent and half woman:

"La tarasca,
Que ya sale por el Corpus,
Medio sierpe y medio dama."
(*Entremeses*, etc., Vol. I, p. 138.)

See Covarrubias, *Tesoro*, ad verb.

[5] For a description of this procession, see Schack, Vol. II, pp. 128, 129, and Ticknor, Vol. II, pp. 293–295. In the succeeding chapter will be found the accounts of eye-witnesses. Ticknor describes the procession as a "sort of rude mumming, which certainly had nothing grave about it," in which we quite agree, and we shall see that it finally degenerated into such license that it called forth the earnest protests of churchmen.

pointed by the city for that purpose, who generally included the "regidores" and "corregidor" of the city,[1] and
who, it seems, had to be approved by the ordinary.[2]

The earliest *autos sacramentales* performed in Madrid,
of which we have any detailed description (so far as I
am aware), were those represented in 1574 by the company of Jerónimo Velazquez. At this time and for some
years thereafter, three *autos* were represented each year
at Madrid. In 1587 there were three *autores de comedias*: Nicolas de los Rios, Miguel Ramirez, and Juan de
Alcozer, each of whom represented an *auto* at the Corpus
festival in Madrid.[3] In 1592 four *autos* were represented, two (*Job* and *Santa Catalina*) by the company of
Gaspar de Porres, and two (titles not given) by Rodrigo
de Saavedra.[4]

There is recorded an obligation dated March 3, 1574,
by Jerónimo Velazquez, to represent at the festival of
the Holy Sacrament of that year at Madrid three *autos*:
La Pesca de San Pedro, La Vendimia celestial, and *El
Rey Baltasar quando en sus Convites profanó los Vasos
del Templo*, and to provide all the personages and
costumes and all other things necessary for the said
representations, "and he shall take part in the said representations himself and shall provide the other necessary
persons; the city to furnish him with three cars (*carros*),
constructed with all the necessary devices and artifices,
without the said Jerónimo Velazquez providing anything
concerning the preparation and machinery of the said
cars, he only to furnish the persons and costumes, and
to provide people to move the said cars from place to
place. The city is to pay him 130 ducats, besides 20 reals
for the persons who move each car, i.e., 60 reals in all.
. . . He is to represent only on the day of Corpus along

[1] Pérez Pastor, *Nuevos Datos*, pp. 210, 216.
[2] *Ibid.*, p. 117.   [3] *Ibid.*, p. 18.   [4] *Ibid.*, p. 29.

the route of the procession and afterward where the "comisarios" may order."[1]

The *autor de comedias* thus appointed to represent the *autos* was obliged to give a trial performance before the "comisarios," generally twenty days before the festival, and the "comisarios" always reserved the right of insisting upon the appearance of such players as they thought especially desirable and obliging the *autor* to hire players for this purpose. Thus in 1585, when Gaspar de Porres was to represent the three *autos* in Madrid, the "comisarios" agreed to furnish him with the three cars provided with *invenciones,* etc., in such manner as the said Porres may require, but "he is to provide the personages and figures which are to represent in the said *autos* with new costumes, and if necessary to provide another *simple* [a character which afterward developed into the *gracioso*] besides the one whom he has in his company, and he must give a trial performance of the said *autos* twenty days before the said festival, for all of which he is to receive 400 ducats. . . . And besides this he is to receive a license from the Council to represent two days in each week (not counting feast-days) from Easter (*Pascua de Resurreccion*) till Corpus Christi, and no other *autor de comedias,* Spaniard or foreigner, shall be permitted to represent in Madrid during the said time."[2] Moreover, the "comisarios" were to be furnished with a list of the players in the company, and they could compel any player whom they desired to be brought from wherever he might be, to take part in the *autos,* and this was to be done at the expense of the manager of the company.[3] Frequently a player

[1] Pérez Pastor, *Nuevos Datos,* pp. 333, 334.   [2] *Ibid.,* pp. 335, 336.

[3] "En la villa de Madrid á quince dias del mes de Marzo de mil y seiscientos y veinte y nueve años, los señores Licenciado Melchor de Molina, del Consejo y Cámara de su Magestad, D. Francisco de Brizuela y Cárdenas, Corregidor de la dicha villa, Francisco Enriquez de Villacorte y Don Francisco de Sardeneta y Mendoza, regidores de la dicha villa y comisarios para las fiestas del Santisimo Sacramento de este año.— Acordaron que los autos que se han de hacer para el dicho dia se den á

bound himself not to leave Madrid, but to "remain in his house as a prison, so that he may take part in the Corpus festival."[1]

A minute description of the *autos* entitled *Job* and *Santa Catalina,* represented by the company of Gaspar de Porres at Madrid in 1592, is given by Pérez Pastor. The costumes to be worn are described in great detail: Job is to wear a long coat of purple damask and a hat of taffeta, and buskins; God the Father appears in a tunic of sateen or taffeta of gold and purple, with a cloak of white taffeta, etc.; and in the *auto* of *Santa Catalina* there are to be three gallants dressed in the Roman fashion, with coats of mail, etc. It is agreed that the rehearsal is to be given twenty days before Corpus, and each *auto* is to have an *entremes;* the city to furnish the cars, prepared and painted at its own cost, with all the inventions necessary for the representation, and the wheels greased with lard or tallow, so that the cars can be moved from place to place. Porres received 600 ducats for the representation, and each player was furnished with a candle.[2]

Bartolomé Romero y Roque de Figueroa, autores de comedias, á cada uno los dos, obligandose y dando fianzas de que haran los dichos autos en la forma acostumbrada y con que para la Pascua de Resurreccion, antes ó despues, quando se les mandare, hayan de dar quenta de sus compañias, y si para hacer las dichas fiestas les faltare ó paresciere á los dichos señores son necesarios algunos personajes, hombres ó mugeres, hayan de recibir los que se les ordenare, trayendolos á su costa de qualesquier partes donde estuvieren, dandoles despachos para ello, y lo señalaron." (*Ibid.,* p. 216.) Three years before this, at the Corpus festival of 1626, Andrés de la Vega, an *autor de comedias,* was required to provide another *gracioso* in the place of the one then in his company, and Cristóbal de Avendaño, the other *autor* representing the festival, had to substitute another actress. (*Ibid.,* p. 210.)

[1] In 1621 Bartolomé de Robles and Micaela Lopez, his wife, were engaged to act in the *autos* of Corpus of that year in Madrid, and bound themselves not to leave the city "dejando el primero su casa por carcel, para trabajar ambos durante las fiestas del Corpus en la corte." (*Ibid.,* p. 189.)

[2] The importance of this document may justify its insertion here in full: "2 Marzo 1592. Obligacion de Gaspar de Porres para hacer dos autos. En la villa de Madrid á dos dias del mes de Marzo de mil y quinientos y

Of these *autos sacramentales* four were represented annually at Madrid, beginning with this year (1592), as nearly as we can determine; prior to this, as we have seen, the number varied. Two *autores de comedias* were chosen by the "comisarios," each company representing two *autos*, which took place at Corpus Christi on the evenings of Thursday and Friday, and for which each *autor* (dur-

noventa y dos años por ante mi el escribano publico e testigos de yuso escritos parecieron presentes Gaspar de Porres, autor de comedias, estante en esta corte como principal deudor y obligado, y Gerónimo Velazquez desta villa de Madrid como su fiador y principal pagador, y ambos a dos juntamente y de mancomun. . . . Otorgaron que se obligaban y obligaron que el dicho Gaspar de Porres hará para la fiesta del Santisimo Sacramento deste presente año de noventa y dos, dos autos, el uno de *Job* en que entren su figura con un gaban de damasco morado y un sombrero de tafetan y sus borceguíes, quatro hijos con quatro baqueros de damasco y brocatel con sus mantos de colores con sus tocados y borceguíes y un criado con una tunicela de damasco con su tocado, y los demas sirvientes que son tres pastores con sus pellicos de damasco de colores, caperuças de lo mismo y çaragüelles y camisas de caniquí blancas; tres amigos con tres tunicelas de damasco y sus mantos de tafetan y tocados y borceguíes, y quatro virtudes con quatro tunicelas de tafetan con cotas y faldones y sus tocados y calçadillas; su muger de Job con un mongil a lo judaico de raso leonado con sus tocas, el demonio principal con una tunicela de tafetan negro, cota, faldin y calçadilla, y los otros tres demonios con tres ropas largas muy bien pintadas de bocas, y una figura de Dios Padre con una tunicela de raso o tafetan que tenga oro y morado y una capa de tafetan blanco, y una figura de un angel como se suele vestir: y otro auto de *Santa Catalina*, en que haya tres galanes vestidos a lo romano con cotas y faldones y tocados con monteras de terciopelo y raso con sus mantos y calçadillas y borceguíes: la figura de Catalina con un vestido a lo romano corto de tela y tocado a lo romano; la criada tambien a lo romano de damasco o de raso; dós senadores con dos tunicelas de damasco y encima dos ropas de terciopelo de colores con sus tocados a lo romano o gorras; otras dos con dos baqueros y mantos y tocados y borceguíes; y una figura de Santo Domingo y su compañero con sus habitos acostumbrados de estameña; una figura de Christo con un sayo baquero bordado con unas cifras que declaren la figura, y el tocado ni mas ni menos, y un angel en habito de paxe de la misma manera que saliere el christo salvo que no ha de llevar bordado el baquero.—Una figura del niño Jesús con su tunicela de tafetan o raso que tenga oro con las insignias de la pasion, y la misma figura de Christo ha de salir otra vez de resurreccion de la forma que se pinta, y una figura de la madre de Dios como se pinta la imagen del rosario vestida de damasco: los quales dichos autos vestidos los dichos personajes como está dicho ha de ser á contento y satisfaccion del Señor Licenciado Alonso Nuñez de Bohorques del Consejo de su magestad y comisario de las cosas de esta villa y de los señores corregidor y comisarios por ella nombrados y ha de dar las muestras

ing the first half of the seventeenth century, at least) received 600 ducats.[1]

It appears that at first (in Madrid, at all events) the *autos* were represented in the morning, and that a change was made by the Council in 1586, which commanded that the performances at the festival of Corpus Christi be held in the afternoon. On April 17, 1587, the President of the Council was, however, petitioned to continue the order of the preceding year, "as experience had shown how much more advantageous this was, and with how much greater solemnity the procession and the divine offices were conducted, which took place on that day." On May 25, 1587, however, it was resolved that the representation

veinte dias antes de la dicha fiesta o el dia que el dicho señor comisario les ordenare y en cada auto ha de hacer un entremes á contento de los dichos señores y ha de representar el dicho dia del sacramento en la parte y lugar que los señores del Consejo les ordenaren y mandaren ora sea por la mañana ora por la tarde, y de alli ha de ir á las demas partes y lugares donde el dicho señor comisario le ordenare por sus autos sin salir del ambitu de la procesion y el viernes siguiente ha de representar a esta villa en la plaza de San Salvador y de alli adonde le mandare el dicho señor comisario, y le ha de dar esta villa los carros aderezados y pintados á costa della con las invenciones que fueren necesarias para las dichas representaciones y untados con sebo o manteca para que puedan andar dicho dia por las partes que han de andar y de alli los ha de hacer sacar el dicho Gaspar de Porres y traerlos por las partes y lugares que se le ordenare y mandare y volvellos á la dicha obreria el viernes en la noche y entregallos á Pedro de la Puente obrero della, y demas desto le ha de dar la dicha villa seiscientos ducados en dineros pagados los dos partes luego y la otra tercia parte la mitad al dia que diere la muestra y la otra mitad acabada la dicha fiesta, ye le han de dar una vela para cada uno de los representantes que hicieren las dichas representaciones, y demas desto han de representar en esta corte el dicho Gaspar de Porres y Rodrigo de Saavedra que tiene los otros dos carros, desde el lunes de Casimodo hasta el dicho dia del Sacramento sin que otro ningun autor pueda representar, y se ha de procurar licencia del Consejo para que representen desde el segundo dia de Pascua de Resurreccion hasta el domingo de Casimodo, y se obligaron de hacer y que harán la dicha fiesta de la manera que dicha es sin que haya falta alguna y si alguna hubiere que á su costa se pueda hacer y haga y se busquen vestidos y personas que hagan las dichas figuras, y por lo que costare se les pueda executar y execute por solo el juramento de qualquiera de los dichos señores comisarios de la dicha villa (*siguen las seguridades*)." (Pérez Pastor, *Nuevos Datos*, pp. 29–31.)

[1] See above, p. 200.

on Friday should take place before the Ayuntamiento of the city in the morning, beginning at seven o'clock.[1] In 1600, when the *autos* of Madrid were presented by the companies of Melchor de Villalba and Gabriel de la Torre, the performance on Thursday took place in the afternoon, first before the Council, and afterward "wherever they may be ordered to perform."[2] Beginning on the afternoon of Corpus Christi, the *autos* continued through the whole of the following day (Friday). In 1609, when Alonso de Heredia represented the *autos* in Madrid, he was required to perform them until two o'clock in the morning. With each *auto* an *entremes* was to be given,[3] and in 1618, when the *autos* were presented by Baltasar Pinedo and Hernan Sanchez de Vargas, it was agreed that "each one of the *autores* was to produce two *autos* and to have them composed at his own cost and approved by the ordinary, furnishing also with each *auto* an *entremes*, and presenting them with new costumes." They were to give a rehearsal ten days before Corpus, and on that day they

---

[1] Pérez Pastor, *Nuevos Datos,* p. 19.

[2] *Ibid.,* p. 52. It appears that at the Corpus festival in Seville in 1582 no less than seven *autos* were represented: *El Testamento del Señor* by the company of Alonso de Capilla; *El Convite que hizo el Rey Salomon á la Reina Saba* by Juan Bautista; *El Triunfo de la Verdad* by Diego Pineda; *Santa Felicitas y otros Mártires* by Marcos de Cardenal; *La Muerte de Orias y Casamiento de David con Bethsabée* by Tomas Gutierrez; *Cuando Nuestra Señora salió de Egipto para Galilea* by the company of Juan Gonzalez; and Cosme de Oviedo represented *El Estado del Hombre desde su Juventud hasta que triunfa la Muerte.* (Sanchez-Arjona, *Anales,* p. 68.) In 1585 five autos were represented: two by Pedro de Saldaña, two by Alonso de Cisneros, and one by Tomas Gutierrez. (*Ibid.,* p. 74.) In general, however, four *autos* were represented here also each year. In 1591 there appeared in the representation at Corpus, in addition to the *autos,* a "carro de apariencias," brought out by Juan Bautista de Aguilar, on which Juan Agustin de Torres and Antonio Veloco "performed sleight-of-hand tricks with living birds, in the manner of the Italians," "y con una armada de galeras y otras piezas de fuego muy curiosas, con su musica y romances y letras á lo divino con un entremes gracioso." (*Ibid.,* p. 82.) For four *autos* represented by Diego de Santander in 1596, he received 1200 ducats. (*Ibid.,* p. 94.)

[3] *Ibid.,* p. 112.

were to represent from noon until ten o'clock at night, and on Friday from ten in the morning till midnight, in such places as should be assigned to them. In this case, besides providing the cars (*carros*) and paying to the *autores* 600 ducats each, the city agreed to furnish a wax candle of half a pound to each actor and two wax candles of one pound each to the *autor* and *autora*.[1] In 1621 it was stipulated that Pedro de Valdes, who presented two of the *autos*, "is to represent on Corpus day from two in the afternoon till midnight, and on Friday from six o'clock in the morning until midnight, and if he represent on Saturday, he is to receive the customary gratuity." Besides, his company and that of Cristóbal de Avendaño (who presented the other two *autos*) were to have the exclusive right of performing in the theaters of Madrid from the date of granting the license until Corpus Christi.[2]

As already stated, the Corpus Christi celebration always began with a procession through the streets of the city, and the stopping-places where the *autos* were to be represented were designated by the civic authorities, who provided the *carros*. In Seville, in 1609, the *autos* were first to be represented "before the Most Holy Sacrament, and afterward, during the whole of that day until the bell for evening prayers rings, going through the streets along which the procession passes, and if any car should break down, the actors and all the paraphernalia for the representation are to wait on the spot for two hours until the car be repaired," and the places for representation are designated "in case a car cannot proceed because one in front of it be broken down."[3] Besides the

---

[1] Pérez Pastor, *Nuevos Datos*, p. 166.   [2] *Ibid.*, p. 188.

[3] "Si en algun carro se quebrase alguna rueda viniendo detrás otro carro que haya menester pasar adelante, si se quebrase en la calle de Génova, le hayan de sacar á la plaza de San Francisco; y si en la calle de la Sierpe, á la entrada de lo ancho de la cárcel ó á la dicha plaza de San Francisco; y si fuere á los Sileros, le saquen á la plazuela que está

representations which were to be given on the day of Corpus, another was to be given in the Plaza de San Francisco on the following Monday, and it was expressly provided that no player was to pass from one car to another, but that each car be furnished with all necessary actors. Each *auto* had to be accompanied by a new *entremes*, and a rehearsal had to be given thirty days before Corpus.

In addition to the 600 ducats received by each *autor* (sometimes this sum was 350 ducats for each *auto*, as in Seville in 1609) for his two *autos*, a prize of 100 ducats was generally awarded by the city to the *autor de comedias* whose company gave the best representations with the finest costumes, and sometimes various sums were awarded to individual players.

It was greatly to the advantage of the manager of a company to be selected to represent the *autos* in Madrid, for besides the large sum received therefor, he and the other manager so selected were also granted the sole and exclusive privilege of representing comedias in the Madrid theaters from the day on which he received the license (generally Easter) until Corpus Christi.[1] When the court was in Madrid it was generally necessary to give additional representations of the *autos* on the following Saturday, for which a gratuity was always received by the manager of the company.[2] It was an invariable condition that the *autos* represented in Madrid and Seville should be new and should never have been seen before.[3] The remuneration received by poets for writing *autos* doubtless varied, as did their honorarium for comedias, but, being a shorter composition, the amount paid was

---

frente de la botica; y si en la calle de Carpinteros, á la plazuela de San Salvador, para que se aderecen y prosigan la representacion." (Sanchez-Arjona, *Anales*, p. 137.)

[1] Peréz Pastor, *Nuevos Datos*, pp. 49, 52, 123, 132, 162, 188 *et passim*.

[2] *Ibid.*, pp. 112, 123, 129 *et passim*.

[3] Sanchez-Arjona, *Anales*, pp. 125, 136, 215.

much less than for a comedia. In 1611 Lope de Vega,
then at the height of his popularity, received 1200 reals
for four *autos* represented at the Corpus festival of that
year in Seville.[1] In 1618 Bartolomé de Enciso received
200 reals for an *auto* entitled *La Montañesa,* while Jusepa

[1] Three years before, in 1608, Lope had also written the four *autos* which
were represented at Madrid in that year: *El Adulterio de la Esposa* and
El Caballero del Fenix, performed by the company of Juan de Morales
Medrano, and *Los Casamientos de Joseph* and *La Niñez de Cristo,* by the
company of Alonso Riquelme. The scenic appliances of the *carros* are
thus described:

"Para el auto del *Adulterio de la Esposa:*

—En el medio carro en lo alto ha de haber una nube ó globo que se abra
en quartos á modo de azucena que sea bastante para que quepan tres personas dentro: ha de estar pintado de azul y estrellas, en este medio carro
ha de haber pintados algunos pesos y llamas de fuego porque es el carro
de la Justicia divina.

—En el otro medio carro ha de haber en lo alto un trono á modo de
capilla ó yglesia, porque aqui se ha de representar la Iglesia; ha de haber
un dragon de siete cabezas, si pudiere ser, echando fuego por las bocas,
y si no pudiere ser vivo, sea pintado: este capilla ha de ser bastante para
que én ella esté una muger sobre este dragon.

—En este medio carro ha de haber dos bofetones que salgan con dos
hombres hasta la mitad de los carros y los vuelvan arriba.

—Ha de haber unas plomadas para subir una muger arriba. Dirá el
modo de esta invencion Jaraba, cobrador de la comedia.

"Para el auto del *Caballero del Fenix:*

—En el medio carro sean quatro bastidores sobre la casa, que se abran
en la frente del carro: esté una mesa con asiento y sea todo lo alto un
guerto con una peña sobre que pueda estar un Angel.

—El otro medio carro sea un Globo pintado de mar y tierra por defuera
y por dentro de tinieblas, con un sol y luna eclisados y sangrientos, una
cruz grande en medio sobre un calvario, bastante á que esté echada en él
una figura.

"Para el auto de *Los Casamientos de Joseph:*

—El medio carro sea un Palacio con un corredor y un altar con unos
ydolos: sea el Palacio el mas rico que sea posible, y si puede estar en
medio de quatro corredores la capilla del altar que dije, será mejor.

—El otro medio carro tenga un cielo sobre la casa con una subida por
donde pueda descender dél y volver á él una figura. Si hubiere pintura
por defuera sea el Carro de Pharaon y Joseph en él vestido de Rey.
Haya una mesa con invencion para que los platos que estén en ella se
desaparezcan á la vista.

"Para el auto de *La Niñez de* Xpo:

—En el medio carro sea un templo con asientos y una silla en medio:
hanle de cubrir quatro bastidores que se caygan á su tiempo.

—El otro medio carro ha de ser un jardin y una palma en medio dél con

Vaca and her daughter Mariana de Morales were paid a gratuity of 300 reals "por lo bien que en el trabajaron,"[1] and in the same year Salustio del Poyo received 200 reals for *Las Fuerzas de Sanson*.[2]

No expense seems to have been spared in the preparation of the *autos*, which were presented with a splendor of decoration and costume that must have greatly pleased the *populacho*, especially as these representations, being on the streets and in the public squares, were free to all.

For the representation of *El Naufragio de Jonás profeta*, at Plasencia in 1578, a large stage was built in the square of the city, and upon it a tank was constructed sixty

todos los pasos de la Pasion por razimos ó en cada razimo de dátiles el suyo: tenga el tronco como escalera por que se pueda subir, y sea muy alta: esté una cabaña paxiza á un lado y una fuente. Pongase cuydado en este porque es notable. Si hubiere pintura por de fuera, sea toda de niños angelitos, ocupados en diversos juegos de muchachos.

"Pintura de los carros para la fiesta del Santisimo Sacramento deste año de 1608.

"*Condiciones de la pintura de los carros:*

—Hanse de pintar los carros á contento del señor Corregidor y comisarios, etc.

—Hanse de pintar ocho medios carros conforme los autos lo requieren dellos de arquitectura bien ordenada y compuesta y colorida de colores finos y á cada arquitectura de carro conforme la historia del auto lo requiere.

—Hanse de pintar todas las apariencias dentro y fuera de los carros y todo lo que se hubiere de hacer demás de lo dicho conforme las memorias que tienen dadas Riquelme y Morales, autores.

—Han de ir las puertas de los carros pintadas conforme los carros lo requieren, cada una diferente de la otra, con sus peinazos y cruzeros contrahechas al natural, y las ventanas han de ir contrahechas á ventanas naturales, unas. diferentes de otras.

—Han de ir los rodapies de los carros pintados cada uno conforme al carro que ha de ir puesto y que sea conforme á lo de arriba.

—Hanse de dorar todos los remates de los carros y pintar los balustres y verjuelas de azul fino, y dorar los botoncillos dellas.

—Han de ir enlosados de pintura y enladrillados con sus colores los suelos de los carros donde se han de representar altos y baxos, y los dos medios carros que se añaden se ha de hacer lo mismo.

—Hase de dar de azul la reja donde se pone la Custodia en la Plaza de Santa Maria y dorar las manzanas della," etc. (Pérez Pastor, *Nuevos Datos*, pp. 106–109.)

[1] Sanchez-Arjona, *El Teatro en Sevilla*, Madrid, 1887, p. 303.
[2] *Ibid.*, p. 293.

feet long and twenty feet wide, which was filled with water, upon which a ship floated, with its sails and tackle, large enough to hold a number of sailors and passengers.[1]

At an early period, however, the *autos*, besides being performed in the public squares, were also represented at the theaters. On June 22, 1601, we find that Gaspar de Porres presented *autos* in one of the theaters of Madrid, and on the next two following days we read: "Autos á los semaneros en el teatro."[2] Besides, *autos* were frequently represented privately before the King, as in June, 1609, when Domingo Balbin and Alonso de Heredia presented the *autos* of that year before Philip the Third in the Escurial.[3]

The cars were beautifully painted and were frequently of great magnificence; in 1611 the amount paid for painting them was 1350 reals.[4]

The number of cars for the *autos* seems to have varied: to represent four *autos*, eight *medios carros* were required, as we have seen above, in the case of the *autos* of 1608. In 1619 we read of "eight *medios carros* on which the representation is to be given, to be handsomely painted, and . . . likewise the four *medios carrillos* which are put in between for the representations,"[5] and

---

[1] "En las fiestas del dia de Corpus Christi de aquel año se hizo en medio de la plaza un gran tablado, que parecia hecho para muchos dias, y en lo alto un mar de sesenta pies de longitud y veinte de latitud, con abundancia de agua que con mucho artificio habian hecho subir alli. En el mar estaba una muy lucida nave, con sus velas y jarcias, de tanta grandeza que estaban dentro muchos marineros y pasajeros vestidos de librea. Aqui se representó el *Naufragio de Jonás profeta*, y se vió la nao ir por el agua, con la qual hubo gran conmocion y tormenta con artificio de pólvora que debajo del tablado se encendió." (Sanchez-Arjona, p. 97.)

[2] *Bulletin Hispanique* (1907), p. 365.

[3] *Bulletin Hispanique* (1907), p. 375.

[4] *Nuevos Datos*, p. 125.

[5] "Se obliga á pintar los ocho medios carros, en que se hace la representacion, de pinturas finas . . . y tambien en los quatro medios carrillos que se meten en medio para las representaciones." (*Ibid.*, p. 182.) The term *medio carro* (middle car) is explained by a document dated Madrid, May 15, 1593: "Obligacion de Nicolas Granelo, criado de S. M., pintor resi-

in 1620 a *medio carro* was built "with its two bridges, upon which the stage is to be placed, and the stage is to have the same form as it has in the others [i.e., cars] with its balustrades and railings."[1]

That a stage was built at the various points along the streets where the *auto* was to be represented, and that the *carros* were grouped around this stage, is evident from many descriptions of the *autos*. Still, the word here used for stage (*tablado*) seems sometimes to have the meaning of scaffold or stand for spectators.[2] It is probable that representations also took place upon one of the *carros*, so, at all events, we should infer from the fact that in 1593 eight cars were ordered to be painted for the festival of Corpus, beside "the one in the middle which serves for the representations."[3] Moreover, above (p. 308) we read of the "floors of the cars on which they are to act." Perhaps it was the custom to set up the stage on the bridges of one of the cars, as was done in 1620, as we have just seen. When Rios represented a comedia and

dente en Madrid, de hacer la pintura de los 8 carros que esta Villa hace para la fiesta del Santisimo y la del 'que sirve en medio para las representaciones,' en precio de 230 ducados" (*ibid.*, p. 35), and another record dated Madrid, April 5, 1595: "Fianza de Pedro de la Puente, obrero de la villa de Madrid, en favor de Fabricio Castello, pintor de su Magestad, que hará la pintura de los ocho carros que esta villa hace para la fiesta del Santisimo Sacramento deste presente año de noventa y cinco, asi los cuerpos principales como el que sirve en medio para las representaciones." (*Ibid.*, p. 343.) For the *auto* entitled *El Meson del Alma*, represented at Seville in 1607 by the company of Riquelme, the following description of the *medio carro* was furnished by the city authorities: "Para el auto *El Meson del Alma* se dispuso que en un medio carro ha de haber una casa grande, donde va toda la compañia deste auto, con sus torres, chapiteles y remates, en la qual han de ir pintados atributos de la Gracia y Virtudes y lo demas que dijere el poeta. Item esta casa ha de tener quatro lienzos en quadrado con la largura y anchura que le convenga." (Sanchez-Arjona, *Anales*, p. 128.)

[1] *Ibid.*, p. 186. 3 Junio 1620.—Condiciones de un medio carro que se ha de hacer para las fiestas del Santisimo Sacramento del año 1620, "con sus dos puentes en que ha de ir el tablado encima y el tablado ha de ser de la misma forma que está en los otros con sus balustres y antepechos."

[2] See *Nuevos Datos*, pp. 13, 14, 17.

[3] *Nuevos Datos*, p. 35, and *ibid.*, p. 40: Abril 1595. "Fianza para los 8 carros triunfales y el de las representaciones en las fiestas del Corpus."

an *auto* in the village of Fuenlabrada in August, 1603, it
was especially stipulated that "el tablado se ha de pagar y
aderezar por cuenta de la Cofradia."[1] Here *tablado*
could only have meant the acting stage. At the close of
the first scene of Josef de Valdivielso's *El Peregrino,* an
auto published in 1622, is the direction *"Cierrase el
tablado, y queda dentro la Tierra."*[2]

Calderon's *autos* show clearly that there were fixed
stages or *tablados,* the cars being arranged around them,
the actors facing the select company before which the
auto is presented, while the great mass of the populace
see only their backs. In Calderon's *El sacro Parnaso*
(1659) the stage is referred to as "el tablado de la representacion," and in the same author's *Quien hallará Mujer
fuerte* (1672), in the "Memoria de las Apariencias," we
read: "El segundo carro ha de tener tambien bajada para
el tablado, por donde pueda subir una muger."[3]

The properties on these cars were of pasteboard
(*pasta*) and were made "as the poets requested" (*conforme lo pidieren los poetas*).[4] The costumes worn by
the players were of the richest and costliest stuffs. In
1624, when Antonio de Prado represented two of the
autos at Madrid, it was especially stipulated that "he
shall provide the costumes for the said *autos* and *entremeses,* and they are to be of brocatel and velvet and
damask and sateen, trimmed with gold passementerie,
all new and to the satisfaction of the *comisarios.*"[5]

Like the comedia, the *autos sacramentales* were invariably accompanied by *bayles* and *entremeses.* Cervantes

---

[1] *Nuevos Datos,* p. 81.
[2] Gonzalez Pedroso, in *Bibl. de Autores Esp.,* Vol. 58, p. 203.
[3] *Ibid.,* p. 403. See also Calderon's *La Nave del Mercader:* "baja la
Culpa al tablado." *Ibid.,* p. 441, and *La Viña del Señor. Ibid.,* pp. 464,
475. For an account of the *autos* and their representation, see Schack,
Geschichte, etc., Vol. II, p. 129, and Julio Monreal, *Cuadros viejos,* pp.
203 ff., and especially p. 230.
[4] Pérez Pastor, *Nuevos Datos,* p. 182.
[5] *Ibid.,* p. 205, and see above, p. 107.

gives a description of a traveling company which was representing the *auto* entitled *Las Cortes de la Muerte* in various small towns during the octave of Corpus Christi (we copy from the excellent translation of John Ormsby)[1]:

Don Quixote was about to reply to Sancho Panza, but he was prevented by a cart crossing the road full of the most diverse and strange personages and figures that could be imagined. He who led the mules and acted as carter was a hideous demon; the cart was open to the sky, with a tilt or cane roof, and the first figure that presented itself to Don Quixote's eyes was that of Death itself with a human face; next to it was an angel with large painted wings, and at one side an emperor, with a crown, to all appearance of gold, on his head. At the feet of Death was the god called Cupid, without his bandage, but with his bow, quiver, and arrows; there was also a knight in full armour, except that he had no morion or helmet, but only a hat decked with plumes of divers colours; and along with these there were others with a variety of costumes and faces. All this, unexpectedly encountered, took Don Quixote somewhat aback, and struck terror into the heart of Sancho; but the next instant Don Quixote was glad of it, believing that some new perilous adventure was presenting itself to him, and under this impression, and with a spirit prepared to face any danger, he planted himself in front of the cart, and, in a loud and menacing tone, exclaimed, "Carter or coachman, or devil, or whatever thou art, tell me at once who thou art, whither thou art going, and who these folk are thou carriest in thy waggon, which looks more like Charon's boat than an ordinary cart." To which the devil, stopping the cart, answered quietly, "Señor, we are players of Angulo el Malo's company [a theatrical manager and dramatist who flourished about 1580]; we have been acting the *auto* of 'The Cortes of Death' this morning, which is the octave of Corpus Christi, in a village behind that hill, and we have to act it this afternoon in that village which you can see from this; and as it is so near, and to save the trouble of undressing and dressing again, we go in the costumes in which we perform. That lad there appears as Death, that other as an angel, that woman, the manager's

[1] *Don Quixote,* Part II, chap. xi.

wife, plays the queen, this one the soldier, that the emperor, and I the devil; and I am one of the principal characters of the *auto,* for in this company I take the leading parts. If you want to know anything more about us, ask me, and I will answer with the utmost exactitude, for, as I am a devil, I am up to everything." Belonging to this company also was "a merry-andrew, in a mummer's dress with a great number of bells, and armed with three blown ox-bladders at the end of a stick."

The above-mentioned *Cortes de la Muerte* was probably the *auto* which, begun by Miguel de Carvajal and finished by Luis Hurtado de Toledo, was published in 1557, and represented in Seville in 1570 and again in 1571.[1]

As in the performance of comedias, there was also, even on such solemn occasions as the representation of *autos sacramentales* at Corpus Christi, much noise and disorder among the motley crowds that thronged the streets and the public squares to see them. Nor was this disorder confined to the mob (*populacho*). Under date of June 16, 1615, we read the following: "In this Council [Madrid] attention being drawn to the disorder which is wont to be created on the stage (*tablado*) erected for the purpose of enabling the wives of the *regidores* to view the *autos* at the festival of the Holy Sacrament, the *corregidor* commands that the said stage or stand be apportioned in the same manner as the windows in the plaza are assigned for the bull-fights, according to seniority (*por su antiguedad*), beginning from the middle of the stage and giving to the four most ancient gentlemen five feet of stage, and in this manner to continue the apportionment on both sides, . . . making the division by means of wooden frames," etc.[2]

How these processions degenerated into mere mummery through the license and abuse of the participants,

---

[1] Sanchez-Arjona, *Anales,* p. 44. It has been republished by Don Justo de Sancha in Vol. XXXV of the *Biblioteca de Autores Españoles.*
[2] *Nuevos Datos,* p. 158.

and how the religious significance and solemnity of the representations was greatly impaired and almost destroyed by the boisterous and unruly conduct of the crowd, is shown by an edict of the Bishop of Badajoz in 1605. To this decree the city of Badajoz objected, and petitioned the King that the comedias and dances on the day of Corpus should be allowed, as heretofore, "upon a stage erected for that purpose, on which is revealed the Most Holy Sacrament, and that the Corregidor, Bishop, Dean, and Chapter of the said church take part."

Among other things, the edict of the Bishop[1] prohibited the clothing of the image of Our Lady in borrowed bridal garments; "(1) that no ruffed collars or other adornments in fashion among women be put on such images, under penalty of excommunication and a fine of 20 ducats. (2) That no one dress himself as a saint or take part as such in any procession or on a car unless he be acting in some devotional *auto* in which a saint takes part, and then he must have a license to do so; nor shall he stand at an altar or in any other place, unless in some devotional *auto* that is being acted, for besides the great indecency of such an action, we have seen and know that for the said representations beautiful girls are sought, who, as they are generally poor and are seen

---

[1] The Bishop's edict contains the following prohibitions:

(1) "Que se vistan las imágenes de Nuestra Señora con prestados que llevan puestos para los casamientos las desposadas, que no se le pongan lechuguillos ni otros adornos de moda entre las mugeres, so pena de excomunion mayor, 20 ducados para la guerra contra infieles y pérdida de los tales vestidos."

(2) Que ninguno se vista de santo y asista vestido de tal, "en procesion alguna ni en carro si no fuere habiendo de representar algun auto de deuocion en que intervenga algun santo, y esto con licencia de nuestro provisor dada en escrito, mas que de ninguna manera no puedan estar en altares ni en otros puestos no habiendo auto en que se hable y represente algo de devocion, porque fuera de la grande indecencia que esto tiene, avemos visto y sabido que se andan buscando muchachas hermosas y de buenos pareceres para las dichas representaciones, las quales, como ordinariamente son pobres, y son vistas de todo el pueblo, somos informado de ·las ofensas á Dios y pecados que resultan dello."

by all the people, we are informed that offenses to God and sins result therefrom. (3) That no cars in these processions be drawn by oxen, mules, or horses, on account of the shouts of the drivers and the disorder resulting from the confusion of the cars with the saints who are carried on litters, and the disputes which arise, as in the past year, when swords were drawn and blows were exchanged, producing great scandal; wherefore the said cars may be brought out and the representations made to the people either before or after the procession. (4) That no profane comedia be performed at the festival of Corpus Christi, but only devout *autos,* without profane *entremeses,* nor any other thing that may divert the people from the devotion and adoration of the Holy Sacrament or from the reverence which is due to the presence of so great a Lord [the Host], or which may incite the people to laughter, shouts, or any other unseemly actions which are repugnant to representations of this kind."

Down to the year 1635 these Corpus processions in Seville had always taken place in the morning, but in this year they were changed to the afternoon, and the *autos* were represented on the cars in the morning, after high mass.[1]

We have, in a previous chapter, referred to the objec-

---

(3) "Que no se saquen para esta procesion carros con bueyes, mulas o caballos, por los gritos que dan los carreteros y por el desorden que hay en ello por estar á veces confundidos los carros con los santos que van en andas y promoverse questiones como la del año anterior en que se sacaron las espadas y andaron á cuchilladas, promoviendo un fuerte escandalo; por lo qual podrian salir dichos carros y hacer las representaciones al pueblo antes o despues de la procesion."

(4) "Que en las fiestas del Corpus Christi no se haga comedia ninguna profana sino algunos autos devotos sin mezcla de entremeses profanos ni de cosa que no sea para mejor enderezar el pueblo á devocion y adorar al Santisimo Sacramento, é conforme á la reuerencia que se debe en presencia de tan gran Señor e no para mover el pueblo á risa y hacer otras descomposiciones, gritos, ruidos y alborotos indebidos con semejantes representaciones." Todo esto so pena de excomunion mayor, 20 ducados para la cera del Santisimo. (*Ibid.,* pp. 103, 104.)

[1] Sanchez-Arjona, *Anales,* p. 253.

tions and protests of the historian Padre Juan de Mariana
to the manner in which the *autos sacramentales* were
represented, and to these the testimony of many other
writers might be added. In 1600 Fray José de Jesus
Mariana, a barefoot Carmelite of Madrid,[1] objects not
only, as we have seen,[2] to "vile and infamous men," as he
calls them, representing the *autos sacramentales,* but protests earnestly against the introduction of worldly and irreverent *entremeses* into such sacred representations. He
says that these actors, "accustomed to their evil manner of
living, frequently do and say things before the Holy Sacrament which are wholly foreign to the name of Christian
and worthy of severe punishment. And even if it were
tolerable that persons so infamous should represent such
lofty mysteries, what have holy festivals to do with *entremeses* treating of robberies and adulteries, which are
ordinarily mingled with the *autos sacramentales?* If this
is justly intolerable in profane comedias, how can it be
endured in those which treat of sacred subjects? It is
this admixture, in Spain, of the sacred and profane, which
offends all foreigners and all good and pious natives."

Despite these protests, of which we might cite many
more from the work of Sr. Cotarelo, *autos sacramentales*
continued to be represented in the public squares and
theaters of the principal cities until 1765. On June 10
of that year a royal decree was issued declaring that the
theaters were not proper places and the comedians were
unfit and unworthy persons to represent the sacred mysteries of which the *autos sacramentales* treat, and that
the King has therefore determined to prohibit absolutely
all representations of *autos sacramentales* and to renew
the prohibition of *comedias de santos.*[3] Thus there
passed from the popular stage a kind of religious drama

---

[1] In his *Primera Parte de las Excelencias de la Virtud de la Castidad,*
Alcalá, 1601, chap. xvii; see Cotarelo y Mori, *Controversias,* p. 377.
[2] Above, p. 262.   [3] *Controversias,* p. 657.

that was peculiar to Spain and which, in the hands of
some of its dramatists, notably Calderon, had reached
the highest point of beauty and perfection.

We have already[1] alluded to the fact that *autos sacramentales* were not only represented in the public squares,
but also in the theaters of Madrid as early as 1601.
Under what conditions these *autos* in the theaters took
place, we do not know. That an admission fee was
paid, however, in this event, is certain. It appears
that originally the *autos* were represented on only two
days: Corpus Christi day and the next day (Friday).
In 1574 Jerónimo Velazquez stipulated to represent three
autos "only on Corpus day and afterward wherever he
may be commanded."[2] But all the representations were
confined to these two days. So in 1594 the representations were to be on Corpus and the day following,[3] and
in 1599, when Gaspar de Porres presented the *autos,*
they were to be performed only on Corpus day and on the
following day, and it was expressly agreed that the *carros*
were to be returned on Saturday.[4] In 1600, when Melchor de Villalba and Gabriel de la Torre represented the
autos at Madrid, they received for two *autos* each 650
ducats, to be represented on Thursday and Friday,[5]
and in 1609, when the *autos* in Madrid were in charge
of Alonso de Heredia and Domingo Balbin, each was
to represent two *autos* on Thursday and Friday for
600 ducats, and if the court should be in Madrid on
Saturday they were to receive a gratuity for the representations on that day.[6] This latter stipulation occurs
constantly in the succeeding years down to 1638.[7] In
1612 Juan de Morales Medrano and Tomas Fernandez
de Cabredo represented the *autos,* and "because they had

[1] P. 250.
[2] *Nuevos Datos,* p. 334.
[3] *Ibid.,* p. 38.   [4] *Ibid.,* p. 49.   [5] *Ibid.,* p. 52.
[6] *Ibid.,* p. 112. See also above, p. 200.
[7] *Nuevos Datos,* pp. 132, 134, 156, 160, 161, 166, 188, 206, 224.

given more representations than they were obliged to give (Morales five and Cabredo seven) on Saturday, besides those on Thursday and Friday," the former received 700 and the latter 800 reals extra.[1]

In 1639 the *autos* were represented in Madrid in the following order: On Thursday afternoon (Corpus day) all four *autos* were to be given in the presence of the King before the royal palace at such an hour as the King should fix; then the four *autos* were to be performed before the Princess of Carignan, wife of Prince Thomas, in front of the monastery of the Incarnation. On Friday before the "casas del Ayuntamiento" in the Plazuela de San Salvador, then two *autos* before the Council of Aragon and two before the Council of Italy. On Saturday before the "Consejos de Inquisicion y Cruzada," and in the afternoon to the Villa de Madrid, before the "casas del Ayuntamiento," etc., and on Sunday, in the afternoon, before the Archbishop of Granada, etc.[2]

In 1649 there is specific information of the representation of *autos* in the public theaters. In that year "Diego Osorio began to represent the *auto sacramental* which fell to the lot of his company in the *Corral del Príncipe*, on Wednesday, June 23, and he gave twelve representations in the theater until July 4. The said Osorio ceased to perform in the said *Corral del Príncipe*, and Antonio de Prado entered it and began on Saturday, July 10, giving fifteen representations of the *auto sacramental* which he was to give, until July 25, for on July 24 there was no representation. Osorio did not [again] represent until July 16, when he began in the *Corral de la Cruz*, where he gave thirteen representations until July 30. On August 5 Prado began to represent the *auto La Vacante* in the *Príncipe*, where he gave nine representations of the said *auto* until August 13, and then rested

[1] *Nuevos Datos*, p. 130.
[2] Pérez Pastor, *Calderon Documentos*, Vol. I, p. 119.

until the 24th, when he began in the said *corral* the *auto*
La Magdalena, of which he alone gave in this *corral*
fifteen representations until September 8, so that there
were twenty-four representations of the said two *autos* in
the said *corral*. Between September 14 and September
29 Prado gave ten representations. From October 3 to
October 16 he alone represented and then ceased. On
August 6 Osorio began in *La Cruz* and gave two representations to August 10. On September 20 he again
represented in the *Corral del Príncipe* and gave seven
representations. From October 16 to November 1 Osorio
gave twelve representations."[1]

Whether the *autos* were afterward conducted on the
scale of magnificence which they attained in 1649, or
whether they were represented for as long a period as
they were given in the theaters in this year, we have no
means of determining. The Dutch traveler Francis van
Aerssen, who visited Spain in 1655, tells us that when

---

[1] Pérez Pastor, *Calderon Documentos*, Vol. I, pp. 166, 167. It is interesting to add a list of the expenses incurred for the *autos* at Madrid in
this year, 1649, showing the enormous costs which these entertainments,
fostered by the idle and show-loving Philip IV, brought upon his exhausted
country.

Fiesta del Santísimo Sacramento. Año 1649.

Gastos:

A los autores por las representaciones	710,600 mrs.
Al que compone los autos	112,200 "
Al cerero	644,470 "
A Juan de Caramanchel para hacer los carros	319,600 "
A Gaspar Flores y compañia por las danzas	421,600 "
A Adrian Lopez por el lienzo de los toldos	366,656 "
Por traer la Tarasca	27,200 "
Hermanos de la Dotrina	112,200 "
La musica	76,296 "
Por llevar los carros y aderezos para ellos	14,012 "
Al mayordomo de propios para gastos menudos	17,760 "
Al obrero para unos palos	21,760 "
Al dicho para coser los toldos y hacerlos	105,944 "
A Juan Blanco por el tablado de la plaza	127,500 "
Tablado de Palacio	51,000 "
Carried forward	3,128,798 mrs.

the *autos* were represented the theaters were closed for a month. The money derived from the entrance fees to the theaters during these representations may have helped to defray the expenses of these festivals; it was undoubtedly a source of profit for the *autores* who represented the *autos,* for the sum of 950 ducats, which they received, could only have compensated them for the free representations on the first three days of the Corpus festival.

These festivals were a very considerable financial help to Calderon. Acknowledged as the foremost religious poet of Spain, his services were in great demand on these occasions, and he received a much larger honorarium for his *autos sacramentales* than any other poet had yet obtained. In 1639 he wrote for the Corpus celebration of that year two *autos: Santa Maria Egipciaca* and *El mejor Huesped de España,* and in 1640 *Los Misterios de la Misa* and *El Juicio final.* In 1645 he wrote the four *autos* for the festival, re-

Brought forward	3,128,798 mrs.
A Francisco de Mena, por la escalera que se hace en casa del Marques de Cañete	22,200 "
Por poner los toldos	95,200 "
De colgar el tablado	34,000 "
Atajos	11,050 "
A los escuderos de a pie	11,220 "
Traer los Gigantes	37,944 "
Puntas y valonas para los Gigantes	14,416 "
Atajo primero de Santa Maria	6,800 "
Ministriles	5,580 "
Alguaciles	13,056 "
Limpiar la custodia	17,000 "
A los porteros que se ocupan	9,520 "
Al alguacil mayor	6,800 "
Al cura de Santa Maria	3,400 "
Tablados para representar a el pueblo	6,732 "
Propina a los señores del Consejo y a la Villa	710,100 "
Total	4,133,816 mrs.

From this it will be seen that Calderon, who wrote the four *autos* for the festival of this year, received 112,200 maravedís = 300 ducats, and the *autores de comedias* each 950 ducats.

ceiving 3300 reals *vellon* (copper), which sum was also paid him in the years 1648 to 1653, while in 1654 to 1656 he received 4000 reals.[1] During this time and, I believe, thereafter until his death, he alone was honored with the privilege of writing the *autos* for the Madrid festival. But besides the 3300 reals *vellon* which Calderon received from the city for the *autos,* a document of 1652 shows that each of the two *autores de comedias* who represented them was obliged to pay him 700 reals, i.e., he then received 4700 reals.[2] In 1654–56 he was paid 4000 reals *vellon,*[3] while from 1657 to 1665 he received 4400 reals, i.e., 3000 from the city and 1400 from the *autores.* In the latter year the sum paid him was 5800 reals, and this sum he continued to receive until 1680, the year before his death, when 5500 reals were paid him for two *autos.*[4] It appears that as early as 1658,[5] and perhaps in the previous year, only two *autos sacramentales* were represented each year at Madrid, and this was the rule thereafter until the death of Calderon. Four *autos* were also represented annually in Seville down to the year 1648, when only two were given, and the same number thereafter.[6] Calderon continued to write the *autos* for the Madrid festival until 1681, the year of his death, when he left an *auto* unfinished, which was completed by Don Manuel de Leon Marchante.[7]

---

[1] Pérez Pastor, *Calderon Documentos*, Vol. I, pp. 120, 122, 127, 163, 168, 187, 196, 206, 224, 240.

[2] *Ibid.*, pp. 196, 333, 337.   [3] *Ibid.*, pp. 224, 238, 240.

[4] *Ibid.*, pp. 249, 315, 336 *et passim.*   [5] *Ibid.*, p. 257.

[6] Sanchez-Arjona, *Anales*, p. 449.

[7] See above, p. 295.

CHAPTER XV

Contemporary accounts of the representation of comedias and *autos*. Francis van Aerssen. The Comtesse d'Aulnoy. The behavior of audiences. Scenes in the theaters. Spanish players abroad. Conclusion.

THE accounts of persons who were eye-witnesses of the representation of a comedia at a time when some of the great dramatists were still living and when several of the greatest among them had not long since passed away, always possess an exceeding interest. When these accounts are due to the pen of a foreigner, some allowance must necessarily be made, not only for national prejudice, which is apt to warp his judgment somewhat, but also for a nore or less imperfect knowledge of the language. Nevertheless, they furnish us with a living picture of the scene as it passed before the eyes of the spectator, and herein they possess the definite value of contemporary documents. With their aid it requires no very great flight of the imagination to picture ourselves in one of the *corrales* of Madrid, in the very place and atmosphere in which these immortal productions of the great masters of the Spanish drama were enacted, and to view them once more, through the long vista of nearly three hundred years. The very realistic description of the interior of the *Corral de la Olivera* in Valencia, given in the comedia *La Baltasara,* has already been alluded to in a previous chapter. The other accounts which we possess belong, with two exceptions, to the middle of the seventeenth century or somewhat later. It may not be without interest, however, to give the earliest of these contemporary notices, slight as it is. The simple narrative is taken from a MS. formerly in the possession of Don Pascual de Gayangos—a name ever to be recorded with gratitude in the annals of Spanish literature. This manuscript, written by a Morisco of the time of Philip the Third, contains all sorts of moral observations mingled with other matters and descriptions of passing events, among them an account of a representation of Mira de Mescua's comedia *La Rueda de la Fortuna,* which our author had witnessed. We do not know when Mescua's play was written, but Lope de Vega, in a letter to a friend, mentions that it was acted in Toledo by the company of Juan de Morales before August, 1604.[1]

The Morisco's account is as follows:

I passed through the door of a house which I saw many people entering—men as well as women. Having gone in, I saw a large *patio,* where, upon chairs and benches, men and women were sitting; in a gallery sat the women of the common people, and there were, besides, a number of balconies occupied by the distinguished persons with their wives. In the *patio* a stage was erected, upon which all eyes were fixed, and when the house was full, I saw two ladies (*damas*) and two gallants (*galanes*) come out upon the stage with their *vihuelas,* who sang these *decimas*:

> "Quien se bió en prosperidad
> Y se be en misero estado
> Considere ques prestado
> El bien y la adbersidad," etc.

Having finished singing, they retired, and an actor entered, clad in a garment of damask, and recited the *loa.* After he had finished and had withdrawn, other players entered to represent "The Wheel

---

[1] See the writer's *Life of Lope de Vega,* pp. 153, 154. As now printed the *loa* shows that the comedia was also acted by the company of Riquelme. (*Dramaticos contemporaneos de Lope de Vega,* Tomo II, *Bibl. de Aut. Esp.*)

of Fortune," which sets forth the various conditions of the world, and how they are subject to change, etc.

A detailed description of the comedia follows.[1]

AMONG the narratives of travelers in Spain who have left any account of theatrical representations, one of the most interesting is that of a Dutchman, Francis van Aerssen, who visited Spain in 1654–55, though his account[2] was not published till eleven years afterward. In 1670 an English translation of this work appeared in London, entitled *A Journey into Spain*, though it is nowhere indicated that this little book is a translation.[3] I shall quote from this English version:

On one side of the Town [Madrid] is the *Prado,* a large Walk made use of for the *Tour;* near it is a great Fabrick, but low, called *Buen Retiro.* The Duke of *Olivares,* during his administration, spent many Millions on a Structure that is not very considerable: I saw but part of it, where a Comedy was preparing with Scenes, that would amount to a great expence; a *Florentine* was the Undertaker. For ordinary Comedies here are two Theaters, where they act every day. The Players have to themselves not above three half pence for every person, the Hospital as much, and as much the Town-house; [the French original says: and for a seat on the benches one pays besides about two sous, which are for the city, to which the theaters belong]; to set down costs seven pence, the whole amounting to fifteen pence. I can say little to the Lines or Plots, not being skilful enough in the language to understand

---

[1] Schack, *Nachträge,* p. 57.

[2] *Voyage d'Espagne, Contenant entre plusieurs particularitez de ce Royaume, trois Discours Politiques, etc., avec une Relation de l'Estat & Gouvernement de cette Monarchie; & une Relation particulière de Madrid.* A Cologne, chez Pierre Marteau, 1666. The real author of this work, according to R. Foulché-Delbosc, was Antoine de Brunel. (See *Revue Hispanique,* Vol. III, p. 65.)

[3] *A Journey into Spain.* (Here follows a quotation from Seneca, *de Vita beata.*) London. Printed for Henry Herringman, and are to be sold at the Sign of the *Blew Anchor* in the Lower Walk of the *New Exchange,* 1670. 6 + 247 pp.

Poetry, nor the figurative fashion of speaking that belongs to it: but know they play their parts ill, few or none having either the meen or genius of true Actors. [They do not play by the light of torches, but] They present by day-light, so that their Scenes appear not with advantage. Their Clothes are neither rich, nor appropriated to their Subject; and the Spanish habit serves where the Scene is *Greece* or *Rome*. The Playes I have seen have but three Acts, called *Jornadas*. They usually begin by a Prologue in Musick, but sing so ill, that their harmony resembles little Childrens whinings. Between the Acts there is some little Farce, Dance, or Intrigue, the most diverting of the whole Piece. The People are so taken with them it is hard to get a place, the best being bespoken, and the excessive idleness of this Country is made evident in that in Paris it self, though there are not Playes every day, there is no such crowding to them.[1]

The Dutch traveler's description of the Corpus Christi procession and the *autos* is as follows:

As the publick sports, the Moors introduced in Spain, whilst they possessed it, continue after their exile; the Church also retains something of their superstition, especially on *Corpus Christi* day. The Twenty seventh of *May* we saw all its Ceremonies, which are many, and last long; they begin by a procession, whose first ranks are intermixed with several Hoboies, Tabors, and Castanettas; a great many habited in party coloured clothes, skip and dance as extravagantly as at a Morrice. The King goes to *St Maries* Church not far from his Palace, and after Mass, returns with a Torch in his hand, following a silver Tabernacle, in which is the Holy Wafer, attended by the Grandes of *Spain,* and his several Councils. This day to avoid dispute, they observe not order, so that the Counsellors *de la Hazienda,* joyn with those of the *Indies;* before these Counsellors and certain other persons, move Machines, representing Giants; these are Statues of Pasboard carried by men concealed under them: they are of several shapes, some very hideous; all of them represent Femals, except the first, which is only the Figure of a great head painted, within which is concealed a little man that gives it meen and motion: it being a *Colossus* over the body of a Pigmie. Amongst these chimerical Monsters, there is one which represents two Giantesses, Moors, or Aethiopians, such having really been if we may beleeve the vulgar, who call them *Hijos de Vecinos,* that is, neighbors children. The people are so taken with these Gothick figures, that there is scarce any Village without them. They report the Giantesses to have lived in the time of King *Mammelin,* and on that account sometimes call them *Mammelins,* after the name of that Gothick or Moorish King who once Reigned in *Spain.* I was told of another terrible Pageant (*machine épouvantable qui roule ce jour là*) which they call *Tarasca,* from a wood that was formerly in *Province,* where at present stands the City of *Tarascon* on the banks of *Rosne,* over against *Beaucaire.* They fancy that in this place was once a Serpent (no less enemy of Mankind, then that which seduced our first Ancestors in Paradise) called *Behemoth,* and report that *St Martha* by oraisons triumphed over it, leading it prisoner in her apron strings. Be this History or Fable, the *Tarasca* is a Serpent of enormous greatness in form of a Woman, moving on wheels, the body covered with scales, a vast belly, long tail, short feet, sharp talons, fiery eyes, gaping mouth, out of which extend three tongues, and long tusks. This Bulbegger stalks up and down and they which are under the pastboard and paper, of which it is composed, by certain Springs, cause it to move so dexterously, that it puts off the Hat to the Sots that stare at it, and sometimes lays hold on Countrey fellows, whose fright moves laughter amongst the people. Such as please themselves in telling wonders of this foppery, relate that a certain Town having sent to some of its neighbors six of these paper Giants, two Pigmies and the *Tarasca* to be made use of on *Corpus Christi* day, they which give them their motion being entered, to divert themselves in the passage, caused them to dance as at processions by couples: they were met by certain Muliters or Carriers, who (Moonshine discovering at a distance, these imaginary Monsters,) marching with a great deal of prattle and loud laughter, (for their merrier passing two or three Leagues) not recollecting what was to be done the day after, were so affrighted, that the terror still augmenting, by their contemplating those fantasmes, they at last run away with all their might. The conductors of the Monsters perceiving this, casting off their Vizards, went out of the

Machines to disabuse them, running after them to cause them to come back to their Mules and charges; this increased their astonishment, and hastened their pace, which aided by the wings of fear, soon transported them cross the fields to a village, which they allarmed to free the Countrey of highway men, so hideous, they could be little less then Devils: the other in the mean time slipping their cases, and perceiving themselves masters of the spoils, the muletiers had abandoned, began to visit the baggage, and finding Wine, drank so much they fell fast asleep till morning. The Muletiers after their raising the Village, and bringing the Justice to the place, perceived their mistake, and the Countrey fellows laughing heartily at them, drank the remainder of the Wine in recompence of their trouble. The Village of the solemnity, a great while waited for those grim Puppets, which came too late, and by their excuse and relation of what had happened, disordered the whole procession, changing it into a Ring of such as abandoned the Cross and Banner, to hearken to their story. The pleasantest posture of these Mammelinas that I saw was, when they made their salutes before the Queens Balcony, besides some feats of activity by address of those that danced them. The King passing by it, salutes the Queen with a smile, and the Queen and Infanta rise a little before he comes at them, to return his compliment. The Procession having filed to the Piazza, returns by the High street or Calle Mayor, adorned by many Tapestries waving on the Balconies, filled with men and women of all conditions: the crowd is so great one cannot pass without difficulty, and we had much ado to return to *St Maries* Church where the procession ended. As soon as free from it we went to the Palace, and there saw the King, Queen, and Infanta, return with all the Court Ladies. I think I have mentioned all that is worth notice, unless it be that as on this day all the men put on Summer cloaths, so do all the Ladies, and those new and very rich, of several fashions and colours. In the afternoon about five a clock, *Autos* are represented: these are ghostly Comedies (*Comedies spirituelles*), with interludes, very ridiculous to give rellish to what is serious and tedious in the pieces themselves.

The two companies of Players that belong to Madrid at this time, shut their theatres, and for a month represent these Holy Poems: this they do every evening in publick on Scaffolds erected to that purpose in the streets before the houses of the Presidents of several Councils. They begin at Court the day of the Solemnity, when a seat under a State is provided for their Majesties: the Stage is at the foot of these Scaffolds, and [because the players act with their backs turned toward the crowd, which is in the square] little painted Booths are rowled to it, environ it [the stage] and serve as tiring houses [where they dress, from which they enter upon the stage and to which they retire at the end of each scene]. This is continued certain days, every President having one [day] and a Stage and Scaffold erected before his house. Before these *Autos* begin, all the foppery of the Procession dances, and the Gigantine Machines make the people sport; but what I most admired in that which I saw at a distance in the old *Prado,* is, that in the streets and open air they use Torches to those pieces, which in the daily Theaters, and within doors, they represent without other light then that of the Sun: all these antick ceremonies appeared much more ridiculous to those that beheld them, then they can possibly do in my describing them, and confirm me in what I often observed, that the Spaniards, and other wise and grave nations seem fondest in their diversions, as Misers at their feasts sometimes become most prodigal.[1]

In a little work entitled *Relation de l'Estat & Gouvernement d'Espagne,* printed at Cologne in 1666, and generally bound in the above-mentioned *Voyage d'Espagne,* the author, François Bertaut,[2] who accompanied the Maréchal de Gramont to Spain in 1659, gives a description of the Madrid theaters, which I here copy:

Concerning the Comedia, there are troupes of players in nearly all the towns, and they are better, in comparison, than our own, but there are none in the pay of the King. They represent in a court-yard, where a number of private houses join together, so that the windows of the rooms, which they call *rexas,* because the most of them are provided with iron gratings, do not belong to them [the players] but to the owners of the houses. They repre-

[1] *A Journey into Spain,* pp. 83–88; *Voyage d'Espagne,* pp. 118–124.
[2] See the excellent Bibliography of works of Travel in Spain by R. Foulché-Delbosc, in the *Revue Hispanique,* Vol. III, pp. 65, 69.

sent by day and without torches, and their theaters (except in the *Buen Retiro,* where there are three or four distinct salons) have not such fine decorations as ours, but they have an amphitheater and a parterre. There are two places or *Salles* in Madrid, which they call *Corrales,* and which are always filled with merchants and artisans, who leave their shops and repair thither with cloak, sword, and poniard, and who all call themselves *Cavalleros,* even down to the cobblers, and it is these who decide whether the comedia is good or not. And because they now hiss and now applaud the play and are drawn up on both sides in ranks, and as this is a sort of salvo, they are called *Mosqueteros.* It is on these that the fortune of the author depends. . . . Some of the spectators have seats close to the stage, which places they preserve from father to son like an entailed estate (*mayorazgo*), which cannot be sold or pledged, so great a passion have they for the theater. The women all sit together in a gallery at one end [of the theater], which the men are not allowed to enter.[1]

The *Memoirs de Madame de Motteville* (Françoise Bertaut) contain a letter written to her from Madrid, on October 21, 1659, by her brother, François Bertaut, who, as already noted, accompanied the Maréchal de Gramont on his mission to Spain in reference to the Peace of the Pyrenees and the marriage of Louis the Fourteenth to the Infanta Maria Teresa, daughter of Philip the Fourth of Spain. In this letter Bertaut gives a brief account of a play which he saw performed before the royal family at the Buen Retiro:

The best thing of all and the most interesting, I reserve for the last; it was the comedia which was acted at the palace by the light of six large torches of white wax, contained in huge silver candlesticks. On the two sides of the room were two alcoves, closed by a curtain. In one of them were the Infantas and other persons of the palace, while in the other one opposite was the Maréchal. Along the two sides were only two long benches covered with Persian carpets. The ladies, to the number of ten or twelve, took

---

[1] *Relation de l'Estat & Gouvernement d'Espagne,* pp. 59, 60.

seats upon these carpets on both sides, their backs leaning against the bench. Behind them, on the side where the Infanta sat, but further on, toward where the players were, and almost behind them, some gentlemen were standing, and a grandee was on the side where the Maréchal sat. The rest of us Frenchmen stood behind the benches against which the ladies were leaning. The King, Queen, and Infanta entered after one of the ladies who bore a torch. As the King entered he took off his hat to all these ladies and then took a seat in front of a screen, the Queen on his left and the Infanta on the left of the Queen. During the whole comedy, save a single word which he spoke to the Queen, the King moved neither foot, hand, nor head, only casting his eyes about once in a while, nobody being near him except a dwarf. When the comedy was over, all the ladies arose and left their places one by one, assembling in the middle of the room like canons leaving their seats after a service, and joining hands they made their reverences, which lasted for some minutes; then they went out one after another, while the King was still uncovered. Finally he arose and made a moderate bow (*une réverence raisonnable*) to the Queen, the latter bowed to the Infanta, and taking one another by the hand, as it seemed to me, they went out.[1]

In 1679 the Comtesse d'Aulnoy journeyed through Spain, and in her second letter, dated at San Sebastian. writes:

After I had rested somewhat from the fatigue of the journey, it was proposed that we go to the comedia. . . . When I entered the theater there was a cry of *mira! mira!* i.e., look! look! The decorations of the theater were not brilliant. The stage was raised, resting upon barrels, over which were boards, ill arranged. The windows were all open, for they do not use torches, and you can im-

---

[1] *Memoirs,* etc., Maestricht, 1782, Vol. V, pp. 360, 361. The Infanta was Doña María Teresa, the bride of Louis XIV., and the comedia, from the fact that the *galan* was an Archbishop of Toledo, was probably, according to Pellicer (Vol. I, p. 192), *La Conquista de Oran,* which he ascribes to Lope de Vega. Doubtless this is the comedia by Luis Vélez de Guevara, *La Conquista de Oran, ó El Gran Cardenal de España Fray Francisco Jimenez de Cisneros,* published in *Comedias Escogidas,* Part XXXV, Madrid, 1671. When the Prince of Wales, afterward Charles I., "undertook his romantic wooing journey" to Spain with Buckingham, the contemporary account of the royal entry into Madrid, on March 23, 1623, informs us that: "in the streets of the passage divers representations were

agine how much this detracts from the spectacle. They represented
the "Life of St. Anthony," and when the players said anything
which pleased the audience, everybody cried out *victor! victor!* I
learned that this was the custom in this country. I noticed that the
devil was not dressed differently from the other actors, save that
his hose were flame-colored and that he wore a pair of horns, to
distinguish him from the rest. The comedia was in three acts, as
they all are. At the end of each serious act they played a farce
with some pleasantries, in which the *gracioso* or clown appeared,
who, amid a great number of dull jests, occasionally uttered some
that were not so bad. These interludes were mingled with dances
to the music of harps and guitars. The actresses had castanets and
wore little hats. This is the custom when they dance, and when
they dance the *Zarabanda,* it seemed that they did not touch the
ground, so lightly did they glide. Their manner is quite different
from ours; they move their arms too much, and often pass their
hands over their hats and faces with a very pleasing grace, and they
play the castanets admirably.

Moreover, one must not think that these players—because San
Sebastian is a small place—are very different from those of Madrid.
I have been told that the King's players are somewhat better, for,
after all, they, too, play what they call *Comedias famosas,* that is,
the best and most famous comedies, and in truth the greater part
of them are quite ridiculous. For example, when St. Anthony said
the *confiteor,* which was quite frequent, everybody kneeled, and
each one gave himself such a violent *mea culpa* that one thought
they would crush their breasts.[1]

In her tenth letter, written from Madrid on May 29,
1679, Madame d'Aulnoy gives the following description
of the opera of *Alcina,*[2] which she witnessed:

made of the best comedians, dancers and men of musicke, to give con-
tentment to the Royal paire [Charles and Philip IV.] as they passed it."
The scene is presented in a rare German print in the Grenville library,
which shows the players on a rude platform or stage raised about five
feet from the ground, with a curtain at the back and on the sides. (See
W. B. Rye, *England as seen by Foreigners in the Days of Elizabeth and
James I.,* etc., London, 1865, p. cx. Also Nichols, *The Progress of James
I.,* Vol. IV, pp. 824 and 877.)

[1] *Relation du Voyage d'Espagne,* à La Haye, chez Henry van Bulderen,
Tome Premier, 1693, p. 55.

[2] Founded on an episode in the *Orlando Furioso.*

I never saw such wretched machinery. The gods descended on horseback upon a beam which extended from one end of the stage to the other; the sun was lighted up by means of a dozen lanterns of oiled paper in each of which was a lamp. When Alcina practised her enchantments and evoked the demons, the latter arose leisurely out of hell upon ladders. The *gracioso* or clown made countless rude jests. The musicians have rather good voices, but sing too much from the throat. Formerly all sorts of persons were permitted to enter [the Buen Retiro, where the opera of *Alcina* was presented before the King], although the King was present, but this custom is changed now and only great lords, or at least titled persons or knights of the three military orders, are admitted. The building is certainly very beautiful and handsomely painted and gilded; the boxes are furnished with blinds (*grillées de jalousies*) like those we have at the Opera, but they reach from top to bottom, so that they seem to form a kind of room. The side on which the King sits is magnificent. Moreover, the finest comedy in the world, I mean of those which they play in the city [i.e., in the public theaters], is often approved or hissed, according to the caprice of some wretch.

At this time, as already related,[1] the fate of a new comedia on the Madrid boards generally depended upon the whim of a shoemaker.

The writer continues:

There is a certain place in the theater, a kind of amphitheater, called the *cazuela*. Hither flock all the women of a mediocre virtue, and all the great lords also repair to it to speak with them. Sometimes so much noise is made there that the thunder cannot be heard. They say so many witty things that one almost dies of laughter, for their vivacity is not restrained by good breeding.[2]

Madame d'Aulnoy gives a brief account of an *auto* which she saw represented in Madrid in June, 1679. After describing summarily the procession which always precedes

---

[1] See above, pp. 121, 122.
[2] *Relation du Voyage d'Espagne*, La Haye, 1693, Tome III, p. 21.

the *auto,* she says that the King went to the church of
Santa Maria, near the palace, to meet the procession.

On that day all the ladies put on their summer clothes and appear in all their finery on the balconies, with baskets of flowers and
bottles of scented water, which they throw down when the procession passes. . . . When the Holy Sacrament, which had been
carried in the procession, is returned to the church, the people repair
to their houses to dine and then to attend the *auto.* . . . These are
tragedies upon sacred subjects, the execution of which is very
bizarre. They are represented in the yard or in the street of the
President of each Council, to whom this is due. The King comes
there, and all the persons of quality receive tickets on the previous
evening. We were also invited, and I was surprised that they
should have lighted an extraordinary number of torches while the
sun was shining brightly on the comedians, and made the candles
melt like butter. They played the most absurd piece that I have
ever seen. Here is the plot of it: The Knights of St. James are
assembled, and our Lord comes to beg them to receive him into
their order. There are several who are quite willing, but the elders
represent to the others the wrong which they would commit by
admitting among their number a person of lowly birth, for St.
Joseph, his father, was a poor carpenter and the Holy Virgin had
worked as a seamstress. Our Lord awaits the decision with much
anxiety, and is at length refused, but the Order of Christ is
finally instituted for him, and all are satisfied. This is a Portuguese
order. . . . These *autos* last a month.[1]

Of the character of Spanish audiences and of their behavior, we have already spoken. Alonso Lopez Pinciano
gives an amusing account of the scenes enacted among the
spectators in the *Corral de la Cruz* about 1595 or perhaps earlier. With his friends Ugo and Fadrique, the
Pincian had gone to see a tragedy of Euripides at the
above theater. While waiting for the performance to
begin, Fadrique says: "This is by no means a poor pastime,
—for here we can enjoy many and various things, observ-

[1] *Ibid.,* p. 55.

ing these people gathered together. One throws a handkerchief from above into the *patio*, and a seller of fruits or confections picks it up, unties the knot in the corner, takes out the coin and, wrapping in it the fruit demanded, tosses it up and perchance it alights in the mouth of some one for whom it was not intended, who involuntarily bites into it—handkerchief and all. Then, to watch the wrangling over the *bancos:* this banco is mine; this seat was reserved by my servant, etc., and the arguments pro and contra. To watch some fellow cross the whole theater to reach his seat, and see how they shout at him and twit him. Or to see blows exchanged in the women's gallery in a quarrel over a seat or in a fit of jealousy,"[1] etc.

A very animated description of the scenes in a Spanish theater at about the middle of the seventeenth century is given by the dramatist Juan de Zabaleta, in his *Dia de Fiesta por la Tarde,* Madrid, 1692, p. 236 (the first edition is of Zaragoza, 1666). He says:

He must dine hurriedly at noon, who intends to go to the comedia in the afternoon. His anxiety to get a good seat hardly permits him to warm the chair at the dinner-table. He reaches the door of the theater, and the first thing he does is to try to enter without paying. The first misfortune of players is to work much and to have but few persons pay. For twenty persons to enter on three quartos would not do much harm if it were not an occasion for many others to do the same. For if only one has not paid, countless others will also refuse to pay. All wish to enjoy the privilege of free admission in order that others may see that they are worthy of it. This they desire with such intense eagerness that they will fight to obtain it, and by fighting they achieve their object. Rarely does a man who has once quarreled to avoid paying ever pay at any subsequent time. A fine reason to quarrel, in order to profit by the sweat of those who labor to entertain one! And then, because he does not pay, will he be easy to please? On the contrary, if a player wears a poor costume he insults him or hisses him.

[1] *Philosophia Antigua*, Madrid, 1596, pp. 529, 530.

I should like to know how this fellow and those who imitate him can expect a player to wear fine clothes, when they refuse to pay him. . . . Our idler moves on into the theater and approaches the person who assigns the seats and benches, and asks for a place.[1] He is met with the reply that there are none, but that a certain seat which has been engaged has not yet been occupied, and that he should wait until the guitar-players appear, and if it be still vacant, he may then occupy it. Our man argues, but to amuse himself, in the meanwhile, he goes to the dressing-room. There he finds women taking off their street clothes and putting on their theatrical costumes. Some are so far disrobed as though they were about to retire to bed. He takes his place in front of a woman who, having come to the theater on foot, is having her shoes and stockings put on by her maid. This cannot be done without some sacrifice of modesty. The poor actress must suffer this and does not dare to protest, for, as her chief object is to win applause, she is afraid to offend any one. A hiss, no matter how unjust, discredits her, since all believe that the judgment of him who accuses is better than their own. The actress continues to dress, enduring his presence with patience. The most indecorous woman on the stage has some modesty in the green-room, for here her immodesty is a vice, while there it is of her profession.

The fellow never takes his eyes off her. . . . He approaches the hangings (*paños*) to see whether the doubtful seat is occupied, and finds it vacant. As it appears that the owner will not come, he goes and takes the seat. Scarcely has he been seated when the owner arrives and defends his claim. The one already seated resists, and a quarrel ensues. Did this fellow not come to amuse himself, when he left his home? And what has quarreling to do with amusement? . . . Finally the quarrel is adjusted, and the one who has paid for the seat yields and takes another place which has been offered him by the peacemakers. The commotion caused by the struggle having subsided, our intruder is also quieted and now turns his eyes to the gallery occupied by the women (*cazuela*), carefully scrutinizing their faces until he finds one who particularly strikes his fancy, and guardedly makes signs to her.

The *cazuela*, my dear sir, is not what you came to see, but the

---

[1] The sum paid at the door (*entrada*) only entitles the person to admission, not to a seat, for which an extra sum must be paid.

comedia. . . . He is looking round in every direction, when he feels some one pull his cloak from behind. He turns and sees a fruit-seller, who, leaning forward between two men, whispers to him that the woman who is tapping her knee with her fan says that she has much admired the spirit which he has shown in the quarrel and asks him to pay for a dozen oranges for her. The fellow looks again at the *cazuela,* sees that the woman is the one that caught his fancy before, pays the money for the fruit, and sends word that she may have anything else she pleases. As the fruit-seller leaves, the fellow immediately plans that he will wait for the woman at the exit of the theater, and he begins to think that there is an interminable delay in beginning the play. In a loud and peevish manner he signifies his disapproval, exciting the *mosqueteros,* who are standing below, to break forth with insulting shouts, in order to hasten the players. Why do they do this? . . . Not one of those who are shouting would run the risk of saying a word to a player in the street. And besides being foolish and cowardly to treat them thus, it is most ungrateful, for of all people actors are those who strive hardest to please. The rehearsals for a comedia are so frequent and so long that it is often a positive torment. And when the time for the first performance arrives, every one of them would willingly give a year's pay to make a good appearance on that day. And when they come upon the stage, what fatigue, what loss would they not willingly undergo to acquit themselves well of their task? If they are to cast themselves from a rock they do it with the fearlessness of despair, yet their bodies are human, and they feel pain like any other. And if in a comedia a death-struggle is to be represented, the actor to whose lot it falls writhes upon the dirty stage, which is full of projecting nails and splinters, with no more regard for his costume than if it were the coarsest leather, while often it is very costly. . . . And I have seen an actress of great repute (who died only a short while ago) representing a passage where, in a rage, she tears a garment to tatters to heighten the effect of her acting, though the article torn may cost twice as much as the money she receives for the performance. . . .

But women also go to see the comedia. On feast-days men go to the play *after* lunching, but women go *before.* The woman who goes to the comedia on a holiday generally makes it an affair of a whole day. She meets one of her friends, and they take a bite of breakfast, reserving the midday meal for the evening. Then they go to mass, and from the church straight to the *cazuela* to get a good seat. There is no money-taker at the door yet. They enter and find a sprinkling of women as foolish as themselves already in the *cazuela*. They avoid the front seats, for these are for the women who come to see and be seen; so they take a modest seat in the middle. They express their pleasure at having found so comfortable a place and cast their eyes about for some pastime. Finding none, the rest from the hurry of the morning serves as a satisfaction. Other women enter, and some of the more brazen sit by the front railing of the *cazuela,* thus shutting out the light from those in the middle. Now the merry-making is let loose. The money-takers enter. One of our friends draws a handkerchief from beneath the folds of her petticoat, and with her teeth looses a knot tied in the corner of it, and takes out a real (34 maravedís) and asks for the return of ten maravedís. While she is doing this the other takes from her bosom a paper containing ten quartos (40 maravedís), and hands her money to the doorkeeper, who passes on. The one with the ten maravedís in her hand now buys a package of filberts for two quartos, and, like a child, does not know what to do with the remaining ochavo (2 maravedís) which she has received in change; finally she drops it in her bosom, with the remark that it is for the poor. Now the two friends begin to crack the filberts, and you can hear them munching them; but one of the filberts is full of dust, the other contains a dry kernel, while another has an oily taste. . . . Now more women are crowding in. One of those who are in front makes signs to two others who are standing behind our two friends, and without asking permission the newcomers pass between the two, stepping on their skirts and disarranging their cloaks, which provokes the exclamation: "Did you ever see such rudeness!" and they begin to shake and fleck the dust from their skirts. Those in the front seats begin to eat sandwiches, and presently one of the two friends remarks: "Do you see that man down there with grayish hair who is taking a seat on one of the benches on the left?" etc. . . . Here follows some scandal, for which she is reproved by another woman sitting near. . . .

The *cazuela* being now full, the *apretador* enters (he is the doorkeeper, who makes the women sit closer so that they may make more room), accompanied by four women, well dressed and thickly veiled, whom he wants to accommodate, for they have given him eight quartos. He approaches our friends and tells them to sit closer; they protest; he insists, and they reply that the women should have come earlier, when they would have found seats. Finally the newcomers let themselves fall upon those already seated, who, to get away from under them, unconsciously make room. There is grumbling on all sides, but at last quiet is restored. . . . It is now half-past two o'clock, and the friends, who had not dined, begin to get hungry. At length one of the women who had been accommodated by the *apretador* gives to our friends each a handful of prunes and some candied yolks of eggs, with the remark: "Come, let us be friends and eat these sweets which some booby gave me." They begin to eat and want to strike up a conversation, but say nothing, as they cannot stop eating. Presently there is an altercation at the door of the *cazuela* between the doorkeeper and a number of youths who want some women to enter free, and they burst into the *cazuela* quarreling. A great commotion and uproar ensues. The women rise excitedly, and in their anxiety to avoid those who are quarreling they fall over one another. . . . Those who rush up from the *patio* to lend aid or restore order push into the jumbling mass and bowl the women over. All now take to the corners as the best place in the *cazuela,* and some on all fours and others running seek a place of safety. Finally the police expel the men, and every woman takes a seat where she happens to be, none occupying the one she had at first. One of the two friends is now on the last bench, while the other is near the door. The former has lost her gloves and finds that her gown is torn; her friend is bleeding at the nose as the result of the scuffle, and, having lost her handkerchief, makes use of her petticoat. All is lamentation, when the guitar-players enter, and quiet is once more restored. . . .[1]

In no country, as already observed, had the drama received greater encouragement than in Spain, nor was its popularity limited to any one class, but all, from the highest to the lowest, favored and supported it. As developed and perfected by the great Phenix, Lope de Vega,

---

[1] *Obras de D. Juan de Zabaleta*, Madrid, 1692, "El Dia de Fiesta por la Tarde," pp. 296 ff.

it was a genuine product of the Spanish soil. Whatever
its subject-matter, whether mythology, history, or legend,
all was translated into the Spain of the day; its characters
not only spoke Spanish, but they were Spaniards in every
vein and fiber. In a word, it was truly national in character, and herein lies one of the chief glories of the
Spanish drama, which is shared only by England among
the countries of modern Europe. Such a rapid and
extraordinary development of the drama necessitated a
vast number of players for its exposition, and the names
of nearly two thousand actors have come down to us,
who, from the rude beginnings of Lope de Rueda upon
an improvised stage in the public square, to the magnificent
and costly entertainments of Philip the Fourth in the Buen
Retiro, represented the uninterrupted productions of the
Spanish Muse, from the simple *pasos, églogas,* and *farsas*
to the great masterpieces of Lope de Vega and his host
of followers. And yet, great as was the number of
Spanish players, they seem to have limited their sphere
of action almost exclusively to their own country or to
the Spanish possessions in Italy. During the long occupation of the Netherlands by Spain the Spanish language
gained great currency through that country,[1] and Spanish
players certainly visited the Netherlands frequently.[2]
Our information as to their journeys in the remaining
countries of Europe is also very slight when compared
with the records left by the many companies of traveling
players from England and Italy during the latter part of

---

[1] "In de zestiende en zeventiende eeuw was de Spaansche taal in ons
vaterland bijna zoo gemeenzaam als tegenwoordig de Fransche." (Geys-
beek, *Anthologisch en Critisch Woordenboek,* Bd. III, quoted by Schwe-
ring, *Zur Geschichte des niederländischen und spanischen Dramas in
Deutschland,* Münster, 1895, p. 76.)

[2] I have been unable to consult the following article, which may contain
some information on this point: Te Winkel, "De invloed der Spaansche
Letterkunde op de Nederlandsche in de zeventiende eeuw," in the *Tijd-
schrift voor Nederlandsche Taal- en Letterkunde,* Eerste Jaargang, Leiden,
1881, S. 59. Melchor de Leon seems to have been in Brussels with his company in 1629. See Appendix,—*List of Actors and Actresses.*

the sixteenth and beginning of the seventeenth centuries. The earliest notice of Spanish players abroad that I have found falls in the year 1604. On August 2 of that year a Spanish actress was found murdered at Saint-Germain-des-Prés, and two Spanish actors were convicted of the crime and executed.[1] Some Spanish players also appeared at the Port Saint-Germain on October 27, 1613, but met with no success.[2] A company also visited Paris in 1618, but we know nothing further about them.[3] In 1643 Pedro de la Rosa and his company visited Paris, and returned thither in 1674, and in 1660 Sebastian de Prado took a troupe of players to Paris at the instance of Maria Teresa, daughter of Philip IV. and wife of Louis XIV., whom she had married the previous year. Some members of this company are said to have remained in France twelve years; Prado certainly did not, for we find him in Spain in the following year. In 1666 we again hear of Spanish players who gave a *Ballet des Muses* at Saint-Germain-en-Laye on December 2, among them Jerónima de Olmedo and Maria de Anaya.[4]

The only record of the visit of a Spanish company to London has already been mentioned (above, p. 139,

---

[1] *Mémoires et Journal de Pierre de l'Estoile,* ed. Michaud et Poujolat, Paris, 1857, p. 378. See Rigal, *Le Théâtre Français avant la période classique,* Paris, 1901, p. 50, note 3.

[2] In a letter dated October 27, 1613, Malherbe says: "Je viens tout à cette heure de la comédie des Espagnols, qui ont aujourd'hui commencé à jouer à la porte Saint-Germain dans le faubourg; ils ont fait des merveilles en sottises et impertinences, et n'y a eu personne qui ne s'en soit revenu avec mal de tête; mais pour une fois il n'y a point eu de mal de savoir ce que c'est. Je suis de ceux qui s'y sont excellemment ennuyés," etc. (*Lettres de Malherbe,* ed. Lalanne (*Grands Ecrivains*), Paris, 1862, Vol. III, p. 350.) And in a letter of November 24 (p. 358) he remarks: "Les Espagnols ne plaisent à personne; ils jouent au faubourg Saint-Germain, mais ils ne gagnent pas le louage du jeu de paume où ils jouent."

[3] *Mémoires du Maréchal de Bassompierre,* ed. Petitot, Tome XX, Paris, 1822, p. 157, who merely remarks: "Nous eûmes les comédies espagnoles cet hiver-la."

[4] Rouanet, *Intermèdes Espagnols,* Paris, 1897, p. 316, quoting Fournel, *Les Contemporains de Molière,* Tome II.

note 1), when Juan Navarro Oliver represented a play before the King on December 23, 1635, for which he received ten pounds.

But great as the popularity of the drama was in Spain, and rapid as was its rise, its decline and fall were almost equally rapid, and by the middle of the seventeenth century it was clearly on the wane. Indeed, a change is perceptible a decade earlier. The death of the great founder of the national drama, Lope de Vega, in 1635, withdrew from it a support which caused the magnificent structure to waver. By the middle of the century all the greatest dramatists, with the single exception of Calderon, were dead. Guillen de Castro died in 1631; Alarcon's death occurred in 1639, followed by Mira de Mescua in 1644. Tirso de Molina died in 1648, although he had ceased to write for the stage even before Lope's death. Of the lesser lights of the drama, Montalvan died in 1638, and Luis Velez de Guevara in 1644. All these had passed from the stage of life, and Calderon alone, of those who had helped to rear the imposing fabric of the drama, was still writing comedias after the middle of the century, and even of his followers, Rojas and Moreto had written their best plays by that time. No great Spanish comedia dates after 1650. And here, once more, at the close as at the beginning, the Spanish national drama exhibits a striking parallel to the English, which had also produced all that was best in it before the closing of the theaters in 1642.

That the Spanish theater was on the decline by 1650, a glance at the list of the great leaders of the theatrical companies convincingly shows. The older ones, who had taken part in the great renascence under the magical touch of Lope—Velazquez, Cisneros, Rios, Porres, Antonio de Villegas, Vergara, Melchor de Villalba, etc.— had long been dead, while those who shared in the greatest glory of the stage—Baltasar Pinedo, Domingo Balbin,

Cristóbal Ortiz de Villazan, Alonso de Riquelme, Cristóbal de Avendaño, Tomas Fernandez de Cabredo, Manuel Vallejo, Antonio Granados, Pedro de Valdes, Hernan Sanchez de Vargas, and Juan de Morales Medrano—had also passed away, and Antonio de Prado, Alonso de Olmedo, and Roque de Figueroa all died in 1651. Those who were left, like the surviving dramatists, were but the smaller lights that still shone for a while in the glow cast behind them as the great stars one by one disappeared beneath the horizon.

And it was, perhaps, not unfitting that this should be so. These famous *autores* had been the friends and associates of the great poets who created this vast and wonderful drama; for particular players of their companies many of the most celebrated comedias had been written; the rehearsals were often conducted in the presence of the poet, and the parts perfected under his eye. For them the business of the stage was an actual and living thing, not a dead and dry tradition. But the sun had set, and while one great star was still refulgent in the gathering gloom, it was only a question of a little while when it, too, should disappear, and all be enveloped in darkness.

APPENDIX A

REPRESENTATIONS IN THE CORRALES OF MADRID,
1579-1602.
(From an article by Sr. Pérez Pastor, in the *Bulletin Hispanique* (1906).)

1579

Producto de comedias para el Hospital civil de la Pasión desde 30 de Mayo de 1579 hasta 31 de Diciembre de el:

Mayo.—"En treinta de Mayo de 1579 años se nombró por comisario de las comedias al señor Francisco de Prado el qual ha de usar desta comision desde 7 de Junio del dicho año por dexacion que hizo dello Luis de Barahona, comisario que fué de las dichas comedias hasta este dicho dia."

Junio.—"En 7 dia del mes de Junio del dicho año estando en el Hospital de la Sagrada Pasion juntos en su cabildo D. Alonso Enriquez, Pedro de Ledesma y Gonzalo de Monzon, diputados, y Juan Lopez y Pedro Alvarez de Casasola y Gaspar de la Torre y Valdivieso y Juan Diaz, cofrades, Francisco de Prado, comisario de las comedias, dixo que Francisco Osorio, autor de comedias, ha venido á esta corte y le ha pedido le dé corral en que represente sus comedias, y que él le ha señalado el corral de Valdivieso, y que el dicho Francisco Osorio se ha obligado á hacer el teatro y dos tablados a los lados a su costa y que el aprovechamiento dellos sea para los Hospitales sin que se les descuente cosa alguna, y demas desto le da el dicho Francisco Osorio diez reales cada dia que representare y destos diez reales se dan siete reales á la de Valdivieso cada dia que se representare, y hoy dicho dia es el primero que representa el dicho Osorio y que ansi mesmo halla que en el corral de la Pacheca está Salcedo y en el de Puente Ganasa que ansi mesmo representan hoy dicho dia y firmaron de sus nombres.—Juan Lopez—Gonzalo de Monzon."

"El dicho Osorio comediante representó en el dicho corral de la de Valdivieso segundo y tercero dia de Pascua que fueron á los ocho y nueve de Junio del dicho año y por respeto de la poca gente que tuvo no hubo aprovechamiento ninguno mas de los diez reales que dió del corral, de los quales de los dichos dos dias se dieron á la de Valdivieso catorce reales y quedaron seis y cupo á esta casa quatro, los quales se metieron con la quenta de Salcedo y el susdicho Osorio se fué luego sin representar más.—Francisco de Prado— Gonzalo de Monzon."

Domingo 7 de Junio de 1579 representaron Ganasa y Salcedo, y el Hospital de la Pasion tuvo de aprovechamiento de las dos comedias 221 reales y 10 maravedíses de las dos tercias partes que le pertenecen.

En 8 de Junio segundo dia de pascua, 156 reales y 12 maravedís de las comedias de Ganasa y Salcedo.

En 8 de Junio pagó Ganasa 20 reales de las representaciones de los dias 1º y 2º de Pascua.

En 9 de Junio 195 reales y 10 maravedíses de las comedias que en dicho dia hicieron Ganasa y Salcedo.

11 de Junio.   Representaron Ganasa y Salcedo.

14 de Junio, domingo de la Trinidad.   Representaron Ganasa y Salcedo.

"Jueves dia del Corpus Christi diez y ocho del mes de Junio de 1579 años, de pedimento de Francisco de Prado, vecino desta villa de Madrid, comisario nombrado para los aprovechamientos que procedieren de las comedias tocantes al Hospital de la Pasion desta corte, yo el presente escribano fui al corral de Puente, que es en la calle del Lobo, donde representa hasta ahora Ganasa, italiano, y al corral de la Pacheca para ver si habia representacion e pidio por testimonio como no habia representacion en el un corral ni en el otro porque Ganasa es ido a Toledo y Salcedo tiene las fiestas del Corpus que se hicieron hoy en esta villa, y de su pedimento doy fee que hoy dicho dia é las quatro de la tarde al punto fui a los dichos corrales y no habia gente en ellos y estaban vacios de manera que se entiende no haber comedias este dia, y yo el presente escribano doy fee que en la sala de los señores alcaldes de la casa y corte de su Magestad anteayer martes de mañana se dixo que por mandado de su Magestad llevaban á Toledo al dicho Ganasa y sus compañeros para la fiesta de hoy dicho dia y ansi por mandado de los dichos señores alcaldes se les dieron mulas para el dicho efecto, y doy fee que el dicho Salcedo ha fecho hoy las fiestas desta villa, y de pedimento del dicho Francisco de Prado lo firmé y signé.— Diego Verdugo de Leon."

En 21 de Junio de 1579 Francisco de Prado hace saber á los diputados de la Pasion que Ganasa no ha vuelto de Toledo, ni sabe quando vendrá Salcedo y que no hay comedias en la corte.

En 24 de Junio Ganasa, vuelto ya de Toledo, representó en el corral de Puente.

En 28 y 29 Junio representó Ganasa en el corral de la Pacheca.

Julio, 2.—"Yo Alonso de Robles, escribano de su majestad en la su corte, doy fee que Ganasa, italiano, representó en el corral de la Pacheca hoy Jueves dos del mes de Julio deste año de setenta y nueve dia de trabajo, y que en la dicha representacion declaró que se le habia dado licencia de representar dos dias en la semana por los Señores del Consejo de su Magestad, y en fee de ello di esta el dicho dia mes y año de pedimento de Francisco de Prado y lo firmé de mi nombre.—Alonso de Robles, escribano."

5 de Julio, Domingo. Representó Ganasa en la Pacheca. (*Id.* martes 7 Julio.)

"Domingo 12 de Julio. Representó Cisneros en el corral de la calle del Lobo, que es el de Puente, y fue la primera representacion que hizo en Madrid despues que salió de la corte."

En el mismo dia representó Ganasa en el corral de la Pacheca.

16 de Julio. Representó Ganasa en la Pacheca.

22 de Julio. Representaron Ganasa y Cisneros cada uno una comedia. (*Id.* 25 y domingo 26.)

28 y 30. Ganasa.

Agosto.—Domingo 2. Ganasa y Cisneros. (*Id.* 5, 6, 9 y 10.)

15 Agosto. Alonso Rodriguez, el Toledano, representó en el corral de Puente porque Cisneros no estaba en la corte. Representó tambien Ganasa en la Pacheca.

Domingo 16 de Agosto. Representó Ganasa. No hubo representacion en el corral de Cristobal de Puente por no haber autor en Madrid.

18 de Agosto de 1579. No hubo representacion en la Pacheca por estar fuera de Madrid los italianos, ni en el corral de Puente por no haber autor en Madrid.

20 Agosto. Representó Ganasa en la Pacheca.

Domingo 23. Representaron Ganasa y Cisneros. (*Id*. 24.)

27 de Agosto. No hubo representacion en la calle del Lobo porque Cisneros estaba ausente, ni en el de la Pacheca porque Ganasa no quiso representar al ver que habia poca gente en el corral, y se devolvió el dinero á las personas que habian entrado.

30 Agosto. Representó Ganasa en la Pacheca y hubo un volteador en la calle del Lobo.

Setiembre.—En 6 de Setiembre de 1579 representó Velazquez la primera vez de esta temporada en el corral de Puente; y los dias anteriores no hubo representacion porque la licencia que se dió á los autores para representar dos dias de trabajo fue solamente para los meses de Julio y Agosto. En el mismo dia representó Ganasa en la Pacheca.

8 de Setiembre. Hubo dos comedias una de Ganasa y otra de Velazquez.

10 de Setiembre. Representó Velazquez. (*Id*. 15.)

13 de Setiembre. Ganasa y Velazquez.

17 de Setiembre. Representó Ganasa aunque fue dia de trabajo y es la primera vez que lo hace en este mes.

20 de Setiembre, Domingo. Hubo comedia de Ganasa y de Velazquez. (*Id*. 21 y 24.)

27. Velazquez en la calle del Lobo. En el corral de la Pacheca hubo mucha gente y mucha mas en la calle esperando la representacion que no se hizo porque Juan Alberto Ganasa no habia tenido licencia para ello.

29. Ganasa y Velazquez.

Octubre.—1º. Ganasa y Velazquez. (*Id*. 4, 6, 8 y 11.)

13. Ganasa en la Pacheca. Velazquez estaba fuera de Madrid.

15. No hubo representacion en la Pacheca "por lo mucho que llovio."

18 y 20. Ganasa.

22. "No hubo comedia a causa de los toros que hubo."

25 Octubre. Representó por primera vez en el corral de Puente Rivas, maestro de comedias y no representó mas que este dia. Ganasa representó en la Pacheca.

28 y 29. Ganasa.

Noviembre.—Domingo 1º. Representó Ganasa. (*Id*. 3, 7, 8, 10, 12, 15.)

18. Ganasa y Salcedo (1er dia). (*Id*. Domingo 22.)

24 y 26. Ganasa.

Domingo 29. Ganasa, Salcedo y Granado.

"Yo Francisco de Olea doy fee . . . en como hoy domingo 29 dias del mes de Noviembre de 1579 años fue el primero dia que se representó en el corral que las cofradias de la Sagrada Pasion y Nuestra Señora de la Soledad tienen en esta dicha villa en la calle de la Cruz, en el qual asi mismo representó la primera vez Juan Granado e Galvez, autores de comedias, esta ultima vez que vinieron a esta corte sin que hubiesen representado en el ni en otro corral donde se acostumbra hacer las dichas comedias otra vez desta postrera venida . . . Francisco de Olea."

Lunes 30 de Noviembre. Representaron Ganasa, Salcedo y Granado.

Diciembre.—3. Representó Ganasa.

Domingo 6. Ganasa, Salcedo y Granado.

8. Ganasa y Velazquez. En este dia se notificó á Cristobal de Puente dueño del corral de la calle del Lobo, que tenian alquilado las cofradias, que cesaba este arrendamiento y que los asientos, tablados y pertrechos que a costa de las cofradias se habian hecho en dicho corral se transladarían al nuevo teatro de la calle de la Cruz ya por evitar gastos ya tambien porque Francisco Salcedo, que representaba en la calle del Lobo, se ha ausentado.

10. No hubo representacion en ningun corral por haber llovido mucho.

13. Representaron Ganasa y Granado.

17. Representaron Ganasa y Granado y fue la primera vez que se representó por Granado en la Cruz en dia de trabajo.

18. Ganasa en la Pacheca y Granado en la Cruz.

20. Ganasa y Granado.

21. Ganasa.

22 y 23. Granado.

25 y 26. Granado y Ganasa.

Domingo 27. No representaron los Italianos ni Granado en los corrales públicos porque lo hicieron á los señores del Consejo de S. M.

28. Ganasa y Granado.

29. Se dió licencia á Granado y Galvez para que pudiesen representar todos los dias hasta el de Reyes proximo.

29 y 30. Representó Granado en el corral de la Cruz.

31. Ganasa en la Pacheca "y no representó Granado en la Cruz." (*Archivo de la Diputacion provincial de Madrid. Libros de cuentas del Hospital de la Pasion*, VII, 115, 2.)

—"Razon puntual de la ejecucion del corral de la Cruz para las comedias el año 1579": Empezó la obra el 13 de Octubre de 1579 por cuenta de las dos obras pias, la Sagrada Pasion y Nuestra Señora de la Soledad. El edificio y gastos del mismo estuvieron á cargo de Getino de Guzman, fiador que habia sido de Dª Leonor de Cortinas para el rescate de Miguel de Cervantes.

1580

Cargo de las comedias del año 1580 para el Hospital de la Pasion:

Enero.—En 1º de Enero hubo representacion por Ganasa. (*Id.* 3, 5, 6.) 10. Granado. 12. Ganasa. 14. Ganasa y Granado. (*Id.* 17 y 20.) 23. Cisneros y Ganasa. 24. Ganasa y Granado. (*Id.* 26 y 27.) 28. Empezó Cisneros á representar en el corral de Puente que habia estado desbaratado; y además trabajaron hasta Carnestolendas Granado en la Cruz y Ganasa en la Pacheca. 29. Cisneros y Granado. 31. Cisneros, Granado y Ganasa.

Febrero.—3. Cisneros y Granado. 4. Cisneros, Granado y Ganasa. 5. Cisneros en la Cruz. 7. Cisneros, Granado y Ganasa. 8. Cisneros en la Cruz y dió "para ayuda de costa del corral" 200 reales que le correspondian de su aprovechamiento como autor. 9. Ganasa y Granado (Cisneros se habia ido á Alcalá de Henares). 10, 11, 12, 13, 14, 15 y 16. Ganasa y Granado. 17, miércoles de Ceniza. Se suspenden las representaciones.

Septiembre.—11. Empezó á representar Rivas en la Pacheca. 12. Rivas. 14. Empieza Cisneros en la Pacheca. 15 á 25. Cisneros. 26, 28. No hubo representacion. 27, 29 y 30. Cisneros.

Octubre.—1º á 10, 16 á 19. Cisneros. 20 á 22. No hubo comedia. 23 á 25. Representó Juan Granado. 26. No hubo comedia. 27. Granado. 28. Juan Granado y Alonso Rodriguez. Se suspenden las representaciones por muerte de la Reina Dª Ana. (*Archivo de la Diputacion provincial*, VII, 115, 2.)

1581

Cargo de las comedias del año 1581 para el Hospital de la Pasion y cofradia de la Soledad:

30 noviembre 1581.—Ganasa representó en la Cruz y fue el primer dia que hubo comedia despues de la muerte de la Reina Ana. "Y de todo el aprovechamiento de la comedia, sin la representacion, se allegaron ducientos y setenta reales y medio de que cupo á la cofradia de la Soledad de la tercia parte que lleva noventa reales y cinco maravedís, y a la Pasion le cupo de sus dos tercias partes ciento y ochenta reales y doce maravedís."

Diciembre.—3. No representó Ganasa en el teatro de la Cruz porque lo hizo al Consejo de Cruzada en casa del Comisario general; Galvez representó en el corral de la Pacheca "la primera comedia que en este año hizo." 4. Ganasa en la Cruz. 5, 7, 8. Ganasa en la Cruz y Galvez en la Pacheca. 10. *Id.* "Este dia representó Alonso Rodriguez, el de Toledo, la primera farsa en el corral de Puente y envió de todo aprovechamiento, con la representacion, 54 reales." 12, 14 y 16. Ganasa en la Cruz, y Galvez en la Pacheca. 17, 18. Ganasa en la Cruz, Galvez en la Pacheca, y Rodriguez en el Puente. 19, 20 y 21. Ganasa en la Cruz, y Galvez en la Pacheca. 22. Granado en la Pacheca. 23. Saldaña en la Cruz. 24. Ganasa en la Cruz, Galvez en la Pacheca y Saldaña, por primera vez, en el corral de Puente. 25. Ganasa, Galvez y Saldaña en la Cruz, Pacheca y Puente. 26. Saldaña en la Cruz, Galvez en la Pacheca. Ganasa representó al presidente del Consejo. 27 y 28. Ganasa, Galvez y Saldaña. 29. Saldaña. 30. Ganasa, Galvez y Saldaña. 31. Ganasa y Galvez. "No representó Saldaña porque el y su compañia estuvieron en la Cruz viendo a los Italianos." (*Archivo de la Diputacion,* VII, 115, 2, y 59, 2, XII, 17.)

1582

Cargo de las comedias del año 1582 para el Hospital de la Pasion y cofradia de la Soledad:

Enero.—1. Representaron Ganasa, Galvez y Saldaña. 2. Galvez. 3 y 4. Ganasa y Galvez. 5. Saldaña en la Pacheca. 6. Ganasa, Galvez y Saldaña. 7. Ganasa y Galvez. 8. Saldaña en la Cruz. Galvez y Juan Granado salieron para Valladolid. 9.

Ganasa en la Cruz. 10. Saldaña en la Cruz. 11. Ganasa en la Cruz. 12. Saldaña en la Pacheca. 14. Saldaña en la Cruz. No representaron los Italianos por estar enfermos algunos de ellos. 15. Saldaña en la Pacheca, Velazquez en la Cruz "y fue su primera representacion." 16. Ganasa en la Cruz, "que es el de las obras pias"; Saldaña en la Pacheca. 17. Velazquez en la Cruz. 20. Velazquez en la Cruz, Saldaña en la Pacheca. No representaron los Italianos en la Cruz por estar en Guadalajara a la boda de D. Rodrigo de Mendoza.[1] 21. Saldaña en la Cruz, Velazquez en la Pacheca. 22. Velazquez en la Cruz. 23. Velazquez en la Cruz, Saldaña en la Pacheca. 24. Saldaña en la Cruz. 25. Velazquez en la Cruz. 26. Saldaña en la Cruz. 28 y 29. Saldaña en la Cruz, Velazquez en la Pacheca. 30. Velazquez en la Cruz. 31. Saldaña en la Cruz.

Febrero.—2. Saldaña en la Cruz. 4. No hubo representaciones por la procesion general para recoger los pobres mendigos en el Hospital general. 5. Velazquez en la Cruz. 6. Ganasa en la Cruz "y fue la primera que hizo despues que vino de Guadalajara." 7. Saldaña en la Cruz. 8. Ganasa en la Cruz. 9. Velazquez en la Cruz. 10. Saldaña en la Cruz. 11. Domingo. Velazquez en la Pacheca, Ganasa en la Cruz y Saldaña en el corral de Puente. 12. Velazquez en la Cruz. 13. Ganasa en la Cruz. 14. Saldaña en la Cruz. 15. Ganasa en la Cruz. 16. Velazquez en la Cruz. 17. Saldaña en la Cruz. 18. Domingo. Ganasa en la Cruz, Velazquez en el Puente, y Saldaña en la Pacheca. 19. Ganasa en la Cruz, Velazquez en la Pacheca. 20. Ganasa en la Cruz, Saldaña en la Pacheca. 21. Velazquez en la Pacheca, Ganasa en la Cruz. 22. Ganasa en la Cruz, Saldaña en la Pacheca. 23. Ganasa en la Cruz, Velazquez en la Pacheca. 24. Velazquez en la Cruz, Saldaña en la Pacheca. 25 y 26. Saldaña en la Cruz, Velazquez en la Pacheca. 27. Saldaña en la

[1] (Enero 1582, sábado.) "Salió a representar Ganasa el italiano una comedia, la qual . . . oyeron con mucho aplauso y por haber tanta gente no se pudo representar en el tablado que para ello estaba hecho . . ."— "Domingo siguiente . . . á la noche representó Ganasa el italiano, con que se entretuvieron hasta fue hora de cenar." (Relacion de todo lo sucedido en los casamientos de los señores Don Rodrigo y Doña Ana de Mendoza, hijo y hermano del señor Marques de Cenete y Duque del Infantado, que se celebraron en la ciudad de Guadalajara á 20 de Enero de 1582. *Relaciones historicas de los siglos XVI y XVII*, Madrid, 1896.)

Pacheca, Velazquez en la Cruz. "No representó Ganasa a causa de su prision."

Abril.—16. Segundo dia de Pascua. Velazquez en la Cruz "y fue el primero dia de representacion despues de la quaresma deste dicho año." 17. Cisneros en la Cruz, Velazquez en la Pacheca. 18. Cisneros en la Cruz. 19. Velazquez en la Cruz. 20. Cisneros en la Cruz. 21, 22 y 23. Velazquez en la Cruz. 24. Cisneros en la Cruz. 25. Cisneros en la Cruz, Velazquez en la Pacheca. 26. Velazquez en la Cruz. 27. Cisneros en la Cruz. 29. Velazquez en la Cruz, Cisneros en la Pacheca. 30. Cisneros en la Cruz.

Mayo.—1. Cisneros en la Cruz, Velazquez en la Pacheca. 2 y 3. Velazquez en la Cruz. 4. Cisneros en la Cruz. 5. Velazquez en la Cruz. 6. Cisneros en la Cruz, Velazquez en la Pacheca. 7. Cisneros en la Cruz. 8 y 10. Velazquez en la Cruz. 11. Cisneros en la Cruz. 13. Velazquez en la Cruz, Cisneros en la Pacheca. 14. Velazquez en la Cruz. 15. Cisneros en la Cruz. 16. Velazquez en la Cruz. 17. Cisneros en la Cruz. 20. Cisneros en la Cruz, Velazquez en la Pacheca. 21. Cisneros en la Cruz. 23. Velazquez en la Cruz. 24. Velazquez en la Cruz, Cisneros en la Pacheca. 25. Cisneros en la Cruz. 26. Velazquez en la Cruz. 27. Velazquez en la Pacheca, Cisneros en la Cruz. 28. Velazquez en la Cruz. 29. Cisneros en la Cruz.

Junio.—1. Cisneros en la Cruz. 2. Velazquez en la Cruz. 3. Velazquez en la Cruz, Cisneros en la Pacheca. 4. Velazquez en la Cruz. 5 y 6. Cisneros en la Cruz. 7. Velazquez en la Cruz. 8. Cisneros en la Cruz. 9. Velazquez en la Cruz. 10. Velazquez en la Pacheca,-Cisneros en la Cruz. 11. Velazquez en la Cruz, Cisneros en la Pacheca. 19 y 20. Cisneros en la Cruz. 29. Un italiano volteó en la Pacheca y siguió trabajando con sus volteadores hasta el dia de Santiago.

Julio.—En 29 de Julio hubo *juego de manos* y siguió durante algunos dias.

Agosto.—5. Hizo Saldaña "una comedia en el teatro de las obras pias, que fue la primera que representó despues de la tasa del quartillo." El volteador trabajó en la Pacheca. 6. Saldaña en la Cruz. El volteador en la Pacheca. 10, 13 y 15. Saldaña hizo comedia en la Cruz. El volteador trabajó en la Pacheca. 16 y 19.

Saldaña en la Cruz. 24. Saldaña represèntó en la Cruz y los *Italianos nuevos* hicieron otra comedia en la Pacheca. 26. Saldaña en la Cruz y los *Corteses* en la Pacheca.

Septiembre.—2, 8, 9, 16, 21 y 23. Saldaña en la Cruz y los *Corteses* en la Pacheca. 29 y 30. Los *Italianos nuevos*.

Octubre.—17 y 18. Los Italianos. 28. Osorio y los Italianos. 31. Osorio y los Italianos.

Noviembre.—1. Osorio y los Italianos. 7, 14 y 15. Angulo y los *Corteses*.

Diciembre.—12. Alonso Rodriguez. 18 y 19. Alonso Rodriguez. Hubo títeres en la Pacheca. 21, 25, 26, 27, 28. Alonso Rodriguez. (*Archivo de la Diputacion provincial*, VII, 115, 2, y 59, 2, XII (2400), 17.)

1590

Aprovechamiento de las comedias para el Hospital general:

Enero, lunes 1º—Entraron 458 reales de las dos comedias de Velazquez y Rios. 2. Velazquez y Cisneros. 3. Rios y Cisneros. 4. Velazquez y Rios. 5. Cisneros y Rios. 6. Cisneros y Velazquez. 7. Velazquez y Rios. 9. Velazquez y Cisneros. 11 y 12. Velazquez y Rios. 13. Rios y Cisneros. 14 y 15. Velazquez y Rios. 16. Rios y Cisneros. 17 á 31. Velazquez y Rios.

Febrero.—2, 3, 4 y 5. Velazquez y Rios. 6. Porras, Velazquez y Rios. 7, 8 y 9. Velazquez y Rios. 10. Velazquez. 11 á 20. Rios y Velazquez. 21. Velazquez y Cisneros. 22. Velazquez y Rios. 23. Velazquez y Cisneros. 24. Rios y Cisneros. 25. Velazquez y Cisneros. 26. Velazquez y Rios. 27. Rios y Cisneros.

Marzo.—1º Velazquez y Rios. 2. Rios y Cisneros. 3. Velazquez. 5. Rios y Velazquez. 6. Velazquez y Cisneros.

Mayo.—3 á 7. Cisneros. 9. Rios. 11 y 12. Cisneros. 13 á 31. Cisneros y Rios.

Junio.—1, 2 y 3. Rios y Cisneros. 6. Cisneros. 7. Rios. 10 á 16. Rios y Cisneros. 18 y 19. Cisneros.

Julio.—15. Alcocer. 17. Villalba. 19. Alcocer y Villalba. 20. Alcocer. 21. Villalba y Alcocer. 23. Alcocer. 24, 25, 28 y 31. Villalba.

Agosto.—2. Villalba. 4 y 5. Villalba. 19 á 31. Osorio.

Septiembre.—2 á 30. Osorio.

Octubre.—2 á 30. Osorio.

Noviembre.—1 á 25. Osorio. 26 á 30. Cisneros.

Diciembre.—1° Cisneros. 2. Osorio. 3. Cisneros. 4 y 5. Cisneros. 6 y 7. Melchor de Leon. 8 á 15. Cisneros y Leon. 17. Cisneros y Osorio. 18 y 19. Leon y Cisneros. 20. Cisneros. 21. Leon y Cisneros. Trabajo tambien un *volador*. 23. Cisneros y Leon. 25. Cisneros. 26 y 27. Cisneros y Leon. 28. Leon. Hubo comedia en casa de Gonzalo de Monzon. 30. Cisneros y Leon.

Total de ingresos en el año 1590: 1,840,613 maravedís. Gastos: igual cantidad. (*Archivo de la Diputacion. Manual del Hospital general*, II, 158, 8.)

1601

Enero.—1° Gaspar de Porres y Baltasar Pinedo. 3 á 24. Porres y Pinedo. 25 y 26. Pinedo. 28, 30 y 31. Porres y Pinedo.

Febrero.—1° Porres y Diego Lopez de Alcaraz. 2. Porres y Pinedo. 3. Alcaraz. 4. Porres y Pinedo. 5 á 8. Porres y Alcaraz. 9. Pinedo y Alcaraz. 10. Porres y Pinedo. 11. Pinedo y Alcaraz. 13 á 16. Porres y Alcaraz. 17 y 18. Porres y Pinedo. 19. Porres y Alcaraz. 20. Porres y Pinedo. 21. Porres y Alcaraz. 22. Porres y Pinedo. 23 á 25. Pinedo y Alcaraz. 26 y 27. Porres y Pinedo. 28. Alcaraz y Pinedo.

Marzo.—1° Porres y Pinedo. 2. Porres y Alcaraz. 3. Pinedo y Alcaraz. 4. Porres y Pinedo. 5. Porres y Alcaraz. 6. Pinedo y Alcaraz.

Abril.—29 á 30. Gaspar de Porres.

Mayo.—1° á 7. Gaspar de Porres. 9. Pedro Jiménez de Valenzuela. 10 y 11. Porres y Gabriel Vaca. 12. Porres. 13 á 15. Porres y Vaca. 16. Vaca. 18. Porres. 19 á 22. Porres y Vaca. 23 á 31. Porres.

Junio.—3 á 17. Gaspar de Porres. 22. Porres (Autos en el teatro). 23 y 24. Autos á los semaneros en el teatro.

Julio.—12, 13, 18 y 22. Gabriel de la Torre. 23 y 30. Antonio de Villegas.

Agosto.—3 á 31. Villegas.

Septiembre.—3 á 30. Villegas.

Octubre.—2 á 18. Villegas. 19. Los *Franceses*. 20 y 21. Villegas. 26, 27 y 28. Gabriel de la Torre.

Noviembre.—2 á 13. Gabriel de la Torre. 14 á 23. Gabriel Vaca y Pedro Jiménez de Valenzuela [these two *autores* managed a company in partnership].

Diciembre.—2 á 18. Vaca y Jiménez de Valenzuela. 21 á 31. Villegas. (*Archivo de la Diputacion. Manual del Hospital general*, II, 158, 8.)

1602

Enero.—4 á 29. Jerónimo Lopez.

Abril.—8 y 9. Pedro Jiménez de Valenzuela.

Mayo.—3. Pedro Jiménez de Valenzuela. 23, 24. Los *Españoles* [this company was formed by Pedro Rodriguez, Diego de Rojas, and Gaspar de los Reyes]. 26 á 28. Pedro Jiménez de Valenzuela.

Junio.—16 y 18. Los *Españoles*.

Agosto.—11 á 30. Villegas.

Septiembre.—3 á 30. Villegas.

Octubre.—1 á 9. Villegas. 31. Villegas.

Noviembre.—1 á 7. Antonio Granados. 8. Gabriel de la Torre. 10 á 27. Granados.

Diciembre.—4 á 29. Juan de Morales. (*Archivo de la Diputacion. Manual del Hospital general*, II, 198, 8.)

APPENDIX B

1574   Jerónimo Velazquez represented three *autos* at the Corpus festival of this year.

1578   Alonso de Cisneros, three *autos*.

1579   Mateo de Salcedo.

1580   Alonso de Cisneros.

1581   Jerónimo Velazquez.

1582   Alonso de Cisneros and Jerónimo Velazquez.

1585   Gaspar de Porres, three *autos*.

1586   Jerónimo Velazquez represented three *autos*.

1587   Nicolas de los Rios, Miguel Ramirez, and Juan de Alcozer.

1589   Jerónimo Velazquez, three *autos*.

1590   Nicolas de los Rios and Alonso de Cisneros.

1591   Alonso de Cisneros.

1592   Gaspar de Porres and Rodrigo de Saavedra, each two *autos*.

1593   Alonso de Cisneros and Gaspar de Porres.

1594   Jerónimo Velazquez, two *autos*.

1595   Alonso de Cisneros and Antonio de Villegas. [Porres?]

1596   Nicolas de los Rios and Antonio de Villegas, each two *autos*.

1597   Nicolas de los Rios.

1598   Antonio de Villegas and Diego Lopez de Alcaraz.

1599   Gaspar de Porres (two *autos*); Diego Lopez de Alcaraz and Luis de Vergara, each an *auto*.

1600   Melchor de Villalba and Gabriel de la Torre, each two *autos*.

1602   Pedro Jimenez de Valenzuela.

1603   Juan de Morales Medrano.

1604   Gaspar de Porres.

1605 Gaspar de Porres. In this year only two *autos* were represented, both by Porres. For these he received 3700 reals. (*Bull Hisp.* (1907), p. 372.)

1606 Baltasar Pinedo and Juan de Morales Medrano.

1607 Baltasar Pinedo and Nicolas de los Rios.

1608 Alonso Riquelme and Juan de Morales Medrano.

1609 Alonso de Heredia and Domingo Balbin.

1610 Alonso Riquelme and Hernan Sanchez de Vargas.

1611 Hernan Sanchez de Vargas and Tomas Fernandez de Cabredo.

1612 Juan de Morales Medrano and Tomas Fernandez de Cabredo.

1613 Alonso de Riquelme and Antonio de Villegas.

1614 Juan de Morales Medrano and Baltasar Pinedo. (*Bull. Hisp.* (1907), p. 379.)

1615 Hernan Sanchez de Vargas and Pedro de Valdes.

1616 Pedro Cebrian and Pedro Cerezo de Guevara. In Paz y Melia, *Catálogo,* No. 1641, we read that Alonso de Riquelme represented Lope's *auto La Isla del Sol* in this year.

1617 Cristóbal de Leon and Baltasar Pinedo.

1618 Baltasar Pinedo and Hernan Sanchez de Vargas.

1619 Baltasar Pinedo and Hernan Sanchez de Vargas.

1620 Alonso de Olmedo and Cristobal de Avendaño.

1621 Pedro de Valdes and Cristobal de Avendaño. (*Bull. Hisp.* (1908), p. 244.)

1622 Manuel Vallejo.

1623 Juan de Morales Medrano and Antonio de Prado.

1624 Juan de Morales Medrano and Antonio de Prado.

1625 Andrés de la Vega, Tomas Fernandez de Cabredo, and Juan de Morales Medrano. In this year each *autor* represented one *auto* and a part of the fourth *auto.* (*Bull. Hisp.* (1908), p. 252.)

1626 Cristobal de Avendaño and Andrés de la Vega.

1627 Roque de Figueroa and Andrés de la Vega.

1628 Andrés de la Vega and Bartolomé Romero.

1629 Bartolomé Romero and Roque de Figueroa.

1630 Andrés de la Vega and Roque de Figueroa.

1632 Manuel Vallejo and Francisco Lopez.

1633 Antonio de Prado and Manuel Vallejo.
1637 Pedro de la Rosa and Tomas Fernandez de Cabredo.
1638 Bartolomé Romero (two *autos*) and Antonio de Rueda and
       Pedro Ascanio (each one).
1639 Antonio de Rueda and Manuel Vallejo.
1640 Bartolomé Romero.

APPENDIX C

___

CASTS OF COMEDIAS

The following casts of comedias of the seventeenth century have been collected from various sources, the most of them from manuscripts in the Biblioteca Nacional. They are arranged in chronological order.

La bella Ester (1610)

Lope de Vega. Autog. MS. in British Museum, dated at Madrid, April 5, 1610. This comedia was afterward published in Part XV of Lope's *Comedias* under the title *La hermosa Ester*.

Bassan .... Morales
Egeo .... Vicente
Tarses .... Torres
Marsanes .... Carrillo
Adamasa .... Fuentes
Setar .... Morales
El Rey Assuero .... Sanchez
Un Capitan .... Carrillo
Mardoqueo .... Toledo
La Reyna Vasti ....
Ester .... Sª Polonia
Selvagio .... Vicente
Sirena, *labradora* .... Clara
Musica .... Villaverde
Aman .... Rosales

In Act III the part of Marsanes is assigned to Antonio. This is the company of Hernan Sanchez de Vargas.

La buena Guarda ó la Encomienda bien guardada (1610)

Lope de Vega. Autog. MS. dated at Madrid, April 16, 1610, formerly in the possession of the Marquis Pidal.

Personas del P⁰ Acto:

Leonarda .... Catalina [de Valcázar]
Doña Luisa .... Mariana [de Herbias?]
Un Escudero .... [Martin de?] Vivar
Don Juan .... Luis
Don Luis .... [Pedro de] España
El hermano Carrizo, *sacristan* .... [Diego Lopez] Basurto
Felix, *mayordomo* .... [Alonso de] Olmedo
Doña Clara .... Maria de Argüello
Doña Elena .... Catalina
Don Pedro, *su padre* .... [Luis de] Quiñones
Ricardo, *viejo* .... España
Don Carlos .... Benito [de Castro]
Musicos ....

Hablan en el Segundo Acto:

Felix .... [Alonso de] Olmedo
Carrizo .... [Diego Lopez] Basurto
Doña Clara .... Maria de Argüello
Un Angel .... Mariana
Una Voz .... Catalina Valcacer
Portera ....
Don Carlos .... Benito [de Castro]
Ginés .... [Agustin] Coronel
Carrizo, *fingido* .... Vivar
Un pastor .... [Alonso de] Riquelme
Un huesped .... [Pedro de] Callenueva

Hablan en el 3⁰ Acto:

Carrizo .... Basurto
Felix .... Olmedo
Tres bandoleros .... Coronel, España, Callenueva

Liseno
Cosme } *villanos* .... Argüello
.... Luis

Dos damas...................................... { Catalina
Jerónima

Dos galanes .... { España
Luis

Dos musicos ....

Dos nadadores............................... { Vivar
Callenueva

Don Carlos .... Benito
Un pastor .... Riquelme
Un Angel .... Mariana
Don Pedro .... Quiñones
Ginés .... Coronel
La hortelana .... Jerónima
La portera .... Catalina
Carrizo, *fingido* .... Vivar
Un platero .... Callenueva

This is the company of Alonso Riquelme. *Comedias escogidas de Lope de Vega,* ed. Hartzenbusch (*Bibl. de Aut. Esp.*), Vol. III, p. 326.

La Discordia en los Casados (1611)

Lope de Vega. Autog. MS. (Osuna) dated at Madrid, August 2, 1611, with licenses to 1618. Paz y Melia, *Catálogo,* No. 933.

Alberto .... Arellano. Soria
Aurelio .... Quiñones
Musico .... Quiñones

Personas del 3º Acto:

Cenardo .... Arellano. Soria
Panfilo .... Herrera

El Bastardo Mudarra (1612)

Lope de Vega. Autog. MS. signed at Madrid, April 27, 1612, formerly in the possession of Sr. Olózaga. I have an excellent photo-zincograph of it, published in 1886.

Personas del P⁰ Acto:

Doña Alanbra .... Ana Maria
Gonzalo Bustos .... Cintor
Rui Velazquez .... Benito
Gonzalo Gonzalez .... Cintorico

The remaining characters are unassigned. The MS. contains licenses to represent dated Madrid, May 17, 1612; Çaragoça, January 29, 1613, and Antequera, May 13, 1616, and in 1617.

La Dama boba (1613)

Lope de Vega. Autog. MS. (Osuna) dated at Madrid, April 28, 1613. Paz y Melia, *Catálogo,* No. 810.

Liseo, *caballero* .... Ortiz [de Villazan]
Leandro, *caballero* .... Almonte
Turin, *lacayo* .... [Baltasar de?] Carvajal
Octavio, *viejo* .... [Luis de] Quiñones
Miseno, *su amigo* .... [Juan de] Villanueva
Duardo .... Guebara
Laurencio .... Benito [de Castro]
Feniso, *caballero* .... [Manuel] Simon
Rufino, *maestro* .... [Pedro] Aguado
Nise, *dama* .... Jeronima [de Burgos]
Finea, *su hermana* .... Maria [de los Angeles?]
Celia, *criada* .... Isabel [Rodriguez?]
Clara, *criada* .... Ana Maria [de Ribero]

This is the company of Pedro de Valdes. Perhaps the "Isabel" is Isabel de Velasco, who married Luis Quiñones in 1614.

La Tercera de la Sancta Juana (1614)

Tirso de Molina. Autog. MS. inedited [since published by Sr. Cotarelo], dated at Toledo, August 6, 1614. *Catálogo,* No. 3035. I have a copy of this MS. made years ago. The cast is in Tirso's hand. It was represented, apparently, by two companies. The characters of the play are in the middle column:

Bernardo . . . . Don Luis . . . . [Luis de] Toledo
[Iñigo de] Loaisa . . . . Çesar . . . . [Juan de] Montemayor
Diego . . . . Don Diego, *viejo* . . . . Cristobal
Nauarete . . . . Lillo . . . . . . [Antonio de] Sanpayo
                                   Xρo. nr̄o Sr. . . . . Montemayor
Mᵃ . . . . La Sancta . . . . Mᵃ de Morales
Lorenzo . . . . S. Laruel . . . . Antᵒ de Prado
Ana Mᵃ . . . . Aldonça . La Sᵃ Petronila[de Loaysa]
                                   Peynado, *pastor* . . . . [Pedro] Aguado
Isabel . . . . Doña Ines
                                   La Sᵃ Ana Maria[de Ulloa?]
Montemayor . . . . Crespo, *pastor* . . . . Aguado
                                   Mingo, *pastor* . . [Cristobal de] S. Pedro
                                   Berrueco *pastor* . . . . Juan Ximenez

2º Acto. Personas:

Don Luis . . . . Toledo
Aldonça . . . . la Sʳᵃ Petronila
Don Diego . . . . S. Pedro
Lillo . . . . Sanpayo
D. Jorge . . . . Xρōbal
Maria, *monja* . . . . la Sʳᵃ Anna Maria
Doña Ines . . . . la dicha
Çesar . . . . Montemayor
Nr̄a Señora . . . . la Sʳᵃ Petronila
El niño Jesus . . . . Sanpaico
El Angel . . . . Antonio del Prado

3º Acto. Personas de el:

D. Diego . . . . Alonso fre. [Alonso Fernandez de Guardo?]
D. Luis . . . . Toledo

Lillo .... Sanpayo. Guardia
Crespo .... Aguado
Berrueco .... Ju⁰ Ximenez
Mingo .... S. P⁰ [i.e. San Pedro]
Çesar .... Mᵗᵉmayor
Doña Ynes .... Ana Cabello
La Santa .... Mᵃ de Morales
El Angel .... Antonio de Prado. Juan de Madrid
Nuestra Señora .... la Sᵃ Petronila [de Loaysa]
Jesus Niño .... Sanpaico
Maria, *monja* .... la Sᵃ Ana Maria
Otra monja .... la Sᵃ Madalena [de Oviedo]
Una niña .... Sanpaico
Un Alma .... Ju⁰ Ximenez

En Toledo, a 24 de Agosto de 1614 años.

El Sembrar en buena Tierra (1616)

Lope de Vega. Autog. MS. in British Museum, dated Madrid, January 6, 1616. It contains a license to perform, signed by Tomas Gracian Dantisco on January 12, 1616.

Personas del P⁰ Acto:

Don Felix .... [Cristóbal] Ortiz [de Villazan]
Florencio .... Benito
Galindo, *criado* .... Sanchez
Doña Prudencia .... Eugenia [de Villegas?]
Ynes ....
Celia .... Luçia
Elena ....
Fabio .... [Francisco Muñoz de la] Plaza
Felino .... [Antonio] Ramos
Don Alonso .... [Juan de] Valdivieso
Lizardo .... Herrera
Liseo .... Escruela[?]
Fidelio .... Rā

Personas del 2º Acto:

Arseno .... Ceruela
Otavio .... Ramon
Un escriuano .... Ramos
Un alguacil .... Plaza

The other characters are unassigned.

3º Acto:

Florencio .... Benito

The name of one of these actors once appears as Escruela, then as Ceruela. This name is otherwise unknown. Escoriguela was a well-known player.

Quien mas no puede (1616)

Lope de Vega. Autog. MS. dated at Madrid, September 1, 1616, in the possession of Mr. John Murray.

Personas del Pº Acto:

Ramiro, *Rey de Nauarra* .... Zancado
Don Beltran, *criado suyo* .... Bernardino
El Conde Henrriq̄ .... Xρōbal
Nuño, *criado del Conde* .... Ossorio
Doña Eluira, *ynfanta* .... Ana
Lucinda, *donzella suya* .... Francisca
Ordoño, *Rey de Leon* .... Pº Zebrian
Laynez, *criado del Rey* .... Cuebas
Yñigo, *criado del Conde* .... el q̄ bayla, Alº
Doña Blanca, *hermᵃ del Conde* .... Maritardia

Personas del 2º Acto:

Doña Blanca ....
Don Yñigo ....
Celio .... Antonio
Laynez ....
Don Sancho .... Cuebas

Don Arias .... Antonio
Lisis .... Francisca o Ana Muñoz
Riselo .... o Cuebas o Bernardino
Menandro Villanas .... el q̄ bayle q̄ no se el nonbre

Luzinda, El Conde Henrriq̄, Doña. Eluira, Nuño, Rey Ramiro, Don Beltran, unassigned. In the third act only one character is assigned: Estela to Francisca.

Las Paredes oyen· (1617)

Juan Ruiz de Alarcon. D. Luis Fernandez Guerra, *D. Juan Ruiz de Alarcon,* Madrid, 1871, p. 257, says that the MS., apparently an autograph, is preserved in the Osuna library. But between this date and 1882, when Rocamora published his Catalogue of the Osuna manuscripts, it must have disappeared, for it is not mentioned by Rocamora and never passed into the possession of the Biblioteca Nacional. See *ibid.,* p. 497.

Celia .... Dorotea [de Sierra]
D. Juan .... [Damian] Arias
Beltran .... Pedro de Villegas
Doña Ana .... Maria de Cordoba
Ortiz .... Frasquito
D. Mendo .... [Luis Bernardo de] Bobadilla
Lucrecia .... Maria de Vitoria
Conde .... Azua
Duque .... [Gabriel] Cintor
Escudero ....
Marcelo ....
Leonido .... Francisco de Robles
Un arriero .... Bernardino [Alvarez?]
Una musica .... Maria de Vitoria
Otro musico .... [Juan] Mazana
Otro musico .... Navarrete

La Guarda cuidadosa

Miguel Sanchez, *el Divino.* The comedia was first printed at Alcalá in 1615. The manuscript from which the following cast is taken, and which was formerly in the Osuna collection, is now in the Biblioteca Nacional. Paz y Melia, *Catálogo*, No. 1431. It is of the early seventeenth century. See *La Isla barbara* and *La Guarda cuidadosa*, two comedies by Miguel Sanchez (*el Divino*), ed. by H. A. Rennert, Boston and Halle, 1896.

Trebacio .... Lorenzo [Hurtado?]
Leucato .... Diego
Príncipe .... [Juan de] Montemayor
Roberto .... [Iñigo de] Loaysa
Nisea .... Maria [de Jesus? de Vitoria?]
Arsinda .... Ana Maria [de Ulloa?]
Florela, *labradora* .... Isabelica
Ariadeno .... Navarrete
Fileno .... Miñano
Florencio .... Bernardo

In a MS. comedia of the beginning of the seventeenth century, *Como a de usarse del Bien y a de preuenirse el Mal,* existing in the Biblioteca Palatina at Parma and described by Professor Restori in *Studj di Filologia Romanza,* fasc. 15, Roma, 1891, p. 129, occur the names of the following players: Sotomayor, Olmedo(?), Isabelica, Naba[rrete], La Sª Bernarda, Tapia, Perez, and Loaysa. This comedia, which was afterward published (Halle, 1899) by Professor Restori with the title:

Los Guzmanes de Toral,

was written by Lope de Vega, and, as the title occurs in the first list of his *Peregrino en su Patria,* is prior to 1604. The third act is in Lope's hand and has the following cast:

Rey Don Alfonso .... Sotomayor
Doña Greida .... Mª
Don Payo .... Obredo [Olmedo?]
Doña Aldonza .... Isabelica
Tirso .... Trebiño
Godinez, *lacayo* .... Naba[rrete]
Urgel .... Diego
Alvaro .... Olmedo

Pascuala .... la Sª Bernarda
Doña Ana de Haro .... Isabel bª
Don Garcia ....
Don Lope Diaz de Haro .... Diego
Sancho Manrique .... Diego
Verveco .... Tapia
Mireno .... Juanico
Soldado 1° .... Tapia
Soldado 2° .... Juanico
Soldado 3° .... Perez
Alonso Ansurez .... Loaisa

El Desden vengado (1617)

Lope de Vega. Autog. MS. signed at Madrid, August 4, 1617, formerly in the Osuna library, now in the Biblioteca Nacional. Paz y Melia, *Catálogo*, No. 871.

El Conde Lucindo .... Fadrique
Tomin, *criado* .... [Agustin] Coronel
Feniso .... Juan Jeronimo [Valenciano]
Roberto, *caballero* .... Juan de Vargas
Leonardo .... Cosme
Rugero, *Rey de Napoles* .... Juan Bautista [Valenciano]
Lisena, *dama* .... Dª Maria [Coronel?]
Celia, *dama* .... Manuela [Enriquez]
Evandro, *su padre* ....
Ynarda, *criada* .... Vincenta [de Borja?]

Schack, *Nachträge,.* p. 46. This is probably the company of Juan Bautista Valenciano.

El Martir de Madrid (1619)

Mira de Amescua. Partly autograph, with a license to perform dated 1619. Paz y Melia, *Catálogo*, No. 2029. There are other licenses as late as 1641.

Alvaro Ramirez .... Jusepe
D. Fernando .... Lorenzo [Hurtado] el autor

La infelice Dorotea (1620)

Andres de Claramonte wrote it for Juan Bautista Valenciano. Sanchez-Arjona, *Anales del Teatro en Sevilla*, p. 214. MS. copy in the Biblioteca Nacional. Paz y Melia, *Catálogo*, No. 1594.

D. Garcinuñez .... Fadrique
El Rey .... Juan Jerónimo [Valenciano]
D. Fernando .... Juan Bautista [Valenciano]
Nuño de Lemos .... Andres [de Claramonte?]
Arnao .... [Agustin] Coronel
Solano .... Miguel
Layn .... [Cristobal de?] Avendaño
Mendo .... Jusepe
Teodora .... Sª Maria [Candau?]
Dorotea .... Sª Manuela [Enriquez]
Leonor .... Sʳᵃ Maria de los Angeles
D. Juan .... Manuel de Coca

Amor, Pleito y Desafio (1621)

Lope de Vega. Autog. MS. dated at Madrid, November 23, 1621, with a license of January 14, 1622. Formerly in the Durán collection and now in the Biblioteca Nacional. *Catálogo*, No. 171.

D. Alvaro de Rojas .... [Pedro] Maldonado
D. Juan de Padilla .... Lorenzo Hurtado
D. Juan de Aragon .... Francisco Triviño
El Rey Alfonso .... Juan Bautista [Valenciano]
Doña Beatriz .... la Señora Angela [de Toledo?]
Dª Ana .... la Sʳᵃ Francisca de Soria(?)
Martin, *escudero* .... Antonio Rodriguez
Tello, *criado* .... Vicente
Sancho, *criado* .... Pedro de Valdes
Leonor .... la Señora Jeronima [de Burgos]

La nueva Victoria de D. Gonzalo de Cordoba (1622)

Lope de Vega. Autog. MS. in the Biblioteca Nacional, dated at Madrid, October 8, 1622. *Catálogo,* No. 2409.

Lisarda, *dama* .... la S^{ra} Manuela [Enriquez]
Fulgencia, *criada* .... S^{ra} Ana
D. Juan Ramirez .... Fadrique
Bernabé, *lacayo* .... [Agustin] Coronel
El Capitan Medrano .... Cosme
Estevan, *criado* .... Jusepe
El Bastardo .... Juan Jeronimo [Valenciano]
El Obispo de Holstad .... [Juan de] Vargas
El Duque de Bullon .... Jusepe
D. Gonzalo de Cordoba .... Juan Bautista [Valenciano]
D. Francisco de Harras .... Manuel
El Baron de Tili .... Naruaez
Musico .... [Manuel] Simon

El Poder en el Discreto (1623)

Lope de Vega. Autog. MS. in the Biblioteca Nacional, dated at Madrid, May 8, 1623. Paz y Melia, *Catálogo,* No. 2649. There are two casts given in the MS.

Serafina, *dama* .... Maria Calderon ...... Josefa [Vaca?]
Rosela, *criada* .... Dª Isabel ....
Teodosio, *Rey de Sicilia* ... Lezcano .... Bracamonte
Celio, *de su camara* .... Morales .... Arias
Alejo, *criado de Celio* ...... Castro .... Triviño
El Conde de Augusta ...... Suarez .... Morales
Flora, *dama* .... Mariana [Vaca] ..... Mariana [Vaca]

The MS. contains a license dated 1624, and the company on the right was in all probability that of Juan de Morales Medrano, in which both his wife and his daughter Mariana appeared. My copy gives the name "Bracamonte," not Vacamonte.

Celos con Celos se curan (1625)

Tirso de Molina. MS. copy, formerly in the Osuna collection, now in the Biblioteca Nacional. Paz y Melia, *Cátalogo,* No. 563. It contains licenses dated 1625. There are two casts:

Çesar .... [Cristobal] de Avendaño .... Gutierrez
Carlos .... Viera .... Segobia
Gascon .... Bernardo .... Matias
Sirena .... Maria de Montesinos .. Juana de los Reyes
Diana .... Catalina Moreno .... Ines
Marco Antonio .... Lezcano .... Francisco Alonso
Alejandro .... [?] .... Juan Alonso
Narcisa .... Mª Candáu .... Luisa
Un grande chico ...... [Balt.] Moreno .... [?]
Un jardinero .... Ordoñez .... Marcos

The first of these companies seems to be that of Cristóbal de Avendaño about the year 1632.

El Brasil restituido (1625)

Lope de Vega. Autog. MS. dated at Madrid, October 23, 1625, now in the Lenox Library, New York.

Personas del Pº Acto:

Doña Guiomar .... Mª de Vitoria
Don Diego .... [Gabriel?] Cintor
Bernardo .... Bernardino [Alvarez?]
Laurencio .... [Juan] Antonio
Leonardo .... [Luis Bernardo de] Bobadilla
El Coronel de Olanda .... Arias con barba Françesa
Alberto, *su hijo* .... El Spir santo del Auto
El Gobernador .... El Autor
Machado .... Pedro [de Villegas?]
La Monarquia de España ....
Ongol ....
Darin ....
Soldados ....
El Brasil .... Maria de Cordoba

Personas del 2º Acto:

La religion Catolica .... Dorotea [de Sierra]
El Brasil .... La Autora
D. Manuel de Meneses .... Musico
D. Fadrique de Toledo .... Arias
Leonardo .... Bobadilla
Machado .... Pedro
Dª Guiomar .... Mª de Vitoria
D. Juan de Orellana .... [Juan] Mazana
D. Diego Ramirez ....
El Coronel electo .... Bernardino
Don Enrique de Alagon .... Cintor
Don Diego de Espinosa .... Antonio
Don Pedro de Santisteban .... frᶜᵒ de rro [Francisco de Robles?]
Apolo .... Arias
La heregia .... Mª de Vitoria
Un soldado .... el niño

This is probably the company of Andres de la Vega. See my
article in the *Mod. Lang. Review* for January, 1906, p. 108.

El piadoso Aragones (1626)

Lope de Vega. Autog. MS. dated at Madrid, August 17, 1626,
now in the Biblioteca Nacional. Paz y Melia, *Catálogo,* No. 2607.
Licenses of Madrid, September 15, 1626; Zaragoza, 1627, and Lisbon, 1631.

Almirante .... Vicente
D. Bernardo .... [Pedro?] Jordan
D. Pedro Agramonte .... Quadrado
Alcalde .... Lorenzo

These names are crossed out, and the following are added:

D. Pedro Agramonte .... Felipe
Bernardo .... Jordan
Raymundo de Luna .... Mateo
Mendoza .... Tapia

Musico .... Leon
D. Juan de Beamonte .... Max°

El Favor en la Sentencia (1626)

Jacinto Cordeiro. Autog. MS. in the Biblioteca Nacional. Paz
y Melia, *Catálogo,* No. 1242. Written for Bartolomé Romero.

Porcia .... la Autora [Antonia Manuela Catalan]
Arminda .... Dorotea
Rey .... Estrada[?]
El Principe .... [Gabriel] Zintor
Conde .... [Alonso de] Osuna
Rosando .... Autor [Bartolome Romero]
Dª Linda .... Micaela
Gascon .... Tomas [Enriquez?]

Sanchez-Arjona, *Anales,* p. 272.

Amor con vista (1626)

Lope de Vega. Autog. MS. signed at Madrid on December 10,
1626. Licenses to perform in Madrid, of 1627, and in Lisbon,
1630. In the Biblioteca Nacional. Paz y Melia, *Catálogo,* No.
149.
El Conde Otabio .... Autor [Antonio de Prado]
Tome, *criado suyo* .... [Luis Bernardo de] Bobadilla
Celia .... Mª de Calderon [this is crossed out] Vitoria
Lisena .... Autora [Mariana Vaca de Morales]

2° Acto:
Julio .... Jeronimo

Sin Secreto no ay Amor (1626)

Lope de Vega. Autog. MS. signed at Madrid, July 18, 1626,
with licenses to perform of Madrid, August 2, 1626; Zaragoza,
October 13, 1626, and Granada, April 28, 1630. British Museum.
Published by me, Baltimore, 1894 (Mod. Lang. Assoc.).
Celio .... Tapia
Fabricio .... Jeronimo

Del Monte sale quien el Monte quema (1627)

Lope de Vega. Autog. MS. signed at Madrid, October 20, 1627. Licenses of Madrid, May 17, 1628; Valencia, September 28, 1628; Granada, October 1, 1636. In the Biblioteca Nacional. *Catálogo*, No. 848.

El Conde Henrrique	Arias
Feliciano	Jusepe
Narcisa, *labradora*	Sra Maria de Heredia
Tirso, *villano*	Heredia
Juana, *labradora*	Sra Catalina [de Medina?]
Celia, *dama*	Sra Ana Maria [de Ulloa?]
Clara, *criada*	Sra Francisca
El Rey de Francia	[Francisco de] Salas
Mauricio, *Gobernador*	[Juan de] Montemayor
El Marques Roselo	Sr Marcos. Rueda
Leonelo, *Capitan*	Alvarez

The names Valdes, Mencos, and Francisca also occur.

La Conpetencia en los Nobles (1628?)

Lope de Vega. MS. in the British Museum with corrections supposed to be in the hand of Lope.

Acto 2°:

D. Juan	[Juan] Antonio
D. Pedro	[Manuel] Simon
Hernando	Autor
Guzman	Canobas
Don Luis	Damian [Arias?]
Don Diego	Luis de Salaçar
El Rey	Nabarrete
Beltran	Saçedo
Doña Juana	Ana de Moya
Doña Maria	Catalina [de Peralta?]
Leonor	su muger de Nabarrete
Toreadores	Marcos y Grajales

According to the *suelta* of this comedia, it was first represented by Tomas Fernandez. It was in the repertory of the companies of Rueda and Ascanio in 1638–40. See Rosell, *Entremeses de Benavente,* Vol. I, p. 377.

La gran Columna fogosa (1629?)

Lope de Vega. MS. copy in Biblioteca Nacional. Paz y Melia, *Catálogo,* No. 1412. The MS. contains original licenses dated at Plasencia, 1629.

El Enperador Valente, *ereje* .... Al° Gomez
Pretoriano, *ereje* .... P° Gonçalez
Agustulo, *ereje* .... Dominguez
Posidonio, *ereje* ....Domingo Hernandez
San Basio, *Obispo* .... Fernando Lopez
Eraclio, *cauallero biejo* .... Gaspar Serrano
Antonia, *hija de Eraclio* .... Antonio
Sabina, *criada de Ant^a* .... Martin
Patricio .... P° de Bonilla
Un encantador .... Diego Lopez
Satan .... Juan Martinez
Otro demonio .... Diego Lopez
Emerencio, *biejo* .... Diego Lopez
Leonicio, *criado* .... Juan Martinez
Fulbino, *criado* .... Domingo Hernandez
Telemarco .... Francisco Rodriguez
Decio, *criado* .... Luis
Un hebreo .... Dominguez

El Castigo sin Venganza (1631)

Lope de Vega. Autog. MS. dated at Madrid, August 1, 1631, in the Ticknor Library, Boston. See my article, "Ueber Lope de Vega's *El Castigo sin Venganza*," in *Zeitschrift für Rom. Phil.,* 1901, p. 411.

El Duque de Ferrara .... Autor [Manuel Vallejo]
El Conde Federico .... Arias
Albano ....
Rutilio ....
Floro ....
Luzindo ....

El Marques Gonzaga .... [Francisco de] Salas
Casandra .... Autora [Maria de Riquelme]
Aurora .... Ber[nar]da
Lucrezia .... Geronima [de Valcázar]
Batin .... [Pedro Garcia] Salinas
Cintia .... Maria de Ceballos
Febo y Ricardo ....

The Bernarda mentioned above is probably Bernarda Ramirez de Robles.

Peligrar en los Remedios (1634)

D. Francisco de Rojas Zorrilla. MS. partly autog. in Biblioteca Nacional. Paz y Melia, *Catálogo*, No. 2552. At the end, in the hand of Rojas: "Finished on Saturday, December 9, 1634, for Roque de Figueroa."

La Duquesa Violante .... la Señora Isabel [Blanco?]
Celia, *criada* .... Bernarda [Ramirez?]
Bojeton, *criado* .... [Francisco] Tribiño
Conde Federico .... [Manuel] Coca
El Almirante de Sicilia .... Paz
El Marques Alberto, *privado* .... Roque [de Figueroa]
El Rey de Napoles Sigismundo .... Francisco de la Calle
Carlos, *su hermano* .... Jacinto Varela
Infanta de Sicilia .... Maria de San Pedro
Duque Conrado .... Bargas

La Desdicha de la Voz (1639)

Calderon. Autog. MS. dated at Madrid, May 14, 1639, with licenses of June 1 and November 3, 1639. In the Biblioteca Nacional. Paz y Melia, *Catálogo*, No. 873.

Don Juan .... Pedro Manuel de Castilla
Don Pedro .... el Autor [Antonio de Rueda]
Don Diego .... [Diego de] Leon
Don Luis, *viejo* .... Jusepe [de Carrion]
Feliciano .... Pedro [Ascanio]

Luquete .... [Diego] Ossorio
Dª Beatriz .... Ma. de [Heredia]

Schack, *Nachträge,* p. 87. This is the company of Antonio de Rueda.

A un tiempo Rey y Vasallo (1642)

Comedia de Luis de Belmonte Bermúdez, del Dr. Manuel Antonio de Vargas y de D. . . . MS. of the first act in the hand of Vargas and nearly the whole third act in the hand of Belmonte. See Paz y Melia, *Catálogo,* No. 19. The author of the second act is probably Geronimo Cancer; v. Stiefel, in *Ztft. für Roman. Philol., XXXII,* p. 486; Sanchez-Arjona, *Anales,* p. 295.

Rey de Sicilia .... Iñigo
Duque de Calabria .... Francisco Garcia
Almirante .... Mejia
La Infanta Beatriz .... la Sʳᵃ Maria de Jesus
Belisarda, *labradora* .... Jusepa de Salazar
Silena .... Sʳᵃ Antonia de Santiago
Laura, *dama* .... Jusepa Roman
Pasquin, *gracioso* .... Bernardo
Julio, *criado* .... Salvador
Príncipe, 7 años .... Sʳᵃ Francisca Berdugo

This is the company of Pedro de la Rosa. This play was written for Juana de Espinosa, then (1642) the widow of Tomas Fernandez, and the manager of a company.

La belligera Española (?)

Pedro Juan de Rejaule y Toledo (who wrote under the pseudonym Ricardo de Turia). MS. copy in the Palatina at Parma, belonging to the early seventeenth century. The play was first printed in the *Norte de la Poesia española,* at Valencia, in 1616, a copy of which I possess. See A. Restori in *Studj di Filologia Romanza,* fasc. 15, Roma, 1891, p. 92.

Guacolda .... la Sʳᵃ Ana Maria
Dª Mencia .... la Sʳᵃ Juana [de Espinosa? or de Segura?]
D. Pedro .... Tomas Fernandez
Lantaro .... Aldana [Aldama?]

Rengo .... Simon Gutierrez
Valdiuia .... Pedro Maldonado
Laupí y Aluarado .... Villanueva
Rauco ...:... Lastra
Pillan y Bouadilla .... Barco
Gracolano y otro Indio moço .... Aranda

Paciencia en la Fortuna (?)

Anonymous. Copy of the first half of the seventeenth century in the Biblioteca Palatina at Parma. See Restori, *ibid.*, p. 143. The names of the actors are:

Luis de Estrada, Carlos, Juan Gonçalez, Pedro Perez, Cuebas, Nabarete, Berio, Belasco, Caçeres, Barionuebo, and Juan Mazana (added in a different hand).

Troya abrasada (1644)

Calderon. Autog. MS. in the Biblioteca Nacional, Madrid. Paz y Melia, *Catálogo*, No. 3371.

Paris .... Pedro Manuel
Hector .... Dª Veatriz
Priamo ....
Rey de Troya, *varba* .... Juan Matias
Casandra .... Maria Maçana
Elena ....Autora
Ismenia, *criada* .... Jusepa
Achiles .... Najara
Sinon .... Francisco Albarez
Menelao, *Rey de Esparta* .... Mexia
Agamemnon, *Rey de Atenas* .... Juan Antonio
Un criado de Ector ....
Viznaga .... Marin

ADDENDA ET CORRIGENDA

p. 7, n. 1.   On the *Auto Sacramental* (1520) of López de Yanguas, v. Cotarelo in *Revista de Archivos* (1902), pp. 251, ff.

p. 13.   Naharro is mentioned by Cueva in the third *Epistola* of his *Exemplar poetico:*

> "De fabula procede la comedia,
> Y en ella es la inuencion licenciosa,
> Cual vemos en Naharro y Heredia."
> (Sedano, *Parnaso Español,* VIII, p. 66.)

p. 71, n. 2.   *La Casa confusa* was represented by Pinedo's company on October 16, 1618, Baltasar Osorio and Maria Flores also taking part. (Barrera, *Catálogo,* p. 210.)

p. 122, l. 23.   Lope de Rueda concludes his *Colloquio de Camila* with the words: "Señores, perdonen, porque aqui se da fin á nuestro Colloquio," and his *Colloquio de Tymbria* with: "Señores, perdonen, que con bailar se dió fin á nuestro Colloquio." His comedia *Armelina* ends with a similar phrase, but the appeal to the audience as "El ilustre Senado," I do not remember to have seen in any dramatist before Lope de Vega.

p. 164, l. 5.   For Villahermoso read Vallehermoso.

p. 176, note, l. 2.   Strike out the words "years before," as the *Plaza universal* was published in 1615.

p. 177. To what is here said concerning the sums received by a dramatist for a comedia we may add that in 1634 eight hundred reals was paid for a comedia by Montalvan, and nine hundred for a comedia by Francisco de Rojas and Antonio Coello. (Pérez Pastor, *Bibliografia Madrileña*, III, pp. 452, 463.)

p. 232, n. To the playwrights mentioned may be added Antonio Coello, Antonio Solis, Geronimo de Cuellar, and Luis Velez de Guevara, who writes in 1633 that he is unable to leave his house for want of a garment to cover him. (Pérez Pastor, *Bibliografia Madrileña*, III, p. 512.)

p. 238, n. 1. The episode related by Hume, it may be remarked, was related by François van Aerssen, *Voyage d'Espagne*, Cologne, 1666, pp. 47–49, and repeated by Madame d'Aulnoy, who gives the Countess of Lemos as authority for her story. (*Relation du Voyage d'Espagne*, La Haye, 1693, Vol. II, p. 20.) It is, of course, indignantly rejected by Barrera, *Catálogo*, p. 483. It may not be amiss to add the following, concerning the comedia, also from Madame d'Aulnoy: "Autrefois, continua-t-il [D. Agustin Pacheco], les personnes vertueuses ne se pouvoient resoudre d'aller à la Comedie; on n'y voyait que des actions opposées à la modestie; on y entendoit des discours qui blessoient la liberté, les Acteurs faisoient honte aux gens de bien; on y flatoit le vice, on y condamnoit la Vertu; les combats ensanglantoient la Scene; le plus foible étoit toûjours opprimé par le plus fort, & l'usage autorisoit le crime: Mais depuis que Lopes (*sic*) de Vega a travaillé avec succez à reformer le Theâtre Espagnol, il ne s'y passe plus rien de contraire aux bonnes mœurs; & le Confident, le Valet, ou le Villageois, gardant leur simplicité naturelle, & la rendant agreable par un enjoüement naïf trouvent le secret de guerir nos Princes, & même nos Rois, de la maladie de ne point entendre les veritez où leurs défauts peuvent avoir part. C'est lui qui prescrivit des regles à ses éléves, & qui leur enseigna de faire des Comedies en trois Jornadas, qui veut dire en trois Actes. Nous avons vû depuis briller les Montalvanes, Mendozas, Rojas, Alarcones, Velez, Mira de Mescuas, Coellos, Villaizanes; mais enfin Don Pedro Calderon excella dans le serieux, & dans le comique, & il passa tous ceux qui l'avoient precedé." (*Relation du Voyage d'Espagne,* II, p. 98.)

p. 266. Among the early defenders of the comedia Andres Rey de Artieda might have been mentioned.

p. 339. In 1620 Sancho de Paz, *autor de comedias,* obtained a privilege from Cardinal Borgia to form a company of Spanish players in Naples; "and nobody else nor any other company may represent in Naples except he." (Croce, *I Teatri di Napoli,* p. 91.) In 1621 Francisco de Leon obtained a similar privilege, and in 1620 and 1621 Sancho de Paz and Francisco de Leon represented in the *Teatro dei Fiorentini.* (*Ibid.,* p. 92.) In 1630 and 1631 Francisco Malhelo and Gregorio Laredo had companies in Naples.

The Biblioteca Nacional also contains a MS. of Lope de Vega's *Quien todo lo quiere,* undated, new No. 16798. Paz y Melia, *Catálogo,* No. 2810, with the following cast:

don Juⁿ . . . . Pᵒ Mᵉ [Pedro Manuel de Castilla]
don fernando . . . . [Antonio de] Rueda
d. pᵒ leon. i.e. Don Pedro . . . . [Diego de] Leon

fabio ....

bernal .... osorio [Diego Osorio de Velasco]

octabia .... bisenta [Vicenta ......?]

julia .... Catalina [de Acosta]

Ines .... Antª [Antonia Infante]

Dª Ana .... Jasinta [Jacinta de Herbias y Flores]

Leonarda ....

This is the company of Antonio de Rueda, about 1639–40.

The following cast of an *entremes* of the sixteenth century I owe to the kindness of Dr. Crawford. It is entitled *Entremes de un Hijo que negó á su Padre,* manuscript of two leaves in folio in the Biblioteca Nacional, in a hand of the sixteenth century.

Padre del licenciado .... Gaspar de huerta

licenciado .... Christoual de castro

muger .... michael

amo .... alº robleño

villano .... torres

There is nothing in the manuscript to indicate the date of representation. The above cast is interesting, however, from the fact that the rôle of the woman (*muger*) is played by a man (michael), which is an evidence of the early representation of this *entremes*.

INDEX

LITERATURE

WORLD DRAMA, B. H. Clark. 46 plays from Ancient Greece, Rome, to India, China, Japan. Plays by Aeschylus, Sophocles, Euripides, Aristophanes, Plautus, Marlowe, Jonson, Farquhar, Goldsmith, Cervantes, Molière, Dumas, Goethe, Schiller, Ibsen, many others. One of the most comprehensive collections of important plays from all literature available in English. Over ⅓ of this material is unavailable in any other current edition. Reading lists. 2 volumes. Total of 1364pp. 5⅜ x 8. Vol. I, T57 Paperbound **$2.00**
Vol. II, T59 Paperbound **$2.00**

MASTERS OF THE DRAMA, John Gassner. The most comprehensive history of the drama in print. Covers more than 800 dramatists and over 2000 plays from the Greeks to modern Western, Near Eastern, Oriental drama. Plot summaries, theatre history, etc. "Best of its kind in English," NEW REPUBLIC. 35 pages of bibliography. 77 photos and drawings. Deluxe edition. xxii + 890pp. 5⅜ x 8. T100 Clothbound **$5.95**

THE DRAMA OF LUIGI PIRANDELLO, D. Vittorini. All 38 of Pirandello's plays (to 1935) summarized and analyzed in terms of symbolic techniques, plot structure, etc. The only authorized work. Foreword by Pirandello. Biography. Bibliography. xiii + 350pp. 5⅜ x 8.
T435 Paperbound **$1.98**

ARISTOTLE'S THEORY OF POETRY AND THE FINE ARTS, S. H. Butcher, ed. The celebrated "Butcher translation" faced page by page with the Greek text; Butcher's 300-page introduction to Greek poetic, dramatic thought. Modern Aristotelian criticism discussed by John Gassner. lxxvi + 421pp. 5⅜ x 8.
T42 Paperbound **$2.00**

EUGENE O'NEILL: THE MAN AND HIS PLAYS, B. H. Clark. The first published source-book on O'Neill's life and work. Analyzes each play from the early THE WEB up to THE ICEMAN COMETH. Supplies much information about environmental and dramatic influences. ix + 182pp. 5⅜ x 8. T379 Paperbound **$1.25**

INTRODUCTION TO ENGLISH LITERATURE, B. Dobrée, ed. Most compendious literary aid in its price range. Extensive, categorized bibliography (with entries up to 1949) of more than 5,000 poets, dramatists, novelists, as well as historians, philosophers, economists, religious writers, travellers, and scientists of literary stature. Information about manuscripts, important biographical data. Critical, historical, background works not simply listed, but evaluated. Each volume also contains a long introduction to the period it covers.

Vol. I: **THE BEGINNINGS OF ENGLISH LITERATURE TO SKELTON, 1509, W. L. Renwick. H. Orton.** 450pp. 5⅛ x 7⅛. T75 Clothbound **$3.50**
Vol. II: **THE ENGLISH RENAISSANCE, 1510-1688, V. de Sola Pinto.** 381pp. 5⅛ x 7⅛.
T76 Clothbound **$3.50**
Vol. III: **THE AUGUSTANS AND ROMANTICS, 1689-1830, H. Dyson, J. Butt.** 320pp. 5⅛ x 7⅛.
T77 Clothbound **$3.50**
Vol. IV: **THE VICTORIANS AND AFTER, 1830-1914, E. Batho, B. Dobrée.** 360pp. 5⅛ x 7⅛.
T78 Clothbound **$3.50**

EPIC AND ROMANCE, W. P. Ker. The standard survey of Medieval epic and romance by a foremost authority on Medieval literature. Covers historical background, plot, literary analysis, significance of Teutonic epics, Icelandic sagas, Beowulf, French chansons de geste, the Niebelungenlied, Arthurian romances, much more. 422pp. 5⅜ x 8. T355 Paperbound **$1.95**

THE HEART OF EMERSON'S JOURNALS, Bliss Perry, ed. Emerson's most intimate thoughts, impressions, records of conversations with Channing, Hawthorne, Thoreau, etc., carefully chosen from the 10 volumes of The Journals. "The essays do not reveal the power of Emerson's mind . . . as do these hasty and informal writings," N. Y. TIMES. Preface by B. Perry. 370pp. 5⅜ x 8. T447 Paperbound **$1.85**

A SOURCE BOOK IN THEATRICAL HISTORY, A. M. Nagler. (Formerly, "Sources of Theatrical History.") Over 300 selected passages by contemporary observers tell about styles of acting, direction, make-up, scene designing, etc., in the theatre's great periods from ancient Greece to the Théâtre Libre. "Indispensable complement to the study of drama," EDUCATIONAL THEATRE JOURNAL. Prof. Nagler, Yale Univ. School of Drama, also supplies notes, references. 85 illustrations. 611pp. 5⅜ x 8. T515 Paperbound **$2.75**

THE ART OF THE STORY-TELLER, M. L. Shedlock. Regarded as the finest, most helpful book on telling stories to children, by a great story-teller. How to catch, hold, recapture attention; how to choose material; many other aspects. Also includes: a 99-page selection of Miss Shedlock's most successful stories; extensive bibliography of other stories. xxi + 320pp. 5⅜ x 8. T245 Clothbound **$3.50**

THE DEVIL'S DICTIONARY, Ambrose Bierce. Over 1000 short, ironic definitions in alphabetical order, by America's greatest satirist in the classical tradition. "Some of the most gorgeous witticisms in the English language," H. L. Mencken. 144pp. 5⅜ x 8. T487 Paperbound **$1.00**

DOVER BOOKS

THE BIRTH AND DEVELOPMENT OF THE GEOLOGICAL SCIENCES, F. D. Adams. The most complete and thorough history of the earth sciences in print. Covers over 300 geological thinkers and systems; treats fossils, theories of stone growth, paleontology, earthquakes, vulcanists vs. neptunists, odd theories, etc. 91 illustrations, including medieval, Renaissance wood cuts, etc. 632 footnotes and bibliographic notes. 511pp. 308pp. 5⅜ x 8. T5 Paperbound **$2.00**

FROM MAGIC TO SCIENCE, Charles Singer. A close study of aspects of medical science from the Roman Empire through the Renaissance. The sections on early herbals, and "The Visions of Hildegarde of Bingen," are probably the best studies of these subjects available. 158 unusual classic and medieval illustrations. xxvii + 365pp. 5⅜ x 8. T390 Paperbound **$2.00**

SAILING ALONE AROUND THE WORLD, Captain Joshua Slocum. Captain Slocum's personal account of his single-handed voyage around the world in a 34-foot boat he rebuilt himself. A classic of both seamanship and descriptive writing. "A nautical equivalent of Thoreau's account," Van Wyck Brooks. 67 illus. 308pp. 5⅜ x 8. T326 Paperbound **$1.00**

TREES OF THE EASTERN AND CENTRAL UNITED STATES AND CANADA, W. M. Harlow. Standard middle-level guide designed to help you know the characteristics of Eastern trees and identify them at sight by means of an 8-page synoptic key. More than 600 drawings and photographs of twigs, leaves, fruit, other features. xiii + 288pp. 4⅝ x 6½. T395 Paperbound **$1.35**

FRUIT KEY AND TWIG KEY ("Fruit Key to Northeastern Trees," "Twig Key to Deciduous Woody Plants of Eastern North America"), **W. M. Harlow.** Identify trees in fall, winter, spring. Easy-to-use, synoptic keys, with photographs of every twig and fruit identified. Covers 120 different fruits, 160 different twigs. Over 350 photos. Bibliographies. Glossaries. Total of 143pp. 5⅝ x 8⅜. T511 Paperbound **$1.25**

INTRODUCTION TO THE STUDY OF EXPERIMENTAL MEDICINE, Claude Bernard. This classic records Bernard's far-reaching efforts to transform physiology into an exact science. It covers problems of vivisection, the limits of physiological experiment, hypotheses in medical experimentation, hundreds of others. Many of his own famous experiments on the liver, the pancreas, etc., are used as examples. Foreword by I. B. Cohen. xxv + 266pp. 5⅜ x 8. T400 Paperbound **$1.50**

THE ORIGIN OF LIFE, A. I. Oparin. The first modern statement that life evolved from complex nitro-carbon compounds, carefully presented according to modern biochemical knowledge of primary colloids, organic molecules, etc. Begins with historical introduction to the problem of the origin of life. Bibliography. xxv + 270pp. 5⅜ x 8. S213 Paperbound **$1.75**

A HISTORY OF ASTRONOMY FROM THALES TO KEPLER, J. L. E. Dreyer. The only work in English which provides a detailed picture of man's cosmological views from Egypt, Babylonia, Greece, and Alexandria to Copernicus, Tycho Brahe and Kepler. "Standard reference on Greek astronomy and the Copernican revolution," SKY AND TELESCOPE. Formerly called "A History of Planetary Systems From Thales to Kepler." Bibliography. 21 diagrams. xvii + 430pp. 5⅜ x 8. S79 Paperbound **$1.98**

URANIUM PROSPECTING, H. L. Barnes. A professional geologist tells you what you need to know. Hundreds of facts about minerals, tests, detectors, sampling, assays, claiming, developing, government regulations, etc. Glossary of technical terms. Annotated bibliography. x + 117pp. 5⅜ x 8. T309 Paperbound **$1.00**

DE RE METALLICA, Georgius Agricola. All 12 books of this 400 year old classic on metals and metal production, fully annotated, and containing all 289 of the 16th century woodcuts which made the original an artistic masterpiece. A superb gift for geologists, engineers, libraries, artists, historians. Translated by Herbert Hoover & L. H. Hoover. Bibliography, survey of ancient authors. 289 illustrations of the excavating, assaying, smelting, refining, and countless other metal production operations described in the text. 672pp. 6¾ x 10¾. Deluxe library edition. S6 Clothbound **$10.00**

DE MAGNETE, William Gilbert. A landmark of science by the man who first used the word "electricity," distinguished between static electricity and magnetism, and founded a new science. P. F. Mottelay translation. 90 figures. lix + 368pp. 5⅜ x 8. S470 Paperbound **$2.00**

THE AUTOBIOGRAPHY OF CHARLES DARWIN AND SELECTED LETTERS, Francis Darwin, ed. Fascinating documents on Darwin's early life, the voyage of the "Beagle," the discovery of evolution, Darwin's thought on mimicry, plant development, vivisection, evolution, many other subjects Letters to Henslow, Lyell, Hooker, Wallace, Kingsley, etc. Appendix. 365pp. 5⅜ x 8. T479 Paperbound **$1.65**

A WAY OF LIFE AND OTHER SELECTED WRITINGS OF SIR WILLIAM OSLER. 16 of the great physician, teacher and humanist's most inspiring writings on a practical philosophy of life, science and the humanities, and the history of medicine. 5 photographs. Introduction by G. L. Keynes, M.D., F.R.C.S. xx + 278pp. 5⅜ x 8. T488 Paperbound **$1.50**

Catalog
of
DOVER BOOKS

BOOKS EXPLAINING SCIENCE

(Note: The books listed under this category are general introductions, surveys, reviews, and non-technical expositions of science for the interested layman or scientist who wishes to brush up. Dover also publishes the largest list of inexpensive reprints of books on intermediate and higher mathematics, mathematical physics, engineering, chemistry, astronomy, etc., for the professional mathematician or scientist. For our complete Science Catalog, write Dept. catrr., Dover Publications, Inc., 180 Varick Street, New York 14, N. Y.)

CONCERNING THE NATURE OF THINGS, Sir William Bragg. Royal Institute Christmas Lectures by Nobel Laureate. Excellent plain-language introduction to gases, molecules, crystal structure, etc. explains "building blocks" of universe, basic properties of matter, with simplest, clearest examples, demonstrations. 32pp. of photos; 57 figures. 244pp. 5⅜ x 8.
T31 Paperbound **$1.35**

MATTER AND LIGHT, THE NEW PHYSICS, Louis de Broglie. Non-technical explanations by a Nobel Laureate of electro-magnetic theory, relativity, wave mechanics, quantum physics, philosophies of science, etc. Simple, yet accurate introduction to work of Planck, Bohr, Einstein, other modern physicists. Only 2 of 12 chapters require mathematics. 300pp. 5⅜ x 8.
T35 Paperbound **$1.60**

THE COMMON SENSE OF THE EXACT SCIENCES, W. K. Clifford. For 70 years, Clifford's work has been acclaimed as one of the clearest, yet most precise introductions to mathematical symbolism, measurement, surface boundaries, position, space, motion, mass and force, etc. Prefaces by Bertrand Russell and Karl Pearson. Introduction by James Newman. 130 figures. 249pp. 5⅜ x 8.
T61 Paperbound **$1.60**

THE NATURE OF LIGHT AND COLOUR IN THE OPEN AIR, M. Minnaert. What causes mirages? haloes? "multiple" suns and moons? Professor Minnaert explains these and hundreds of other fascinating natural optical phenomena in simple terms, tells how to observe them, suggests hundreds of experiments. 200 illus; 42 photos. xvi + 362pp.
T196 Paperbound **$1.95**

SPINNING TOPS AND GYROSCOPIC MOTION, John Perry. Classic elementary text on dynamics of rotation treats gyroscopes, tops, how quasi-rigidity is induced in paper disks, smoke rings, chains, etc, by rapid motion, precession, earth's motion, etc. Contains many easy-to-perform experiments. Appendix on practical uses of gyroscopes. 62 figures. 128pp.
T416 Paperbound **$1.00**

A CONCISE HISTORY OF MATHEMATICS, D. Struik. This lucid, easily followed history of mathematics from the Ancient Near East to modern times requires no mathematical background itself, yet introduces both mathematicians and laymen to basic concepts and discoveries and the men who made them. Contains a collection of 31 portraits of eminent mathematicians. Bibliography. xix + 299pp. 5⅜ x 8.
T255 Paperbound **$1.75**

THE RESTLESS UNIVERSE, Max Born. A remarkably clear, thorough exposition of gases, electrons, ions, waves and particles, electronic structure of the atom, nuclear physics, written for the layman by a Nobel Laureate. "Much more thorough and deep than most attempts . . . easy and delightful," CHEMICAL AND ENGINEERING NEWS. Includes 7 animated sequences showing motion of molecules, alpha particles, etc. 11 full-page plates of photographs. Total of nearly 600 illus. 315pp. 6⅛ x 9¼.
T412 Paperbound **$2.00**

WHAT IS SCIENCE?, N. Campbell. The role of experiment, the function of mathematics, the nature of scientific laws, the limitations of science, and many other provocative topics are explored without technicalities by an eminent scientist. "Still an excellent introduction to scientific philosophy," H. Margenau in PHYSICS TODAY. 192pp. 5⅜ x 8.
S43 Paperbound **$1.25**

FADS AND FALLACIES IN THE NAME OF SCIENCE, Martin Gardner. The standard account of the various cults, quack systems and delusions which have recently masqueraded as science: hollow earth theory, Atlantis, dianetics, Reich's orgone theory, flying saucers, Bridey Murphy, psionics, irridiagnosis, many other fascinating fallacies that deluded tens of thousands. "Should be read by everyone, scientist and non-scientist alike," R. T. Birge, Prof. Emeritus, Univ. of California; Former President, American Physical Society. Formerly titled, "In the Name of Science." Revised and enlarged edition. x + 365pp. 5⅜ x 8.
T394 Paperbound **$1.50**

THE STUDY OF THE HISTORY OF MATHEMATICS, THE STUDY OF THE HISTORY OF SCIENCE, G. Sarton. Two books bound as one. Both volumes are standard introductions to their fields by an eminent science historian. They discuss problems of historical research, teaching, pitfalls, other matters of interest to the historically oriented writer, teacher, or student. Both have extensive bibliographies. 10 illustrations. 188pp. 5⅜ x 8.   T240 Paperbound **$1.25**

THE PRINCIPLES OF SCIENCE, W. S. Jevons. Unabridged reprinting of a milestone in the development of symbolic logic and other subjects concerning scientific methodology, probability, inferential validity, etc. Also describes Jevons' "logic machine," an early precursor of modern electronic calculators. Preface by E. Nagel. 839pp. 5⅜ x 8.   S446 Paperbound **$2.98**

SCIENCE THEORY AND MAN, Erwin Schroedinger. Complete, unabridged reprinting of "Science and the Human Temperament" plus an additional essay "What is an Elementary Particle?" Nobel Laureate Schroedinger discusses many aspects of modern physics from novel points of view which provide unusual insights for both laymen and physicists. 192 pp. 5⅜ x 8.
T428 Paperbound **$1.35**

BRIDGES AND THEIR BUILDERS, D. B. Steinman & S. R. Watson. Information about ancient, medieval, modern bridges; how they were built; who built them; the structural principles employed; the materials they are built of; etc. Written by one of the world's leading authorities on bridge design and construction. New, revised, expanded edition. 23 photos; 26 line drawings, xvii + 401pp. 5⅜ x 8.   T431 Paperbound **$1.95**

HISTORY OF MATHEMATICS, D. E. Smith. Most comprehensive non-technical history of math in English. In two volumes. Vol. I: A chronological examination of the growth of mathematics from primitive concepts up to 1900. Vol. II: The development of ideas in specific fields and areas, up through elementary calculus. The lives and works of over a thousand mathematicians are covered; thousands of specific historical problems and their solutions are clearly explained. Total of 510 illustrations, 1355pp. 5⅜ x 8. Set boxed in attractive container.   T429, T430 Paperbound, the set **$5.00**

PHILOSOPHY AND THE PHYSICISTS, L. S. Stebbing. A philosopher examines the philosophical implications of modern science by posing a lively critical attack on the popular science expositions of Sir James Jeans and Arthur Eddington. xvi + 295pp. 5⅜ x 8.
T480 Paperbound **$1.65**

ON MATHEMATICS AND MATHEMATICIANS, R. E. Moritz. The first collection of quotations by and about mathematicians in English. 1140 anecdotes, aphorisms, definitions, speculations, etc. give both mathematicians and layman stimulating new insights into what mathematics is, and into the personalities of the great mathematicians from Archimedes to Euler, Gauss, Klein, Weierstrass. Invaluable to teachers, writers. Extensive cross index. 410pp. 5⅜ x 8.
T489 Paperbound **$1.95**

NATURAL SCIENCE, BIOLOGY, GEOLOGY, TRAVEL

A SHORT HISTORY OF ANATOMY AND PHYSIOLOGY FROM THE GREEKS TO HARVEY, C. Singer. A great medical historian's fascinating intermediate account of the slow advance of anatomical and physiological knowledge from pre-scientific times to Vesalius, Harvey. 139 unusually interesting illustrations. 221pp. 5⅜ x 8.   T389 Paperbound **$1.75**

THE BEHAVIOUR AND SOCIAL LIFE OF HONEYBEES, Ronald Ribbands. The most comprehensive, lucid and authoritative book on bee habits, communication, duties, cell life, motivations, etc. "A MUST for every scientist, experimenter, and educator, and a happy and valuable selection for all interested in the honeybee," AMERICAN BEE JOURNAL. 690-item bibliography. 127 illus.; 11 photographic plates. 352pp. 5⅜ x 8⅜.   S410 Clothbound **$4.50**

TRAVELS OF WILLIAM BARTRAM, edited by Mark Van Doren. One of the 18th century's most delightful books, and one of the few first-hand sources of information about American geography, natural history, and anthropology of American Indian tribes of the time. "The mind of a scientist with the soul of a poet," John Livingston Lowes. 13 original illustrations, maps. Introduction by Mark Van Doren. 448pp. 5⅜ x 8.   T326 Paperbound **$2.00**▼

STUDIES ON THE STRUCTURE AND DEVELOPMENT OF VERTEBRATES, Edwin Goodrich. The definitive study of the skeleton, fins and limbs, head region, divisions of the body cavity, vascular, respiratory, excretory systems, etc., of vertebrates from fish to higher mammals, by the greatest comparative anatomist of recent times. "The standard textbook," JOURNAL OF ANATOMY. 754 illus. 69-page biographical study. 1186-item bibliography. 2 vols. Total of 906pp. 5⅜ x 8.
Vol. I: S449 Paperbound **$2.50**
Vol. II: S450 Paperbound **$2.50**

MUSIC

A DICTIONARY OF HYMNOLOGY, John Julian. More than 30,000 entries on individual hymns, their authorship, textual variations, location of texts, dates and circumstances of composition, denominational and ritual usages, the biographies of more than 9,000 hymn writers, essays on important topics such as children's hymns and Christmas carols, and hundreds of thousands of other important facts about hymns which are virtually impossible to find anywhere else. Convenient alphabetical listing, and a 200-page double-columned index of first lines enable you to track down virtually any hymn ever written. Total of 1786pp. 6¼ x 9¼. 2 volumes.   T133. The Set, Clothbound **$15.00**

STRUCTURAL HEARING, TONAL COHERENCE IN MUSIC, Felix Salzer. Extends the well-known Schenker approach to include modern music, music of the middle ages, and Renaissance music. Explores the phenomenon of tonal organization by discussing more than 500 compositions, and offers unusual new insights into the theory of composition and musical relationships. "The foundation on which all teaching in music theory has been based at this college," Leopold Mannes, President, The Mannes College of Music. Total of 658pp. 6½ x 9¼. 2 volumes.   S418 The set, Clothbound **$8.00**

A GENERAL HISTORY OF MUSIC, Charles Burney. The complete history of music from the Greeks up to 1789 by the 18th century musical historian who personally knew the great Baroque composers. Covers sacred and secular, vocal and instrumental, operatic and symphonic music; treats theory, notation, forms, instruments; discusses composers, performers, important works. Invaluable as a source of information on the period for students, historians, musicians. "Surprisingly few of Burney's statements have been invalidated by modern research . . . still of great value," NEW YORK TIMES. Edited and corrected by Frank Mercer. 35 figures. 1915pp. 5½ x 8½. 2 volumes.   T36 The set, Clothbound **$12.50**

JOHANN SEBASTIAN BACH, Phillip Spitta. Recognized as one of the greatest accomplishments of musical scholarship and far and away the definitive coverage of Bach's works. Hundreds of individual pieces are analyzed. Major works, such as the B Minor Mass and the St. Matthew Passion are examined in minute detail. Spitta also deals with the works of Buxtehude, Pachelbel, and others of the period. Can be read with profit even by those without a knowledge of the technicalities of musical composition. "Unchallenged as the last word on one of the supreme geniuses of music," John Barkham, SATURDAY REVIEW SYNDICATE. Total of 1819pp. 5⅜ x 8. 2 volumes.   T252 The set, Clothbound **$10.00**

HISTORY

THE IDEA OF PROGRESS, J. B. Bury. Prof. Bury traces the evolution of a central concept of Western civilization in Greek, Roman, Medieval, and Renaissance thought to its flowering in the 17th and 18th centuries. Introduction by Charles Beard. xl + 357pp. 5⅜ x 8.
T39 Clothbound **$3.95**
T40 Paperbound **$1.95**

THE ANCIENT GREEK HISTORIANS, J. B. Bury. Greek historians such as Herodotus, Thucydides, Xenophon; Roman historians such as Tacitus, Caesar, Livy; scores of others fully analyzed in terms of sources, concepts, influences, etc., by a great scholar and historian. 291pp. 5⅜ x 8.   T397 Paperbound **$1.50**

HISTORY OF THE LATER ROMAN EMPIRE, J. B. Bury. The standard work on the Byzantine Empire from 395 A.D. to the death of Justinian in 565 A.D., by the leading Byzantine scholar of our time. Covers political, social, cultural, theological, military history. Quotes contemporary documents extensively. "Most unlikely that it will ever be superseded," Glanville Downey, Dumbarton Oaks Research Library. Genealogical tables. 5 maps. Bibliography. 2 vols. Total of 965pp. 5⅜ x 8.   T398, T399 Paperbound, the set **$4.00**

GARDNER'S PHOTOGRAPHIC SKETCH BOOK OF THE CIVIL WAR, Alexander Gardner. One of the rarest and most valuable Civil War photographic collections exactly reproduced for the first time since 1866. Scenes of Manassas, Bull Run, Harper's Ferry, Appomattox, Mechanicsville, Fredericksburg, Gettysburg, etc.; battle ruins, prisons, arsenals, a slave pen, fortifications; Lincoln on the field, officers, men, corpses. By one of the most famous pioneers in documentary photography. Original copies of the "Sketch Book" sold for $425 in 1952. Introduction by E. Bleiler. 100 full-page 7 x 10 photographs (original size). 244pp. 10¾ x 8½
T476 Clothbound **$6.00**

THE WORLD'S GREAT SPEECHES, L. Copeland and L. Lamm, eds. 255 speeches from Pericles to Churchill, Dylan Thomas. Invaluable as a guide to speakers; fascinating as history past and present; a source of much difficult-to-find material. Includes an extensive section of informal and humorous speeches. 3 indices: Topic, Author, Nation. xx + 745pp. 5⅜ x 8.
T468 Paperbound **$2.49**

FOUNDERS OF THE MIDDLE AGES, E. K. Rand. The best non-technical discussion of the transformation of Latin paganism into medieval civilization. Tertullian, Gregory, Jerome, Boethius, Augustine, the Neoplatonists, other crucial figures, philosophies examined. Excellent for the intelligent non-specialist. "Extraordinarily accurate," Richard McKeon, THE NATION. ix + 365pp. 5⅜ x 8.   T369 Paperbound **$1.85**

THE POLITICAL THOUGHT OF PLATO AND ARISTOTLE, Ernest Barker. The standard, comprehensive exposition of Greek political thought. Covers every aspect of the "Republic" and the "Politics" as well as minor writings, other philosophers, theorists of the period, and the later history of Greek political thought. Unabridged edition. 584pp. 5⅜ x 8.
T521 Paperbound $1.85

PHILOSOPHY

THE GIFT OF LANGUAGE, M. Schlauch. (Formerly, "The Gift of Tongues.") A sound, middle-level treatment of linguistic families, word histories, grammatical processes, semantics, language taboos, word-coining of Joyce, Cummings, Stein, etc. 232 bibliographical notes. 350pp. 5⅜ x 8.
T243 Paperbound $1.85

THE PHILOSOPHY OF HEGEL, W. T. Stace. The first work in English to give a complete and connected view of Hegel's entire system. Especially valuable to those who do not have time to study the highly complicated original texts, yet want an accurate presentation by a most reputable scholar of one of the most influential 19th century thinkers. Includes a 14 x 20 fold-out chart of Hegelian system. 536pp. 5⅜ x 8.
T254 Paperbound $2.00

ARISTOTLE, A. E. Taylor. A lucid, non-technical account of Aristotle written by a foremost Platonist. Covers life and works; thought on matter, form, causes, logic, God, physics, metaphysics, etc. Bibliography. New index compiled for this edition. 128pp. 5⅜ x 8.
T280 Paperbound $1.00

GUIDE TO PHILOSOPHY, C. E. M. Joad. This basic work describes the major philosophic problems and evaluates the answers propounded by great philosophers from the Greeks to Whitehead, Russell. "The finest introduction," BOSTON TRANSCRIPT. Bibliography, 592pp. 5⅜ x 8.
T297 Paperbound $2.00

LANGUAGE AND MYTH, E. Cassirer. Cassirer's brilliant demonstration that beneath both language and myth lies an unconscious "grammar" of experience whose categories and canons are not those of logical thought. Introduction and translation by Susanne Langer. Index. x + 103pp. 5⅜ x 8.
T51 Paperbound $1.25

SUBSTANCE AND FUNCTION, EINSTEIN'S THEORY OF RELATIVITY, E. Cassirer. This double volume contains the German philosopher's profound philosophical formulation of the differences between traditional logic and the new logic of science. Number, space, energy, relativity, many other topics are treated in detail. Authorized translation by W. C. and M. C. Swabey. xii + 465pp. 5⅜ x 8.
T50 Paperbound $2.00

THE PHILOSOPHICAL WORKS OF DESCARTES. The definitive English edition, in two volumes, of all major philosophical works and letters of René Descartes, father of modern philosophy of knowledge and science. Translated by E. S. Haldane and G. Ross. Introductory notes. Total of 842pp. 5⅜ x 8.
T71 Vol. 1, Paperbound $2.00
T72 Vol. 2, Paperbound $2.00

ESSAYS IN EXPERIMENTAL LOGIC, J. Dewey. Based upon Dewey's theory that knowledge implies a judgment which in turn implies an inquiry, these papers consider such topics as the thought of Bertrand Russell, pragmatism, the logic of values, antecedents of thought, data and meanings. 452pp. 5⅜ x 8.
T73 Paperbound $1.95

THE PHILOSOPHY OF HISTORY, G. W. F. Hegel. This classic of Western thought is Hegel's detailed formulation of the thesis that history is not chance but a rational process, the realization of the Spirit of Freedom. Translated and introduced by J. Sibree. Introduction by C. Hegel. Special introduction for this edition by Prof. Carl Friedrich, Harvard University. xxxix + 447pp. 5⅜ x 8.
T112 Paperbound $1.85

THE WILL TO BELIEVE and HUMAN IMMORTALITY, W. James. Two of James's most profound investigations of human belief in God and immortality, bound as one volume. Both are powerful expressions of James's views on chance vs. determinism, pluralism vs. monism, will and intellect, arguments for survival after death, etc. Two prefaces. 429pp. 5⅜ x 8.
T294 Clothbound $3.75
T291 Paperbound $1.65

INTRODUCTION TO SYMBOLIC LOGIC, S. Langer. A lucid, general introduction to modern logic, covering forms, classes, the use of symbols, the calculus of propositions, the Boole-Schroeder and the Russell-Whitehead systems, etc. "One of the clearest and simplest introductions," MATHEMATICS GAZETTE. Second, enlarged, revised edition. 368pp. 5⅜ x 8.
S164 Paperbound $1.75

MIND AND THE WORLD-ORDER, C. I. Lewis. Building upon the work of Peirce, James, and Dewey, Professor Lewis outlines a theory of knowledge in terms of "conceptual pragmatism," and demonstrates why the traditional understanding of the a priori must be abandoned. Appendices. xiv + 446pp. 5⅜ x 8.
T359 Paperbound $1.95

THE GUIDE FOR THE PERPLEXED. M. Maimonides One of the great philosophical works of all time, Maimonides' formulation of the meeting-ground between Old Testament and Aristotelian thought is essential to anyone interested in Jewish, Christian, and Moslem thought in the Middle Ages. 2nd revised edition of the Friedlander translation. Extensive introduction. lix + 414pp. 5⅜ x 8.
T351 Paperbound $1.85

DOVER BOOKS

THE PHILOSOPHICAL WRITINGS OF PEIRCE, J. Buchler, ed. (Formerly, "The Philosophy of Peirce.") This carefully integrated selection of Peirce's papers is considered the best coverage of the complete thought of one of the greatest philosophers of modern times. Covers Peirce's work on the theory of signs, pragmatism, epistemology, symbolic logic, the scientific method, chance, etc. xvi + 386pp. 5 ⅜ x 8. T216 Clothbound **$5.00**
T217 Paperbound **$1.95**

HISTORY OF ANCIENT PHILOSOPHY, W. Windelband. Considered the clearest survey of Greek and Roman philosophy. Examines Thales, Anaximander, Anaximenes, Heraclitus, the Eleatics, Empedocles, the Pythagoreans, the Sophists, Socrates, Democritus, Stoics, Epicureans, Sceptics, Neo-platonists, etc. 50 pages on Plato; 70 on Aristotle. 2nd German edition tr. by H. E. Cushman. xv + 393pp. 5⅜ x 8. T357 Paperbound **$1.75**

INTRODUCTION TO SYMBOLIC LOGIC AND ITS APPLICATIONS, R. Carnap. A comprehensive, rigorous introduction to modern logic by perhaps its greatest living master. Includes demonstrations of applications in mathematics, physics, biology. "Of the rank of a masterpiece," Z. für Mathematik und ihre Grenzgebiete. Over 300 exercises. xvi + 241pp. 5⅜ x 8. Clothbound **$4.00**
S453 Paperbound **$1.85**

SCEPTICISM AND ANIMAL FAITH, G. Santayana. Santayana's unusually lucid exposition of the difference between the independent existence of objects and the essence our mind attributes to them, and of the necessity of scepticism as a form of belief and animal faith as a necessary condition of knowledge. Discusses belief, memory, intuition, symbols, etc. xii + 314pp. 5⅜ x 8. T235 Clothbound **$3.50**
T236 Paperbound **$1.50**

THE ANALYSIS OF MATTER, B. Russell. With his usual brilliance, Russell analyzes physics, causality, scientific inference, Weyl's theory, tensors, invariants, periodicity, etc. in order to discover the basic concepts of scientific thought about matter. "Most thorough treatment of the subject," THE NATION. Introduction. 8 figures. viii + 408pp. 5⅜ x 8.
T231 Paperbound **$1.95**

THE SENSE OF BEAUTY, G. Santayana. This important philosophical study of why, when, and how beauty appears, and what conditions must be fulfilled, is in itself a revelation of the beauty of language. "It is doubtful if a better treatment of the subject has since appeared," PEABODY JOURNAL. ix + 275pp. 5⅜ x 8. T238 Paperbound **$1.00**

THE CHIEF WORKS OF SPINOZA. In two volumes. Vol. I: The Theologico-Political Treatise and the Political Treatise. Vol. II: On the Improvement of Understanding, The Ethics, and Selected Letters. The permanent and enduring ideas in these works on God, the universe, religion, society, etc., have had tremendous impact on later philosophical works. Introduction. Total of 862pp. 5⅜ x 8. T249 Vol. I, Paperbound **$1.50**
T250 Vol. II, Paperbound **$1.50**

TRAGIC SENSE OF LIFE, M. de Unamuno. The acknowledged masterpiece of one of Spain's most influential thinkers. Between the despair at the inevitable death of man and all his works, and the desire for immortality, Unamuno finds a "saving incertitude." Called "a masterpiece," by the ENCYCLOPAEDIA BRITANNICA. xxx + 332pp. 5⅜ x 8.
T257 Paperbound **$1.95**

EXPERIENCE AND NATURE, John Dewey. The enlarged, revised edition of the Paul Carus lectures (1925). One of Dewey's clearest presentations of the philosophy of empirical naturalism which reestablishes the continuity between "inner" experience and "outer" nature. These lectures are among the most significant ever delivered by an American philosopher. 457pp. 5⅜ x 8. T471 Paperbound **$1.85**

PHILOSOPHY AND CIVILIZATION IN THE MIDDLE AGES, M. de Wulf. A semi-popular survey of medieval intellectual life, religion, philosophy, science, the arts, etc. that covers feudalism vs. Catholicism, rise of the universities, mendicant orders, and similar topics. Bibliography. viii + 320pp. 5⅜ x 8. T284 Paperbound **$1.75**

AN INTRODUCTION TO SCHOLASTIC PHILOSOPHY, M. de Wulf. (Formerly, "Scholasticism Old and New.") Prof. de Wulf covers the central scholastic tradition from St. Anselm, Albertus Magnus, Thomas Aquinas, up to Suarez in the 17th century; and then treats the modern revival of scholasticism, the Louvain position, relations with Kantianism and positivism, etc. xvi + 271pp. 5⅜ x 8. T296 Clothbound **$3.50**
T283 Paperbound **$1.75**

A HISTORY OF MODERN PHILOSOPHY, H. Höffding. An exceptionally clear and detailed coverage of Western philosophy from the Renaissance to the end of the 19th century. Both major and minor figures are examined in terms of theory of knowledge, logic, cosmology, psychology. Covers Pomponazzi, Bodin, Boehme, Telesius, Bruno, Copernicus, Descartes, Spinoza, Hobbes, Locke, Hume, Kant, Fichte, Schopenhauer, Mill, Spencer, Langer, scores of others. A standard reference work. 2 volumes. Total of 1159pp. 5⅜ x 8. T117 Vol. 1, Paperbound **$2.00**
T118 Vol. 2, Paperbound **$2.00**

LANGUAGE, TRUTH AND LOGIC, A. J. Ayer. The first full-length development of Logical Positivism in English. Building on the work of Schlick, Russell, Carnap, and the Vienna school, Ayer presents the tenets of one of the most important systems of modern philosophical thought. 160pp. 5⅜ x 8. T10 Paperbound **$1.25**

ORIENTALIA AND RELIGION

THE MYSTERIES OF MITHRA, F. Cumont. The great Belgian scholar's definitive study of the Persian mystery religion that almost vanquished Christianity in the ideological struggle for the Roman Empire. A masterpiece of scholarly detection that reconstructs secret doctrines, organization, rites. Mithraic art is discussed and analyzed. 70 illus. 239pp. 5⅜ x 8.
T323 Paperbound **$1.85**

CHRISTIAN AND ORIENTAL PHILOSOPHY OF ART. A. K. Coomaraswamy. The late art historian and orientalist discusses artistic symbolism, the role of traditional culture in enriching art, medieval art, folklore, philosophy of art, other similar topics. Bibliography. 148pp. 5⅜ x 8.
T378 Paperbound **$1.25**

TRANSFORMATION OF NATURE IN ART, A. K. Coomaraswamy. A basic work on Asiatic religious art. Includes discussions of religious art in Asia and Medieval Europe (exemplified by Meister Eckhart), the origin and use of images in Indian art, Indian Medieval aesthetic manuals, and other fascinating, little known topics. Glossaries of Sanskrit and Chinese terms. Bibliography. 41pp. of notes. 245pp. 5⅜ x 8.
T368 Paperbound **$1.75**

ORIENTAL RELIGIONS IN ROMAN PAGANISM, F. Cumont. This well-known study treats the ecstatic cults of Syria and Phrygia (Cybele, Attis, Adonis, their orgies and mutilatory rites); the mysteries of Egypt (Serapis, Isis, Osiris); Persian dualism; Mithraic cults; Hermes Trismegistus, Ishtar, Astarte, etc. and their influence on the religious thought of the Roman Empire. Introduction. 55pp. of notes; extensive bibliography. xxiv + 298pp. 5⅜ x 8.
T321 Paperbound **$1.75**

ANTHROPOLOGY, SOCIOLOGY, AND PSYCHOLOGY

PRIMITIVE MAN AS PHILOSOPHER, P. Radin. A standard anthropological work based on Radin's investigations of the Winnebago, Maori, Batak, Zuni, other primitive tribes. Describes primitive thought on the purpose of life, marital relations, death, personality, gods, etc. Extensive selections of õriginal primitive documents. Bibliography. xviii + 420pp. 5⅜ x 8.
T392 Paperbound **$2.00**

PRIMITIVE RELIGION, P. Radin. Radin's thoroughgoing treatment of supernatural beliefs, shamanism, initiations, religious expression, etc. in primitive societies. Arunta, Ashanti, Aztec, Bushman, Crow, Fijian, many other tribes examined. "Excellent," NATURE. New preface by the author. Bibliographic notes. x + 322pp. 5⅜ x 8.   T393 Paperbound **$1.85**

SEX IN PSYCHO-ANALYSIS, S. Ferenczi. (Formerly, "Contributions to Psycho-analysis.") 14 selected papers on impotence, transference, analysis and children, dreams, obscene words, homosexuality, paranoia, etc. by an associate of Freud. Also included: THE DEVELOPMENT OF PSYCHO-ANALYSIS, by Ferenczi and Otto Rank. Two books bound as one. Total of 406pp. 5⅜ x 8.   T324 Paperbound **$1.85**

THE PRINCIPLES OF PSYCHOLOGY, William James. The complete text of the famous "long course," one of the great books of Western thought. An almost incredible amount of information about psychological processes, the stream of consciousness, habit, time perception, memory, emotions, reason, consciousness of self, abnormal phenomena, and similar topics. Based on James's own discoveries integrated with the work of Descartes, Locke, Hume, Royce, Wundt, Berkeley, Lotse, Herbart, scores of others. "A classic of interpretation," PSYCHIATRIC QUARTERLY. 94 illus. 1408pp. 2 volumes. 5⅜ x 8.
T381 Vol. 1, Paperbound **$2.50**
T382 Vol. 2, Paperbound **$2.50**

THE POLISH PEASANT IN EUROPE AND AMERICA, W. I. Thomas, F. Znaniecki. Monumental sociological study of peasant primary groups (family and community) and the disruptions produced by·a new industrial system and emigration to America, by two of the foremost sociologists of recent times. One of the most important works in sociological thought. Includes hundreds of pages of primary documentation; point by point analysis of causes of social decay, breakdown of morality, crime, drunkenness, prostitution, etc. 2nd revised edition. 2 volumes. Total of 2250pp. 6 x 9.   T478 2 volume set, Clothbound **$12.50**

FOLKWAYS, W. G. Sumner. The great Yale sociologist's detailed exposition of thousands of social, sexual, and religious customs in hundreds of cultures from ancient Greece to Modern Western societies. Preface by A. G. Keller. Introduction by William Lyon Phelps. 705pp. 5⅜ x 8.   S508 Paperbound **$2.49**

BEYOND PSYCHOLOGY, Otto Rank. The author, an early associate of Freud, uses psychoanalytic techniques of myth-analysis to explore ultimates of human existence. Treats love, immortality, the soul, sexual identity, kingship, sources of state power, many other topics which illuminate the irrational basis of human existence. 291pp. 5⅜ x 8.   T485 Paperbound **$1.75**

ILLUSIONS AND DELUSIONS OF THE SUPERNATURAL AND THE OCCULT, D. H. Rawcliffe. A rational, scientific examination of crystal gazing, automatic writing, table turning, stigmata, the Indian rope trick, dowsing, telepathy, clairvoyance, ghosts, ESP, PK, thousands of other supposedly occult phenomena. Originally titled "The Psychology of the Occult." 14 illustrations. 551pp. 5⅜ x 8.   T503 Paperbound **$2.00**

DOVER BOOKS

YOGA: A SCIENTIFIC EVALUATION, Kovoor T. Behanan. A scientific study of the physiological and psychological effects of Yoga discipline, written under the auspices of the Yale University Institute of Human Relations. Foreword by W. A. Miles, Yale Univ. 17 photographs. 290pp. 5⅜ x 8.   T505 Paperbound **$1.65**

HOAXES, C. D. MacDougall. Delightful, entertaining, yet scholarly exposition of how hoaxes start, why they succeed, documented with stories of hundreds of the most famous hoaxes. "A stupendous collection . . . and shrewd analysis, "NEW YORKER. New, revised edition. 54 photographs. 320pp. 5⅜ x 8.   T465 Paperbound **$1.75**

CREATIVE POWER: THE EDUCATION OF YOUTH IN THE CREATIVE ARTS, Hughes Mearns. Named by the National Education Association as one of the 20 foremost books on education in recent times. Tells how to help children express themselves in drama, poetry, music, art, develop latent creative power. Should be read by every parent, teacher. New, enlarged, revised edition. Introduction. 272pp. 5⅜ x 8.   T490 Paperbound **$1.50**

LANGUAGES

NEW RUSSIAN-ENGLISH, ENGLISH-RUSSIAN DICTIONARY, M. A. O'Brien. Over 70,000 entries in new orthography! Idiomatic usages, colloquialisms. One of the few dictionaries that indicate accent changes in conjugation and declension. "One of the best," Prof. E. J. Simmons, Cornell. First names, geographical terms, bibliography, many other features. 738pp. 4½ x 6¼.
T208 Paperbound **$2.00**

MONEY CONVERTER AND TIPPING GUIDE FOR EUROPEAN TRAVEL, C. Vomacka. Invaluable, handy source of currency regulations, conversion tables, tipping rules, postal rates, much other travel information for every European country plus Israel, Egypt and Turkey. 128pp. 3½ x 5¼.
T260 Paperbound **60¢**

MONEY CONVERTER AND TIPPING GUIDE FOR TRAVEL IN THE AMERICAS (including the United States and Canada), **C. Vomacka.** The information you need for informed and confident travel in the Americas: money conversion tables, tipping guide, postal, telephone rates, etc. 128pp. 3½ x 5¼.   T261 Paperbound **65¢**

DUTCH-ENGLISH, ENGLISH-DUTCH DICTIONARY, F. G. Renier. The most convenient, practical Dutch-English dictionary on the market. New orthography. More than 60,000 entries: idioms, compounds, technical terms, etc. Gender of nouns indicated. xviii + 571pp. 5½ x 6¼.
T224 Clothbound **$2.50**

LEARN DUTCH!, F. G. Renier. The most satisfactory and easily-used grammar of modern Dutch. Used and recommended by the Fulbright Committee in the Netherlands. Over 1200 simple exercises lead to mastery of spoken and written Dutch. Dutch-English, English-Dutch vocabularies. 181pp. 4¼ x 7¼.   T441 Clothbound **$1.75**

PHRASE AND SENTENCE DICTIONARY OF SPOKEN RUSSIAN, English-Russian, Russian-English. Based on phrases and complete sentences, rather than isolated words; recognized as one of the best methods of learning the idiomatic speech of a country. Over 11,500 entries, indexed by single words, with more than 32,000 English and Russian sentences and phrases, in immediately usable form. Probably the largest list ever published. Shows accent changes in conjugation and declension; irregular forms listed in both alphabetical place and under main form of word. 15,000 word introduction covering Russian sounds, writing, grammar, syntax. 15-page appendix of geographical names, money, important signs, given names, foods, special Soviet terms, etc. Travellers, businessmen, students, government employees have found this their best source for Russian expressions. Originally published as U.S. Government Technical Manual TM 30-944. iv + 573pp. 5⅝ x 8⅜.   T496 Paperbound **$2.75**

PHRASE AND SENTENCE DICTIONARY OF SPOKEN SPANISH, Spanish-English, English-Spanish. Compiled from spoken Spanish, emphasizing idiom and colloquial usage in both Castilian and Latin-American. More than 16,000 entries containing over 25,000 idioms—the largest list of idiomatic constructions ever published. Complete sentences given, indexed under single words —language in immediately usable form, for travellers, businessmen, students, etc. 25-page introduction provides rapid survey of sounds, grammar, syntax, with full consideration of irregular verbs. Especially apt in modern treatment of phrases and structure. 17-page glossary gives translations of geographical names, money values, numbers, national holidays, important street signs, useful expressions of high frequency, plus unique 7-page glossary of Spanish and Spanish-American foods and dishes. Originally published as U.S. Government Technical Manual TM 30-900. iv + 513pp. 5⅝ x 8⅜.   T495 Paperbound **$1.75**

SAY IT language phrase books

"SAY IT" in the foreign language of your choice! We have sold over ½ million copies of these popular, useful language books. They will not make you an expert linguist overnight, but they do cover most practical matters of everyday life abroad.

Over 1000 useful phrases, expressions, with additional variants, substitutions.

Modern! Useful! Hundreds of phrases not available in other texts: "Nylon," "air-conditioned," etc.

The ONLY inexpensive phrase book **completely indexed.** Everything is available at a flip of your finger, ready for use.

Prepared by native linguists, travel experts.

Based on years of travel experience abroad.

This handy phrase book may be used by itself, or it may supplement any other text or course; it provides a living element. Used by many colleges and institutions: Hunter College; Barnard College; Army Ordnance School, Aberdeen; and many others.

Available, 1 book per language:

Danish (T818) 75¢	**Italian** (T806) 60¢
Dutch T(817) 75¢	**Japanese** (T807) 60¢
English (for German-speaking people) (T801) 60¢	**Norwegian** (T814) 75¢
English (for Italian-speaking people) (T816) 60¢	**Russian** (T810) 75¢
English (for Spanish-speaking people) (T802) 60¢	**Spanish** (T811) 60¢
Esperanto (T820) 75¢	**Turkish** (T821) 75¢
French (T803) 60¢	**Yiddish** (T815) 75¢
German (T804) 60¢	**Swedish** (T812) 75¢
Modern Greek (T813) 75¢	**Polish** (T808) 75¢
Hebrew (T805) 60¢	**Portuguese** (T809) 75¢

LISTEN & LEARN language record sets

LISTEN & LEARN is the only language record course designed especially to meet your travel needs, or help you learn essential foreign language quickly by yourself, or in conjunction with any school course, by means of the automatic association method. Each set contains three 33⅓ rpm long-playing records — 1½ hours of recorded speech by eminent native speakers who are professors at Columbia, N.Y.U., Queens College and other leading universities. The sets are priced far below other sets of similar quality, yet they contain many special features not found in other record sets:

* Over 800 selected phrases and sentences, a basic vocabulary of over 3200 words.
* Both English and foreign language recorded; with a pause for your repetition.
* Designed for persons with limited time; no time wasted on material you cannot use immediately.
* Living, modern expressions that answer modern needs: drugstore items, "air-conditioned," etc.
* 128-196 page manuals contain everything on the records, plus simple pronunciation guides.
* Manual is fully indexed; find the phrase you want instantly.
* High fidelity recording—equal to any records costing up to $6 each.

The phrases on these records cover 41 different categories useful to the traveller or student interested in learning the living, spoken language: greetings, introductions, making yourself understood, passing customs, planes, trains, boats, buses, taxis, nightclubs, restaurants, menu items, sports, concerts, cameras, automobile travel, repairs, drugstores, doctors, dentists, medicines, barber shops, beauty parlors, laundries, many, many more.

"Excellent . . . among the very best on the market," Prof. Mario Pei, Dept. of Romance Languages, Columbia University. "Inexpensive and well-done . . . an ideal present," CHICAGO SUNDAY TRIBUNE. "More genuinely helpful than anything of its kind which I have previously encountered," Sidney Clark, well-known author of "ALL THE BEST" travel books. Each set contains 3 33⅓ rpm pure vinyl records, 128-196 page with full record text, and album. One language per set. LISTEN & LEARN record sets are now available in—

FRENCH	the set $4.95		**GERMAN**	the set $4.95
ITALIAN	the set $4.95		**SPANISH**	the set $4.95
RUSSIAN	the set $5.95		**JAPANESE** *	the set $5.95

* Available Sept. 1, 1959

UNCONDITIONAL GUARANTEE: Dover Publications stands behind every Listen and Learn record set. If you are dissatisfied with these sets for any reason whatever, return them within 10 days and your money will be refunded in full.

ART HISTORY

STICKS AND STONES, Lewis Mumford. An examination of forces influencing American architecture: the medieval tradition in early New England, the classical influence in Jefferson's time, the Brown Decades, the imperial facade, the machine age, etc. "A truly remarkable book," SAT. REV. OF LITERATURE. 2nd revised edition. 21 illus. xvii + 228pp. 5⅜ x 8.
T202 Paperbound **$1.60**

THE AUTOBIOGRAPHY OF AN IDEA, Louis Sullivan. The architect whom Frank Lloyd Wright called "the master," records the development of the theories that revolutionized America's skyline. 34 full-page plates of Sullivan's finest work. New introduction by R. M. Line. xiv + 335pp. 5⅜ x 8.
T281 Paperbound **$1.85**

THE MATERIALS AND TECHNIQUES OF MEDIEVAL PAINTING, D. V. Thompson. An invaluable study of carriers and grounds, binding media, pigments, metals used in painting, al fresco and al secco techniques, burnishing, etc. used by the medieval masters. Preface by Bernard Berenson. 239pp. 5⅜ x 8.
T327 Paperbound **$1.85**

PRINCIPLES OF ART HISTORY, H. Wölfflin. This remarkably instructive work demonstrates the tremendous change in artistic conception from the 14th to the 18th centuries, by analyzing 164 works by Botticelli, Dürer, Hobbema, Holbein, Hals, Titian, Rembrandt, Vermeer, etc., and pointing out exactly what is meant by "baroque," "classic," "primitive," "picturesque," and other basic terms of art history and criticism. "A remarkable lesson in the art of seeing," SAT. REV. OF LITERATURE. Translated from the 7th German edition. 150 illus. 254pp. 6⅛ x 9¼.
T276 Paperbound **$2.00**

FOUNDATIONS OF MODERN ART, A. Ozenfant. Stimulating discussion of human creativity from paleolithic cave painting to modern painting, architecture, decorative arts. Fully illustrated with works of Gris, Lipchitz, Léger, Picasso, primitive, modern artifacts, architecture, industrial art, much more. 226 illustrations. 368pp. 6⅛ x 9¼.
T215 Paperbound **$1.95**

HANDICRAFTS, APPLIED ART, ART SOURCES, ETC.

WILD FOWL DECOYS, J. Barber. The standard work on this fascinating branch of folk art, ranging from Indian mud and grass devices to realistic wooden decoys. Discusses styles, types, periods; gives full information on how to make decoys. 140 illustrations (including 14 new plates) show decoys and provide full sets of plans for handicrafters, artists, hunters, and students of folk art. 281pp. 7⅞ x 10¾. Deluxe edition.
T11 Clothbound **$8.50**

METALWORK AND ENAMELLING, H. Maryon. Probably the best book ever written on the subject. Tells everything necessary for the home manufacture of jewelry, rings, ear pendants, bowls, etc. Covers materials, tools, soldering, filigree, setting stones, raising patterns, repoussé work, damascening, niello, cloisonné, polishing, assaying, casting, and dozens of other techniques. The best substitute for apprenticeship to a master metalworker. 363 photos and figures. 374pp. 5½ x 8½.
T183 Clothbound **$7.50**

SHAKER FURNITURE, E. D. and F. Andrews. The most illuminating study of Shaker furniture ever written. Covers chronology, craftsmanship, houses, shops, etc. Includes over 200 photographs of chairs, tables, clocks, beds, benches, etc. "Mr. & Mrs. Andrews know all there is to know about Shaker furniture," Mark Van Doren, NATION. 48 full-page plates. 192pp. Deluxe cloth binding. 7⅞ x 10¾.
T7 Clothbound **$6.00**

PRIMITIVE ART, Franz Boas. A great American anthropologist covers theory, technical virtuosity, styles, symbolism, patterns, etc. of primitive art. The more than 900 illustrations will interest artists, designers, craftworkers. Over 900 illustrations. 376pp. 5⅜ x 8.
T25 Paperbound **$1.95**

ON THE LAWS OF JAPANESE PAINTING, H. Bowie. The best possible substitute for lessons from an oriental master. Treats both spirit and technique; exercises for control of the brush; inks, brushes, colors; use of dots, lines to express whole moods, etc. 220 illus. 132pp. 6⅛ x 9¼.
T30 Paperbound **$1.95**

HANDBOOK OF ORNAMENT, F. S. Meyer. One of the largest collections of copyright-free traditional art: over 3300 line cuts of Greek, Roman, Medieval, Renaissance, Baroque, 18th and 19th century art motifs (tracery, geometric elements, flower and animal motifs, etc.) and decorated objects (chairs, thrones, weapons, vases, jewelry, armor, etc.). Full text. 3300 illustrations. 562pp. 5⅜ x 8.
T302 Paperbound **$2.00**

THREE CLASSICS OF ITALIAN CALLIGRAPHY. Oscar Ogg, ed. Exact reproductions of three famous Renaissance calligraphic works: Arrighi's OPERINA and IL MODO, Tagliente's LO PRESENTE LIBRO, and Palatino's LIBRO NUOVO. More than 200 complete alphabets, thousands of lettered specimens, in Papal Chancery and other beautiful, ornate handwriting. Introduction. 245 plates. 282pp. 6⅛ x 9¼.
T212 Paperbound **$1.95**

THE HISTORY AND TECHNIQUES OF LETTERING, A. Nesbitt. A thorough history of lettering from the ancient Egyptians to the present, and a 65-page course in lettering for artists. Every major development in lettering history is illustrated by a complete alphabet. Fully analyzes such masters as Caslon, Koch, Garamont, Jenson, and many more. 89 alphabets, 165 other specimens. 317pp. 5⅜ x 8.
T427 Paperbound **$2.00**

LETTERING AND ALPHABETS, J. A. Cavanagh. An unabridged reissue of "Lettering," containing the full discussion, analysis, illustration of 89 basic hand lettering tyles based on Caslon, Bodoni, Gothic, many other types. Hundreds of technical hints on construction, strokes, pens, brushes, etc. 89 alphabets, 72 lettered specimens, which may be reproduced permission-free. 121pp. 9¾ x 8. **T53 Paperbound $1.25**

THE HUMAN FIGURE IN MOTION, Eadweard Muybridge. The largest collection in print of Muybridge's famous high-speed action photos. 4789 photographs in more than 500 action-strip-sequences (at shutter speeds up to 1/6000th of a second) illustrate men, women, children—mostly undraped—performing such actions as walking, running, getting up, lying down, carrying objects, throwing, etc. "An unparalleled dictionary of action for all artists," AMERICAN ARTIST. 390 full-page plates, with 4789 photographs. Heavy glossy stock, reinforced binding with headbands. 7⅞ x 10¾. **T204 Clothbound $10.00**

ANIMALS IN MOTION, Eadweard Muybridge. The largest collection of animal action photos in print. 34 different animals (horses, mules, oxen, goats, camels, pigs, cats, lions, gnus, deer, monkeys, eagles—and 22 others) in 132 characteristic actions. All 3919 photographs are taken in series at speeds up to 1/1600th of a second, offering artists, biologists, cartoonists a remarkable opportunity to see exactly how an ostrich's head bobs when running, how a lion puts his foot down, how an elephant's knee bends, how a bird flaps his wings, thousands of other hard-to-catch details. "A really marvelous series of plates," NATURE. 380 full-pages of plates. Heavy glossy stock, reinforced binding with headbands. 7⅞ x 10¾. **T203 Clothbound $10.00**

THE BOOK OF SIGNS, R. Koch. 493 symbols—crosses, monograms, astrological, biological symbols, runes, etc.—from ancient manuscripts, cathedrals, coins, catacombs, pottery. May be reproduced permission-free. 493 illustrations by Fritz Kredel. 104pp. 6⅛ x 9¼. **T162 Paperbound $1.00**

A HANDBOOK OF EARLY ADVERTISING ART, C. P. Hornung. The largest collection of copyright-free early advertising art ever compiled. Vol. I: 2,000 illustrations of animals, old automobiles, buildings, allegorical figures, fire engines, Indians, ships, trains, more than 33 other categories! Vol II: Over 4,000 typographical specimens; 600 Roman, Gothic, Barnum, Old English faces; 630 ornamental type faces; hundreds of scrolls, initials, flourishes, etc. "A remarkable collection," PRINTERS' INK.

Vol. I: Pictorial Volume. Over 2000 illustrations. 256pp. 9 x 12. **T122 Clothbound $10.00**
Vol. II: Typographical Volume. Over 4000 specimens. 319pp. 9 x 12. **T123 Clothbound $10.00**
Two volume set, Clothbound, only **$18.50**

DESIGN FOR ARTISTS AND CRAFTSMEN, L. Wolchonok. The most thorough course on the creation of art motifs and designs. Shows you step-by-step, with hundreds of examples and 113 detailed exercises, how to create original designs from geometric patterns, plants, birds, animals, humans, and man-made objects. "A great contribution to the field of design and crafts," N. Y. SOCIETY OF CRAFTSMEN. More than 1300 entirely new illustrations. xv + 207pp. 7⅞ x 10¾. **T274 Clothbound $4.95**

HANDBOOK OF DESIGNS AND DEVICES, C. P. Hornung. A remarkable working collection of 1836 basic designs and variations, all copyright-free. Variations of circle, line, cross, diamond, swastika, star, scroll, shield, many more. Notes on symbolism. "A necessity to every designer who would be original without having to labor heavily," ARTIST and ADVERTISER. 204 plates. 240pp. 5⅜ x 8.

T125 Paperbound $1.90

THE UNIVERSAL PENMAN, George Bickham. Exact reproduction of beautiful 18th century book of handwriting. 22 complete alphabets in finest English roundhand, other scripts, over 2000 elaborate flourishes, 122 calligraphic illustrations, etc. Material is copyright-free. "An essential part of any art library, and a book of permanent value," AMERICAN ARTIST. 212 plates. 224pp. 9 x 13¾. **T20 Clothbound $10.00**

AN ATLAS OF ANATOMY FOR ARTISTS, F. Schider. This standard work contains 189 full-page plates, more than 647 illustrations of all aspects of the human skeleton, musculature, cutaway portions of the body, each part of the anatomy, hand forms, eyelids, breasts, location of muscles under the flesh, etc. 59 plates illustrate how Michelangelo, da Vinci, Goya, 15 others, drew human anatomy. New 3rd edition enlarged by 52 new illustrations by Cloquet, Barcsay. "The standard reference tool," AMERICAN LIBRARY ASSOCIATION. "Excellent," AMERICAN ARTIST. 189 plates, 647 illustrations. xxvi + 192pp. 7⅞ x 10⅝. **T241 Clothbound $6.00**

AN ATLAS OF ANIMAL ANATOMY FOR ARTISTS, W. Ellenberger, H. Baum, H. Dittrich. The largest, richest animal anatomy for artists in English. Form, musculature, tendons, bone structure, expression, detailed cross sections of head, other features, of the horse, lion, dog, cat, deer, seal, kangaroo, cow, bull, goat, monkey, hare, many other animals. "Highly recommended," DESIGN. Second, revised, enlarged edition with new plates from Cuvier, Stubbs, etc. 288 illustrations. 153pp. 11⅜ x 9. **T82 Clothbound $6.00**

ANIMAL DRAWING: ANATOMY AND ACTION FOR ARTISTS, C. R. Knight. 158 studies, with full accompanying text, of such animals as the gorilla, bear, bison, dromedary, camel, vulture, pelican, iguana, shark, etc., by one of the greatest modern masters of animal drawing. Innumerable tips on how to get life expression into your work. "An excellent reference work,' SAN FRANCISCO CHRONICLE. 158 illustrations. 156pp. 10½ x 8½. **T426 Paperbound $2.00**

DOVER BOOKS

THE CRAFTSMAN'S HANDBOOK, Cennino Cennini. The finest English translation of IL LIBRO DELL' ARTE, the 15th century introduction to art technique that is both a mirror of Quatrocento life and a source of many useful but nearly forgotten facets of the painter's art. 4 illustrations. xxvii + 142pp. D. V. Thompson, translator. 6⅛ x 9¼.   T54 Paperbound **$1.50**

THE BROWN DECADES, Lewis Mumford. A picture of the "buried renaissance" of the post-Civil War period, and the founding of modern architecture (Sullivan, Richardson, Root, Roebling), landscape development (Marsh, Olmstead, Eliot), and the graphic arts (Homer, Eakins, Ryder). 2nd revised, enlarged edition. Bibliography. 12 illustrations. xiv + 266 pp. 5⅜ x 8.   T200 Paperbound **$1.65**

STIEGEL GLASS, F. W. Hunter. The story of the most highly esteemed early American glassware, fully illustrated. How a German adventurer, "Baron" Stiegel, founded a glass empire; detailed accounts of individual glasswork. "This pioneer work is reprinted in an edition even more beautiful than the original," ANTIQUES DEALER. New introduction by Helen McKearin. 171 illustrations, 12 in full color. xxii + 338pp. 7⅞ x 10¾.   T128 Clothbound **$10.00**

THE HUMAN FIGURE, J. H. Vanderpoel. Not just a picture book, but a complete course by a famous figure artist. Extensive text, illustrated by 430 pencil and charcoal drawings of both male and female anatomy. 2nd enlarged edition. Foreword. 430 illus. 143pp. 6⅛ x 9¼.   T432 Paperbound **$1.45**

PINE FURNITURE OF EARLY NEW ENGLAND, R. H. Kettell. Over 400 illustrations, over 50 working drawings of early New England chairs, benches, beds cupboards, mirrors, shelves, tables, other furniture esteemed for simple beauty and character. "Rich store of illustrations . . . emphasizes the individuality and varied design," ANTIQUES. 413 illustrations, 55 working drawings. 475pp. 8 x 10¾.   T145 Clothbound **$10.00**

BASIC BOOKBINDING, A. W. Lewis. Enables both beginners and experts to rebind old books or bind paperbacks in hard covers. Treats materials, tools; gives step-by-step instruction in how to collate a book, sew it, back it, make boards, etc. 261 illus. Appendices. 155pp. 5⅜ x 8.   T169 Paperbound **$1.35**

DESIGN MOTIFS OF ANCIENT MEXICO, J. Enciso. Nearly 90% of these 766 superb designs from Aztec, Olmec, Totonac, Maya, and Toltec origins are unobtainable elsewhere! Contains plumed serpents, wind gods, animals, demons, dancers, monsters, etc. Excellent applied design source. Originally $17.50. 766 illustrations, thousands of motifs. 192pp. 6⅛ x 9¼.   T84 Paperbound **$1.85**

AFRICAN SCULPTURE, Ladislas Segy. 163 full-page plates illustrating masks, fertility figures, ceremonial objects, etc., of 50 West and Central African tribes—95% never before illustrated. 34-page introduction to African sculpture. "Mr. Segy is one of its top authorities," NEW YORKER. 164 full-page photographic plates. Introduction. Bibliography. 244pp. 6⅛ x 9¼.   T396 Paperbound **$2.00**

THE PROCESSES OF GRAPHIC REPRODUCTION IN PRINTING, H. Curwen. A thorough and practical survey of wood, linoleum, and rubber engraving; copper engraving; drypoint, mezzotint, etching, aquatint, steel engraving, die sinking, stencilling, lithography (extensively); photographic reproduction utilizing line, continuous tone, photoengravure, collotype; every other process in general use. Note on color reproduction. Section on bookbinding. Over 200 illustrations, 25 in color. 143pp. 5½ x 8½.   T512 Clothbound **$4.00**

CALLIGRAPHY, J. G. Schwandner. First reprinting in 200 years of this legendary book of beautiful handwriting. Over 300 ornamental initials, 12 complete calligraphic alphabets, over 150 ornate frames and panels, 75 calligraphic pictures of cherubs, stags, lions, etc., thousands of flourishes, scrolls, etc., by the greatest 18th century masters. All material can be copied or adapted without permission. Historical introduction. 158 full-page plates. 368pp. 9 x 13.   T475 Clothbound **$10.00**

* * *

A DIDEROT PICTORIAL ENCYCLOPEDIA OF TRADES AND INDUSTRY, Manufacturing and the Technical Arts in Plates Selected from "L'Encyclopédie ou Dictionnaire Raisonné des Sciences, des Arts, et des Métiers," of Denis Diderot, edited with text by C. Gillispie. Over 2000 illustrations on 485 full-page plates. Magnificent 18th century engravings of men, women, and children working at such trades as milling flour, cheesemaking, charcoal burning, mining, silverplating, shoeing horses, making fine glass, printing, hundreds more, showing details of machinery, different steps in sequence, etc. A remarkable art work, but also the largest collection of working figures in print, copyright-free, for art directors, designers, etc. Two vols. 920pp. 9 x 12. Heavy library cloth.   T421 Two volume set **$18.50**

* * *

SILK SCREEN TECHNIQUES, J. Biegeleisen, M. Cohn. A practical step-by-step home course in one of the most versatile, least expensive graphic arts processes. How to build an inexpensive silk screen, prepare stencils, print, achieve special textures, use color, etc. Every step explained, diagrammed. 149 illustrations, 8 in color. 201pp. 6⅛ x 9¼.   T433 Paperbound **$1.45**

PUZZLES, GAMES, AND ENTERTAINMENTS

MATHEMATICS, MAGIC AND MYSTERY, Martin Gardner. Astonishing feats of mind reading, mystifying "magic" tricks, are often based on mathematical principles anyone can learn. This book shows you how to perform scores of tricks with cards, dice, coins, knots, numbers, etc., by using simple principles from set theory, theory of numbers, topology, other areas of mathematics, fascinating in themselves. No special knowledge required. 135 illus. 186pp. 5⅜ x 8.   T335 Paperbound **$1.00**

MATHEMATICAL PUZZLES FOR BEGINNERS AND ENTHUSIASTS, G. Mott-Smith. Test your problem-solving techniques and powers of inference on 188 challenging, amusing puzzles based on algebra, dissection of plane figures, permutations, probabilities, etc. Appendix of primes, square roots, etc. 135 illus. 2nd revised edition. 248pp. 5⅜ x 8.
T198 Paperbound **$1.00**

LEARN CHESS FROM THE MASTERS, F. Reinfeld. Play 10 games against Marshall, Bronstein, Najdorf, other masters, and grade yourself on each move. Detailed annotations reveal principles of play, strategy, etc. as you proceed. An excellent way to get a real insight into the game. Formerly titled, "Chess by Yourself." 91 diagrams. vii + 144pp. 5⅜ x 8.
T362 Paperbound **$1.00**

REINFELD ON THE END GAME IN CHESS, F. Reinfeld. 62 end games of Alekhine, Tarrasch, Morphy, other masters, are carefully analyzed with emphasis on transition from middle game to end play. Tempo moves, queen endings, weak squares, other basic principles clearly illustrated. Excellent for understanding why some moves are weak or incorrect, how to avoid errors. Formerly titled, "Practical End-game Play." 62 diagrams. vi + 177pp. 5⅜ x 8.
T417 Paperbound **$1.25**

101 PUZZLES IN THOUGHT AND LOGIC, C. R. Wylie, Jr. Brand new puzzles you need no special knowledge to solve! Each one is a gem of ingenuity that will really challenge your problem-solving technique. Introduction with simplified explanation of scientic puzzle solving. 128pp. 5⅜ x 8.   T167 Paperbound **$1.00**

THE COMPLETE NONSENSE OF EDWARD LEAR. The only complete edition of this master of gentle madness at a popular price. The Dong with the Luminous Nose, The Jumblies, The Owl and the Pussycat, hundreds of other bits of wonderful nonsense. 214 limericks, 3 sets of Nonsense Botany, 5 Nonsense Alphabets, 546 fantastic drawings, much more. 320pp. 5⅜ x 8.   T167 Paperbound **$1.00**

28 SCIENCE FICTION STORIES OF H. G. WELLS. Two complete novels, "Men Like Gods" and "Star Begotten," plus 26 short stories by the master science-fiction writer of all time. Stories of space, time, future adventure that are among the all-time classics of science fiction. 928pp. 5⅜ x 8.   T265 Clothbound **$3.95**

SEVEN SCIENCE FICTION NOVELS, H. G. Wells. Unabridged texts of "The Time Machine," "The Island of Dr. Moreau," "First Men in the Moon," "The Invisible Man," "The War of the Worlds," "The Food of the Gods," "In the Days of the Comet." "One will have to go far to match this for entertainment, excitement, and sheer pleasure," N. Y. TIMES. 1015pp. 5⅜ x 8.   T264 Clothbound **$3.95**

MATHEMAGIC, MAGIC PUZZLES, AND GAMES WITH NUMBERS, R. V. Heath. More than 60 new puzzles and stunts based on number properties: multiplying large numbers mentally, finding the date of any day in the year, etc. Edited by J. S. Meyer. 76 illus. 129pp. 5⅜ x 8.
T110 Paperbound **$1.00**

FIVE ADVENTURE NOVELS OF H. RIDER HAGGARD. The master story-teller's five best tales of mystery and adventure set against authentic African backgrounds: "She," "King Solomon's Mines," "Allan Quatermain," "Allan's Wife," "Maiwa's Revenge." 821pp. 5⅜ x 8.
T108 Clothbound **$3.95**

WIN AT CHECKERS, M. Hopper. (Formerly "Checkers.") The former World's Unrestricted Checker Champion gives you valuable lessons in openings, traps, end games, ways to draw when you are behind, etc. More than 100 questions and answers anticipate your problems. Appendix. 75 problems diagrammed, solved. 79 figures. xi + 107pp. 5⅜ x 8.
T363 Paperbound **$1.00**

CRYPTOGRAPHY, L. D. Smith. Excellent introductory work on ciphers and their solution, history of secret writing, techniques, etc. Appendices on Japanese methods, the Baconian cipher, frequency tables. Bibliography. Over 150 problems, solutions. 160pp. 5⅜ x 8.
T247 Paperbound **$1.00**

CRYPTANALYSIS, H. F. Gaines. (Formerly, "Elementary Cryptanalysis.") The best book available on cryptograms and how to solve them. Contains all major techniques: substitution, transposition, mixed alphabets, multafid, Kasiski and Vignere methods, etc. Word frequency appendix. 167 problems, solutions. 173 figures. 236pp. 5⅜ x 8.   T97 Paperbound **$1.95**

FLATLAND, E. A. Abbot. The science-fiction classic of life in a 2-dimensional world that is considered a first-rate introduction to relativity and hyperspace, as well as a scathing satire on society, politics and religion. 7th edition. 16 illus. 128pp. 5⅜ x 8.
T1 Paperbound **$1.00**

DOVER BOOKS

HOW TO FORCE CHECKMATE, F. Reinfeld. (Formerly "Challenge to Chessplayers.") No board needed to sharpen your checkmate skill on 300 checkmate situations. Learn to plan up to 3 moves ahead and play a superior end game. 300 situations diagrammed; notes and full solutions. 111pp. 5⅜ x 8.   T439 Paperbound **$1.25**

MORPHY'S GAMES OF CHESS, P. W. Sergeant, ed. Play forcefully by following the techniques used by one of the greatest chess champions. 300 of Morphy's games carefully annotated to reveal principles. Bibliography. New introduction by F. Reinfeld. 235 diagrams. x + 352pp. 5⅜ x 8.   T386 Paperbound **$1.75**

MATHEMATICAL RECREATIONS, M. Kraitchik. Hundreds of unusual mathematical puzzlers and odd bypaths of math, elementary and advanced. Greek, Medieval, Arabic, Hindu problems; figurate numbers, Fermat numbers, primes; magic, Euler, Latin squares; fairy chess, latruncles, reversi, jinx, ruma, tetrachrome other positional and permutational games. Rigorous solutions. Revised second edition. 181 illus. 330pp. 5⅜ x 8.   T163 Paperbound **$1.75**

MATHEMATICAL EXCURSIONS, H. A. Merrill. Revealing stimulating insights into elementary math, not usually taught in school. 90 problems demonstrate Russian peasant multiplication, memory systems for pi, magic squares, dyadic systems, division by inspection, many more. Solutions to difficult problems. 50 illus. 5⅜ x 8.   T350 Paperbound **$1.00**

MAGIC TRICKS & CARD TRICKS, W. Jonson. Best introduction to tricks with coins, bills, eggs, ribbons, slates, cards, easily performed without elaborate equipment. Professional routines, tips on presentation, misdirection, etc. Two books bound as one: 52 tricks with cards, 37 tricks with common objects. 106 figures. 224pp. 5⅜ x 8.   T909 Paperbound **$1.00**

MATHEMATICAL PUZZLES OF SAM LOYD, selected and edited by **M. Gardner.** 177 most ingenious mathematical puzzles of America's greatest puzzle originator, based on arithmetic, algebra, game theory, dissection, route tracing, operations research, probability, etc. 120 drawings, diagrams. Solutions. 187pp. 5⅜ x 8.   T498 Paperbound **$1.00**

THE ART OF CHESS, J. Mason. The most famous general study of chess ever written. More than 90 openings, middle game, end game, how to attack, sacrifice, defend, exchange, form general strategy. Supplement on "How Do You Play Chess?" by F. Reinfeld. 448 diagrams. 356pp. 5⅜ x 8.   T463 Paperbound **$1.85**

HYPERMODERN CHESS as Developed in the Games of its Greatest Exponent, ARON NIMZOVICH, F. Reinfeld, ed. Learn how the game's greatest innovator defeated Alekhine, Lasker, and many others; and use these methods in your own game. 180 diagrams. 228pp. 5⅜ x 8.
T448 Paperbound **$1.35**

A TREASURY OF CHESS LORE, F. Reinfeld, ed. Hundreds of fascinating stories by and about the masters, accounts of tournaments and famous games, aphorisms, word portraits, little known incidents, photographs, etc., that will delight the chess enthusiast, captivate the beginner. 49 photographs (14 full-page plates), 12 diagrams. 315pp. 5⅜ x 8.
T458 Paperbound **$1.75**

A NONSENSE ANTHOLOGY, collected by **Carolyn Wells.** 245 of the best nonsense verses ever written: nonsense puns, absurd arguments, mock epics, nonsense ballads, "sick" verses, dog-Latin verses, French nonsense verses, limericks. Lear, Carroll, Belloc, Burgess, nearly 100 other writers. Introduction by Carolyn Wells. 3 indices: Title, Author, First Lines. xxxiii + 279pp. 5⅜ x 8.   T499 Paperbound **$1.25**

SYMBOLIC LOGIC and THE GAME OF LOGIC, Lewis Carroll. Two delightful puzzle books by the author of "Alice," bound as one. Both works concern the symbolic representation of traditional logic and together contain more than 500 ingenious, amusing and instructive syllogistic puzzlers. Total of 326pp. 5⅜ x 8.   T492 Paperbound **$1.50**

PILLOW PROBLEMS and A TANGLED TALE, Lewis Carroll. Two of Carroll's rare puzzle works bound as one. "Pillow Problems" contain 72 original math puzzles. The puzzles in "A Tangled Tale" are given in delightful story form. Total of 291pp. 5⅜ x 8.   T493 Paperbound **$1.50**

PECK'S BAD BOY AND HIS PA, G. W. Peck. Both volumes of one of the most widely read of all American humor books. A classic of American folk humor, also invaluable as a portrait of an age. 100 original illustrations. Introduction by E. Bleiler. 347pp. 5⅜ x 8.
T497 Paperbound **$1.35**

Dover publishes books on art, music, philosophy, literature, languages, history, social sciences, psychology, handcrafts, orientalia, puzzles and entertainments, chess, pets and gardens, books explaining science, intermediate and higher mathematics mathematical physics, engineering, biological sciences, earth sciences, classics of science, etc. Write to:

Dept. catrr.
Dover Publications, Inc.
180 Varick Street, N. Y. 14, N. Y.